Corporate Finance

This book introduces corporate finance to first-year students in business schools. Basic subjects such as marketing, human resources and finance are fundamental to the learning of a business manager. A book on these subjects must emphasize learning that is conceptual in nature and, at the same time, application oriented. This book attempts to achieve this in a manner that is comprehensive and shorn of complexity. It examines the practice of finance without diluting theory and conceptual knowledge. Corporate finance is necessarily quantitative in nature, and the book duly places emphasis on that aspect. It ensures the primacy of ideas and concepts, utilizing numbers as supportive elements. Grounded in fundamental concepts, it is application oriented with global, real-world examples and contains corporate snippets and insights aiding the understanding of theoretical frameworks.

Sunil Mahajan is visiting professor of finance in the Hope Foundation's International Institute of Information Technology, Pune. His areas of expertise include portfolio management, corporate finance and the fixed income securities market.

Corporate Finance

Theory and Practice in Emerging Economies

Sunil Mahajan

CAMBRIDGE
UNIVERSITY PRESS

CAMBRIDGE
UNIVERSITY PRESS

University Printing House, Cambridge CB2 8BS, United Kingdom

One Liberty Plaza, 20th Floor, New York, NY 10006, USA

477 Williamstown Road, Port Melbourne, VIC 3207, Australia

314–321, 3rd Floor, Plot 3, Splendor Forum, Jasola District Centre, New Delhi–110025, India

79 Anson Road, #06–04/06, Singapore 079906

Cambridge University Press is part of the University of Cambridge.

It furthers the University's mission by disseminating knowledge in the pursuit of education, learning and research at the highest international levels of excellence.

www.cambridge.org
Information on this title: www.cambridge.org/9781108486965

First published 2020

Printed in India by Nutech Print Services, New Delhi 110020

A catalogue record for this publication is available from the British Library

Library of Congress Cataloging-in-Publication Data
Names: Mahajan, Sunil, 1961- author.
Title: Corporate finance : theory and practice in emerging economies / Sunil Mahajan.
Description: New York : Cambridge University Press, 2020. | Includes bibliographical references and index.
Identifiers: LCCN 2020010165 (print) | LCCN 2020010166 (ebook) | ISBN 9781108486965 (hardback) | ISBN 9781108732024 (paperback) | ISBN 9781108764957 (ebook)
Subjects: LCSH: Corporations--Developing countries--Finance. | Business enterprises--Developing countries--Finance.
Classification: LCC HG4285 .M34 2020 (print) | LCC HG4285 (ebook) | DDC 658.1509172/4--dc23
LC record available at https://lccn.loc.gov/2020010165
LC ebook record available at https://lccn.loc.gov/2020010166

ISBN 978-1-108-48696-5 Hardback

ISBN 978-1-108-73202-4 Paperback

Contents

Figures

Tables

Corporate Snippets

I have made extensive use of what can be termed *corporate snippets* in each chapter.

These have been positioned close to the concept they refer to and are used for the following purposes:

1. Practical illustration of the concept being discussed: For instance, the concept of corporate governance is illustrated with an example of how the Securities and Exchange Board of India's (SEBI's) efforts helped to protect minority interest at Raymonds Ltd. Similarly, the concept of intermediation is illustrated with details of HDFC Bank intermediation.
2. Complexity of a concept: While the basic concept is explained in the main chapter, corporate snippets will expose the students to a little more intricacy. For instance, while discussing intra-year compounding in the main body of the chapter, continuous compounding has been explained as a snippet.
3. To explain a little extra, relating to a topic, without disturbing the flow of the chapter.

Abbreviations

ADR	American depository receipts
AGM	annual general meeting
APV	adjusted present value
ARR	accounting rate of return
BG	bank guarantee
BOP	balance of payments
BSE	Bombay Stock Exchange
CA	current assets
CAGR	compounded annual growth rate
CAP	competitive advantage period
CAPM	capital asset pricing model
CDMA	code division multiple access
CKD	completely knocked down
CL	current liability
COC	cost of capital
CP	commercial paper
CSR	corporate social responsibility
DCF	discounted cash flow
DDM	dividend discount model
DDT	dividend distribution tax
DF	discount factor
DRIP	Dividend Reinvestment Plan
DTH	direct-to-home
EBIT	earnings before interest and taxes
EBITDA	earnings before interest, tax, depreciation and amortization
ECB	external commercial borrowing
ECGC	Export Credit Guarantee Corporation
EMH	efficient markets hypothesis
EPC	engineering, procurement and construction
EPS	earnings per share
ERP	enterprise resource planning

ESOP	employee stock option plan
EVA	economic value added
FC	fixed costs
FCF	free cash flows
FDA	Food and Drug Administration
FDI	foreign direct investment
FEMA	Foreign Exchange Management Act
FII	foreign institutional investment
Fintech	financial technology
FMCG	fast-moving consumer goods
forex	foreign exchange
FPI	foreign portfolio investment
FVIF	future value interest factor
GAAP	generally accepted accounting principles
GDR	global depository receipts
GMAC	General Motors Acceptance Corporation
GSM	global system for mobile communications
HUL	Hindustan Unilever Ltd
IIAS	Institutional Investor Advisory Services India Limited
IMF	International Monetary Fund
IPO	initial public offering
IRR	internal rate of return
ITM	in the money
JV	joint venture
KFA	Kingfisher Airlines
LC	letter of credit
LEAPS	long-term equity anticipation securities
LRS	Liberalized Remittance Scheme
MIBOR	Mumbai inter-bank offered rate
MIRR	modified internal rate of return
MM Model	Modigliani–Miller Model
MNC	multinational company
NABARD	National Bank for Agriculture and Rural Development
NDTL	net demand and term liabilities
NOPAT	net operating profits after tax
NPA	non-performing asset
NPV	net present value
NSE	National Stock Exchange
OTC	over the counter
OTM	out of the money
PAT	profit after tax
PBT	profit before tax
P&L	profit and loss
P/E ratio	price earnings ratio

PE	private equity
PI	profitability index
PIGS	Portugal, Ireland, Greece and Spain
PIK	payment-in-kind
PVIF	present value interest factor
R&D	research and development
ROE	return on equity
SEBI	Securities and Exchange Board of India
SLR	Statutory Liquidity Ratio
SME	small and medium enterprises
SWIFT	Society for Worldwide Interbank Financial Telecommunication
TIPS	treasury inflation protected securities
TSI	total societal impact
UK	United Kingdom
USA	United States of America
VIX	volatility index
WACC	weighted average cost of capital
WDV	written down value
YTM	yield to maturity

Preface

I have been teaching for over two decades. During this period, I have witnessed a quantum jump in the number of students pursuing business management in India and a significant decline in standards. Maybe, there is a correlation between the two. Business management as a course and the corporate sector as a career choice are demanding. Not everyone has the competence, or the inclination, to pursue it successfully. In our desire to be inclusive and to pass on the benefit of business management as a career to everyone, we may have diluted the standards significantly.

Management education in India presents a contrast. The top few business schools are demanding in terms of who they accept and the inputs they provide during the two years of the course. Only the best and the toughest emerge unscathed, ready to take on the challenges the corporate sector throws at them. They compete with the best global business schools on equal terms and the students have, over time, proven their competence in the corporate world throughout the world.

At the bottom are a large number of schools lacking in funding, competent faculty, infrastructure and, of course, students who can stand up to the rigour demanded by the study and practice of management. Of course, the desire to establish standards may also be lacking. The consequent dilution in quality has created a wide chasm, which has destroyed the credibility of management education in the country. MBA is not an inclusive course; by trying to make it inclusive, we have diluted its core and it no longer commands the respect it earlier did.

At the same time, management education in the country cannot be restricted to the top few. Not only would that be an elitist approach, it would ensure that the country is unable to provide for and meet the rising demand for professionals for a fast-expanding corporate sector.

This demand is currently fulfilled by business schools in the mid-range that may not match the best in the country but are able to provide inputs to students that enable them to pursue a lucrative career. My book is designed for students from these institutes, who are desirous of learning, imbibing and applying management theories and concepts but may not have the inclination or the capability to master the esoteric books and cases that are the bread and butter of the Indian Institute of Management (IIM) students.

The attempt has been to write a book that is simple and easy to read, without in any manner compromising on the conceptual knowledge required by a management student. Some of the books on the subject, written by well-known authors, are the finest one can come across. Books by Brealey and Myers; Ross, Westerfield and Jaffe; Damodaran; Vanhorne and others open up a new world that leads to lifelong fascination with the subject. But these books are also daunting, and quite frankly many would-be corporate sector managers are likely to be put off, as they usually are, by the size and complexity of these books.

What we need is a book that is relatively short and easy to read, current in terms of its coverage, elaborating on the latest developments in the subject, extensively incorporating quantitative aspects and throwing sufficient light on the practice of finance, without in any way diluting theory and conceptual knowledge. That has, in a nutshell, been the objective with which I have ventured into writing a textbook on a subject that otherwise presents a wide choice.

The book is primarily based on my teaching of the subject over the years. My first interaction with management students of a new batch is always in the second trimester/semester when they study corporate finance. The discussed objectives have been firmed up over many years of experience in teaching the subject. Students who intend to specialize in finance will find that the book provides sufficient expertise for them to pursue specialization subjects in the latter part of the course, while others will gain the requisite fundamental knowledge they may need on the subject.

The idea for the book germinated many years back when one of my students 'advised' me to write a book encapsulating what I usually teach in my classes. I had resisted the urge but now feel the need for such a book is imminent. I leave it to the students to judge whether it serves the purpose it is intended for.

Acknowledgements

Writing a book can be an exhausting and, at times, a lonely and tortuous experience. Often, it seems to be an endless task; there is always scope for improvement. One never realizes how onerous it can be until one starts. I would not advise it for the faint-hearted.

I am happy I was unaware it would take so much out of me; probably that is why the eventual satisfaction is much greater. Hopefully, the final output will justify the efforts that have gone into writing it. And, hopefully, it will encourage some students to take up finance as a career path, while others will be able to appreciate the role and influence of finance in their own streams of choice and in their work.

I have been fortunate to have received help from many people, directly and indirectly. The late Prof. P. L. Arya, my senior from IIM Ahmedabad, was instrumental in my shift from the corporate sector to academics and gave me the initial breathing space to make the changeover. Prof. Aruna Katara, president, the International Institute of Information Technology, Pune, gave the faculty the academic freedom that is so critical to the teaching–learning process. In her own way, she prodded me to write even when I showed reluctance. Prof. Swaminathan Sankaran was quite liberal in helping me, going through some of the chapters and providing advice. He was the first person whose views I sought before embarking on the journey.

Prof. Dhananjay Mallya, a close friend for three decades and a professional colleague, has been of tremendous help in going through the book, suggesting improvements and giving ideas that only a true professional and friend can give.

Prof. Mahendra Singhvi, again a close friend for over a decade and a valued colleague, was profuse with his help. He diligently read and reread substantial parts of the book to provide his own inputs that have helped shape the book in some ways.

With both Prof. Mallya and Prof. Singhvi, I have engaged in animated discussions that have helped a great deal in ensuring a professional output.

My students have, over the years, been responsible for keeping alive my interest in teaching, and challenging me with their inquisitiveness and incisive questioning. To them I owe a big gratitude.

My profuse and heartfelt thanks to Cambridge University Press, Anwesha Rana and Tapajyoti Chaudhuri. This is my first attempt at writing a book, and I was unaware of the many aspects of publishing. It is only with the constant help and assurances provided by Anwesha and Tapajyoti that the book has seen the light of day.

My final thanks are undoubtedly reserved for my son, Arjun, and my wife, Mona. My son has always wished that I write this book and was disappointed that it kept getting delayed. I know he will be delighted to see the book finally in his hands.

My wife has probably suffered the most in the process of writing. As I have mentioned, writing a book can be a tortuous process and she was more tortured than I was during this time. While I cannot say she bore the torture without complaint, she did keep egging me on even while complaining. Hers has been a tremendous help in the whole process, helping me with concepts, structuring, editing, playing the devil's advocate and ensuring that the output is a quality one.

I thank them all. As I thank many others, friends and colleagues, whom I have had the fortune of knowing and who have enriched me in many ways.

Sunil Mahajan

CHAPTER 1

Corporate Finance

A Conceptual Introduction

> Our goal is to make finance the servant, not the master, of the real economy.
>
> —Alistair Darling

Tata Motors Limited (TML) has a capacity to produce 790,000 cars annually. Based on the projected growth of the economy, it must estimate the future demand and decide whether to add another half a million to its capacity. The additional half million vehicles will require substantial investment. If the economy grows at the rate projected by the company's corporate planning department, the investment will prove extremely lucrative. On the other hand, if the growth slackens and other factors do not turn out to be favourable, it can spell doom for the company.

A decision to go ahead with the project would necessitate arrangement of funds for investment. The funds may be raised through either equity or debt. The debt can be short term, to be rolled over on maturity, or for a longer duration. Alternatively, the company can mobilize funds through instruments that are a combination of both debt and equity, as it had done in 1991 by issuing partially convertible bonds. The company can either directly approach a financial institution or it can undertake a public issue whereby it invites the public at large to participate in the financing. There are numerous options available and a choice must be made regarding the best possible combination with which the project can be financed.

An appropriate dividend policy is critical to the company's future success. Shareholder earnings comprise dividends as well as capital gains. Shareholders keenly look forward to receiving dividends from the company. At the same time, the distribution of dividend reduces the cash flows available with the company for investment, besides its implications for capital structure and valuation. A long-term policy must be established that balances the desire of the shareholders to receive dividends on the one hand and the cash flow requirements of the company on the other.

Credit to dealers constitutes a significant proportion of the working capital. Should TML insist on payment on delivery from the dealers, or let them pay only after a vehicle has been sold to the eventual customer? What should be the inventory of vehicles to be stocked with the dealers and in TML's own factory, in addition to the inventory of components it must maintain?

Payment terms negotiated with component suppliers are a crucial determinant of the working capital. Credit, inventory and payables have a bearing on the investment required for working capital, significantly impacting the cash flow position as well as the return on investment of TML.

The Indian economy has recently been going through tough times, with growth having plummeted from 8.2 per cent during 2015–16 to below 5 per cent annualized in the first nine months during 2019–20. Lower growth has quite naturally dented the demand for commercial vehicles as well as passenger cars, the two main segments that TML operates in. Profitability of its operations has declined. It is imperative that the company critically analyses its recent performance and devises ways to improve profitability and generate sufficient cash flows.

- Is it possible to push sales higher by giving dealers longer term credit?
- Can inventories be optimized by reducing the number of suppliers?
- Has the company compromised on margins in order to push sales and whether has this hurt profitability?
- Have the company's cash flows been compromised?
- Does the company's cost of production compare favourably with that of competitors?
- Has tax outgo increased due to reduced investments? Can this be optimized?

Some years back, the iconic Jaguar Land Rover Limited (JLR) was bleeding financially and was up for grabs. Tata Motors decided to acquire it, and JLR now constitutes a significant part of TML's business. Its impact on the overall performance of TML is significant. Mergers and acquisitions (M&As) can be game changers for any company in the long run.

Tata Motors Ltd generates substantial cash flows from its business operations every year which need to be invested efficiently to ensure safety, returns and liquidity. Termed 'treasury management', companies can generate significant returns from the cash flows they have accumulated over the years.

Some of the machinery for the expansion will be imported from Europe, requiring payment in euros. A decision needs to be taken whether to raise funds in the domestic market and convert the rupees into euros at the time of actual payment or to source funds in euros through an issue of global depository receipts or external commercial borrowing. The company also has the option of raising funds in a different currency, such as the US dollar, and then swapping it with the euro. The foreign exchange rates are in a constant state of flux, and the company must decide whether to ride the volatility in foreign exchange rates or hedge its requirements of euros through various derivative instruments such as futures, forwards, options and longer-term swaps.

TML today is a global entity with production, sales and imports in many countries. It has to deal in several currencies on a daily basis. While its sales in China and the United Kingdom (UK) lead to inflows in yuan and pound, investment in a new plant in Mexico requires funds in Mexican peso. Taking care of inflows and outflows of funds in different currencies is a complex task.

The aforementioned are some of the decisions that the chief financial officer (CFO) of TML must take, in conjunction with other departments of the company. Evidently, these decisions have a significant bearing on the company's performance and are all a part of what the CFO of TML handles on a daily basis, constituting what we study as corporate finance.

The Financial Markets

Understanding and interfacing with financial markets is integral to the functioning of a CFO. The CFO relies considerably on financial markets to achieve the company's objectives. As we will discuss later, a company's objective is to maximize its value and, therefore, the pricing of its equity and bonds is critical. The CFO must have expert knowledge of how prices are determined in financial markets. He needs to constantly access the financial markets for satisfying the requirement for funds. Other functions such as treasury investments, risk management, acquisitions and dividends also require deep knowledge of and experience in financial markets. The CFO must communicate effectively with investors. In fact, investor relations have become a priority with most companies today.

While we will discuss financial markets in much greater detail in the next chapter, it is useful to point out its impact on individuals and corporates briefly.

Financial markets enable an individual's earnings pattern and his corresponding spending pattern to be different over his lifespan. Without financial markets, the consumption and earnings pattern must correspond, wherein the individual is able to consume only what he earns during a given period of time.

When a person starts earning, he may wish to save, either for a rainy day or for his post-retirement days. Alternatively, he may be like the generation 'Y', which believes in consumption today rather than in some uncertain future time period; they borrow now against future income to acquire a house, an automobile, an expensive mobile handset or even an exotic holiday abroad. After finishing your MBA and securing a well-paying job, you are unlikely to wait for years to buy your favourite car or a house of your own. The financial markets enable you to borrow to fund the purchase. The borrowing will be paid off from your future income. This implies an exchange of your future income for present consumption. This is unlike the author, who, being at the end of his employment, is consuming less than his current income to pay for past borrowings as well as save for his post-retirement needs.

Mortgage Financing

Ownership of a house was a difficult proposition for people of my generation. Financial institutions lending for purchase of a house were non-existent. The only option was to accumulate sufficient savings, which took a lifetime. Severe shortage of housing ensured that property prices rose faster than accumulation of savings. It was a very frustrating catch-up game.

The establishment of HDFC Limited in the 1980s and its subsequent growth ushered in the mortgage industry in India. Three decades later, the mortgage sector growth shows no sign of abating. Borrowing long term to buy a house is a simple proposition in today's developed financial markets.

Similar to individuals, companies also need not depend only on internally generated cash flows to finance their long-term investments; they can raise money from the financial markets. They may borrow or sell new equity to raise funds that can be paid off through future income. Reliance Infrastructure Limited had huge plans for investment in the mid-2000s. Its internally generated cash flows were insufficient, but it was able to access the financial markets in different ways—public issue of its shares, bank loans, external commercial borrowing amongst others— to finance the projects. On the other hand, there are companies which generate cash flows in excess of what they need. Hindustan Unilever Limited (HUL), with established brands and an extensive distribution network, generates large cash flows every year. Being a mature company, its investment requirements are limited. Hindustan Unilever Limited makes use of the financial markets to park its excess cash flows in financial securities, to be used later when required.

Consumption Choices

Without the existence of financial markets, an individual's consumption is limited by his earnings. Financial markets enable him to save from his current income, earn a return and consume more in the future. Alternatively, an individual can borrow against his future earnings by taking a loan from banks and financial institutions.

Assume that Mr A earns ₹100 each in the current as well as in the subsequent year. If the financial market provides a return of 10 per cent for one year, Mr A can invest his current year earnings of ₹100 at 10 per cent to obtain ₹110 next year. Together with the earnings of ₹100 next year, he can consume ₹210. Alternatively, Mr A can borrow ₹90.91 and pay it back with interest from the next year's earnings of ₹100. His choices, thus, broaden to

- ₹210 next year and nothing in the current year, or
- ₹190.91 now and nothing next year.

In fact, Mr A can enjoy a consumption pattern of any combination represented by Figure 1.1.

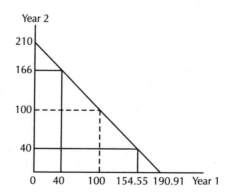

FIGURE 1.1 Consumption choices

Source: Author.

In the real world, Mr A can manoeuvre his choices over his entire lifespan (and not just for the two years, as in the example), depending on expectations of his earnings, applicable interest rate and expected lifespan. Such choices are enabled by the existence of vibrant financial markets.

It is the existence of a vibrant, developed and well-regulated financial market which facilitates an interchange between earnings and consumption and enables individuals as well as corporates to plan their consumption and investment patterns over time to suit their own preferences. Financial market enables both individuals and companies to enjoy spending and investment quite different from their earnings patterns.

There are two distinguishing characteristics of the discussed financial decisions. First, investment decisions entail costs and benefits, usually spread over a long period of time. Spending more than earnings leads to borrowing from the financial markets and paying interest on the borrowings. On the other hand, if the earnings are greater than the expenditure, the surplus can be invested in financial instruments to earn a return on investments.

Second, the associated costs and benefits are not known with certainty. Returns depend on the choice of investments and may neither be fixed nor known in advance. An investor may decide to invest in the equity of a software venture whose returns and cash flows will depend on multiple factors, namely the growth of the US economy, the rupee–dollar exchange rate and several others, which cannot be predicted with certainty. Return on equities for an investor can be very volatile and unpredictable. Markets were booming for a long period of time until 2007. Unbridled optimism all around raised stock prices to dizzying levels. The subsequent crisis witnessed decline in prices by over 50 per cent and destroyed huge wealth. Booms and busts have characterized stocks throughout history, leading to overnight riches or extensive wealth destruction.

Return is what the investor gets from his investment; risk of these investments is what he has to bear. Usually, there is a direct relationship between risk and return; the higher the risk of an investment, the higher is the return and vice versa. The financial markets offer a wide spectrum of risk–return choices. Investors take a decision based on which return and risk combination suits them best.

In making such decisions on where and how to invest/raise funds, economic entities use the financial system in the country and even globally. The financial system refers to the set of markets and institutions which enables 'financial contracting and the exchange of assets and risks' (Zvie and Merton 2000). The financial system comprises the following:

1. Financial markets: markets for trading financial securities such as shares, bonds and financial derivatives.
2. Regulatory bodies that govern the players and the markets: the Reserve Bank of India; the Securities and Exchange Board of India (SEBI); the Insurance Regulatory Development Authority; and the Securities and Exchange Commission, United States of America (USA), amongst others.
3. Financial services firms: investment banks, financial advisory firms, institutional advisory firms.

4. Financial intermediaries: banks, non-banking finance companies, mutual funds, hedge funds, insurance and pension funds.

While there are many reasons for studying finance, in this book we will focus on finance for the corporate sector. An MBA course is designed to prepare students to take up managerial responsibilities in the corporate sector. We will concentrate on financial theory required for the management of a business entity and focus on the company as an organizational form, to the exclusion of say a non-governmental organization (NGO), a start-up entrepreneurial venture or household finance.

Types of Business Organizations

A business enterprise can be organized in three forms. The simplest is the sole proprietorship wherein a single person, the sole proprietor, owns the business in its entirety and has exclusive responsibility of the assets and liabilities of the firm. If the business is unable to pay its dues, the sole proprietor is legally bound to pay from his own personal resources. Technically, the owner has unlimited liability. Thus, his liability is not limited to the amount he has invested in the venture but extends to the overall commitment of the business.

Unlimited liability also characterizes partnership, which is the second form of organizing a business enterprise. A partnership is a business organization owned by two or more partners who share the profits generated by the partnership. Partnership firms in India are governed by the Indian Partnership Act, 1932. In accordance with the Act, there must be a contract between two or more partners who agree to carry on the business with the objective of sharing profits in the partnership. As in the case of sole proprietorship, all partners have unlimited liability. Provision exists in the law, however, to constitute a business as a limited liability partnership.

Both sole proprietorship and partnership have limitations as business organizations. As business grows in size and becomes more complex, it is difficult to raise the large amount of capital that may be required. A limited number of partners cannot be expected to provide the funding that the growth of the business enterprise may necessitate. That is why virtually all large business organizations are structured as corporate entities.

A corporation, also referred to as a limited liability company, is a legal entity distinct from its owners. Being a separate legal entity, it can borrow, own property and enter into contracts on its own. It can sue and be sued. Tax provisions applicable to a company are different from those applicable to other forms of business organizations. In India, companies are incorporated and governed under the Companies Act, 1956.

A company is a legal entity separate from its owners, and funds raised from investors, in the form of either debt or equity, are a liability of the company, something it owes to those investors.

A corporate form of organization has several advantages.

1. A company is a permanent entity which is not impacted by the death of any of its owners. Equity ownership merely passes on to the heir of the deceased. This gives stability to the organization, which is missing in the other forms. Ownership may change on a daily basis, with investors buying and selling shares of the company, without in any way impacting its working. Managers similarly may come and go, without disrupting operations. Many

companies exist today that are more than a hundred years old. Tata Steel Limited, for example, was founded in 1907 and continues to be a vibrant business entity.

2. A company can have an unlimited number of equity shareholders and thus is in a position to raise a vast amount of capital. It is inconceivable that modern business and economy could have grown in the manner and to the extent they have without the corporate structure of organization. Larsen & Toubro (L&T) Ltd, for example, is valued at over ₹1,750,000 million. No single individual or a set of partners could have contributed this vast sum of money. The company has millions of investors who have together put in the required funds, facilitated, of course, by the corporate structure of organization.

3. A corporate structure of organization, with its distinguishing feature of limited liability, is the earliest means of risk management known to investors. Certain in the knowledge that they cannot be asked to pay for the liability of the firm from their own personal assets, their obligation being limited to the investment they have made, investors can leave the management of the company in more competent hands. Limited liability enables investors to diversify their resources by investing in multiple businesses. Portfolio diversification becomes possible. Thus, the corporate form of organization helps the investor in managing the risks of their investments.

   Kingfisher Airlines (KFA) became bankrupt in 2012. The company had in the past raised funds from the public through issue of equity and borrowings from financial institutions including banks. Debt provided by banks and other financial institutions has now become what is technically termed 'non-performing asset'. With the resources it now has, KFA will find it difficult to pay back all the liabilities and the lenders will have to take a hit. At the same time, limited liability safeguards the shareholders of Kingfisher, who cannot be asked to pay the liabilities of the firm from their personal assets. Their losses are limited to the amount they have already invested in the equity of the company. The payment of any liability of the firm is the sole responsibility of the company and not of its shareholders. The two are separate entities.

4. Separation of ownership and management is a significant characteristic feature of the corporate structure. The owners or equity investors, large in numbers and widely dispersed, appoint competent managers to run the business. You do not necessarily need to own a business you are managing. Nor do you have to manage a business you own.

L&T and Britannia

On 5 June 2017, 1,270,946 shares of L&T Ltd exchanged hands, representing a change in ownership of 0.14 per cent of the total shares. It had no impact on the ordinary business of the company, which continued to engage in its regular operations.

On 3 June 2003, Britannia Industries Limited asked its managing director to leave with immediate effect due to differences over strategic issues and replaced him with a new one. The company continued to function normally, of course, with a different strategy.

Objectives of a Company

In order to effectively manage a company, it is essential that all stakeholders agree on and work towards the objectives the company seeks to accomplish. It is widely believed that companies must maximize profits. However, that would be a flawed metric to try and achieve for various reasons.

1. Profits can be easily manipulated, as they sometimes are. Accountants have this wonderful knack of generating the specific profit figure that will please the management. Widely divergent figures can be made to represent a 'true and fair' picture of a company's performance under a broad interpretation of the generally accepted accounting principles (GAAP).
2. For it to be an effective metric, the period over which the company maximizes profits needs to be specified. For instance, if the objective is to maximize profits in the current year, there are many ways of achieving this at the cost of profits in later years. A pharmaceutical company can easily reduce expenditure on research and development (R&D) to inflate immediate profits. Similarly, a fast-moving consumer goods (FMCG) company may show a better picture of earnings by reducing investments in brands in the current year. The management usually has considerable leeway in manipulating profits over different years.

   Such practices are not healthy for business, and such companies are unlikely to survive for long. Companies have been known to declare profits that are always in line with expectations of investors, irrespective of the actual performance. We have often witnessed a new chief executive officer (CEO) 'clean up the books' by recognizing all past losses and liabilities, attribute the same to the previous CEO and start afresh. Cleaning up the books would, of course, not have been undertaken if the previous CEO had continued in his position.
3. It is important to factor in the investments required to generate a certain level of profit. Absolute profit by itself is meaningless. Company A's ₹100 million profit is better than ₹200 million profit by company B if the investment in company A is less than half the amount invested in company B. It is the return on investment which is more significant than just the absolute amount of profit.
4. Finally, the risk assumed to generate the given profit is critical. A higher profit may not be desirable if the company has been exposed to excessive risk in generating that profit. Not only can the profits disappear in the future, such risks can jeopardize the very existence of the company. Risk will be discussed in detail later in the book.

Earnings per share (EPS) is another measure that analysts sometimes look at, especially stock investors. It takes into account the investments required to generate profits. But it suffers from the other three weaknesses mentioned earlier.

The objectives of a company must be well established and unambiguous, have a long-term perspective and be able to guide the management in decision-making. Profit maximization and similar objectives fail these criteria. Value maximization or shareholder wealth maximization has over time been considered, in financial literature, to be the right metric for a company to aim for, despite somewhat successful attacks on it in recent times.

First, the value of a company is market driven, in fact, market determined; it equals the sum of its equity and debt value. The equity and debt values are based on the price of the company's shares and bonds, established by way of purchase and sale by millions of investors in the market. To that extent, the value is not left to the whims and fancies of an accountant, nor to the vagaries of varied interpretations of the GAAP.

Even if a company is not publicly traded, or its price is not otherwise available, it is possible to determine value by applying standard well-known valuation methods. Based on well-established principles of free cash flow, time value of money, discounting, risk, required rate of return and so forth, the model takes into consideration future cash flows of the company rather than accounting-based methods that look at the past.

Second, value maximization leads to efficient allocation of resources. Financial markets facilitate or intermediate funds transfer between households and the corporate sector. Based on value maximization, the financial markets transfer funds to projects that provide the highest possible return on investments commensurate with their risk, resulting in maximization of the growth of the economy. The Government of India invests large amounts regularly in Air India and other unviable businesses owned by it, thereby dampening economic growth. Given a choice, the financial markets will quite evidently decide against such value-destroying investments.

Third, starting a business venture is quite risky, the risk being primarily borne by equity shareholders. If a company does not perform well or becomes bankrupt, it is the shareholders who stand to lose the most. They have the last priority over the assets and the cash flows of the company. The revenues generated by the company are first used to pay the salaries of employees, the cost of raw materials to suppliers and to meet other operating expenses. The cash flow that remains after meeting these expenses, called operating profits, is distributed as interest to lenders and as corporation tax to the government. Only the balance that remains after all these payments have been made accrues to the shareholders. Technically, the claims of the shareholders are inferior to the claims of other stakeholders and thus, the shareholders are exposed to the highest possible risk.

What motivates equity investors to bear such high risk? Clearly, it is the expectation that companies will maximize their wealth in normal times by pursuing value maximization. New ventures would be very unlikely if the risk bearers (the equity investors) are not appropriately rewarded.

Fourth, a company has numerous stakeholders—people who are impacted by what the company does—the customers, the suppliers, the employees, the lenders, the government, the society and, of course, the shareholders. Ideally, the company must maximize the benefits to all the stakeholders. Such a scenario, while highly desirable, is possible only under ideal conditions and is not quite practical. Good intentions are not only suspect but are also difficult to implement. Often, the gains to one stakeholder will be at the expense of other stakeholders. All stakeholders' claims need to be balanced, a task difficult to define, let alone achieve. Moreover, such a balancing act provides no guidance to managers in their decision-making.

Maximizing shareholder wealth automatically implies that other stakeholders' interests have already been taken care of, since their claims are ahead of and superior to that of the shareholders, who are considered the residual owners of the company. Achieving wealth maximization implies that cash flows accruing to the company have already been satisfactorily distributed to other stakeholders, before the shareholders can claim their share. Shareholder wealth maximization thus becomes the single metric that a firm can aim for and be sure of to satisfy all stakeholders. Value maximization should thus be the one objective guiding all decision-making by the company.

Companies have, for long, been stating this as an explicit policy and thus, shareholder wealth maximization becomes the critical metric to achieve. The iconic Coca-Cola Company stated in its annual report a long time back, 'Our mission is to maximize share-owner value over time.'

Lloyds TSB and Value Maximization

Lloyds TSB had a long time back accepted value maximization as its stated goal and explicitly provided a well-argued defence. According to the company,

> putting value creation first can bring huge benefits, not only to the company but to society as a whole. No company can survive for long unless it creates wealth. A sick company is a drag on society. It cannot sustain jobs nor adequately serve customers. It cannot give to philanthropic causes.
>
> We believe there is no better way for us to serve all our stakeholders—not just our shareholders, but our customers, fellow employees, business partners and the community at large—than by creating value over time for those who employ us. It is our success in value creation that has enabled the Lloyds TSB group to become a leader in charity.

Indian companies too have understood the importance of value creation and actively seek to achieve value maximization. As far back as 1999, EID Parry had stated in its annual report, 'At EID Parry, value creation is central to our operations. It is the force that drives our highly focused agenda for growth. It is the insight to find better, more effective ways of doing business. Maximizing value is more than a slogan. It is the cornerstone of our culture.'

Value maximization thus becomes the guiding mantra for managers in decision-making. Should the company

1. invest in a new packaging project or a cement plant?
2. issue bonds or access equity from a private equity investor for its foray into a software project?
3. lower its price to thwart a new entrant or competitor?
4. offer employee stock option plans (ESOPs) to its managers?

All these decisions can be taken by managers keeping in mind the need to maximize the value of the company by explicitly answering three questions:

1. What is the expected return of the decision? Impacts cash flows.

2. What is the change in the risk profile, if any? Impacts discount rate.
3. Therefore, what is the change in expected value? Net impact of cash flows and the discount rate.

Governance

The various forms of business organizations differ significantly in terms of how they are managed. The difference in the governance structure is significant.

Sole proprietorship and partnerships are easy to manage. The proprietor and the partners take all decisions with respect to the business and, in case of disagreement in a partnership, the partners can vote in proportion to their respective stakes.

The governance of companies is more complex. There are a large number of shareholders, sometimes numbering in millions, each with a different stake in the company. The shareholders are located in different parts of the country and even abroad. Despite advancement in technology and means of transportation and communication, it is virtually impossible to get them together on a regular basis to decide on various business issues.

Shareholders resolve the problem by empowering the board of directors (the 'board') as the apex body managing the company on their behalf. The board establishes the vision and mission of the company to guide its current operations and future development. The board has the following responsibilities:

1. It establishes the strategic policy framework of the company.
2. It appoints the managing director and other senior managers for day-to-day operations.
3. It is responsible for overseeing the management and ensuring the highest standards of corporate governance.

The board is empowered to take decisions on important policy matters of the company's business, its strategy and its organization structure to ensure that the will of the shareholders, expressed through the board of directors, is actually implemented by the managers. The board establishes various committees to oversee and monitor specific areas such as audit, compensation, ethics, risk management and others.

The board appoints the managing director who is the CEO, heading the executive functions, of the company. The board also appoints other senior managers to work under him. The managing director and heads of other functional areas report to the board of directors, which has the power to replace them if their performance is unsatisfactory.

The board members are appointed by the shareholders through an election at the general meeting of all stockholders and hold their positions as long as the shareholders approve. The board of directors has executive as well as non-executive members. Executive members are those who hold a managerial position in the company. The managing director is invariably a member of the board whereas the heads of departments may or may not be members of the board. It is the job of the senior management, led by the managing director, to implement the policy framework established by the board on a day-to-day basis.

Non-executive board members are those who, by virtue of their knowledge and expertise in specific fields, provide advice and guidance. Or they may be 'independent directors' who are expected to look at issues independent of the management and act as trustees of the shareholders. They are expected to be fully aware of, and question, the conduct of the organization on relevant issues. The primary function of the non-executive board members is that of effective oversight. Besides, they must ensure that the company pursues the right strategy, that processes are in place to prevent frauds and that the company has established robust risk management systems. The oversight by independent directors leads to checks and balances and ensures that the managing director and his team continuously work in the interests of the company and its shareholders. Independent directors are expected to have no dealings or any kind of relationship with the company which may prejudice them in performing their role with independence.

Decisions of the board must be ratified by the annual general meeting (AGM) of the shareholders. Shareholders, being owners, are supreme in terms of governance. The approval of the shareholders is required for all major decisions. The practice is to call a general meeting of the shareholders wherein all relevant resolutions are put up for voting. As per the company law, at least one general meeting of shareholders, the AGM, must be held every year. Besides the AGM, the board of directors may call for a special general meeting for any other decision that needs urgent approval.

Until recently, shareholders needed to be physically present at the AGM to exercise their vote, but very few were able to do so, distance, time and cost being major constraints. It was rare to see voting taking place against the management, which has over the years taken the shareholders' consent for granted.

In an effort to resolve this problem, SEBI, the regulatory organization for equity markets, has recently made it mandatory for companies to offer shareholders the option of voting through the internet. E-voting makes distance and time immaterial and enables all shareholders to participate in decision-making. E-voting is mandatory for all companies listed on the stock exchange. It is an effective way to overcome the problem of shareholder non-participation, by leveraging modern technology; the process is safe and maintains the confidentiality of data. It has been a shot in the arm for shareholder governance over the last few years.

Two other measures taken by SEBI have helped improve corporate governance in India. First, there are many issues in which the promoters of a company have personal interest. It is natural for the promoters to keep their own personal interest paramount, often at the expense of the company and its shareholders. Shareholders in the past were powerless to block resolutions which unfairly favoured the promoters, given the large stake of the promoters and the limited attendance by ordinary shareholders at the meetings. The Securities and Exchange Board of India has now barred promoters from voting on any resolution in which they have a personal interest; only the remaining shareholders are allowed to vote and decide on the specific issue. The provision has had immediate success, with Maruti Suzuki India Ltd being forced to alter the terms of agreement with its parent company, subsequent to opposition from some institutional shareholders.

Corporate Governance at Raymond Ltd

Raymond Ltd, a premier textiles company, planned to sell real estate owned by it in Breach Candy, Mumbai, one of the poshest and most expensive places in the city, to the promoter family the Singhanias. For this purpose, it presented a resolution in its AGM on 5 June 2017 for the shareholders' approval.

At the then existing market rate of ₹117,000 per square feet, the real estate was valued at ₹7,100 million. The resolution, however, proposed to sell the property to the Singhanias at ₹9,200 per square feet, for a total consideration of only ₹600 million, at less than 10 per cent of the market value.

The proxy advisory firm Institutional Investor Advisory Services India Limited (IIAS) advised the shareholders to vote against the resolution to protect their interest. In a major boost for corporate governance in India, the resolution was defeated, with 97.67 per cent of the shareholders voting against it. This was possible due to the introduction of a law by SEBI in 2013 whereby promoters are barred from voting on any resolution in which they have a personal interest. The role played by the institutional advisory firm IIAS was also critical.

Interestingly, the audit committee of the company, established by the board, had not approved the transaction prior to its being presented to the AGM, as is the usual practice.

Second, mutual funds, which will be discussed later in the book, are now required to provide rationale for the way they vote on various corporate resolutions in companies where they have invested in equity. The report, stating such rationale, must be published on a quarterly basis. Shareholder activism has become a buzzword in recent times and will hopefully lead to better standards of corporate governance.

In practice, it has been observed that even a board comprising of independent and eminent people is unable to ensure corporate governance conforming to the highest standards if the managers decide otherwise. Satyam Computers had internationally reputed board members, drawn from a wide spectrum including academia. They were unable to detect the financial fraud that was taking place right under their noses for many years, which eventually brought down the company when the fraud was revealed. Such cases of misgovernance are not unique to India and, over the years, many globally renowned companies such as Enron, Volkswagen and WorldCom have similarly suffered through acts of misdemeanour.

The functioning of the boards of directors of companies, in general, leaves a lot to be desired. It has been observed that the constitution of the board is very often faulty and its independence is questionable, despite the regulatory mandated provision that more than half of the directors on the board should be independent. The performance record of the board in monitoring the CEO and safeguarding the interests of the shareholders does not inspire confidence and continues to be a major area of concern in corporate governance worldwide.

Board Evaluation

In 2013, the Companies Act, 1956, made the evaluation of the board and each of its directors mandatory. The Act has also made the evaluation of various board committees mandatory.

The provision is likely to be a shot in the arm for corporate governance, in particular the functioning and accountability of the board of directors. Although currently in a nascent stage, it is expected that such evaluation will significantly improve the manner in which the Boards in the Indian corporate sector discharge their responsibility.

Agency Theory and the Problem of Corporate Governance

The large number of equity shareholders cannot manage the affairs of a company on a day-to-day basis, hence they appoint professional managers to run the business on their behalf. Managers are thus agents of the shareholders, appointed to carry out the task of managing the company. They are expected to accomplish what is in the best interest of the shareholders, implying that managers must maximize shareholders' wealth.

While this separation of ownership and management appears fine in theory, there are definite issues of concern in practice. Often, the objectives of shareholders and those of managers are not aligned, and managers may not pursue maximization of shareholders' wealth but instead work to advance their own personal interests. This is termed agency cost, the pursuit of self-interest by managers without maximizing value, the terminology stemming from the principal–agent relationship between shareholders and managers.

Agency cost arises mainly on account of two factors. First, shareholders are unable to closely and effectively monitor managers who, being in charge of day-to-day operations of the company, become extremely powerful at the expense of the shareholders. Second, managers possess far greater information about the company and its performance than shareholders can ever hope to have. Managers may choose to share only selective and sanitized information with the shareholders, holding back what is against their own interests. This is termed 'information asymmetry', and it prevents shareholders from ensuring that managers pursue maximization of shareholders' wealth.

Agency cost manifests itself in many ways. On the one hand, a prospective project may have a negative net present value, and if the company were to invest in the project, it would lose value. Managers may, on the other hand, want to expand the size of operations so that they have greater opportunities for their own growth and advancement. They may thus decide to go ahead and invest in such a project even though the pursuit of shareholders' interest demands otherwise. Self-aggrandizement by managers often results in a propensity to invest in projects that reduce value.

This commonly happens in companies that operate in a mature industry with few investment opportunities but large free cash flow generation year on year. For maximization of shareholders' wealth, free cash flow must be returned to shareholders, letting them find the best opportunities for investment. However, not many companies do so, often preferring to accumulate free cash flows. Many companies in India, and globally, have huge free cash flows accumulated over the years for which they have no current use. Apple Corporation probably has the largest stock of free cash flow, with over US$200 billion on its books. The main discussion its management usually engages in with large investor activists is not about strategy or development of new products, but how to use these free cash flows and return them to the shareholders. Microsoft has been beset with a similar problem for more than a decade. In India, iconic companies such as Infosys Limited and HUL face a similar predicament.

Managers sometimes incur expenditure which benefits them at the cost of the company and the shareholders. The purchase of a high-cost jet for the personal use of the managing director may fall under this category, as do some of the entitlements that corporate executives get addicted to. At times, salaries of the senior executives are disproportionately high and bear little correlation to the contribution made by them. Huge CEO salary has over the years become a hotly debated issue and is a clear demonstration of the disconnect between the benefits to managers and the interest of shareholders.

Shareholders endeavour to minimize the impact of agency cost in several ways. The tried and tested method is close monitoring by the board of directors, through regular audit of performance and by way of various committees that the board may set up for this purpose. Poor performance may eventually lead to the dismissal of the CEO and his team. However, according to a study carried out in 2010 by Wharton School's Professor Luke Taylor, on an average only 2 per cent CEOs of Fortune 500 firms in the USA are fired in any year (*Knowledge@Wharton* 2011). Since then, this percentage has apparently gone up but is unlikely to be very significant. In India, even fewer CEOs are sacked. Removing a CEO is not a very healthy way of resolving the agency problem, since tremendous damage is already inflicted by the time he is replaced. Chief executive officers in most companies become extremely powerful and removing them is not an easy proposition.

The board may require the CEO to acquire substantial equity stake in the company, to align his interests with that of the shareholders. This is not a feasible option in most cases; for the equity stake to be significant and meaningful, the CEO will need to invest a substantial amount which he may either be unable or unwilling to do.

There are other ways to align the interests of the CEO and the shareholders. The best method is to pay the CEO and other managers a substantial part of their compensation by means of employee stock option plans (ESOPs). Awarding managers ESOPs, instead of requiring them to buy actual stocks, solves the problem of investment financing while at the same time ensuring the alignment of the interests of shareholders and managers.

Prerequisites to granting ESOPs are that the company should be listed on a stock exchange and its shares actively traded in the secondary market. That may not always be the case. If it is not possible to provide ESOPs, the board can structure performance-linked incentives in a way that rewards superior performance and penalizes poor outcomes. The success of such an arrangement depends significantly on careful structuring of the rewards for performance.

Takeover and Managerial Performance

Mergers and acquisitions are an integral part of corporate activity in a capitalist economy. They ostensibly help companies generate efficiencies and build up scale without having to invest in fresh capacities. They also help improve performance and overcome value distortions. If the management of a company is underperforming, leading to lower valuation, the company is likely to become a takeover target, jeopardizing the current management's position. The very threat of such a takeover and eventual dismissal of the management should spur improved performance.

ABC Ltd is a company that should be able to achieve a value of ₹100 billion with the best possible management, in line with the pursuit of value maximization. The managers, having become extremely powerful, ignore the interests of the shareholders and instead pursue their own interests, with huge value-destroying investments and indulging in wasteful expenditure for themselves. Not surprisingly, the market values the company at only ₹60 billion, a huge loss in value.

Sensing an opportunity, many buyers—competitors, private equity firms and others— would be willing to pay a price between the current and the potential value, improve performance and manage the company in line with the objective of value maximization, and bring it closer to ₹100 billion. Obviously, the first target of such a takeover will be the existing management which will have to make way for an alternative one. The threat of such a takeover should prove to be a powerful incentive to align the objectives of shareholders with that of the management and improve performance. For this, it is important for an economy to have a free, vibrant market for M&As.

Corporate governance and managerial compensation are extremely controversial issues and have always aroused strong emotions amongst various stakeholders and the public. Quite possibly, a perfect solution that satisfies everyone is non-existent, although the quest for one continues. Maybe agency cost is the price we pay for the substantial benefits derived from the corporate form of organization.

Corporate Finance

The primary purpose of a business firm is to produce and market goods and services to meet the needs of its customers and simultaneously maximize shareholders' wealth. In this section, we introduce the readers to the major decision areas for a CFO.

1. Capital budgeting: Firms invest in buildings, plant and machinery and in other intangibles such as brands and patents. Capital budgeting refers to the decision and process of investing in long-term assets.

Corporate Strategy

The Aditya Birla Group decided a long time back that cement would be a core area of operations for them. Since the beginning of this century, they have built up substantial manufacturing capacity and are currently the leading cement player in the country with a capacity of 93.70 million tons. Larsen & Toubro Ltd decided to concentrate on its main engineering, procurement and construction (EPC) business and not cement. It sold its cement division to the Aditya Birla Group.

2. Working capital: Besides the fixed and long-term investments, a firm also needs to make short-term investments in inventory and accounts receivables, which comprise its working capital. Working capital management is concerned with day-to-day management of the short-term assets and liabilities—the level of inventory to maintain, how much credit to give customers and what should be the terms of payment to the suppliers. Working capital management is a crucial determinant of the performance of the company. If short-term cash flows are not managed properly, the health of the firm can be seriously impaired. Maruti Ltd has established an enterprise resource planning (ERP) system to monitor the components required for manufacturing its cars. The ERP system is linked with its component manufacturers who supply the components as and when required, enabling Maruti Ltd to significantly reduce its stock of inventory and its investments in working capital, thereby improving its cash flow and the return on investment.

3. Funds raising and capital structure: Companies need to raise funds for investment in both long-term assets and working capital. Funds can be raised through equity, debt or instruments that combine the features of both equity and debt. Some securities issued by companies may have attributes partly of debt and partly of equity to produce a return–risk combination that is demanded by investors.

Hybrid Instruments

Companies often resort to what are termed hybrid instruments to fund their need for capital. Hybrid instruments combine features of both debt and equity. A convertible bond is an example of a very popular hybrid instrument.

As the name suggests, a convertible bond is a type of bond which can be converted into equity shares at a future date. It gives the holder the option to exchange the bond for a predetermined number of shares of the company. The terms governing the conversion are pre-decided at the time of the issue. Usually, the bond pays interest until conversion, after which it becomes an equity share.

Contd

contd .

> Many variants of the convertible bond exist in the marketplace. Conversion into equity may be mandatory instead of being optional to the holder of the bond. Or only part of the bond may be convertible, with the balance continuing as a standard debt instrument until maturity. Interestingly, the colloquial term in the Indian markets for the part remaining after the partial equity conversion of the bond is *khokha*. Convertible bonds can also be denominated in foreign currencies and are quite popular.

Companies have a wide array of instruments to choose from, such as convertible bonds, non-voting shares, preference shares, zero-coupon bonds, junk bonds, payment-in-kind (PIK) securities, floating rate instruments, catastrophe bonds and innumerable others.

Some of these instruments, such as bonds and shares, are widely traded in the market. Alternatively, a company can fund itself through non-traded claims such as term loans. Bharti Airtel required funds for investment in spectrum, technology, marketing and branding in 2003. It made a public offer and sold 185.3 million equity shares to raise ₹8,340 million. But when it acquired operations in Africa, it relied largely on internal accruals and borrowings for its funding.

Given here is an illustration of a very complicated bond issued by Citibank in 1978 for raising US$200 million. At this stage, readers need not worry about the features of this instrument. The illustration is only to demonstrate the innovative ways in which the financial markets fund the corporate sector and banks.

Citibank Innovative Instrument

A US$200 million par amount of floating rate notes was issued by Citicorp on 26 June 1978. The coupon of the floater was indexed to the six-month t-bill rates, that is, to the arithmetic average of the weekly market rate of the six-month US treasury bills, as published by the Federal Reserve Bank during the 14 calendar days immediately prior to the last 10 days of February and August.

The actual coupon was this average plus 120 basis points during the period 1979–83, subject to a minimum of 7.5 per cent. For the period 1984–8, the spread over the average was 100 basis points, subject to a minimum of 7 per cent; for the period of 1989–98, the spread was 75 basis points, subject to a minimum of 6.5 per cent. At the time of issue, Citicorp was rated AAA/AA+.

The note matured on 1 September 1998. The floater did not have conversion features but was callable after 1 September 1988 at declining call prices.

A firm generates cash flows from its operations (operating profits). 'Security' is a generic term for a financial instrument that is entitled to the cash flows generated by the firm. The nature of a security and its risk profile is determined by the nature of cash flows the security is entitled to. Capital structure determines the priority of claims over these cash flows. Debt providers usually get regular interest at fixed rates, whereas equity providers are entitled to the net profits of the company.

Many Indian companies invested heavily in their businesses prior to the global financial crisis of 2008, expecting good times prevailing then to last forever. The investment was funded largely through borrowing which made these companies extremely risky and vulnerable. A significant downturn, post-crisis, has bankrupted many of those companies and destroyed substantial value. A greater reliance on equity and a safer capital structure would have helped prevent the crisis that many companies are facing now. Capital structuring decisions have a significant impact on the long-term health and fortunes of companies.

Capital budgeting, working capital management and financing and capital structure broadly constitute the core of corporate finance. Corporate finance can be considered to be the acquisition and use of funds by a company. It determines the following:

1. How fast should a company grow?
2. What should be the composition of its assets?
3. What should be the financing mix?

Besides these three functions, corporate finance also encompasses the following:

1. Financial analysis and planning: analysis of performance and strategizing for the future
2. Investments and treasury management: management of surplus money
3. M&As: acquisition of other companies and integrating the acquired entity, divestment of own assets
4. Foreign exchange: managing foreign exchange requirements/earnings of the company
5. Risk management: managing strategic risk exposure of the company

KEY CONCEPTS

1. The CFO relies substantially on financial markets to achieve his objectives.
2. The objective of a company is value maximization.
3. Most large organizations are incorporated as companies. Corporate structure helps the business in many ways.
4. Governance presents a difficult problem for companies. Substantial reliance is placed on the board of directors to ensure that policies devised by them are efficiently implemented by managers on a day-to-day basis.
5. Separation of ownership and management leads to agency costs that can be significant.
6. Investment, financing and capital structure, and working capital management broadly constitute the core of corporate finance.

CHAPTER QUESTIONS

1. What is the significance of the financial markets to the CFO in achieving his/her objectives? How does he/she interface with the financial markets?
2. How is a corporate form of organization superior to other forms? Why are large organizations almost invariably incorporated as companies?
3. What objectives does a company seek to achieve and why?
4. Why is maximization of profits not the right metric for a company to strive to achieve?
5. The business of business is business. Discuss.
6. Given that a company has a large number of owners, what is the mechanism of governance? What is the role of the board of directors in governance?
7. What is agency cost, and what is its impact? How can shareholders reduce the impact of agency cost?
8. Which of the following always do/does apply to corporations? Mention true or false against each and explain your rationale.
    a. Unlimited liability.
    b. Ownership can be transferred without affecting operations.
    c. Managers can be fired with no effect on ownership.
    d. Shares must be widely traded.
9. Choose a company you know well. Describe some of the key decisions the CFO of the company has taken over the last few years. What has been the impact of those decisions on the company?

CASE FOR DISCUSSION

ABC Ltd is a mid-sized telecom company planning to increase its sales substantially in order to hit the big league. The CEO of the company is having a strenuous time handling different divisions, strategizing and balancing competing demands. The job in hand seems impossible to handle.

Towards shepherding the company to the big league, he attended a short-term programme at the Indian Institute of Management Ahmedabad, which not only energized him but also changed his thinking in the right direction in his quest towards taking the company forward.

One of the key takeaways of the programme was the emphasis on value maximization and concentration on shareholders' interests. He learnt, belatedly he felt, that a company, and by inference its managers, must direct all their efforts towards maximizing the value of the company. He also learnt that value is determined by future free cash flows, which must be discounted at the risk-adjusted cost of capital (COC). The implication is fairly obvious: in order to increase value, the company must either increase free cash flows or reduce COC.

During the next few months, the CEO took the following decisions amongst many others:

1. The company invested ₹60 million in corporate social responsibility (CSR) projects which included

a. maintenance of greenery outside the Mumbai airport,
b. funding an orphan centre,
c. starting a school for underprivileged children and
d. establishing library facilities in villages around its factory.

2. The company invested in a project that had negative cash flows in the first three years.
3. The company dropped prices for its voice calls and data usage that reduced its margins significantly.

Given that none of these projects apparently increase its value, why did the CEO take the listed decisions? How did he justify these decisions to the company's board of directors?

What factors could have prompted these actions, and what could have been the thought process of the management of ABC Ltd?

Please consider each decision independently.

CHAPTER 2

Financial Markets

In Markets, there is no such thing as scarcity or oversupply. There is only price.

—Anonymous

Raising large amount of funds for establishing and running a business enterprise cannot be done through private ownership and limited partnerships. Corporations are the mainstay of modern commerce and business. They tap large and diverse sources of funds such as individuals, government agencies and financial institutions, both national and global. To facilitate the transfer of funds between suppliers and those who need them, we must have a large and well-regulated mechanism. The financial markets provide such a mechanism for the transfer of funds while also performing many other tasks. In this chapter, we will study the nature, organization, operation and regulation of the financial market.

Financial markets are an essential constituent of an economy and have witnessed a boom in recent times throughout the world. Despite being blamed for the crisis in 2008, more and more countries are taking recourse to financial markets in a bid to improve the state of the economy and their people. Very few wealthy nations, if any, are without an efficient and thriving financial market, whereas hardly any poor country can claim to have one.

It is instructive to understand the role markets play in an economy. Human beings have unlimited wants but their capacity to produce is limited. They need to exchange what they produce with what they wish to consume. Markets for products facilitate the exchange of goods and services and thereby enable us to specialize in our respective areas of expertise. If you want a cup of tea, you do not need to own a tea garden, a sugar factory, a cow for providing milk or a gas service agency. All you need is to continue to do what you are good at—an efficient bureaucrat, a sitar player, a top cricketer or even a teacher—and you can exchange these services for a cup of tea from a tea vendor. By enabling the exchange of goods and services, the product and services markets make it possible to separate the decision to consume from the decision to produce.

Specialization in one's area of expertise results in a much higher level of production in an economy than would have been otherwise possible. It is the basis for the vast improvement in living standards experienced throughout history, especially since the Industrial Revolution.

Just as the product markets enable the exchange of goods and services, financial markets enable the exchange of money and thereby divorce the decision to save from the decision to invest.

Individuals are able to pass on their savings to the corporate sector, and the corporate sector need not depend only on internally generated funds to undertake investment in new projects.

Four Economic Entities

Four broad entities constitute the economy (Figure 2.1). First is the household sector, people like you and me. Households in India have been brought up with the save-for-a-rainy-day attitude and do not spend all their earnings; they, in fact, save a large proportion of their incomes. Second is the corporate sector, which is usually in need of funds for investment in various projects. The third player in the pack is the government, which usually has a large deficit, especially in India. The funds that the government appropriates from household savings leave that much less for the corporate sector. Large fiscal deficit over the years has been the primary cause of high interest rates in the Indian economy. A shortfall in domestic funding can be made up by inflows from the rest of the world, which is the fourth constituent of an economy. Taken together, these four equate savings and investments in the economy.

Functions of Financial Markets

The primary objective of financial markets is to facilitate the movement of funds between the four sectors. It is the financial sector that enables the transfer of savings of the households to the corporate sector and the government. And it is the financial sector that facilitates inflow of funds from across the world into India. In the absence of an efficient financial market, it would become virtually impossible for the corporate sector and the government to source funds for their requirements, and the household sector would be devoid of avenues to invest its savings on lucrative terms. In the absence of financial markets, one can imagine a Sunil Mittal or a

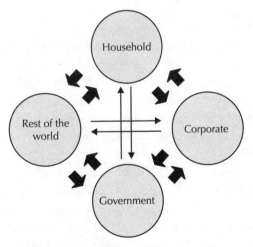

Figure 2.1 Economy: the four entities

Source: Author.

Mukesh Ambani going from house to house, collecting funds for their multi-billion dollar projects! While that may be an exaggeration, with an efficient financial market, all they have to do is to snap their fingers and, hey presto, they have the requisite funding, provided, of course, their projects satisfy the fundamental objective of value creation.

US Institutional Funds

On average, US households directly invest US$230 billion each year in stocks and bonds. They also invest nearly US$350 billion each year in mutual funds that buy stocks and bonds on their behalf. Thus, directly or indirectly, the US households undertake a substantial investment in the financial markets.

The US pension funds are important market participants. In 2012, they held US$8.8 trillion in stocks, or 16.8 per cent of the global equity markets, and US$4.5 trillion in bonds, or 4.5 per cent of the global bond market.

An efficient financial market channels savings from one or more sectors in the economic system to the investors in a timely fashion and at a low cost. It can be safely surmised that the more efficient the financial sector, the greater is the motivation in the economy to save and invest in value-creating assets, resulting in higher economic growth. On the other hand, an underdeveloped financial market is a drag on savings and consequently on investments. This function of the financial markets, of bringing savers and investors together, is termed *intermediation*.

Intermediation by HDFC Bank

HDFC Bank is the second largest private sector bank in India. It has a capital base of ₹1,062.95 billion, on which it has taken deposits of ₹7,887.70 billion in the form of savings and current account and fixed deposits. Its long-term borrowings and other liabilities amount to ₹1,688.69 billion. Thus, the total fund base available with the bank is ₹10,639.34 billion.

HDFC Bank thus intermediates over ₹10,000 billion between savers and investors. Out of this, ₹2,422 billion has been invested in government securities as statutory liquidity ratio (SLR). An amount of ₹6,583.33 billion has been given as advance to the corporate sector and the retail borrowers for various purposes.

This in a nutshell reveals the intermediation function performed by the premier private sector bank in India in 2017–18, which ensures that households have opportunities to save and get lucrative returns on these savings. At the same time, retail borrowers are able to obtain funds for purchasing physical assets such as housing and personal vehicles and the corporate sector for its investment in projects and working capital.

The second function that financial markets perform is the *allocation of resources* in the economy. Financial markets allocate capital efficiently by assigning it to projects which add maximum value, thus maximizing the growth rate of the economy. Given a choice between investing in a highway between Mumbai and Pune and a new airlines venture, financial markets take a decision between the two avenues of investment based on value accretion.

Incremental Capital Output Ratio (ICOR)

The efficiency with which savings are allocated amongst different investment avenues determines the rate of growth of an economy. Efficiency in allocation is primarily a function of what the economists term the incremental capital output ratio (ICOR). It refers to the number of additional units of capital that are required to increase output by one unit. A higher ICOR is an indication of inefficiency, while a low ICOR results in a higher growth from the same amount of capital investment. The growth rate of the economy is equal to the investment rate divided by the ICOR.

Broadly speaking, there are two strands of thoughts on the allocation of funds—a planned economy approach and a market-based one. After independence, India started on the path of a planned economy, with the Planning Commission dictating the flow of funds to different projects. The consequent inefficient allocation of savings ensured a high ICOR for over three decades, ranging between 6 and 8. With a savings rate of 20 per cent, the Indian economy grew at what the economist K. N. Raj had termed the Hindu rate of growth, amounting to 3 to 3.5 per cent per annum, until 1985. A population growth rate of 2 to 2.5 per cent did not leave much room for improvement in per capita income and, consequently, the living standards continued to remain low.

It was only with the liberalization of the Indian economy and the subsequent reliance on the markets for the allocation of investment that our ICOR came down significantly. A combination of high savings rate and low ICOR resulted in a much higher growth rate which, at one point in time, was sprinting towards the double digits.

Historical ICOR in India

Figure 2.2 shows the ICOR for the Indian economy over a twenty-year period from 1993 to 2013. The average has been 4.1, implying that an investment rate of 32.8 per cent is required to achieve a growth rate of 8 per cent. The ICOR which was as high as 6.1 in 2002 dropped significantly to an average of 3.4 over the next five years, providing the Indian economy its best ever phase of growth. Subsequently, there has been a spike in the ICOR resulting in lower growth rates.

Contd

contd

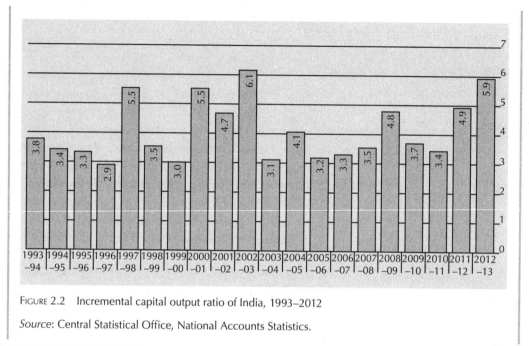

FIGURE 2.2   Incremental capital output ratio of India, 1993–2012

Source: Central Statistical Office, National Accounts Statistics.

The third key function of financial markets is *price discovery*. Price discovery of financial securities enables valuation of companies, thereby helping in allocation of resources, efficient decision-making by managers and high growth rates in the economy.

The price discovery process involves the buyers and sellers trading securities to arrive at a transaction price for any security. Efficient price discovery is predicated on having a large number of buyers and sellers along with an efficient market structure. The market structure refers to the bidding process, settlement procedure, trading structures, timely and relevant information and effective regulatory mechanism. The price of a security thus arrived at reflects an assessment of the future risk and return in an efficient market. Risk and return of a security are incorporated in the price, leading to efficiency in the financial markets.

Finally, financial markets help in *risk management*. Every organization today is exposed to risk, which has no longer remained just a four-letter word. The *Wall Street Journal* had declared in 1993 that an organization which does not have a risk management strategy is a rarity. What was true twenty-five years back of the US economy is even more relevant for the Indian economy today. Companies are increasingly getting exposed to unpredictable changes in foreign exchange rates, interest rates and commodity prices. Any company that does not manage exposure to such risks carefully is unlikely to survive for long. Financial markets enable companies to manage strategic risks by providing tools such as derivatives, enabling them to concentrate on their core business without worrying about the adverse impact of changes in underlying financial variables. Companies are able to survive and, in fact, thrive due to the availability and usage of financial tools to manage their underlying risk exposure.

While individual risk exposure can be reduced, risk for the economy as a whole cannot be reduced. What the markets do is to trade securities and transfer risk from those who are exposed to risk and cannot bear it to those who are best placed to bear such risk. To take a simple example, as individuals, we are exposed to loss of life, health, assets and livelihood. If misfortune befalls us, we will be unable to bear the consequent loss. Insurance companies aggregate the risk of a large number of people and take it on their own account. Overall there is no reduction in risk, but the economy benefits by aggregation of risk and the consequent specialization. Of course, the transfer takes place at a price (the insurance premium), and the pricing of risks becomes one of the most critical functions of financial markets.

To take another example, a student takes an educational loan from a bank for his MBA. In the normal course, the bank would expect the student to pay the interest and maturity amount back once he takes up a job, post MBA. A recession in the economy may result in him being unemployed and unable to pay his dues. Usually, the banks take a personal guarantee from the borrower's parents/relative who will pay up in case the borrower is himself unable to do so. This is a classic case of transfer of risk from the bank to the guarantor.

In general, a financial transaction is a funding as well as a risk transaction. Financial markets enable unbundling of the two so that they may be traded separately. They are thereby able to distribute risks easily and efficiently in the economy. Companies and other entities routinely use derivatives to hedge risks. Derivatives transfer risk from the buyer to the seller, of course at a price. Risk transfer and pricing of risk are critical functions of financial markets which help the real sector (the sector which produces goods and services) undertake innovation and assume risky ventures. Without the ability to transfer and hedge risk, many projects in the real sector would not be undertaken.

Exchange Risk at Wipro Ltd

Wipro Ltd, a software company, derives a large part of its business from the United States of America (USA). Let us assume it bags an order from a large financial services company valued at US$500 million and payable over the next five years. Wipro has expertise and competitive advantage in creating, building, delivering and maintaining software projects which it is confident of doing for its client over the period of the contract.

There is, however, a mismatch between its earnings (in US dollars) and its expenses (largely in Indian rupee). The mismatch creates risk for the company and has the potential to scuttle a project and its profitability. Derivatives enable Wipro Ltd to manage the exchange rate risk so that it is no longer impacted by changes in US dollar/Indian rupee rates and can concentrate on its primary work of providing software services.

Thus, as described, financial markets perform the following critical functions:

1. Intermediation between savers and investors
2. Allocation of investments

3. Price discovery
4. Risk management

Besides, the financial markets also provide for settlement and payment systems to facilitate the exchange of goods and services. Beginning with the barter system, financial markets have come a long way having passed through many stages in the use of money, including gold, metals and others. In the last century, paper money, primarily issued by governments, generally served as a standard payment mechanism. Moving on from the banks' cheque system to ATMs, from plastic cards to online banking, recent times have witnessed significant changes in the way payments can be made. Who knows what the future has in store, with bitcoins and other cryptocurrencies, based on distributed blockchain technology, coming up in a big way?

Institutional Mechanism

There are two kinds of institutional mechanisms in financial markets which enable the intermediation of funds. When the economy is underdeveloped, banks and other finance companies are predominant. These institutions take deposits, primarily from individuals, and pass them on, for investment, to the corporate sector. They accept money on their own account, are responsible to the depositors for repayment and bear the risk of default from borrowing companies. For example, when Alok Industries Ltd defaulted on its loans, the depositors of the State Bank of India (SBI) did not suffer any loss, which was borne completely by the bank. Alok Industries has now been referred to the National Company Law Tribunal for insolvency resolution.

Institutions borrowing money on their own account is not a very efficient mechanism of intermediation as the difference between the lending and the deposit rate, termed 'the spread', is extremely high. Moreover, the resulting allocation of resources is not very efficient, depending as it does on the credit evaluation mechanism of the banks. However, as these are the predominant institutions in the initial stages of the development of an economy, the financial markets depend on them for intermediation.

As the economy develops further, it creates market-based structures and the intermediation takes place through equity and debt markets (the stock exchanges). The government and the corporate sector raise funds directly from the savers, with the stock and debt exchanges providing an interface for this purpose. The savers have a direct relationship with the borrowers and take risks—credit as well as market/price risk—on their own account. In 2009, Mahindra Holidays & Resorts India Ltd (MHRIL), which provides leisure hospitality services, raised funds directly from shareholders by means of an initial public offering. The stock exchanges provided the interface by which MHRIL sold shares to the investors and, subsequently, trading of MHRIL shares was possible on these stock exchanges. This process may be termed 'disintermediation', since the intermediation takes place directly, without any financial institution between the borrowers and lenders.

The mechanism of disintermediation through market-based structures is cost effective and allocates the economy's resources more efficiently. The stage of development of an economy can be gauged by the proportion of funds raised directly through market-based structures vis-à-vis intermediation by financial institutions.

Reintermediation

In many industrialized countries, individuals no longer deposit their savings in banks. Instead, they participate in the markets through mutual funds, insurance companies and pension funds. They also invest in companies through hedge funds, venture capital funds and other forms of private equity. These financial institutions have, in a sense, displaced banks and, according to Raghuram Rajan, former governor of the Reserve Bank of India (RBI), these financial institutions have 'reintermediated' themselves between individuals and markets. In India, although deposits with the banks continue to grow, reintermediation is also gaining momentum.

Funds flow from the surplus units to deficit units in many ways. A surplus unit is one that saves from its current income (individuals) or from its operating cash flows (companies). A deficit unit is one which needs funds—a consumer looking to buy a house/car or a company, considering investment in long-term projects beyond its operating cash flows.

Let us discuss the different ways in which funds move from one unit (surplus) to the other (deficit). Funds may flow from surplus units to deficit units through financial intermediaries such as the banks and insurance companies. For example, SBI accepts deposits from people in small amounts, usually for short periods. Aggregating these deposits, it lends to Reliance Industries Ltd for its investment projects. The risks of lending are borne by SBI which is responsible for the repayment of deposits. The households have no direct claim on Reliance Industries Ltd.

Alternatively, funds can flow through financial markets directly without going through an intermediary. Thyrocare India Ltd, a company specializing in medical diagnostics, made a public issue of shares in 2016, which were purchased directly by investors, through the interface of the stock markets but without an intermediary institution.

Sometimes, intermediaries themselves source funds from the financial markets. L&T Finance Ltd, a non-banking finance company, and hence an intermediary, made a public issue of shares and was able to raise ₹12.45 billion directly from the stock markets in July 2011.

Companies often have excess funds which they may invest in government securities and other instruments. Infosys Ltd, for example, has invested ₹250 billion in government bonds, corporate debt and mutual funds, with varying terms. Funds have thus moved from the corporate sector to the government and other entities through the exchange.

In current times, even global markets are interlinked and funds flow across national boundaries. Companies have the option of raising funds internationally through various kinds of financial securities, from global banks to Euro markets to the Wall Street. Many Indian companies have already done so and continue to access global financial markets for their requirements. HDFC Bank raised US$1.27 billion through American depository receipts from the New York Stock Exchange, and many American citizens and institutions are now shareholders of HDFC Bank.

The Wall Street

Wall Street is a street in Lower Manhattan in New York, USA. It originally housed the New York Stock Exchange as well as the head offices of some of the largest brokerage houses and investment banks in the USA. In a sense, it is synonymous with and represents the financial markets in the USA.

Financial markets may be located anywhere in the world. In the pre-liberalization era, India had 23 stock exchanges, with each stock exchange limited to a specific city. The Bombay Stock Exchange (BSE), located in erstwhile Bombay, now called Mumbai, was predominant, accounting for over 80 per cent of the trading in equity. The money market, the market for trading short-term financial instruments, was also limited to a few banks and institutions, mostly headquartered in Mumbai. It was often said that the financial market of India was limited to the 3.2 square kilometre area in South Bombay. Since the early 1990s, efforts have been made, quite successfully, to broaden and spread the markets to the rest of the 3.2 million square kilometres of India. Spread of trading terminals all over the country and internet penetration has ensured equal opportunity to trade throughout the country. Although much still remains to be done, it would not be wrong to say that significant democratization of financial markets has taken place in India since the early 1990s.

The proliferation of the internet has led to a belief that 'geography is history'. It is doubtful how much this applies to other areas but geography or location has certainly become largely irrelevant in financial markets. In the past, investors and brokers would congregate at a specific location called the trading ring and trade through what was called the open cry system. Now, trading is almost universally electronic and hence not confined to a physical space. Time has also become largely irrelevant, with trading possible 24/7 globally.

The ease and efficiency with which funds flow from various surplus units to deficit units determine the availability and cost of funds for the corporate sector and is a critical determinant of the performance of the economy.

Physical and Financial Assets

Economists usually distinguish between physical and financial assets. The value of a physical asset depends on its physical properties and the utility it provides. Physical assets may include a house, machinery or a computer. A financial asset is a security representing a legal claim to future cash flows. The claim to future cash flows can be fixed, as in the case of a bond. Or such claims can be residual and variable, as in the case of equity. Of course, there are various securities that combine the features of fixed and residual claims.

Types of Financial Markets

Based on the instruments traded, financial markets can be categorized as follows:

1. The fixed income securities market, or the market for debt instruments
2. The equities market
3. The foreign exchange market
4. The derivatives market

The Fixed Income Securities Market

The fixed income securities market is the market for debt instruments. A debt instrument is created when an entity borrows money, whether it is the individual who borrows for funding the purchase of his house, the government which borrows to cover the excess of its spending over revenues (fiscal deficit) or a corporate entity which leverages on its equity and takes on debt for funding its investment requirements.

A typical bond has a face value or par value printed on its face. Nowadays, of course, such securities are held in electronic form and not physically. The issuer of the bond contracts to pay the initial buyer, or any subsequent holder, this par value at the end of a fixed period of time in the future, known as its tenure, or the maturity. The issuer also contracts to pay the holder a certain amount, known as the coupon rate of interest, at fixed intervals, usually every six months. The payback of par value is called redemption.

Innumerable variations in face value, maturity period and value, interest rate and other features are possible on these bonds, leading to a large and a very vibrant market, satisfying diverse needs of investors and borrowers. For example, borrowers may issue zero-coupon bonds, floating rate bonds, option-embedded bonds, foreign currency convertible bonds, catastrophe bonds, payment-in-kind (PIK) bonds, commodity-linked bonds and many other variants. Debt instruments have varying features with respect to return, risk and liquidity. Investors/issuers invest in/issue bonds which satisfy their needs in terms of various features. Many a times, unusual bonds are issued, some of which have interesting antecedents. In 1983, Hungary issued a 6 per cent bond which included a firm promise of a telephone connection in 3 years, the usual waiting period for a phone at that time being 20 years.

Types of Fixed Income Securities Markets

Depending on who the borrower is, the fixed income securities market can be classified as follows:

1. Treasury: Securities issued by the government of a country are termed treasury securities. Since governments have the authority to levy taxes and print currency notes, treasury securities are perceived to be free of the risk of default. It is assumed that sovereign entities would not renege on their commitments and the interest and the maturity value will be paid in accordance with the terms of the borrowing.

While largely true, over the years many governments have defaulted on payment or have had to be bailed out. Traditionally, it was believed that only emerging economies are likely to default and that investment in bonds of developed countries is safe. That does not hold true any longer, with many developed countries having to be bailed out in recent years. The acronym PIGS (Portugal, Ireland, Greece and Spain) had become very popular some years back, referring to European countries which had to be bailed out by the International Monetary Fund (IMF). Else, these countries would have defaulted on their borrowings, an embarrassing event, to say the least. With the US government debt being downgraded two years back from the safest possible rating and no longer enjoying the AAA status, investors have been left wondering where their money can be invested with complete safety!

Treasury securities are large in value and are actively traded in the financial markets. Being risk free, they set the benchmark in terms of rates for other securities. Risk-averse investors find them an attractive proposition for investment. US securities, in particular, have a high demand and many countries, including India, have invested their surplus funds in US government bonds.

2. Corporate: The corporate sector needs large funding for investment in capital goods and working capital. A large proportion of the fund requirement of the corporate sector is met through borrowings. Corporate debt is usually riskier than treasury borrowing. There are credit rating agencies which assess and rate corporate debt to indicate how risky the debt issued by a company is.

Fund Raising in the USA

In 2012, companies raised US$1.36 trillion in corporate debt and US$278.9 billion in equity in the USA.

In 2013, Verizon Communications sold US$49 billion bonds in the biggest corporate debt offering ever. Verizon used the proceeds to finance its US$130 billion buyout of Vodafone's 45 per cent stake in their Verizon Wireless joint venture.

Investors demand a higher return for risky debt than a comparatively safer one, which translates into a higher cost of capital (COC) for the corporate sector. The risk of corporate debt depends on the amount and the uncertainty of the cash flows generated by the company. The higher and more certain the cash flows, the higher is the credit rating and lower the risk. Similarly, the lower and more uncertain the cash flows, the lower is the credit rating and higher the risk.

It is mandatory in India for any corporate debt, longer than 18-month tenure, to be rated by a Securities and Exchange Board of India (SEBI)-recognized rating agency. India has four major credit rating companies, namely CRISIL, IICRA, CARE and Fitch. In the USA, Standard & Poor, Moody and Fitch are the top rating companies.

Masala Bonds

Masala bonds are rupee-denominated bonds, issued by Indian entities in foreign markets. Interestingly, the first such bond was issued by the International Finance Corporation (IFC) to finance its projects in India. It used the term 'masala' to evoke the culture and cuisine of India and create interest for its bond offering. Recently, HDFC raised ₹30 billion through masala bonds.

Usually, when an Indian entity borrows in overseas market, it issues bonds that are denominated in foreign currency—US dollar, euro, pound or yen. Payment of interest and repayment of the principal are in foreign currency, which introduces currency risk for the borrowing company. Masala bonds, being denominated in the local Indian rupee, pass on the exchange risk to the investor and, therefore, can be an attractive proposition for the corporate sector in India.

3. Municipal: Municipal bonds (popularly called munis) are issued by local city or district governments and by local governmental authorities. They have diverse features with respect to redemption, credit risk and liquidity.

Municipal Bonds in the USA

Between 2003 and 2012, US counties, states and other municipalities raised US$3.2 trillion for infrastructure development by issuing municipal bonds.

Municipal securities are issued to cover short-term imbalances and for financing long-term projects. They are popular in the USA and have financed much of the infrastructure in the country. Municipal bonds in the USA are exempt from federal tax, leading to high post-tax return for the investor. Municipal bonds have not made a real mark in India as yet.

Municipal Bonds Issued by PMC

Pune Municipal Corporation (PMC) raised ₹2 billion through a municipal bond issue in June 2017. The bond is listed on the BSE. Pune Municipal Corporation has earned itself a long-term credit rating of AA+, indicating a stable outlook. Pune is the second-largest corporation in Maharashtra and earns the bulk of its revenues from property taxes and local body taxes. The corporation plans to use the funds for a 24/7 water supply project for the city, as it attempts to meet its smart city mission. The bond has been guaranteed by the Maharashtra government.

4. Mortgage backed securities: Mortgage refers to a loan in which property or real estate is provided as a collateral. The purchase of a house is a high-value transaction and usually is several times the annual salary of an individual. Saving for a house used to take an inordinately long time, and most people spent an entire lifetime without owning their own home until the establishment of HDFC Limited in 1977. Housing finance companies like HDFC now enable people to borrow for financing the purchase of their coveted house and pay for it from their future earnings over a period of time.

   Mortgages have two distinguishing features

   i) Mortgage is a loan payable over a long period of time. In the USA, mortgages for 30 years are very common. In India, 20 years used to be the maximum period of a housing loan. Lately, however, housing finance institutions have started disbursing 25 year loans.

   ii) Repayments are through what are termed 'equated monthly instalments', popularly called EMIs. Each month's instalment payment is equal for the entire period of the mortgage. Mortgages are explained later, in greater detail, in Chapter 3.

   Each EMI is too small to interest major players in the financial market. Trust the market to innovate and make mortgages a most sought-after instrument. While each EMI may be small, several mortgages can be combined to create larger cash flows. These cash flows can be used as collateral to fund large institutional requirements by issuing bonds termed mortgage-backed securities (MBS). Over time, MBS have expanded in size, scope and variety and play a significant role in financial markets.

Mortgage-Backed Securities

Assume, HDFC Limited provides a mortgage loan of ₹5 million for 20 years at 10.52 per cent to a single borrower. The EMI for the loan is ₹50,000. The mortgage creates a monthly cash flow of ₹50,000 per month over 240 months. A relatively long cash flow but at a small value of ₹50,000 does not attract the market's attention.

Combine 10,000 similar loans and what we get is a huge cash flow of ₹500 million per month over a period of 240 months. This cash flow can be used as a collateral to raise further funds by HDFC Limited through what is popularly termed an MBS. The cash flows, used as collateral for further borrowing, are rated to determine their risk and consequently the required return on MBS. The financial market has been innovating such securities with different risk and return features. At times, the urge to innovate gets a little too far, leading to a crisis such as the financial meltdown of 2008.

The aforementioned securities have long-term maturity. There also exist short-term instruments such as treasury bills, certificates of deposits and commercial paper which play a significant role in financial markets. The market for short-term securities is known as the money market.

The Equities Market

The equities market is the market for shares issued by the corporate sector. Equity investors are owners of the company and hence all decisions pertaining to its governance must meet their approval. Investment in new projects, funding plans, dividend payments and appointment of board of directors and of senior managers of the company are all decisions that have to ultimately be approved by the shareholders.

Equity as an instrument of investment is risky. The returns on equity are not fixed and can be extremely volatile, even negative during some periods. The claim of equity shareholders on the company's cash flows is residual in nature. They get what remains after all other claimants have received their dues. Sometimes, there may be nothing left, in which case equity shareholders may not receive any returns. At other times, cash flows that remain after satisfying other stakeholders are substantial and shareholders enjoy high returns. Due to the higher risk faced by equity shareholders, the required rate of return on equity is higher than that of debt.

The return to equity holders comprises dividends and capital gains. After all expenses have been incurred and corporate tax has been paid to the government, what remains is the net profit. The net profit belongs to the shareholders, a part of which is paid to them at the discretion of the board of directors and final approval at the annual general meeting (AGM). This is known as dividend. Neither the amount nor the periodicity of dividends is fixed or certain, payable as it is at the discretion of the board of directors and the fund requirements of the company. Dividend policy will be discussed later in Chapter 8.

Depending on the investments undertaken by the company and its performance, the shareholders make capital gains (or capital losses) which add to their total returns. Usually, dividends form only a small portion of the returns to shareholders who depend primarily on the rise in share prices for their returns.

The Foreign Exchange Market

The foreign exchange market is the market where investors and speculators exchange (buy and sell) one currency for another. Each country has its own currency with which purchase and sale of goods can take place. Economic transactions with other countries usually involve payment and receipt in currencies of those countries.

People buy and sell currencies for import and export, investment in capital assets, financing or for pure speculation. Most of us have our first exposure to the foreign exchange market when we travel abroad and have to buy US dollars and GB pounds. These are small-value transactions. Transactions between institutions, banks, governments and companies are of large value, each transaction running into millions of US dollars. The total value of global trading in currencies is extremely high, averaging more than US$4 trillion per day. The foreign exchange market is probably the largest market in the world, financial or otherwise.

Some countries in Europe have decided to have a common currency. These countries, currently 19 in number, have given up their own individual currencies and have chosen one common currency called the euro. All monetary transactions and purchases and sales are conducted with the common euro. The European Central Bank controls the issue of the euro, and individual countries have only a minimal role to play.

There are some currencies which are accepted widely in most parts of the world due to the strength of their economy and the political stability of their governments. These include the US dollar, the pound, the euro, the yen and so forth. These currencies are accepted widely and can be said to be global in nature. Their currency values are determined through free trading in the foreign exchange (forex) markets. On the other hand, the Chinese currency yuan finds little acceptability globally despite a strong Chinese economy, since its price is influenced by the Chinese central bank and is not freely determined.

Currencies of other nations can only be used in the country which issues them. It would be difficult to use the rupee to buy anything in the USA, whereas transactions with the US dollar are possible in India and many other countries. As the Indian economy develops and gains strength, the rupee may become stronger and thus acceptable internationally in the future. For that to happen, the restrictions on converting the rupee to other currencies must be done away with and the rupee must become a fully convertible currency. Currently, the rupee is freely convertible on the current account but not on the capital account. Thus, for short-term transactions such as import and export, there is freedom to convert the rupee into another currency and vice versa. However, for longer term transactions such as purchasing a Greek island, prior permission of the relevant regulatory authority, the RBI, must be obtained.

Derivatives

Derivatives are financial instruments whose pay off structure is determined by the value of some other underlying asset or variable. Derivative instruments are extensively used for the purpose of managing risks by companies and institutions.

Companies face risk because of fluctuations in foreign exchange rates, interest rates and commodity prices, which may impact the cash flows and the value of the company. In an extreme case, even the continued existence of the company may be at stake.

When Bajaj Auto Limited exports a motorcycle, the sales proceeds may be denominated in US dollars. Let us assume that the company prices the motorcycle at US$1,000, payable three months later. Currently, the US dollar–rupee rate is 70 which values the transaction at ₹70,000. During the three-month period before US$1,000 is received by Bajaj Auto Limited, the rate may change. If the rupee appreciates to 60 per US dollar, Bajaj Auto Limited will receive only ₹60,000 when it converts the US$1,000 into rupees. If on the other hand, the US dollar appreciates in value to ₹80, the company will get ₹80,000. Any transaction or economic activity which involves receipt or payment of foreign exchange at a future date faces such a risk. Derivatives can be used to hedge risk of fluctuation in currency values and manage the organization's exposure to changes in underlying variables.

There are four types of derivatives, namely futures, forwards, options and swaps. The underlying variable can be an equity share, a fixed income instrument, foreign exchange or a commodity. Various exotic derivatives have also been designed and created depending on the need of various players. In recent times, there has been a sharp upsurge in the popularity of derivatives and, consequently, the market for derivative instruments is extremely large. Fairly or unfairly, derivatives have been blamed for the financial crisis of 2008, with the legendary investor Warren Buffet calling them 'financial weapons of mass destruction'.

Debt versus Equity

Companies strive to grow by investing in new projects. Projects require vast amount of capital over a long period which can be raised either through equity or by way of debt. Both these instruments are very dissimilar, with divergent characteristics. Let us understand the differing features of debt and equity and how the divergence impacts the investors and the company which issues/sells these instruments. Let us start by looking at the claims to the sales revenue of various stakeholders, as given in Figure 2.3.

A company generates revenues by selling its products and services. Various stakeholders of the company have claims to these cash flows. The cash flows are used to pay salaries to its employees, cost of raw material to suppliers and for general administrative and establishment expenses.

After all the aforementioned expenses have been paid for, the residual operating profits (earnings before interest and taxes [EBIT]) belong to the debt providers (coupon interest payment), the government (corporate tax) and the equity shareholders (net profit—dividends and retained earnings). The debt providers have the first claim, followed by the government, and the balance cash flows belong to the equity shareholders. The returns to the debt providers are predetermined and defined at the time of the issuance of the bonds. Since the returns to debt holders are (a) known, (b) fixed and (c) their claims have priority over the cash flows, debt instruments are a relatively low-risk and safe investment.

On the other hand, returns to equity shareholders are uncertain. Their claims to the company's cash flows are residual in nature, and they get whatever remains after every other stakeholder

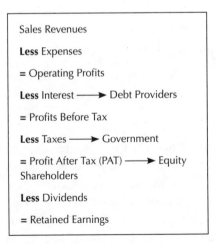

FIGURE 2.3   Claims to corporate cash flows

Source: Author.

TABLE 2.1   Risk: debt versus equity (in ₹)

	XYZ Limited		
	Normal	*Low cost*	*High cost*
Revenues	10,700	10,700	10,700
Costs	8,000	7,000	9,000
Operating profits	2,700	3,700	1,700
Interest	1,200	1,200	1,200
Profit	1,500	2,500	500
Return on equity (ROE)	15%	25%	5%

Capital: 10,000 equity and 10,000 debt at 12% interest.

Source: Author.

has been given his/her due. If the company does not earn sufficient profits, shareholders may not get any return in that year, making equity a very risky form of investment with volatile returns. Required rate of returns to equity shareholders should, therefore, be much higher than returns to debt providers. Let us look at Table 2.1 to understand how the risks of debt and equity are different.

XYZ Limited has a debt of ₹10,000 (at 12 per cent interest) and equity of ₹10,000. Under normal market situation, the profits are ₹1,500 and return on equity is 15 per cent (higher than returns to debt).

If the costs rise, the profits are down to ₹500 and the return to equity reduces to 5 per cent, which is much less than the return to debt providers.

At the same time, if the costs go down, the profits rise to ₹2,500 and the return on equity rises to 25 per cent. Thus, if the company performs well, the residual cash flows may turn out to be substantial. The higher returns go into the kitty of the equity shareholders; the debt providers have no claim over and above what they are entitled to. Equity is a risky instrument whose returns are not only variable but may turn out to be worthless if the performance of the company is poor.

Public Offering

When a company is initially established, the promoters contribute their own funds. Often friends and relatives chip in. But a limited number of associates can only contribute a limited sum, capping the amount of funds available and, therefore, the size of the company remains small. As the organization grows, it needs larger funding, for which it can approach venture capitalists and private equity players. Eventually, the fund requirement becomes huge and a limited set of investors are unable to fulfill the need. The company must invite the public to invest in its equity through what is termed 'initial public offering' (IPO). It is a part of the primary market and results in an inflow of funds to the company and expands its equity base. Most large companies have public shareholding and are listed on the stock exchange.

IPO: Bharati

Bharati Televentures Limited raised ₹8.30 billion through an IPO of 185 million shares in January/February 2002. It was the first public issue based upon 100 per cent book building and the entire bidding was conducted online. The price band was from ₹45 to ₹54. Despite the fact that the issue generated high demand and there were willing buyers at a higher price, the company chose to sell shares at the lower end of the band at ₹45. The 185 million equity share issue formed 10 per cent of the post-equity shareholding. Sixty per cent of the issue was sold to qualified institutional investors. The IPO was oversubscribed 2.5 times. The issue was managed by JM Morgan Stanley and DSP Merrill Lynch.

At times, venture capitalists or private equity investors who have invested in the company may wish to exit. The only way for them to disinvest their holdings is for the company to have an IPO. Alternatively, they can sell later in the secondary market when the shares get listed after the IPO.

Private Equity Investments

Warburg Pincus is a large private equity firm which has been active in India since 1999. It met early success when it sold its initial investment of US$292 million in Bharati Airtel Ltd for US$1.6 billion. This gave a fillip to private equity (PE) investments in India, which has continued to increase steadily. Warburg Pincus has itself invested over a billion US dollars in the first six months of 2017. Private equity investments have a bright future in India.

Companies often provide their management cadre with attractive equity stock options as part of their compensation. Employee stock option plans (ESOPs) are lucrative only if there is an active market for the shares of the company where such options can be valued at the time of allotting the options and can later be sold by the employees.

Sometimes, companies undertake an IPO for higher visibility in the market, as listed companies are better perceived than those which are unlisted. Some of the top Indian information technology companies have undertaken public issues in Nasdaq, USA, as a marketing strategy to improve the perception of their brand in the minds of their US customers. It has been my experience that when a company visits a business school for placement, one of the first things students do is to find out whether the company's shares are listed in the stock market and at what price are they traded.

Public trading of companies also facilitates M&A. Over the years, the size of acquisitions has gone up significantly and financing acquisitions can be a major concern. Acquisitions are likely to be funded by equity only if the shares are publicly traded.

Acquisition by Share Swap

In February 2008, HDFC Bank acquired Centurion Bank of Punjab (CBP) for ₹95.10 billion. This was the largest ever M&A transaction in the financial sector and overall the seventh-largest in India at the time. HDFC Bank did not wish to pay cash to the shareholders of CBP and instead financed the transaction by paying CBP shareholders through its own shares. The CBP shareholders received 1 share of HDFC Bank for every 29 shares of CBP held by them. Financing M&A transactions with the acquirer's shares is a common practice, especially in large value transactions, and is possible only if the shares of the acquiring company are traded in the secondary market and the price of the share is easily obtainable.

Hence, the following are the reasons a company may have an IPO:

1. Raising funds for business
2. Providing exit options to existing investors, including venture capitalists and private equity investors
3. Offer ESOPs to employees
4. Improve the company's brand perception
5. Engage in M&A transactions

SEBI is the regulator for equities, the equity-based derivatives market and now also for the commodity market in India. All public issues by companies must be approved by SEBI. Companies need to submit a document called the prospectus which provides relevant information that an investor may need in order to take an informed decision on investing in the pubic issue. The prospectus includes, inter alia, data on products and services, sales, profits, asset base, end use of the funds planned to be raised through the IPO, information about the management of the company and various other details such as technology, joint ventures and so forth. The prospectus is a highly detailed account of the company and its business and provides information that helps investors assess the company and its worth.

Companies are required to appoint a SEBI-approved investment banker to the public issue. The investment banker is an expert in public issue management and marketing, whose job is to

1. manage the issue in its entirety,
2. help in marketing the public issue and in raising the required funds,
3. ensure that the company conforms to rules and regulations pertaining to the issue.

After the prospectus and the public issue have been approved by SEBI, the issue opens for subscription by the investors. If the company is unable to raise 90 per cent of the targeted amount, the issue fails and the company must return whatever funds it has collected back to the investors. If it raises more money than targeted, it allots shares on a proportionate basis and returns the balance to the investors.

After allotment to the investors, shares can be traded in the stock exchanges where they are listed—the National Stock Exchange (NSE) of India and the BSE. Sometimes, the shares get listed at a price higher than the price at which the public issue was sold, yielding handsome profits to the investors. At other times, the company may have priced its shares optimistically, and the initial price in the secondary market could go below the IPO price which means that investors make a loss on their investment.

The IPO is the first public offer by a company. The company may need further funding in future for which it can approach the market again. A public issue by an already listed company is called a seasoned offering or a follow-on offer. A seasoned offering can be a rights issue in which only the existing investors are given shares in proportion to their existing holdings. Alternatively, it can be a public offer wherein anyone can apply for the shares the company is selling.

Largest IPO in the USA

The largest US IPO ever was by Visa Inc., amounting to US$19.65 billion in March 2008. Each share was priced at US$44. The issue surpassed the earlier record of US$11 billion by AT&T in 2007. The share surged 28 per cent to US$56.50 on the opening day of trading!

The issue was underwritten by JP Morgan and Goldman Sachs. The total fees at 2.80 per cent paid to various intermediaries—the sellers, managers and underwriters—amounted to over US$550 million.

Visa operates the largest electronic retail network in the world. It has the highest number of debit and credit cards in circulation. It is the largest US card company in terms of the number and value of transactions undertaken.

In 2013, Visa was included amongst the 30 shares that comprise the Dow Jones Index.

Subsequently, Alibaba raised an even larger amount at US$25 billion through its IPO in 2014.

Secondary Market

Through an IPO, the company invites the public to invest in its equity. The company lists its shares in a stock exchange such as the NSE and the BSE, enabling trading in these exchanges after the IPO. Trading of a company's shares in the stock exchange, post the public issue, is termed secondary market trading. Secondary market trading is crucial to provide liquidity to investors who may have bought the shares of the company either in its IPO or later. Investors will be reluctant to invest in the primary market if such investments were not liquid and cannot be sold whenever the investor so desires. A vibrant and efficient secondary market provides liquidity to investors and is critical for a successful primary market. Figure 2.4 aptly shows the difference between the primary and secondary markets.

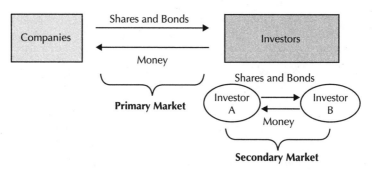

FIGURE 2.4   Financial markets

Source: Author.

Mutual Funds

A mutual fund is a professionally managed investment fund that pools together savings of a large number of investors and invests the pooled funds on their behalf.

Investing funds is not easy; it presupposes knowledge, expertise and access to information which ordinary investors lack. Moreover, a limited size of funds prevents diversification as a strategy.

Mutual funds help overcome these limitations by pooling together savings of a large number of investors. The corpus of funds thus collected enables mutual funds to appoint professional fund managers for investments, gather adequate information required to make informed investment decisions and adequately diversify the investment corpus. The individual investor is the beneficiary of such an arrangement.

The mutual fund industry is large in size and variety, both in India and globally. A wide array of mutual funds is available, satisfying varied needs of the investors.

Market Participants

There are three broad categories of market participants. First are the investors and hedgers whose needs the market primarily seeks to satisfy. They invest in the instruments which are traded in the financial market, seeking returns and bearing risk in doing so. Or they hedge the underlying risks of their business in the derivatives market.

Second are the speculators who bet on the direction they expect the market to move in the very short run. They stake huge amounts while speculating and even a small variation in price yields substantial profits or heavy losses. By speculating large amounts, they provide liquidity to the market, without which trading in the market would not be possible. Without liquidity, the large spread between sale and purchase price makes the execution of orders a difficult task. Usually, stocks that invite speculation have high liquidity and enable investors to trade easily.

Reliance Industries Limited has traditionally been known as a speculator's delight. It attracts huge volumes of trading from speculators who are keen to profit from a change in its price. The stock has always been extremely liquid, resulting in an insignificant spread between buying and selling prices. An investor can invest a large amount in Reliance Industries Limited easily with extremely low impact costs. On the other hand, Siemens Ltd does not attract much speculative interest. Despite being a fundamentally strong company, it becomes difficult and costly to transact large volumes.

Impact Cost

Impact cost is the cost that a buyer or seller of stocks incurs while executing a transaction due to the prevailing liquidity condition on the counter. In other words, impact cost is the cost of executing a transaction in the market. The impact cost is usually calculated for a large transaction value.

At any point in time, there will be a set of buyers and sellers willing to trade a security. The trading terminal of the exchange will show the prices along with the quantity that traders are willing to buy and sell. As an illustration, Table 2.2 may be the trading book for a certain security ABC.

The purchase column shows the price quotes at which the investors have offered to purchase shares. Anyone wishing to sell must hit the purchase quotation; he will receive ₹99 per share. Similarly, the sales column shows the price quotes at which the investors have offered to sell the shares. Anyone wishing to purchase must hit the sale quote and will be able to buy shares by paying ₹101. The difference between the two prices is termed 'the spread' which is the amount an investor loses on a round trip purchase and sale transaction.

The spread is applicable for a small quantum of shares, for only 1,000 shares in the given illustration. For trading in higher quantum of shares, the cost would be even more. A mutual fund which wants to purchase 10,000 shares will need to go up to ₹104. He will be able to purchase

1,500 shares at ₹101,
3,000 shares at ₹102,
1,000 shares at ₹102.50,

TABLE 2.2   Impact cost

Purchase		Sale	
Quantity	*Price*	*Price*	*Quantity*
1,000	99	101	1,500
2,000	98.5	102	3,000
500	98	102.5	1,000
15,000	97.5	103	2,000
500	97	104	5,000
2,000	96	104.5	7,000

Source: Author.

2,000 shares at ₹103,

2,500 shares at ₹104.

His average purchase price is ₹102.60 {(1500 * 101 + 3000 * 102 + 1000 * 102.5 + 2000 * 103 + 2500 * 104)/10,000}.

The average of the best purchase and sale price is ₹100, called the ideal price, and an investor would expect to trade at that price. However, he/she is able to buy 10,000 shares at ₹102.60. The difference between the two is the impact cost. It is useful to remember that

1. impact cost is estimated for a large quantum of shares,
2. impact cost varies for different quantum of transaction, and
3. impact cost may be different for purchase and sale transactions. For instance, in Table 2.2, the impact cost of sale of 10,000 shares is (average purchase price is ₹97.87) is 2.125 per cent

Interestingly, according to one of the criteria for selection in CNX NIFTY 50, the stock must have an impact cost of less than 0.5 per cent for a transaction value of ₹5 million.

The third set of market participants is arbitrageurs. Arbitrageurs take advantage of the difference in pricing to make riskless profits. The law of one price states that a security, or securities with similar risk–return characteristics, must be priced equally in different markets. Violation of the law implies inefficiency. One of the most critical functions of markets is price discovery. Difference in prices would be a manifestation of the market's failure to discover the right price.

Differential pricing offers an opportunity for arbitrageurs to make profits without assuming risk. They buy in the market where the price of a security is lower and sell it in the market where the price is higher. They undertake both the transactions at precisely the same time. Arbitrageurs buy and sell simultaneously and in large quantities in the hope that the prices in the two markets will converge. As long as the prices do converge and become equal, arbitrageurs are not impacted by the movement in security price irrespective of the direction of the movement of the prices. Hence, the profits made by arbitrageurs are free of any risk.

It would be useful to understand the operational details of how arbitrage transactions take place and lead to riskless profits. Transactions in different markets are independent of each other. Transactions undertaken in one market must be concluded and settled in the same market irrespective of what the investor does in any other market. To undertake arbitrage, the arbitrageur buys in one market, say the NSE, at time T_0. He must square up the transaction later by selling an equal number of the same shares in the NSE later at time T_1. The excess of price at T_1 over price at T_0 will determine his profits on the NSE leg of the arbitrage.

The arbitrageur sells in the BSE at time T_0 and must fulfil his commitment by purchasing in the BSE at time T_1. The excess of price at T_0 over the price at T_1 determines his profits at the BSE. His overall arbitrage profits equal the sum of his profits at the NSE and BSE.

Let us take an example to understand the process of arbitrage. If Reliance Industries Limited is priced at ₹1,000 in the NSE and ₹1,100 in the BSE, the law of one price is violated. Arbitrageurs will buy Reliance Industries Limited at the NSE for ₹1,000 and sell at the BSE for ₹1,100. It can be demonstrated that the arbitrageurs' profits are guaranteed as long as the

TABLE 2.3   Arbitrage profit

	Profit in NSE	*Profit in BSE*	*Net profit*
(a)	1,500 – 1,000 = 500	1,100 – 1,500 = –400	100
(b)	800 – 1,000 = –200	1,100 – 800 = 300	100
(c)	1,030 – 1,000 = 30	1,100 – 1,030 = 70	100

Source: Author.

prices in the two markets converge and become equal. It does not matter whether prices go up or decline.

Possible future prices in both the exchanges are (a) ₹1,500, (b) ₹800, (c) ₹1,030 (Table 2.3).

In all three instances, the arbitrageur makes a profit of ₹100, which equals the difference in the initial pricing in the two markets. Since the outcome does not depend on the direction and extent of the movement of prices, the transaction is considered to be risk free. Arbitrageurs must ensure that the sale and purchase transactions are carried out at precisely the same time in different markets.

Interestingly, the arbitrageurs' act of arbitrage leads to the convergence of prices. They buy in the markets where the price is lower, and hence the price goes up. They sell in the markets where the price is high, resulting in a decline in price in these markets. The process goes on until there is a convergence, removing any further opportunity to arbitrage. Arbitrage thus leads to efficient pricing in accordance with the law of one price.

Arbitrageurs take advantage of the differential pricing of the same security. By doing so in large quantities, they remove the difference in pricing and there is no further opportunity to arbitrage. Thus, for arbitrage to take place, markets must price a security differently. The act of arbitrage removes this different pricing and makes the market efficient. The opportunity to arbitrage thus vanishes.

For arbitrage to be effective, markets should be free of any barriers to trade. To the extent that barriers to trade exist, prices will not converge and arbitrage will be limited. The barriers could be

1. physical: in terms of distance,
2. regulatory: in terms of restrictions on trading,
3. financial: in terms of costs of trading.

Common Perception about Financial Markets

Despite the significantly positive and critical role they play in the economy, financial markets have been the target of attack from a large section of people. Financial market excesses have been blamed for the crisis and the subsequent recession of 2008, the impact of which continues to be felt even a decade later. Several reasons can be attributed to the general lack of conviction in the financial markets.

First, the role and importance of the financial markets is little understood by the common man. Benefits of the financial markets are not evident to them. Second, financial markets throughout history have experienced several crises that have destroyed wealth and caused immense misery to people, the 2008 crisis being one of the most vicious in its impact. Such crises strike far and wide, even impacting sections of the economy and individuals who may have no direct links with financial markets. This seems unfair to most people. Third, the compensation of those employed in the financial markets is quite disproportionate to those engaged in other fields. Such significant distortion in compensation seems quite unjustified, especially considering that in many people's eyes financial markets do not seem to add any value in the real sense. Fourth, insider trading and slack enforcement of regulations governing the financial markets result in loss of confidence by market participants. Insider trading refers to trading on stocks by employees of a corporation based on information that is not available to the public. Finally, the importance of the financial markets has grown disproportionately and, over the years, their share as a percentage of the overall economy has increased multifold.

Thomas Philippon (2014), professor of finance at the Stern School of Business, New York University, undertook a study to find out how well financial markets perform their primary task of intermediation. The study covered a period of the last 30 years. According to his study, there has been no significant improvement in the cost of intermediation over the years and the benefits of technology and productivity improvement have not been passed on to the customer by the finance industry. According to Professor Philippon's study, the cost of intermediation has remained largely steady over the years.

Many people believe that finance in recent times is more about secondary market trading than intermediation. Financial market participants need to undertake serious introspection to ensure that financial markets serve the needs of the economy and that of the common man and do not overwhelm the real economy which they are expected to support.

KEY CONCEPTS

1. Financial markets perform critical functions of the intermediation of funds, allocation of investments, price discovery and risk management.
2. Companies can raise funds through equity or debt. Both these instruments have very different features and risk–return characteristics.
3. Stock market, fixed-income securities market, foreign exchange market and the derivatives market are four types of financial markets based on the instruments traded.
4. The IPO is an important event by which a company raises funds from the public by issuing equity shares.
5. Secondary market enables trading of shares previously issued by the company through an IPO or otherwise and provides liquidity to investors.
6. Investors, speculators and arbitrageurs are the three participants who make the financial markets complete.

CHAPTER QUESTIONS

1. What role do financial markets play in an economy? What is likely to happen to an economy that does not have an efficient financial market?
2. Who are the different participants in financial markets that make the markets complete? What would happen to the market if any of them were absent?
3. What do you understand by primary market? What role does it play in an economy?
4. What is an IPO? Why would a company go in for an IPO? What are the considerations before a company when it decides to have an IPO?
5. What do you understand by secondary market? Why is the secondary market essential?
6. What are the diverse features of debt and equity respectively? What impact do these differences have on the investors?
7. What is the role of arbitrage in financial markets?

CASE FOR DISCUSSION

Until the mid-1990s, investing in equities was a nightmarish experience. Each stage of the investment process was uncertain. The whole process was fraught with high risk. The investor could never feel assured if

1. the price paid by him was actually the price at which the shares were purchased by his broker in the stock market,
2. the shares would be delivered to him on the stated date,
3. the shares are genuine or what is technically termed as 'good for delivery', and
4. the investor would be able to transfer the shares in his own name.

The cycle repeated itself on the sell side too when the investor would be uncertain of the sales price, the actual payment of the sales proceeds and the acceptance or non-acceptance of the shares delivered by him. I guess only those with strong hearts could take the pain associated with such investments.

These risks are termed operating risks, referring to the probability that the transaction undertaken may not be completed as per the terms of the contract. High operating risk increased the cost of operation in the Indian equities market and was, in fact, quite substantial.

In addition, the market was largely confined to the BSE and investors from other geographical locations faced significant challenges in transacting in the equities market. The brokerage charged was substantial; compared to the brokerage prevailing currently, rates in those times seem almost unbelievable. The operating uncertainties described here were multiplied, since the transaction had to go through multiple levels for non-Bombay investors.

In the current professional environment, operating risks are quite insignificant and the investor can be certain that his/her transaction will be put through—shares delivered for purchases and sales proceeds paid—on time as per the terms of the contract. Default is non-existent at the exchanges, and the investor can invest with complete assurance. Moreover, the brokerage rates, as already mentioned, have reduced drastically and, for all purposes, have ceased to be a factor in the decision to invest.

Similarly, in the primary market, investment is more assured and whether the shares are allotted to the investor or not is no longer a matter of chance. Investors have far more information on which to base their decision to invest in a new issuance. The transaction moves fairly quickly and with efficiency that could not even be imagined in the decade of the 1980s.

In your view, what is the significance of the discussed trends in the Indian stock markets for the CFO of a company? How have reduced operating risk in both the secondary and primary markets helped him/her achieve his/her objectives?

Appendix: Bond Features

Let us discuss some distinguishing features of bonds.

Covenants

Companies are owned by shareholders who take all major decisions pertaining to the company. Usually, bondholders have no role to play despite the fact that these decisions have the potential to change the risk profile of bonds. For instance, payout of dividends reduces the available cash flows, increasing the risk of bonds issued by the company. Similarly, investment in a risky venture or the sale of an asset of the company could jeopardize the interest of the bondholders.

Bondholders must protect their interests prior to undertaking investment. They do so by way of protective covenants. The covenants describe the responsibilities and commitments of the company, violation of which triggers specific rights of the bondholders. The covenants are a part of the contract between bondholders and the company and are included in the indenture to the bond issue (deed of trust). The indenture specifies in detail the terms and conditions of the bond issue, including the covenants. Typical covenants include a minimum current ratio, maximum debt equity ratio and restrictions on sale of assets. Creditors and bondholders have no say in managing the company as long as payments are being made to them as per the terms of the agreement and no covenants have been violated. However, if the company defaults either in payments or in conforming to any covenant, rights of the bondholders as mentioned in the indenture get activated.

Invoking Debt Covenant

The latter half of the 1990s was a tough period for the Indian economy, especially for the real estate sector. Lok Housing Limited, a small player based in Mumbai, was severely impacted with many projects under construction facing stagnant sales. Cash flows were highly strained.

The company had huge borrowings from the SBI, which it was finding difficult to repay as per the terms of the borrowing. Having defaulted on the loan, it had no qualms however in declaring large dividend to its shareholders. The SBI intervened, exercised its right to priority in cash flows and forced Lok Housing Limited to withdraw the dividend.

Rights in Liquidation

Creditors and bondholders have priority over equity shareholders in receiving their dues if the company is being liquidated. The available cash flow is first paid to the creditors. Only after the dues of the creditors have been paid are the equity shareholders entitled to receive the balance cash flows.

There can be different levels of priority even amongst the creditors, with higher ranking bonds being paid before other subordinate bonds.

Secured Credit

In order to protect their loan in case of a default in payment, lenders often take an asset as a collateral. If the borrower is unable to pay as per the terms of the agreement, the creditor can sell off the asset to realize his/her dues. When an individual borrows from a housing finance company, the house is usually given as a collateral. Similarly, investors in bonds can take an asset of the company (machine and building) as collateral which can be sold off and the ensuing sales consideration used to pay the pending dues.

The collateral need not always be a physical asset but can be future cash flows. Mortgage-backed securities are issued on the strength of future EMI payments. Tata Tea had financed its takeover of Tetley through borrowing, based on the predicted future cash flows.

Call Provision

Call provision refers to the option that an issuer enjoys, to retire the bonds and redeem them prior to their maturity. Such an option is useful for two reasons. First, if the interest rates fall, the company can retire the existing bonds and issue fresh bonds at a lower rate of interest. Second, call provision gives the company flexibility to design and alter its capital structure without being constrained by bonds already issued.

Early redemption is beneficial to the company; hence bonds with call provision pay a higher interest than other bonds with similar risk profile but without a call option.

Traded or Non-traded Debt

Bonds issued by governments, companies or other entities are usually traded in the bond market. On the other hand, term loans taken from a financial institution such as Tourism Finance Corporation of India or National Bank for Agriculture and Rural Development (NABARD) are non-tradable and stay on the books of the lender throughout the life of the debt. Lenders must hold on to a term loan or non-tradable bonds till maturity; therefore, these instruments lack liquidity. Lack of liquidity makes such debts very risky, liquidity being a desired feature of any security. Hence lenders demand a higher interest than for a comparable bond that is tradable and liquid.

CHAPTER 3

The Time Value of Money

> Money makes money and the money that money makes, makes more money.
>
> —Benjamin Franklin

Money is an integral part of modern life. During our lifespan, we receive and pay money at different points in time. At times, we may need to make a choice in terms of the amount, and the timing, of these payments and receipts. It is essential to understand and appreciate the impact of these cash flows in order to make the right choice and get the best value from them. Let us start by appreciating some instances of different patterns of cash flows.

1. You have a choice between two offers.
   a. Receive ₹10,000 now.
   b. Receive ₹11,000 next year.
      Which one would you opt for?
2. You are planning to buy a car for ₹500,000.
   a. Dealer A offers 10 per cent off the price and lends the balance at the regular rate of 9 per cent for seven years.
   b. Dealer B offers to lend you ₹500,000 at 5 per cent for seven years.
      Which of the two financing options would you choose?
3. A firm is contemplating investing ₹10 billion in a project that is expected to generate ₹2 billion per annum over the next seven years. Should the firm accept the proposal?
4. You are planning to buy a house costing ₹7,500,000. The housing finance company offers a loan for 20 years at 10 per cent per annum. Given your monthly income, you can pay an EMI of ₹50,000 only. What is the maximum value of loan that can be availed by you?
5. ABC Ltd has 5 million shares outstanding. Its shares are priced at ₹60. An offer has been made by XYZ Ltd for acquisition of ABC Limited at 25 per cent premium to the existing share price. However, the acquisition price is payable over the next five years. As the CFO of XYZ Ltd, what should be your recommendation to the board of directors?

6. As a senior manager of India Infrastructure Finance Company Ltd, you are evaluating a proposal to finance a project to establish a high-tech entertainment park. The project requires large investment; it is risky but promises huge cash flows if successful. How will you decide on financing the project?

7. On 2 December 1982, General Motors Acceptance Corporation (GMAC), a subsidiary of General Motors Ltd, issued a long-term security. The security was sold for US$500 at that time and was redeemable 30 years later on 1 December 2012 for US$10,000.

    Thus, against the amount of US$500 payable by an investor, he/she would receive US$10,000. During the period of 30 years, GMAC did not pay any interest. Such a security is termed zero-coupon bond. Is this investment worthwhile?

These are some of the typical financial choices that are faced by corporates as well as individuals. Lacking expertise in dealing with cash flows received and paid at different points in time, we are often clueless in dealing with such choices. Caution is warranted since finance companies are known to take advantage of the consumers' ignorance. While the Securities and Exchange Board of India (SEBI) and the Reserve Bank of India, as regulatory organizations, have established norms that banks and finance companies must follow, the best protection against rip-off is our own knowledge.

In any case, managers in the corporate sector must be well-versed with concepts relating to valuation of cash flows at different points in time, since they will face such choices on a regular basis. Value maximization is the objective of a company, and value can be estimated only by an appreciation of the nuances of cash flows and what we term the 'time value of money'.

The time value of money and its calculation is primarily based on the concept of compound interest, which all of us have learnt in school but many of us may have chosen to ignore later on as being of no further use. Now that an attractive career beckons in the corporate sector, we need to dust off that knowledge and build upon it to master the time value of money.

Compound Interest

Simple interest is easy to comprehend and compute; it is the interest only on the principal amount without taking into account any interest earned in previous periods. The interest amount each year remains constant.

While easy to comprehend and calculate, simple interest is conceptually flawed. Financial evaluation is invariably based on the theoretically rigorous compound interest. The difference between the two is instructive and must be clearly understood.

In calculating compound interest,

- interest earned during a time period is added to the original principle, to get
- the amount on which interest will be calculated for the next time period.

TABLE 3.1 Simple interest

Year	Amount at the beginning of the year	Interest earned @ 12%	Amount at the end of the year
1	1,000	120	1,120
2	1,120	120	1,240
3	1,240	120	1,360
4	1,360	120	1,480
5	1,480	120	1,600

Total interest earned = 1,000 * 12% * 5 = ₹600.

Source: Author.

Thus, interest earned during a period depends both on the principal amount as well as the interest earned in the previous periods.

One thousand rupees is invested at an interest rate of 12 per cent per annum for five years. If simple interest rate is applicable, the interest earned and the amount at the end of the period would be as in Table 3.1.

On the other hand, if the interest rate is compounded at the end of every year, the interest earned and the amount at the end of the period would be as in Table 3.2.

You may have observed that simple interest remains constant throughout, whereas compound interest keeps increasing each year. The compound interest in any year depends not only on the original principal but also on the total interest earned up to that period. The compound interest earned during the entire period of five years is ₹762.34, which is substantially higher than the ₹600 earned with simple interest rate. Higher the applicable interest rate and longer the period over which the interest is calculated, greater will be the difference in the total interest earned and, therefore, in the final amount at the end of the period.

This has tremendous implications for any investment over the long term. Albert Einstein is famously said to have remarked that compound interest is the greatest mathematical discovery of

Table 3.2 Compound interest

Year	Amount at the beginning of the year	Interest earned @ 12%	Amount at the end of the year
1	1,000	120	1,120
2	1,120	134.40	1,254.40
3	1,254.40	150.53	1,404.93
4	1,404.93	168.59	1,573.52
5	1,573.52	188.82	1,762.34

Total interest earned = $1,000 * (1 + 0.12)^5 - 1,000 = ₹762.34$.

Source: Author.

mankind, terming it the eighth wonder of the world.[1] Why did he say that? Simply because over a long period of time, compound interest can turn an amount of money into a very large sum.

- Native Indians have always been ridiculed for selling the Manhattan Island for US$24 in 1624. Was the sale really unreasonable? If the Indians had invested US$24 at 6 per cent per annum for the next 392 years, they would have now had US$20 billion!
- If the Indians had been a little more astute and invested the same US$24 at 8 per cent per annum over the same period, they would have now had over US$30 trillion dollars!
- Ibbotson and Sinquefield have calculated that US$1 invested in the US stock markets in 1926 would have had a value of US$7,353 at the end of 2017, over a time span of 92 years (Morningstar Investment Service 2018). While this seems an extremely large increase in value, the annual compounded growth rate implied by this increase in value is only 10.20 per cent per annum. Given an opportunity to grow over a long period (92 years), compound interest has a disproportionate impact on valuation; even a small increase in interest rate has an enormous impact on the final value. For instance, small stocks during the same period returned 12.1 per cent and US$1 became US$36,929!

Given that investment over such long period is rare, these mentioned examples are only for the purpose of illustration, to give an idea of the power of compounding. Recall Benjamin Franklin's quote at the beginning of this chapter.

Money makes money and the money that money makes, makes more money. (quoted in Malkiel and Ellis 2013)

Really Long Term

In 1066, the first Duke of Oxbridge was awarded a square mile of London for his services in assisting the conquest of England. The thirtieth duke wished to live a fast-paced life and sold his holding in 1966 for GB£5,000,000,000. An examination of the original project's cost showed only the entry '1066 a.d.: to repair armor, £5'.

What was the rate of capital appreciation?

While in absolute terms, the appreciation has been phenomenal, the increase has taken place over a really long period of 900 years. The return in fact works out to only 2.33 per cent. Over a long period, even a minor capital gain if compounded can result in a fairly large sum.

A wag once remarked that

the power of compounding can explain why well to do families bequeath their wealth to their grandchildren rather than their children. Parents would rather make their grandchildren very rich

---

[1] See https://quotesonfinance.com/author/20/albert-einstein, accessed 11 July 2019.

than make their children moderately rich. In these families, grandchildren have a more positive view of the power of compounding than do the children.

Manipulation of Cash Flows

We come across countless situations in our lives that involve the time value of money. Transactions that involve receiving money (cash inflows) and/or giving money (cash outflows) at different points in time are quite common.

- Many people of my generation have borrowed for a house or for a car/consumer durables. The calculation of the EMI is based on the time value of money.
- We need to plan our investments to be able to afford a certain lifestyle upon retirement. Without knowledge of the time value of money that would not be possible.
- Your parents had decided to save for your higher education some years back. The amount that they regularly needed to save to finance your MBA involves working with cash flows at different points in time.
- The objective of a company is value maximization. Estimation of value requires similar knowledge of the time value of money.
- Many other functions of finance such as valuation of bonds, capital budgeting and financing decisions are similarly based on the time value of money and would therefore be impossible to understand without a thorough knowledge of the concept.

There are two fundamental ideas which form the basis of the time value of money.

a. Same amount of cash flows at different points in time have different values. Thus, ₹100 today has a different value compared to ₹100 next year. This is intuitively easy to comprehend.

b. It would be incorrect to undertake any mathematical operation, addition, subtraction or others, on cash flows at different time periods. All cash flows must be converted to the same time period which usually is the current period or what we technically term the present value.

Thus, we cannot add ₹100 received next year and ₹100 received two years later; that would be conceptually flawed. Both cash flows must be converted to the same time period, preferably their present value calculated, and only then can they be added. The conversion of the value of cash flows from one period to the other is one of the most fundamental concepts in management. A thorough understanding of the concepts of the time value of money and the ability and skills to undertake calculations involving cash flows at different points in time is critical.

$$
\begin{array}{ccc}
C_0 & C_1 & C_2 \\
& 100 & 100
\end{array}
$$

P < --------------
Q < ------------------------

P is the present value of cash flow at the end of one year, and Q is the present value of cash flow at the end of two years. The total present value of the two cash flows is the sum of P and Q, that is, (P + Q).

Required Rate of Return

The interest rate for converting cash flows from one period to the other is technically termed the required rate of return. This is the return required by an investor, or the return that will persuade an investor to invest his funds in a particular project, given the risk of the investment. Money has a time value associated with it; a rupee received today is worth more than a rupee received in future. Economic theory is premised on the assumption that human beings prefer current consumption to future consumption. If you ask someone whether he would prefer to consume a pizza now rather than one year later, the response would be quite obvious. The utility derived from consuming a pizza at a future date is less than the utility derived from consuming it now. Thus, people can be persuaded to invest money (which is akin to postponing consumption) only if they are assured of getting more in the future than the amount they invest today. They require a return for parting with their money for a certain time period and, thereby, postponing their current consumption. This is the first component of the required rate of return.

Possession of money is not attractive for its own sake. Money is useful because it helps purchase goods and services. Prices, however, do not stay constant and have a tendency to increase. If a pizza costs ₹100 today, with ₹1,000 we can consume 10 pizzas. Let us assume that we postpone the consumption of pizzas for one year and invest ₹1,000 at a 10 per cent interest rate. At the end of one year, we will have ₹1,100. This does not mean that we will be able to consume 11 pizzas. In the meantime, given that there are inflationary pressures in the economy, the price of pizzas may go up. If the price goes up, say by 6 per cent to ₹106, we will be able to consume less than 11 pizzas (technically, 10.38 pizzas to be precise).

To be able to consume 11 pizzas at the end of one year, our investment should yield a *real* return of 10 per cent, that is, a return that has been adjusted for the price increase of 6 per cent. To be able to get a real rate of return of 10 per cent, we need to be compensated for the price increase of 6 per cent too also. Therefore, the nominal return should be ((1.10 * 1.06) – 1) * 100, which equals 16.60 per cent. At this rate, we would have ₹1,166 at the end of one year which will enable us to consume 11 pizzas, giving a real return of 10 per cent.

Investors need to be compensated for the increase in prices, to enable them to purchase the same basket of goods and services which they could do earlier, at the time of initial investment; hence, inflation becomes the second component of the interest or the required rate of return.

Risk

The third component of the required rate of return is risk. Risk refers to the probability that return may turn out to be different from what had been expected. Different investment avenues have varying degree of risks, and investors expect to be compensated adequately for taking such risks. Risk has been explained later in Chapter 5, 'Risk and Return'.

At one end of the risk spectrum are government bonds, also termed treasury bonds. The government of a country is expected to pay the coupons and the principal as per agreed terms of the bond, chances of any default being ruled out. Governments can print currency and raise money through taxation. Therefore, investment in government bonds is considered to be completely safe and risk-free, and their return is termed the risk-free return. Hence treasury bonds provide return only for postponing consumption and for inflation. Currently, the Government of India can borrow at approximately 7 per cent per annum. Returns on all other investments are benchmarked to the returns on government securities and provide a return which is a spread-over and above the returns applicable to government securities. The spread depends upon the risk pertaining to the specific investment.

While all investments usually have the same return for postponing consumption and for inflation, the differentiator is the risk associated with the specific investment. As the risk of investment in different instruments varies, investors require returns which are appropriate to the level of risk inherent in the investment.

For example, investment in bonds issued by ABB Ltd, a company whose bonds enjoy AAA rating would be considered to be very safe. Therefore, the spread is likely to be a few basis points over and above the return from treasury bonds (100 basis points equal 1 per cent and 1 basis point is one-hundredth of 1 per cent). HM Textiles Pvt Ltd is, however, a riskier company with a credit rating of BBB from CRISIL. Investors require a higher spread on investment in HM Textiles Ltd, say 500 basis points leading to the required rate of return being 12 per cent per annum. In order to raise funds through bonds, the company must offer 12 per cent return to investors.

At the other end of the risk spectrum, and in complete contrast to government bonds, is investment in the equities market. Equity investment is extremely volatile, and the return required to persuade investors to invest in equities is even higher. Technically termed the equity risk premium, for the Indian equity markets, it could be as high as 8 per cent. Together with 7 per cent risk-free return, investors require a return of at least 15 per cent per annum to be persuaded to park their savings in equities. Indian equity markets have in fact yielded about 15.4 per cent per annum over the last decade and a half (Sensex 3,469 on 30 March 2002 and 29,910 on 31 March 2017). If the investor invests in a single security with a high risk, technically a beta greater than 1, the required rate of return could be even higher (beta will be explained later in Chapter 5).

If your local grocery store owner asks you for a loan, the chances of getting your money back are remote and, therefore, the spread over the benchmark risk-free rate (G-Sec.) would make the required rate of return quite high. (Presumably, any lending to the writer of this book is fraught with dangerously high risk, ruling out the possibility of such an investment. Conceptual knowledge of the subject does not reduce the risk of investment. It only makes prospective investors even more aware of the risk!)

To sum up, the interest rate on any security is determined by three parameters, namely time (postponement of consumption), inflation and risk. This interest rate is technically termed the required rate of return or the return required by an investor.

An efficient market must provide investors the required rate of return based on the risk profile of the investment. If that does not hold, the market price of the security reduces until such a return becomes available.

Opportunity Cost

The opportunity cost is a measure of cost expressed in terms of the alternative given up. Resources available are limited; spending on a product/ service means giving up something else on which the same money could have been spent. Taking your girlfriend out on a movie date may imply foregoing plans to buy this book. (I suspect the book stands no chance against the opportunity for a date with your girlfriend. Instant gratification of your desires will always score over the long-term benefits of a corporate finance book, learnings from the time value of money notwithstanding!)

Similarly, the opportunity cost of any investment is the return that could be earned from the next best alternative with equivalent risk. Using funds for a certain investment implies foregoing the return on another investment where the funds could have been deployed. If the current investment is unable to provide at least an equivalent return, the investor will withdraw his funds. Hence, that alternative return becomes the minimum return that any investment must provide, and is termed the opportunity cost, equalling the return on the investment foregone.

Investing in Allcargo Logistics Ltd means foregoing the opportunity to invest in EID Parry Ltd since both these companies have the same risk profile. An investment in Allcargo Logistics Ltd is advisable only if returns expected are at least as much as, if not greater than, the returns from EID Parry Ltd, which is the opportunity cost of investing in Allcargo Logistics Ltd.

Intuitively, we know that ₹100 today has a greater value than ₹100 in future. This discussion provides us a conceptual basis of why there is a difference in valuation of money at different points in time. One hundred Indian rupees is worth more today than rupees expected in future because

1. consumption of the same amount of goods in future offers less satisfaction or utility than consumption now,
2. inflation reduces the purchasing power of money, that is, the amount of goods and services that can be purchased with ₹100 at a later date, and
3. there is a risk of actually receiving ₹100 in future.

Annual Period for Comparison

The interest rate is always calculated in annual terms unless otherwise stated. The return stated over the entire period of investment is not only meaningless but can be misleading too. To take an illustration, if an investment of ₹100 gets back ₹200 after five years, the return is not 100 per cent over five years but must be expressed in annual terms. The return can, in fact, be calculated as 14.87 per cent per annum which gives us a fair benchmark for comparative purposes.

Time Value of Money

Cash Flow Depiction

Before we begin to acquire expertise in calculations of time value, we must learn to depict cash flows in a lucid manner. Cash flows can be one time (single cash flows) or they can be over a number of time periods (series of cash flows). Similarly, cash flows can be positive or negative depending on whether

1. we are investing in a project (outflow) which later generates positive cash flows (inflow),
2. we have borrowed money (inflow) which we pay back over a period of time (outflow) and
3. we invest in debt/equity of a company (outflow) which provides return during the period of investment (inflow).

There can be different ways of depicting the listed cash flows. An easy and clearly understandable method is as follows:

End of period	C_0	C_1	C_2	C_3	...	C_n
Cash flow	−1,000	100	100	100		100

The first row represents the year with the number representing the end of the period. Thus, C_0 is the end of the 0th period or the present time, that is, now. C_3 is the end of the 3rd year and C_n is the end of the nth year. The time period of one year can make a significant difference to the value of cash flows. Cash flows at the beginning of the year are significantly more valuable than those at the end of the year. Clarity and consistency are imperative. It is a common practice to represent cash flows at the end of the year.

The second row represents the amount of cash flows that are being paid out or are being received. Outflows are represented as a negative cash flow. This equation represents the end of the 0th year, that is, the present moment, going on to the end of the nth period. The cash flow at the end of the 0th period is negative ₹1,000 which means an outflow of ₹1,000. This is followed by n cash flows in the next n years, each of positive ₹100, which means inflows of ₹100 each year.

Basic Calculations

Let us understand the calculations with the compound interest formula.

$$C_n = C_0 * (1 + r)^n.$$
$$C_1 = C_0 * (1 + r)$$
$$C_0 = C_1/(1 + r).$$

$(1 + r)$ is the critical parameter that is used to convert cash flows from one period to the other. Multiplying by $(1 + r)$ converts a cash flow to a period one year later (compounding). Dividing by $(1 + r)$ converts a cash flow to a period one year earlier (discounting).

Time value of money involves four key parameters, which are required to change the value of a cash flow from one period to the other. These are as follows:

1. Future value (FV): It is the amount of money that an investment will grow to at some future date (that is, after a specific number of years) by earning interest at a specific compound rate of interest. The process of calculating FV from the present value is called *compounding*.
2. Present value (PV): It is the sum needed today to get a certain amount (the FV) after a given number of years at a specific interest rate. The process of computing PV is termed *discounting*.
3. Interest rate (required rate of return as explained earlier).
4. Time period (number of years).

If we know any three parameters, the fourth can be easily determined. The basis of doing so is our old faithful compound interest formula which we took so much pains to learn in our school and should now prove useful.

$$FV = PV (1 + r)^n.$$

(The formula is the same. Only the notations have changed.)
FV = future value,
PV = present value,
r = applicable interest rate in percentage per annum,
n = number of years

Note that we have one equation and four unknowns—PV, FV, interest rate and time period. Given the values of any three of the unknowns, we can find and solve for the fourth unknown.

Discount Factor

The PV of any cash flow, C_n, can be calculated by multiplying it by the discount factor (DF). The DF depends on the interest rate and the time period.

$$DF = 1/(1 + r)^n.$$

Thus, the discount factor for a cash flow of five years from now at an interest rate of 10 per cent is as follows:

$$1/1.10^5 = 0.6209.$$

A cash flow of ₹100 at the end of the fifth year is worth 100 * 0.6209 = ₹62.09 today. The DF can be used to find the PV of any cash flow.

Future Value

Q1. You have invested ₹100 in a fixed deposit with the SBI at 8 per cent for five years. How much amount will you have on maturity?

C_0	C_1	C_2	C_3	C_4	C_5
100					?

A. The problem involves finding the FV from the PV. We know the interest rate (8 per cent) and the time period (5 years). Applying the compound interest formula,

$$FV = 100 \, (1 + 8\%)^5$$
$$= 100 \, (1 + 0.08)^5$$
$$= 100 \, (1.08)^5$$
$$= 100 * 1.4693$$
$$= ₹146.93.$$

If the interest rate was 10 per cent, FV would be

$$100 \, (1 + 10\%)^5 = ₹161.05.$$

If the time period for which the investment was made is 7 years, FV would be

$$100 \, (1 + 8\%)^7 = ₹171.38.$$

As can be observed from the example, higher the interest rate, higher is the FV. Thus, FV and interest rates have a positive and direct relationship.

Present Value

Q2. You have just won a lottery run by the Indian government with a prize money of ₹100,000. However, the lottery prize will be paid in 10 years' time. What is the PV of your win if the applicable interest rate is 10 per cent?

C_0	C_1	C_2	C_3	C_4	...	C_{10}
?						100,000

A. The problem involves finding PV from a known cash flow in future (FV). We know the interest rate (10 per cent) and the time period (10 years). Applying the compound interest formula,

$$FV = PV \, (1 + r)^n$$

$$\Rightarrow \qquad PV = FV/(1 + r)^n.$$

$$PV = 100,000/(1 + 10\%)^{10}$$

$$= 100,000/(1.1)^{10}$$

$$= 100,000/2.5937$$

$$= ₹38,554.43.$$

If the interest rate was 8 per cent, PV would be

$$100,000/(1 + 8\%)^{10} = ₹46,319.35.$$

If the lottery amount is paid to you after 8 years, PV would be

$$100,000/(1 + 10\%)^{8} = ₹46,650.74.$$

As can be observed from the example, higher the interest rate, lower is the PV. Thus, there is an inverse relationship between PV and interest rate.

Interest Rate

Q3. You are planning to do an MBA after 10 years costing ₹500,000. Your parents currently have ₹200,000. At what return should they invest this money to be able to afford your MBA expenses?

$$C_0 \qquad C_1 \qquad C_2 \qquad \dots \qquad C_{10}$$
200,000------------------------------→ 500,000

A. We have a certain cash flow (PV) and require a specific cash flow at a later date (FV). The later date (time period) is known. We have to find the interest rate which will over the time period turn the given PV into the required FV.

$$FV = PV (1 + r)^n.$$
$$500,000 = 200,000 (1 + r)^{10}$$
$$2.5 = (1 + r)^{10}$$
$$2.5^{1/10} = 1 + r$$
$$1.096 = 1 + r$$
$$r = 9.6\%.$$

Period

Q4. You plan to retire after accumulating ₹1 million. Currently you have ₹513,160 which you can invest at 10 per cent per annum. How many years do you need to wait for your retirement?

$$C_0 \qquad C_1 \qquad C_2 \qquad \ldots \qquad C_n$$

513,160------------------------------→ 1,000,000

A. Similar to Q3, we have the PV and the required FV. We also know the interest rate. We need to find the time period over which the investment at the given interest rate will convert the PV to the required FV.

$$1,000,000 = 513,160 * (1 + 10\%)^n$$
$$1.9487 = 1.10^n$$
$$\log 1.9487 = n * \log 1.10$$
$$n = 7 \text{ years.}$$

Nominal versus Real Return

After seven years, ₹1 million is unlikely to have the same value or purchasing power which it currently has. Inflation reduces the quantum of goods and services that can be purchased with the same amount of money. In order to obtain an amount which has the same value in terms of purchasing power as the 1 million today, we need to factor in the increase in prices (inflation) by using the nominal rate of return and not the real rate of return. The nominal rate takes care of inflation and preserves the purchasing power of ₹1 million.

The real rate is 10 per cent. Assuming inflation of 4 per cent, the nominal rate can be derived as follows:

$$(1.10 * 1.04) - 1 = 1.144 - 1 = 14.4\%.$$

Now, the total amount at the end of seven years which will take care of inflation and preserve the purchasing power of the 1 million is

$$513,160 * 1.144^7 = 1,315,937.$$

After seven years, ₹1,315,937 should be able to buy the same basket of goods and services as ₹1 million now. It is not the quantum of money that is critical but what can be purchased with that money. The difference between nominal return and real return has stumped many people. Students of finance should ensure they do not meet a similar fate and clearly understand and distinguish between the two.

The interest rate that investors actually receive, as in the earlier examples, is called the nominal interest rate. If we adjust the nominal rate for inflation, we obtain what is termed as the real return. Real return protects us from inflation in the economy.

The governments of India and the United States of America (USA) have in the past issued bonds which provide return to the investor that is protected in real terms. Termed 'treasury inflation protected security' (TIPS), these bonds provide a return which comprises a fixed real return plus whatever is the prevailing rate of inflation in the economy. For example, if the real return promised is 7 per cent and inflation currently is 3 per cent, the investor will get a 10 per cent coupon. If the inflation rises to 5 per cent, the investor gets 12 per cent. Although not very common, TIPS has a high demand during periods of high inflation.

Special Considerations in Time Value of Money

Real life situations are seldom as simple and straightforward as assumed in the earlier examples. Cash flows accrue over a number of years rather than in a single time period. At times, they accrue multiple times within a year. For example, we take a loan which is payable monthly over a number of years as EMIs. Alternatively, we invest a large sum, and then may be paid monthly pensions over a number of years. Cash flows from a project accrue over a number of years. Valuing a company requires valuing free cash flows, theoretically, over an infinite period.

Sometimes cash flows form a pattern and there may be easier ways to solve some of them.

Annuity

Annuity refers to a series of equal cash flows over a number of time periods.

- A project may involve an initial investment followed by equal cash inflows over the life of the project.
- A housing loan may be repayable in EMIs over 20 years, amounting to an annuity of 240 periods with each period equalling 1 month.
- A bond issued by the Government of India may promise to pay a coupon interest of 8 per cent per annum, payable per 6 months, for 10 years. This is an annuity of 20 periods of 6 months each, with an inflow of ₹4 per period.

An annuity has the following features:

1. The first cash flow occurs exactly one period from now.
2. All subsequent cash flows have a gap of exactly one period.
3. All periods are of equal length. We will be working on annual cash flows but given our concepts of intra-year compounding (discussed later in this chapter), the conversion to any other period is simple.
4. The interest rate applicable for all cash flows is equal. In technical terms, the term structure of interest rates is flat.
5. All cash flows have the same nominal values.

Q5. You save ₹1,000 every year for five years at 10 per cent interest rate. How much will you have at the end of the five years?

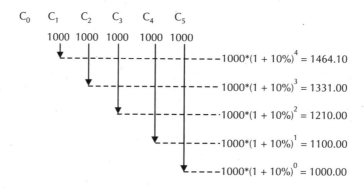

C_0 C_1 C_2 C_3 C_4 C_5

1000 1000 1000 1000 1000

$1000*(1 + 10\%)^4 = 1464.10$

$1000*(1 + 10\%)^3 = 1331.00$

$1000*(1 + 10\%)^2 = 1210.00$

$1000*(1 + 10\%)^1 = 1100.00$

$1000*(1 + 10\%)^0 = 1000.00$

Total = Rs. 6,105

FIGURE 3.1   Future value of an annuity

Source: Author.

Calculating FV of each of these cash flows separately in the given manner is cumbersome. Imagine doing this exercise for 30 years, with six monthly payments (as is the case with US government bonds). The good news is that since the cash flows form a pattern, their value can be calculated with a simple formula. We have constant cash flows over a number of periods, forming an annuity. Future value computation becomes a simple matter with the following formula.

FV of Annuity

$$\text{FV of Annuity} = P\left[\frac{(1+r)^n - 1}{r}\right].$$

FV = future value,
P = present value,
r = discount rate,
n = number of periods.

The formula gives us a value of ₹6,105 which is equal to the previous outcome.

Q6. We can invert the problem to see how much we should invest today to provide us an equal cash flow over a number of specified periods, in this case ₹1,000 over five years (Figure 3.2).

Thus, an investment of ₹3,790.78 today at 10 per cent per annum yields ₹1,000 per annum for five years.

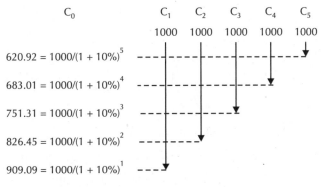

$$620.92 = 1000/(1 + 10\%)^5$$
$$683.01 = 1000/(1 + 10\%)^4$$
$$751.31 = 1000/(1 + 10\%)^3$$
$$826.45 = 1000/(1 + 10\%)^2$$
$$909.09 = 1000/(1 + 10\%)^1$$

3790.78 = Present value

FIGURE 3.2 Present value of an annuity

Source: Author.

As with the computation of FV, the PV can be calculated easily with the following formula:

$$\text{PV of Annuity} = P\left[\frac{1 - (1 + r)^{-n}}{r}\right].$$

P = periodic payment,
r = rate per period,
n = number of periods.

And the formula gives ₹3,790.78 as the PV of the five-year annuity of ₹1,000.

Interestingly, FV of ₹3,790.78 at 10 per cent after five years is ₹6,105.09, which equals the FV as calculated in Figure 3.1. This corroborates the concept of equivalence. The value of ₹3,790.78 at C_0, the five annuity cash flows of ₹1,000 each and ₹6,105.09 at C_5 are all equal (at 10 per cent interest rate).

Making Sense of Sports Contracts

Top sportsmen can make a vital difference to the fortunes of their teams. They also have a short life at the top. Team owners offer them huge compensation over a period of time to attract and retain them. Offers for players have a competitive element. Knowledge of the time value of money enables team owners to attract iconic players with huge nominal salaries whose value may, in fact, be significantly less.

On 12 December 1998, Kevin Brown was signed by Los Angeles Dodgers to play baseball for their team, with the first-ever offer of US$100 million plus. The contract was for US$105 million, with US$15 million being payable annually for the next seven years. If we calculate the worth of the contract, it amounts to (at 10 per cent discount rate)

Contd

contd

$$\text{PV annuity} = P * [1 - (1 + r)^{-n}]/r.$$

Hence, present value equals

$$15 * [1 - (1 + 0.1)^{-7}]/0.1$$

$$= 15 * 4.868$$

$$= \text{US\$73.02 million.}$$

The sum of US\$73.02 million is not exactly small, but far less than the nominal amount of US\$105 million. Knowledge of the time value of money helped Dodgers satisfy Kevin Brown's desire to get more than US\$100 million while at the same time ensuring that Dodgers spent much less in hiring him!

Kinds of Annuity

There are two kinds of annuity:

1. Ordinary annuity where the first cash flow starts from the end of the current period.

$$C_0 \qquad C_1 \qquad C_2 \qquad \dots \qquad C_n$$
$$\quad x \qquad x \qquad\qquad\quad x$$

This is an 'ordinary annuity' since the cash flows start from C_1. The PV calculated will be as at C_0. Similarly, the FV calculated will be as at C_n, that is, the same time period at which the last cash flow accrues.

2. Annuity due where the first cash flow starts at the beginning of the current period.

$$C_0 \qquad C_1 \qquad C_2 \qquad \dots \qquad C_{n-1} \qquad C_n$$
$$x \qquad x \qquad x \qquad\qquad\quad x$$

This is an 'annuity due' since the payment starts at C_0. Cash flows of an annuity due occur one period earlier as compared to an ordinary annuity of a similar period. Hence, the value of an annuity due can be calculated as follows:

Value of an annuity due = Value of an ordinary annuity * (1 + r).

We will be concentrating only on ordinary annuities in this book.

Valuation, Time Value Tables

These formulae are difficult to apply in practice each time. Time value tables simplify the application. The tables are divided into four parts:

1. The FV of a single cash flow (Table A-1) - $FVIF_{r,n}$.

Table A-1 provides FV of a single cash flow. $FVIF_{r,n}$ stands for future value interest factor (FVIF) of a single cash flow at an interest rate of r per cent for n years.

2. The PV of a single cash flow (Table A-2) $PVIF_{r,n}$.

Table A-2 provides PV of a single cash flow. $PVIF_{r,n}$ stands for present value interest factor (PVIF) of a single cash flow at an interest rate of r per cent for n years.

3. The FV of an annuity (Table A-3) $FVIFA_{r,n}$.

Table A-3 provides FV of an annuity. $FVIFA_{r,n}$ stands for FVIF of an annuity at an interest rate of r per cent for n years.

4. The PV of an annuity (Table A-4) $PVIFA_{r,n}$.

Table A-4 provides PV of an annuity. $PVIFA_{r,n}$ stands for PVIF of an annuity at an interest rate of r per cent for n years.

Each table provides the value for ₹1—either a single cash flow of ₹1 or annuity of ₹1 for a certain period. Therefore, the factor given in these tables must be multiplied by the amount of cash flow whose PV/FV needs to be calculated. The table provides valuation for different periods and for different interest rates.

Let us illustrate the use of time value tables by again solving Q1 to Q4, along with Q5 and Q6 on annuities.

Q1. Future value of ₹100 at C_5 at 8 per cent can be calculated by finding $FVIF_{8\%,5}$ from Table A-1 and multiplying that by cash flow of ₹100.

$$FVIF_{8\%,5} = 1.4693.$$

Therefore, ₹100 will be worth 100 * 1.4693 = ₹146.93 after five years.

Q2. Present value of ₹1,000,000 at C_{10} at 10 per cent can be calculated by looking up the value of $PVIF_{10\%,10}$ from Table A-2.

$$PVIF_{10\%,10} = 0.386.$$

$$PV = 1,000,000 * 0.386 = ₹386,000.$$

Q3. We need to find the interest rate that will equate ₹200,000 now to ₹500,000 at C_{10}.

$$500,000 = 200,000 * FVIF_{r,10}$$

$$2.5 = FVIF_{r,10}.$$

We need to look at Table A-1 under 10 years to find out the interest rate which has a yield figure closest to 2.5.

10 per cent yields 2.59, which is slightly higher than 2.5. The actual interest rate should therefore be less than 10 per cent.

We can also find out the interest rate by using the PV table. We find the rate that will make 500,000 at C_{10} equal to 200,000 at C_0, which is exactly the reverse of what we have done.

$$500,000 * PVIF_{r,10} = 200,000$$

$$PVIF_{r,10} = 0.4.$$

If we were to look at Table A-2 under 10 years, the interest rate that is closest to 0.4 is 0.386. The actual interest rate should therefore be less than 10 per cent.

Q4. We need to find the period in which ₹513,160 grows to ₹1,000,000 at 10 per cent interest rate.

$$1,000,000 = 513,160 * FVIF_{10\%,n}$$

$$1.9487 = FVIF_{10\%,n}.$$

We again look at Table A-1 to find the number of years that will yield 1.9487 at 10 per cent interest rate. We find that at seven years the value is 1.949. Hence, the time period is seven years.

Here also, the PV table can be used to determine the time period.

$$513,160 = 1,000,000 * PVIF_{10\%,n}$$

or

$$0.5131 = PVIF_{10\%,n}.$$

Looking under 10 per cent in PV Table A-2, we find seven years yield 0.513. Thus, the actual number of years is seven.

The values obtained by using the time value tables are usually not exact and provide only approximations. Time value tables cannot provide for all interest rates and years. They provide values for whole numbers in terms of years and interest rates which should suffice for a general purpose.

Currently, the purpose is to learn concepts and be able to understand and perform time value calculations. Time value tables serve this purpose rather well. Once the concepts are well understood, actual calculations would obviously be undertaken on Excel or a software specifically designed for this purpose.

Q5. Future value of an annuity of cash flow of ₹1,000 for five years can be calculated by finding the value of $FVIFA_{10\%,5}$ from Table A-3 and multiplying by 1,000.

$$FV = FVIFA_{10\%,5} * 1,000$$

$$= 6.105 * 1,000$$

$$= ₹6,105.$$

Q6. Present value of an annuity of cash flow of ₹1,000 for five years can be calculated by finding the value of $PVIFA_{10\%,5}$ from Table A-4 and multiplying by 1,000.

$$Present\ value = 3.791 * 1000$$

$$= ₹3,791.$$

Clever Use of the Time Value of Money

Lottery sellers have been using the concept of the time value of money and annuity for a long time to meet their objectives. They contribute substantially to charity while at the same time giving prizes that may nominally amount to more than the revenue generated! The revenues are collected now, whereas prizes are given as annuities over a long period.

Assume that the lottery managers have collected ₹500 million in a year and want to pay a prize which is 20 per cent higher at ₹600 million. At the same time, they wish to donate 50 per cent of their revenues to charity. The discount rate is 10 per cent. How do they achieve this?

The lottery owner needs to fulfil two criteria:

1. Nominal value of the annuity (each cash flow * no. of years) should be ₹600 million.
2. The PV of the annuity should be less than ₹250 million.

If they pay ₹24 million per year for 25 years,

$$\text{Nominal value} = ₹600 \text{ million.}$$

Present value of the annuity,

$$\text{PVIFA}_{(10\%,25)} * 24.$$

$$9.0770 * 24 = ₹217.8 \text{ million.}$$

Equivalence

An important concept that applies here is one of equivalence. The PV and the future annuity cash flows are equal and can be substituted for each other. If you have one of these two cash flows, you can obtain the other value by investing/borrowing at the given rate.

Q7. A young upcoming player is bought by a Mumbai franchise for the next five years for ₹200 million, ₹40 million being paid to him annually, with the first payment to be made at the end of the first year. What is the PV of his earnings? Show the equivalence between the two.

A. Cash flows are as follows:

C_0	C_1	C_2	C_3	C_4	C_5
	40	40	40	40	40

We need to find the PV of an annuity for five years.

$$PV = \text{PVIFA}_{10\%,5} * 40.$$

$$3.7908 * 40 = 151.632 \text{ million.}$$

Hence, the value of his contract is approximately ₹150 million, highly lucrative but not ₹200 million which is really the nominal value.

The equivalence of the two can be demonstrated as follows:

$$PV \text{ of earnings is } 151.632.$$

$$\text{Interest for one year} = 151.632 * 10\% = 15.163.$$

$$\text{Value at the end of first year} = 166.795.$$

After subtracting 40 million in year 1, cash flow available = 126.795, which invested at 10 per cent yields 139.474.

After subtracting 40 million in year 2, cash flow available = 99.474, which invested at 10 per cent yields 109.422.

After subtracting 40 million in year 3, cash flow available = 69.422, which invested at 10 per cent yields 76.364.

After subtracting 40 million in year 4, cash flow available = 36.364, which invested at 10 per cent yields 40 million.

Present value amounting to ₹151.632 million at 10 per cent is able to pay ₹40 million per annum for the next five years, demonstrating the equivalence of the PV and the five-year annuity.

Practice Questions

Future Value of an Annuity

Q8. You are 40 years old and plan to retire in 20 years. During these 20 years, you invest ₹100,000 per year in Public Provident Fund (PPF) and expect to get an interest rate of 8 per cent. How much money will you have on retirement?

A.
$$FV = 100,000 * FVIFA_{8\%,\ 20}$$
$$= 100,000 * 45.762$$
$$= ₹4,576,200.$$

Since you need to calculate the future value of an annuity, you will refer to Table A-3. You go down the 8 per cent column until you reach 20 years and you get the figure of 45.762. This implies that an annuity of ₹1 for 20 years at 8 per cent will have an FV of ₹45.762. An annuity amount of ₹100,000 every year will accumulate to ₹4,576,200 at the end of 20 years.

Period of Savings

Q9. Never having gone abroad, you plan a trip to Switzerland. Your travel agency says the trip will cost you ₹500,000 and the cost will remain constant whenever you choose to make the trip. You can invest ₹40,000 per annum, and this money will earn 8 per cent interest. After how many years can you make the trip?

A.
$$500,000 = 40,000 * (1.08^n - 1)/0.08$$
$$12.5 * 0.08 = 1.08^n - 1$$
$$1 + 1 = 2 = 1.08^n$$
$$n = 9 \text{ years.}$$

How Much Should You Save Every Year?

Q10. After completing your MBA, you get placed in a multinational company of your dreams. Your dreams take you to a BMW, you wish to own. The BMW costs ₹5,000,000, and you feel the price will stay constant. You do not wish to wait for more than five years. How much should you save every year to be able to afford the BMW in five years.

A.
$$5,000,000 = A * FVIFA_{10\%, 5}$$
$$5,000,000 = A * 6.105$$
$$A = ₹819,000.$$

Here again, you are looking for the future value of an annuity. You go down the column under 10 per cent for five years and the value you get is 6.105. This implies that ₹1 invested every year for five years will yield ₹6.105. Since your requirement is ₹5,000,000, you need to invest 5,000,000/6.105 = ₹819,000 every year for five years, to be able to afford your dream BMW.

Calculating Implied Interest Rate

Q11. The Government of India announces a pension scheme wherein the investor invests ₹1,000 every year for 20 years. At the end of 20 years, he/she gets ₹51,169 back. What is the implied rate of interest the investor gets?

A.
$$51169 = 1,000 * FVIFA_{r,20}$$
$$51.169 = FVIFA_{r,20}.$$

In Table A-2, the row showing 20 years, 9 per cent yields 51.169.
Hence, the implied rate of interest is 9 per cent.

Present Value of an Annuity

Q12. After completing your MBA, you get placed in a multinational company of your dreams. Instead of waiting to save for purchasing a car, you wish to own it immediately. You calculate that you will be able to pay an EMI of ₹15,000. The finance company charges an interest rate of 12 per cent per annum and lets you pay for the car over five years. What is the value of the car you can purchase, provided the finance company only finances 80 per cent of the value of the car?

$$PV = 15,000 * [1 - 1/(1 + r)^n]/r$$

$$= 1 - (1/1.01^{60})/1\%$$

$$= (1 - 1/1.82)/1\%$$

$$= 45.0549.$$

$$PV = 15,000 * 45.0549$$

$$PV = 675,823.50.$$

Hence, the company will provide you funding up to approximately ₹675,823, and the total value of the car you can purchase after putting in your own 20 per cent will be

$$675,823/80\% = ₹844,779.$$

Financial markets do make dreams come true and much earlier than otherwise possible! However, your knowledge of fundamental financial concepts should be thorough for you to be able to work out the calculations and, more importantly, to bag a job in a multinational company! Opportunities do exist but only for the prepared.

Is Your MBA Worthwhile?

How many students take time out to calculate the benefit of studying for an MBA degree in monetary terms over one's lifespan? Not many, I guess. If anyone could do so, I suspect he/she would not need to pursue MBA!

Let us assume the following.

Q13. If you had not undertaken to study for an MBA, you would have found employment at ₹600,000 per annum in the first year and ₹636,000 in the second year. Let us also assume for the sake of simplicity that your salary would have grown at 6 per cent per annum for the rest of your career spanning 40 years.

Instead, if you pursue an MBA, it would cost ₹1,000,000 in each of the two years. You are now more competent than a non-MBA and are able to secure a job paying ₹800,000 per annum. Also given your greater competence, you secure faster promotions and increments at 8 per cent per annum for the next 38 years.

Are you financially better off doing an MBA or not if the discount rate for your calculations is 12 per cent?

The formula for PV of growing annuity is $\dfrac{P}{r - g}\left[1 - \left(\dfrac{1 + g}{1 + r}\right)^n\right]$.

The examples we have come across until now have been fairly straight forward involving only one-time calculation—calculating either PV or FV of a single cash flow or an annuity. Real life is rarely this simple and involves more than one-step calculations.

Q14. What is the present value of a ten-year annuity of ₹100 per year that makes its first payment two years from today if the discount rate is 10 per cent?

A.

	C_0	C_1	C_2	C_3	...	C_{10}	C_{11}
			100	100	...	100	100

Value of annuity

<.............

Since the cash flow starts from C_2, a 10-year annuity will go on till C_{11}. When we calculate the value of this annuity, the value will be as on C_1. We will have to further take the value of this single cash flow to C_0 to calculate its present value.

$$\text{Value of annuity at } C_1 = 100 * \text{PVIFA}_{10\%,10}$$
$$= 100 * 6.145$$
$$= ₹614.50.$$

Taking this to $C_0 = 614.50/1.1 = ₹558.64$.

Q15. Your uncle is quite impressed with your MBA degree. He wants you to help him in his post-retirement planning. Currently, he has ₹0.5 million with him. He will retire after 10 years. During these 10 years, he will save ₹100,000 per annum. He expects to live for 20 years post-retirement.

1. How much can he consume every year post-retirement? Assume an interest rate of 10 per cent.
2. How much should he save over the next 10 years if he wants ₹500,000 per annum post-retirement?

A. The cash flows can be depicted as the following:

C_0	C_1	C_2	...	C_{10}	C_{11}	C_{12}	...	C_{30}
500,000				?				
	100,000	100,000		100,000	A	A		A

We need to find the value of cash flow in year 10. From that we will be able to find out the cash flow that your uncle would be able to draw for the next 20 years, from year 11 to year 30.

1. The value of ₹500,000 is

$$\text{FVIF}_{10\%,10} * 500,000 = 2.5937 * 500,000$$
$$= 1,296,871 \qquad \qquad ... A$$

2.

$$FVIFA_{10\%,10} * 100{,}000 = 15.937 * 100{,}000$$
$$= 1{,}593{,}700 \qquad \text{... B}$$
$$\text{Total value in year 10} = 2{,}890{,}571 \text{ (A + B)} \qquad \text{... C}$$

3. Annuity cash flow for the next 20 years is

$$2{,}890{,}571/PVIFA_{10\%,20} = 2{,}890{,}571/8.514 = 339{,}508.$$

Every year, ₹339,508 can be drawn for 20 years post-retirement.

In order to draw 500,000 annually, we need to find the amount of money he should have in year 10. We already know how much he will have from the ₹500,000 currently saved. The remaining will help us calculate the annuity required for the next 10 years.

4. Amount required at the end of 10 years is

$$PVIFA_{10\%,20} * 500{,}000 = 8.514 * 500{,}000$$
$$= 4{,}257{,}000 \qquad \text{... D}$$

Available from the single cash flow of ₹500,000 at C_0 = ₹1,296,871.

$$\text{Balance required} = 2{,}960{,}129 \qquad \text{(D – A) ... E}$$
$$\text{Annuity amount} = 2{,}960{,}129/FVIFA_{10\%,10}$$
$$= 2{,}960{,}129/15.937$$
$$= 185{,}739 \qquad \text{... F}$$

Thus, in order to withdraw ₹500,000 every year for 20 years post-retirement, your uncle needs to save ₹185,739 annually for the next 10 years.

Perpetuity

Perpetuity refers to a constant stream of cash flows every year forever. In a way, it is an annuity extended forever. Again, as in the case of ordinary annuities, the first cash flow starts at the end of the first year, that is, at C_1.

Similar to annuity, these cash flows can be valued by a simple formula.

$$PV = CF/r.$$

CF refers to the annual cash flow.

Q16. The Indian Government had issued a ₹100 bond on which it pays a coupon of ₹10 forever but whose principal will never be returned. Today the required rate of return on these bonds is 8 per cent. What price should these bonds trade at?

A. Value of these bonds = CF/r = 10/8% = 125.

A company that has no growth potential and keeps generating the same profit or cash flow every year can be valued as a perpetuity.

$$PV = \frac{C}{(1+r)} + \frac{C}{(1+r)^2} + \frac{C}{(1+r)^3} + \dots$$

$$PV = CF / r.$$

Perpetual Bonds

In April 2017, HDFC Bank issued perpetual bonds amounting to ₹100 billion on a private placement basis. The bond pays a coupon of 8.85 per cent annually. The bonds are callable at par after five years by the bank. The bonds were rated AA+ by three rating agencies, namely CRISIL, CARE and India Ratings & Research Pvt Ltd. The bonds are listed on the wholesale debt segment of the National Stock Exchange (NSE) and the Bombay Stock Exchange (BSE).

Q17. ABC Limited is an old company and has been in operation for 50 years. It has reached a stage of maturity and hardly has any new projects to invest in. It therefore pays out its entire net profit as dividends to shareholders and retains nothing. The annual net profit of the company is a constant ₹60 million forever. The required rate of return is 8 per cent. What is the value of the company?

A. Since the company produces the same cash flow of ₹60 million every year which is expected to continue forever, it can be valued as a perpetuity. Hence,

$$PV = 60/8\% = ₹0.75 \text{ billion.}$$

Growing Perpetuity

A growing perpetuity bond is similar to the perpetuity discussed previosuly; it never matures and the principal is never returned. However, the cash flows do not remain constant but increase every year at a constant rate of growth called 'g'. As against perpetual bonds (perpetuity) in which the cash flows remain constant, in the case of a growing perpetuity, the growth rate of the cash flows is constant. Thus, if the cash flow in the first year is ₹10 and the growth rate is 5 per cent, the second-year cash flow will be

$$10 (1 + 5\%) = 10.50.$$

The third year cash flow would be $10 (1 + 5\%)^2 = 11.025$ and so on.

As always, the first cash flow starts at the end of the first year at C_1.

As in the case of annuity, there is a simple formula to calculate the value of a growing perpetuity.

$$\text{Value} = CF/(r - g),$$

where

$$g < r.$$

The value in the numerator is the cash flow in the first year (CF_1), which equals the previous year's dividend multiplied by $(1 + g)$, g being the constant rate of growth.

Q18. Company XYZ has just given a dividend of ₹10 and this dividend is expected to increase every year by 3 per cent forever. What is the value of the share of this company if the required rate of return for the company is 11 per cent?

A. $\text{Value} = CF_1/(r - g) = [10 * (1 + 3\%)]/(11\% - 3\%)\ ...$

$$10.30/8\% = 128.75.$$

The value of a growing perpetuity is very sensitive to growth rates. Hence, growing companies are very highly valued.

Valuing High Growth Rates

Q19. Let us take a simple example. There are two companies A and B. Both have a required rate of return of 10 per cent. The next year's cash flow for A is expected to be 10 and this cash flow is expected to grow at 3 per cent. For company B, the next years' cash flow is only 6 but is expected to grow at 6 per cent. Their respective values are

$$A = 10/(10\% - 3\%) = 142.86,$$
$$B = 6/(10\% - 6\%) = 150.$$

Despite the much lower initial cash flow of B compared to that of A, B has a higher value due to the higher growth rate.

Intra-year Compounding

Until now, we have been assuming the payment of interest once at the end of the year. In practice, most fixed income securities pay coupons at more frequent intervals. Fixed deposits in a bank receive interest payments quarterly or half-yearly. The bonds issued by the Government of India, and also that of the Government of the USA, pay interest twice a year. Housing loan EMIs are paid monthly. While this does not result in a change in the coupon rate of interest, with the total coupon received annually remaining constant, it has implications for the effective annual rate of interest, since part of the coupon is received earlier than the end of the year. We are aware that the value of a cash flow depends on the quantum as well as the timing of the cash flow. Since the time of receipt of the cash flow has changed, so does the value. Let us understand this with a simple illustration.

An investment is made in a government bond with a coupon rate of 12 per cent per annum. The bond pays interest twice a year which means ₹6 will be paid after 6 months and another ₹6 after 12 months.

The cash flows can be depicted as follows:

C_0	6 months	12 months
	₹6	₹6

Received after six months, ₹6 will not lie idle and will be invested at the prevailing rate of interest of 12 per cent per annum for the remaining period of six months fetching an interest of

$$6 * 12\% * (6/12) = ₹0.36.$$

Effectively, the investor will have ₹12.36 as interest at the end of the year instead of only the coupon of ₹12, as in the case of a one-time payment of the coupon. The total amount at the end of the year will be ₹112.36, instead of ₹112. If the government pays interest more frequently, say every quarter, the effective interest rate will increase even more. The coupons will then be paid as follows:

C_0	3m	6m	9m	12m
₹	3	3	3	3

In this case, the investor will invest

- the first coupon of ₹3 for the balance period of nine months at 12 per cent per annum (₹0.27),
- the second coupon of ₹3 for the balance period of six months at 12 per cent per annum (₹0.18) and
- the third coupon ₹3 for the balance period of three months again at 12 per cent per annum (₹0.09).

The effective interest will amount to ₹12.54, and the investor will have ₹112.54 at the end of the year. More frequent the payment of coupon interest, higher is the effective interest.

This phenomenon is called intra-year compounding, referring to the fact that the coupon interest is being compounded within a year (or intra-year). The number of times the coupon is paid is termed 'm'. The amount at the end of any year can be calculated by the following modification to the compound interest formula:

$$FV = PV \, (1 + r/m)^{n*m}.$$

And the effective interest rate would be

$$[(1 + r/m)^m] - 1.$$

Thus, if the rate of interest is 10 per cent, the amount at the end of the year, on investing ₹100 at different frequency of payment, will be as in Table 3.3.

TABLE 3.3 Effective interest rate

Interest payment	Compounding	Amount	Effective interest
Annually	m = 1	110.00	10.00
Semi-annually	m = 2	110.25	10.25
Quarterly	m = 4	110.38	10.38
Monthly	m = 12	110.47	10.47
Weekly	m = 52	110.51	10.51
Daily	m = 365	110.52	10.52

Source: Author.

Continuous Compounding

As we observe (Table 3.3), more frequent the compounding, higher is the effective interest rate. The limit is reached when the compounding is done continuously, in the sense that the coupon is paid every moment (theoretically speaking).

The formula for intra-year compounding, as given earlier, is

$$FV = PV\ (1 + r/m)^{n*m}.$$

Continuous compounding refers to the limit as m tends to infinity. Hence, $FV = PV\ e^{rn}$.
Where 'e' is the base of the exponential function, with its value approximately equal to 2.71828.

Q20. A finance company promises to pay 10 per cent interest continuously compounded for five years. How much will an investment of ₹1,000 amount to after five years?

A. $\quad\quad\quad\quad FV = PV\ e^{rn}$

$$FV = 1,000 * e^{0.10*5}$$

$$FV = 1,000 * 1.6487 = 1,648.70.$$

And the effective interest rate is $e^{0.1} = 10.52\%$.

Q21. A bank offers 10 per cent interest rate on a deposit of five years; the entire amount to be payable at the end of the period of five years. On a deposit of ₹1,000, what amount will be available after five years? What would be the amount if the interest rate is compounded quarterly, although the entire amount will be paid at the end of five years? What is the effective interest rate?

A. What is FV? Period is five years. Interest rate is 10 per cent. PV = 1,000.

$$FV = 1,000 * (1 + 10\%)^5 = 1610.51.$$

$$\text{Quarterly compounded value} = 1,000 * (1 + 10\%/4)^{5*4}.$$

$$FV = 1,000 * 1.025^{20} = 1,638.61.$$

$$\text{Effective interest rate} = (1 + r/m)^{n*m} - 1$$

$$= (1 + 10\%/4)^{4} - 1$$

$$= 1.1038 - 1$$

$$= 10.38\%.$$

Q22. The interest rate is 12 per cent. What is the effective rate if the coupon is paid

1. semi-annually,
2. quarterly,
3. monthly,

4. weekly,
5. daily,
6. continuously?

For each listed criterion, how much would ₹100 amount to after five years?

Let us put it all together.

Q23. Assume it is 1 January 2017. And you will need ₹10,000 on 1 January 2022. Interest rate is 10 per cent per annum.

1. How much should you deposit today to have ₹10,000 on 1 January 2022? How much should you deposit on 1 January 2018 to have ₹10,000 on 1 January 2022?
2. If you want to make equal payments on each 1 January from 2018 through 2022 to accumulate ₹10,000, how much should this deposited amount be?
3. Your father offers to help you accumulate the required balance. He offers to make the payments as in point 2 or to give you a lump sum of ₹7,000 on 1 January 2018. Which one would you choose?
4. If you can deposit only ₹1,574.06 for each 1 January from 2018 to 2022, what should the interest be for you to have the required balance of ₹10,000 on 1 January 2022?
5. To help you reach ₹10,000 on 1 January 2022, your father offers to give you ₹3,000 on 1 January 2018. You plan to make eight additional payments of equal amount every six months thereafter. What should be the size of each payment?

A. Cash flows can be depicted as follows:

$$C_0 \qquad C_1 \qquad C_2 \qquad C_3 \qquad C_4 \qquad C_5$$
$$10,000$$

C_0 represents the present time period 1 January 2017. C_1 represents 1 January 2018 and so on with C_5 representing 1 January 2022. The objective is to have ₹10,000 at C_5.

1. $PV = FV/(1 + r)^n$.
   a. $PV = 10,000/(1 + 10\%)^5$
                                      $= 10,000/1.6105$
                                      $= ₹6,209.21$.
   b. $PV = 10,000/(1 + 10\%)^4$
                                        $= 10,000/1.4641$
                                      $= ₹6,830.13$.
2. Annuity, five years. FV, ₹10,000. Find annuity cash flow.
   $FVIFA_{10\%,5} * A = 10,000$.
   Annuity $= 10,000/6.105 = ₹1,638.00$.
3. Future value at C_5 of annuity cash flows in point 2 is ₹10,000.
   Future value of ₹7,000 on 1 January 2018 is

$$7,000 * (1 + 10\%)^4 = ₹10,248.70.$$

Hence, a payment of ₹7,000 on 1 January 2018 is preferable.

4. Future value, ₹10,000. Annuity, five years. Annuity cash flow, ₹1,574.06. Find the interest rate.

$$FVIFA_{r,5} = 10,000$$
$$FVIFA_{r,5} = 6.353$$
$$r = 12\%.$$

5. Value of 3,000 at $C_5 = 3,000 * (1 + 10\%)^4 = 4392.30$. Balance required = ₹5,607.70.

$$FVIFA_{5\%,8} * A = 5,607.70$$
$$9.549 * A = 5,607.70$$
$$A = 587.26.$$

Assumption.

The year is divided into two.

Hence, the interest rate applicable is 10%/2 = 5 %.

Number of periods = 4 * 2 = 8.

Amortizing a Loan

It has now become commonplace to borrow for long term to purchase a high value asset such as a house, a car or even a trip abroad. Repayment is by way of what are popularly called EMIs. Typically, a housing loan in India can be taken for up to 20 years, although, in recent times, loans of a longer period have also become a reality. In the USA, 30-year mortgages are quite common. A loan of 20 years implies repayment in 240 months and the EMI, as the name suggests, is constant for the entire period of 240 months.

Housing loans are termed mortgages. Mortgages have two distinguishing features:

1. Mortgages are loans payable over a long period of time.
2. The repayments are through EMIs. Each month's instalment payment is equal for the entire period of the mortgage.

Equated monthly installments, being equal, are like an annuity, with each period being one month (and not one year). Hence, there would be 240 periods of one month for an annuity of 20 years. The monthly interest rate is simply one-twelfth of the annual applicable interest rate.

Housing finance companies, typically, calculate the EMI per ₹10 million for a given interest rate and time period. The actual EMI is a simple calculation based on the loan amount and can be easily derived.

Housing loans are different from standard debt instruments wherein the borrower pays regular interest and the principal amount is repaid towards the end of the loan tenure. That may be an acceptable risk for companies or even borrowing countries. An individual, however, may not find it easy to repay the loan as a lump sum amount towards the end of the tenure.

Housing loans typically amortize the principal over the entire period of the loan. Part of the EMI pays the interest and the balance repays the principal. The repayment of the principal starts with the first EMI and continues each month over the entire duration of the loan, removing the undue burden of large repayment on maturity. In the beginning, a larger proportion of the EMI consists of the interest payment. Over time, as the principal is repaid and gets reduced, the interest component in the EMI decreases while the principal repayment component increases. The loan repayment is structured in such a way that the last EMI is just sufficient to pay the interest for the last month and the remainder of the principal. This process is known as the amortization of a loan.

Let us understand the workings with an example.

Amortization Schedule

Principal is ₹1,000,000, period is 15 years (180 months) and interest is 10 per cent per annum (Table 3.4).

A prospective customer approaches a housing finance company for a loan of ₹1,000,000 to finance the purchase of a house. Considering his advanced age of 45 years, the housing finance company agrees to provide the loan for a period of 15 years at an annual interest rate of 10 per cent. Being an ordinary annuity, the EMI begins from the next month. (That is not the usual practice, but we are assuming an ordinary annuity for illustration purpose.)

Following are the details of the loan structuring:
Loan amount: ₹1,000,000
Period: 180 months (15 * 12)
Interest rate: 0.8333 per cent per month (10/12)
EMI: ₹10,746

The EMI of ₹10,746 comprises both the interest amount and the principal repayment. The interest for the first month is ₹8,333 (0.8333 per cent of 1,000,000). The balance ₹2,413 repays the principal, reducing the amount due (principal outstanding) to ₹997,587. The next month's interest, calculated on ₹997,587, is now only ₹8,313. The principal repayment is higher at

TABLE 3.4   Amortization schedule I

Period	Opening balance	EMI	Interest component @10% per annum	Principal component	Closing balance
1	1,000,000	10,746	8,333	2,413	997,587
2	997,587	10,746	8,313	2,433	995,154
3	995,154	10,746	8,293	2,453	992,701
...	...	...	...	...	...
...	...	...	...	...	...
179	21,243	10,746	177	10,569	10,674
180	10,674	10,746	89	10,657	17

Source: Author.

₹2,433. The next month's interest will be calculated on ₹995,154. The interest component in the next EMI will be further reduced to ₹8,293 and principal repayment increased to ₹2,453.

The process of principal amortization is carried on for the entire period of 180 months. Each period the EMI remains constant, the interest component in the EMI keeps getting reduced and the principal repayment component keeps increasing. The last EMI is sufficient to pay that month's interest and the remaining principal.

Initially, the interest is high and principal repayment portion of the EMI is low. As months pass by and as the principal remaining to be paid back reduces, the interest component of the EMI, calculated on the remaining principal amount, also decreases.

Hence, the principal repayment keeps increasing. Consequently, the principal outstanding decreases at a low rate initially. It is only after a substantive period has elapsed that there is a significant decrease in the principal outstanding.

For example, even after the 60th month, ₹813,171 is outstanding, that is, more than 81 per cent of the loan. Similarly, even after 96 months, ₹647,313 is outstanding. Despite the fact that more than 50 per cent of the period has elapsed, only a little over one-third of the principal has been repaid.

This aspect leaves many people stumped. MBA students should ensure that they understand the concept and have a firm grip on these calculations and interpret them properly.

Negative Amortization

Amortization refers to the repayment of the principal amount and interest over time. An equal EMI is paid every month, part of which pays the interest and the balance repays the principal.

The interest applicable on a loan can be fixed or variable. In the case of a fixed-rate amortization, all parameters and values are known and stated upfront, as in the previous example. For a variable-interest amortization, the interest rate keeps changing, impacting various parameters.

Let us assume that in the previous illustration, the interest rate was variable. Assume after the loan is taken, the interest rate increases to 12 per cent. There are two options available. Increase either the EMI or the period of payment. If the period remains the same, the EMI would need to increase to ₹12,002. Alternatively, we can keep the EMI constant and increase the payment period to a little over 22 years. A third option is increasing both so that neither the period gets extended to 22 years nor does the EMI increases to ₹12,002.

There is a very interesting situation where the interest rate goes up to say 15 per cent. The interest on the principal amount of ₹1 million amounts to ₹12,500, which is more than the EMI itself. Instead of reducing, the principal increases every month and will, in fact, never get paid. This phenomenon is termed as negative amortization. Such a situation is clearly not sustainable, and the borrower will either have to increase his EMI payment substantially or pay part of the loan to reduce the borrowed amount.

Period of Mortgage Loan

Q24. You are planning to buy a house and need a mortgage loan of ₹5,000,000. The interest rate on housing loans is 10 per cent and you can pay an EMI of ₹50,000 only. What will be the period of mortgage?

$$5,000,000 = 50,000 * (1 - 1/1.00833^n)/0.00833$$

$$0.833 = 1 - 1/(1.00833)^n$$

$$0.1667 = 1/(1.00833)^n$$

$$1.00833^n = 1/0.1667 = 6.$$

$$n = 216 \text{ months or } 18 \text{ years.}$$

How Long Will the Money Last?

Q25. Your uncle retires with a corpus of ₹4,868,418, which he invests in a fund giving 10 per cent per annum. He needs ₹1 million for his expenses every year. How long will the money last?

$$4,868,418 = 1,000,000 * (1 - 1/1.10^n)/0.1$$

$$0.4868418 = 1 - 1/1.10^n$$

$$0.5131582 = 1/1.10^n$$

$$1.10^n = 1.948717.$$

$$n = 7 \text{ years.}$$

Let us see how amortization takes place over the seven years in Table 3.5.

TABLE 3.5 Amortization schedule II

Year	Beginning amount	Withdrawl amount	Interest	Principal	Ending amount
1	4,868,418	1,000,000	486,842	513,158	4,355,260
2	4,355,260	1,000,000	435,526	564,474	3,790,786
3	3,790,786	1,000,000	379,079	620,921	3,169,865
4	3,169,865	1,000,000	316,987	683,013	2,486,852
5	2,486,852	1,000,000	248,685	751,315	1,735,537
6	1,735,537	1,000,000	173,554	826,446	909,091
7	909,091	1,000,000	90,909	909,091	0

Source: Author.

Finding the Rate of Interest

Q26. A finance company runs a scheme wherein on a deposit of ₹100,000, the company gives you ₹31,547 annually for four years. What is the interest rate being offered by the company?

$$100,000 = 31547 * PVIFA_{r,4}$$
$$3.1699 = PVIFA_{r,4}.$$

r = 10% approx. (Table A-4 row under 4 years = 3.1699.)

The market for financing is, no doubt, very complex but the concepts learnt help us navigate our way through these complexities without being overwhelmed. Banks and finance companies often present data and calculations in a manner that may not be completely above board. An understanding of the time value of money should help us calculate real returns/costs and not be caught in a trap laid by banks.

Finding the Effective Cost of a Loan

Banks often charge a processing fee for the loans they sanction. Such fees have the potential to impact the real cost of the loan significantly. For example, a borrower approaches two banks A and B for a loan for one year.

Q27. Bank A charges 8 per cent per annum. On a loan of ₹100, the borrower needs to pay back ₹108 at the end of the year.

Bank B charges 6 per cent per annum but also has a loan-processing fee of 4 per cent. For each ₹100, the borrower actually gets only ₹96. Hence, in order to obtain a net cash flow of ₹100, the borrower must take a loan of (100/96) * 100 = ₹104.17. At 6 per cent interest, the borrower will have to return ₹110.42 at the end of the year. Thus, the effective cost is 10.42 per cent.

Payment of EMI in Advance

We have discussed ordinary annuities until now and all the calculations are based on payments commencing from the first year. In most cases, EMIs are payable in advance which increases the effective cost.

Q28. Assume a borrowing of ₹1,000 at an interest rate of 10 per cent for four years payable by equal annual instalments. Each instalment would be ₹315.46.

Thus, the cash flows are

C_0	C_1	C_2	C_3	C_4
–1,000	315.46	315.46	315.46	315.46

However, payment in advance implies that the payment actually starts at the same time that the loan is taken, effectively reducing the quantum of the loan.

The showed amounts to a loan of $1,000 - 315.46 = ₹684.54$, with repayments in three annual instalments. The resultant cash flows are:

C_0	C_1	C_2	C_3	C_4
-684.54	315.46	315.46	315.46	

And the effective interest rate is approximately 18 per cent.

In order to have an inflow or net borrowing of ₹1,000 initially, the borrowed amount should be ₹1,461. The annual instalments then would be ₹461 for three years from C_1 to C_3.

Monthly Payments for Loans

While throughout this chapter we have been assuming annual cash flows, in the real world cash flows are almost invariably more frequent. For housing loans, car loans and consumer loans, we generally pay by way of EMIs. This changes the effective annual interest cost.

Q29. Assume a loan of ₹1,000.

Bank A quotes 15 per cent payable annually. Bank B quotes 14.4 per cent payable monthly.
Bank A: For a loan of ₹1,000, ₹1,150 is required to be paid back at the end of one year.
Bank B: The effective annualized cost is

$$\text{EAR} = 1 + (14.4\%/12)^{12} - 1$$
$$1.012^{12} - 1 = 1.1539 - 1$$
$$= 15.39\%.$$

The borrower ends up paying ₹12 per month for 12 months, with an effective cost of 15.39 per cent!

KEY CONCEPTS

1. Money has time value. The value of a cash flow is determined by the quantum and the time period.
2. A rupee today is worth more than a rupee tomorrow and a rupee today cannot be worth more than a rupee yesterday.
3. Managers should use the present value of cash flows to compare and evaluate payments made and received at different times.
4. Returns are always compounded and are, usually, expressed in annual terms.
5. Cash flows often form a pattern such as annuity, perpetuity and growing perpetuity.
6. Repayment of loan and its interest through equated instalments is a very significant innovation.
7. The conversion of the value of cash flows from one period to the other is one of the most fundamental concepts in financial management. Conversion of PV to FV is termed compounding. Conversion of a future cash flow to PV is called discounting.

8. The discount rate incorporates compensation for time, inflation and risk.
9. Inflation can have a significant impact on the purchasing power of a cash flow and must be carefully incorporated in our analysis.
10. The payment of interest more than once in a year is termed intra-year compounding and may significantly increase the effective annual interest rate.

CHAPTER QUESTIONS

1. Assume an interest rate of 10 per cent for all the following problems:
   a. You have ₹10,000 now. How much will you have after five years? After 10 years? Does the amount increase or decrease? Why?
   b. A lottery won by you promises ₹10,000 after four years, ₹15,000 after eight years and ₹20,000 after 12 years. Your friend offers to pay you in exchange for the lottery: (i) ₹18,000, (ii) ₹22,000. Should you accept the offer? At what amount will you break-even?
   c. A lottery promises ₹10,000 every year, starting from the end of the first year hence, for the next 10 years. What is it worth? What if the lottery payment starts immediately?
   d. Your daughter is keen to pursue her MBA. She is currently in the 5th standard and will be able to pursue her MBA after 10 years. An MBA is expected to cost ₹1 million per annum for the two years. How much should you save every year to be able to fund her MBA?
   e. You expect to obtain a loan of ₹400,000 per year for the two years of her MBA. You expect to save the same amount every year. How many years prior to her MBA do you need to start saving?
   f. The loan needs to be paid back in 10 years but starting 1 year after her MBA is completed. What is the annual repayment amount?
   g. How long must a stream of ₹10,000 payments last to justify a price of ₹61,446? Suppose, the payments lasted only 7 years. How large should the salvage value be to justify the initial investment of ₹61,446?
2. Find FV and PV of the following annuities. What is the relationship between the FVs and PVs?
   a. ₹100 per year at 9 per cent for 10 years
   b. ₹500 per year for eight years at 15 per cent
   c. ₹800 per year for 20 years at 7 per cent
   d. ₹1,000 per year for five years at 0 per cent
   e. ₹100 per month for five years at 10 per cent
3. What are the values of ₹5,000 invested under the following assumptions?
   a. 10 per cent compounded annually for seven years
   b. 10 per cent compounded semi-annually for seven years
   c. 10 per cent compounded quarterly for seven years
   d. 10 per cent compounded monthly for seven years
   e. 10 per cent compounded daily for seven years
   f. 10 per cent compounded continuously for seven years

4. As the finance manager of your company, you need to decide where to invest.
   - A project that pays ₹100,000 one year later; the cost of the project is ₹90,000.
   - Alternatively, you can invest in a bank that pays 10 per cent interest.
   a. Would you invest in the project or with the bank?
   b. What happens if the bank increases its interest rate to 12 per cent?
   c. What is the bank interest rate at which you would be indifferent between the two rates?
   d. What other aspect will you take into account in determining which of the two options to invest in?

5. You have four loans outstanding to your friend: ₹100,000 after 3 years, ₹50,000 after 5 years, ₹150,000 after 7 years and ₹200,000 after 10 years. You wish to consolidate the loans and pay him with six annual instalments starting at the end of the year. What would be the annual payment?

6. What is the present value of a cash flow of ₹100 per year for 10 years starting at the end of one year? What happens if one cash flow is added in the 11th year? What if it is added today? What is the FV of all these three cash flows at the end of 11th years? What is the relationship of the PV with the FV?

7. You need ₹100,000 after 10 years. You start making equal annual deposits starting at the end of four years (seven annual instalments). What should be the size of each deposit? How large should the instalments be if you make the seven instalments starting at the end of the first year?

8. You have been offered a share in a running business. The business is expected to generate cash flows of ₹10 million, growing at 4 per cent forever. What is the value of the business? How much should the business grow annually to justify a valuation of ₹200 million?

9. A company is in a high growth phase and is expected to grow its cash flows at 8 per cent per annum for six years from the present ₹10 million per annum. After that, the company reaches a mature phase and is expected to grow at 3 per cent in perpetuity.
   a. What is the value of the company?
   b. What if the high growth phase lasts for 10 years?
   c. What if the perpetuity growth is 4 per cent per annum?

10. There are two friends, A and B. Both are 25 years old and are planning for their retirement in 40 years. A plans to invest ₹10,000 per annum for the next 10 years and stop thereafter. However, this money will continue to stay invested for the balance period of 30 years till his retirement.

    B does not plan to save immediately. He plans to start saving ₹10,000 per annum after 20 years and continue to do that for the next 20 years till his retirement.

    Who will be richer on retirement?

    What are your learnings from here?

11. Immediately after completing your MBA, you wish to buy a house for ₹1,000,000. You plan to take a loan for the entire amount for a period of 10 years from the housing finance company. The instalments are on annual basis, starting at the end of the year, and the interest rate is 10 per cent. What is the annual instalment?

    After three years, you receive ₹300,000 as the will amount on the death of your beloved aunt. You pay up this amount to the housing finance company and ask them to reduce this from the principal outstanding on the loan and rework the annual instalment for a period of only five years instead of the remaining seven years. What is the reworked annual instalment?

12. A zero-coupon ₹1,000 par value bond is currently selling for ₹540. It matures in exactly eight years. What is the discount rate on this bond? What should the price be to yield 10 per cent? What would the price be after three years? What rate of return do you obtain if you hold the bond for this period of three years?

    If after three years the discount rate reduces to 6 per cent, what will be the price of the bond? What rate of return do you get if you hold the bond for this period of three years?

13. You are 35 years old and will retire at 65. Currently, you have ₹100,000 with you and your aunt has promised to give you another ₹100,000 in her will. She is currently 70 years old. You have looked up the mortality tables applicable and, accordingly, expect her to live for another 10 years.

    You expect to live for 20 years after your retirement. In accordance with your lifestyle and expected inflation, you wish to have ₹800,000 every year post-retirement. How much should you save every year from the end of the current year till retirement in order to have the desired sum post-retirement?

    Your aunt actually expires in five years but has willed you ₹200,000 (bless her soul!). How much do you need to save for the balance period in order to have the same amount as you had originally planned every year after retirement?

14. You are an investment advisor who has been approached by a client for help on his financial strategy. He has savings of ₹250,000. He is 55 years old and expects to work for 10 years more.
    a. Once he retires in 10 years from now, he would like to withdraw ₹80,000 per annum for the next 25 years. (His actuary tells him he will live up to the age of 90 years.) How much would he need 10 years from now to be able to withdraw the said amount?
    b. How much of his income would he need to save each year for the next 10 years to be able to afford these planned withdrawals (₹80,000 per year)?
    c. Assume that in 10 years from now, the interest rates decline to 8 per cent. How much, if any, would your client have to lower his withdrawal every year assuming that he still plans to withdraw cash each year for the next twenty-five years?

15. You borrow ₹10,000 for a period of four years at 14 per cent for your car. The loan is repayable in four equal annual instalments payable at the end of each year.
    a. What is the annual payment that will completely amortize the loan over four years?
    b. Of each equal payment, what is the amount of interest and the amount of principal repayment?

16. Which of the following will decrease or increase with an increase in interest rates? Mention I or D for each.
    a. FV interest factor
    b. FV interest factor of annuity
    c. PV interest factor
    d. Value of a perpetuity

17. If you pay 1 per cent per month in interest on a loan, what is your annual effective interest rate?
18. The PVIF for a rupee on hand is ____.

19. You are 25 years old and not unexpectedly have just bagged a prestigious placement at a multinational company (MNC) from your campus. You recall your professor's advice to start saving early for your retirement needs. You envisage that you will work till the age of 65 years and that in line with increasing life expectancy, you expect to live till the age of 105 years. You wish to move to your own mansion in a luxurious villa scheme currently being planned by one of your classmates. This mansion will cost you ₹10,000,000 when you retire at 65. Your expenses will be ₹2,000,000 per annum starting at the end of the 66th year and continuing till the end of the 105th year. Assume an interest rate of 10 per cent in all your calculations.

    a. How much will you need to have saved by your retirement date to be able to afford the planned course of action?

    b. How much do you need to save every year until retirement to be able to afford the retirement plan?

    c. You suddenly remember that you already have ₹100,000 in savings accumulated over the years. How does that change the amount that you need to save every year?

CASE FOR DISCUSSION

Having completed your MBA at a relatively young age of 20 years, you land a dream job with an MNC operating in fast-moving consumer goods (FMCG) industry and are looking forward to a fulfilling career. You have been a model student, with conservative values, a legacy of your grandfather who was a freedom fighter and who inculcated a sense of discipline in your life.

You have a few days left before taking up your assignment. The celebrations are over as are the congratulatory messages from friends, relatives and well-wishers, known and unknown. You start thinking ahead about your career, your personal life and the problems you may encounter. While the compensation is highly attractive, your spending habits are no longer conservative; you do like to live your life in some style, an outcome of bad habits picked up after the demise of your grandfather a few years back. Your thoughts turn to what the great man Einstein opined about compound interest being the greatest discovery of mankind. You are also suddenly reminded of your professor who had advised your class to start investing early and benefit from the magic of compounding of money over long period of time.

You think hard about financial planning for the future and remember that your professor had, in fact, advised you to start saving from your first year. Any time you lose by postponing such savings will have a disproportionately large impact on your prospective wealth.

Assume a rate of return of 10 per cent per annum.

1. Your objective is to have ₹100 million on retirement at 70 years. (You are currently 20 years old. The first cash flow accrues at the end of the year.) How much do you need to save annually?

2. What should your savings be if the return changes to 8 per cent? 12 per cent?

3. You become lazy and greedy. You have postponed your savings to the time you turn 40. How much do you need to save annually to have ₹100 million on retirement?

4. Let us assume that you do not save in the last 25 years and save regularly in the first 25 years. But the savings in the first 25 years keep earning interest at 10 per cent for the later 25 years. How much do you need to save for those initial 25 years?

5. You also realize that inflation is a fact of life and is likely to reduce the value of the ₹100 million you will have on retirement. If you are expecting inflation to average 4 per cent over this period, what will be the value of your retirement kitty in real terms? If you want the purchasing power to remain at ₹100 million, what nominal amount should you target to have at 70 years?

6. What are your learnings from the preceding exercise?

CHAPTER 4

Capital Budgeting

Companies strive to grow by investing in projects. Growth is a key objective of any business and the only way to grow is to keep investing in projects. Identifying and selecting projects that add value to the firm is called capital budgeting. It refers to the decision and process of investing in long-term assets—buildings, plant and machinery, and intangibles such as brands and patents. As the name suggests, the company is budgeting for capital to be invested for long-term growth.

Investment in long-term projects is amongst the most critical decisions that a company takes. Capital investment is a high-value, high-impact decision which has the potential to significantly alter the fortunes of a company. When Nokia decided to invest in mobile telephones, using the Global system for mobile communication (GSM) technology, it was quite a change from paper products, footwear, tires and radio telephony that comprised the company's product portfolio at the time. The decision paved the way for its global dominance for two decades, from the mid-1990s to the 2000s. Recently, however, it was unable to correctly judge the shift in market preference to smartphones, and Nokia decided not to invest wholeheartedly in this space. The decision proved fatal and the company not only lost its leadership position but had to sell its mobile business to Microsoft Ltd in 2014.

Investment in long-term projects may fall under any of the following categories:

1. Expansion in existing capacities: a cement company increasing its capacity, from the existing 10 million to 15 million tons
2. Diversifying into new products: the Mahindra Group diversifying into real estate in the early years of the twenty-first century through Mahindra Lifespace Developers Ltd
3. Expanding to new markets/customers: an Indian bank going global and opening branches in the United Kingdom (UK), Maruti Ltd moving to the premium car segment and targeting a new set of customers
4. Acquisition: Kotak Mahindra Bank acquiring Vysya Bank for approximately ₹150 billion, Facebook's acquisition of WhatsApp for US$19 billion
5. Changes in the way business is run: installing an enterprise resource planning (ERP) system
6. Replacement of old machinery
7. Investing in research and development (R&D)
8. Others: pollution related, investing for regulatory compliance

Capital Budgeting

Capital investments are long-term in nature, with cash flows occurring over many years. Typically, there are cash outflows in the initial years when the project is established, followed by cash inflows in subsequent years after the project takes off. However, many different patterns are possible depending on the nature of projects undertaken. The distinguishing feature is that projects have a long life and lead to cash inflows and outflows over a number of years.

A company needs to evaluate which projects to invest in and which ones to forego. If it invests in the right kind of projects, it will not only keep growing but also add to the shareholders' wealth. On the other hand, investment in wrong projects will reduce value and take it fast on the path of extinction. While it may not be a day-to-day activity, capital budgeting is arguably the most critical function, significantly impacting a company's long-term performance.

Capital budgeting must be aligned to the strategy of the company in terms of products, markets, customers and technology. The Aditya Birla Group decided a few years back that commodities and metals would be a strategic area for the group. Since then it has been investing in cement and aluminum, both through greenfield investments and by acquiring existing capacities. In 2017, UltraTech Cement Ltd, a group company, acquired six integrated cement plants and five grinding units of the JP Group, with a capacity of 21.2 million tons for ₹161.89 billion, taking the group capacity to 93 million tons. In the process, it has become the largest cement company in India and the fourth-largest global cement company outside China. The JP Group which has been in a financial crunch, reduced its debt substantially, taking a major step towards restoring its financial health.

Hindalco Ltd, another Aditya Birla Group company, acquired Novelis Inc., a Mexican company, for US$6 billion in 2007. This was one of the largest acquisitions in the Indian corporate sector. Hindalco Ltd has now become a leading player in the aluminum space in India.

United Breweries was a market leader in the liquor industry. The promoter, Vijay Mallya, got taken in by the apparently lucrative prospects and prestige associated with owning an airline. Despite strong advice to the contrary, he went ahead and established the high-profile Kingfisher Airlines. The outcome was predictable, with Kingfisher Airlines becoming defunct in a few years' time. In fact, Vijay Mallya had to sell even his flagship company United Breweries Holdings Limited to Diageo PLC. Currently, he is facing court cases for non-payment of dues to creditors, bankers, employees and the government.

The Process

Capital budgeting encompasses the following process.

Generation of Investment Proposals

Most large companies have a formal process of identifying and generating project opportunities, based on their strategy for the future. The Tata Group planned to become a global player and its corporate planning department identified Tetley Tea PLC in the UK as a potential target. Tetley was acquired by Tata Tea Ltd in the year 2000 and the group took its first tentative step towards establishing a global imprint. Reliance Industries Ltd recently decided to enter the telecom business and made its well-publicized entry through Reliance Jio. DishTV wanted to increase its customer base, it acquired Videocon d2h and has now become the largest player in the business, surpassing Tata Sky Ltd. Various such proposals for investment may be generated, and the company selects those which add value and conform to its strategic vision.

In 2008, Infosys Ltd wanted to acquire Axon PLC and made a bid at a price of GB£407 million. HCL Ltd bid higher at GB£441 million. While Infosys Ltd felt Axon Ltd will be aligned with its strategy, the acquisition price was much higher than it was willing to pay. Hence, the company decided not to increase its bid price for Axon Ltd which was then acquired by HCL Ltd.

Most organizations, at least the large ones, have a formal corporate planning department, with the responsibility of scouting for opportunities in line with the company's strategy. Alternatively, proposals may come to the company without a formal process in place. In either case, many proposals are generated initiating the process of capital budgeting.

Generation of Cash Flows

Once a project proposal is initiated, it must be transformed in a form that enables clear evaluation. This involves estimating future cash flows—inflows and outflows—over the lifespan of the project. Cash flow estimation is a critical part of the overall capital budgeting process, requiring sound judgement that comes only with experience.

A project entails investment in plant and machinery, technology, patents and brands, subsequently generating sales revenues and profits, over the life of the project. These must be converted into cash flows—yearly outflows and inflows. Analysis of projects can be undertaken only with cash flows. Later in the chapter, we will learn how to generate cash flows for a project.

Evaluation

The estimated cash flows must be evaluated to decide whether the project should be undertaken or not. The evaluation is based on standard techniques available—net present value (NPV), internal rate of return (IRR), accounting rate of return (ARR) and payback period amongst others—which are standard tools for any management expert.

Broadly speaking, methods to evaluate projects can be divided into two. One set takes into consideration the time value of money. There are other methods which lack rigour as they do not take into account the time value of money. At the same time, they are simple to understand and calculate and are widely used. Hence, it is essential for us to understand them despite their limitations.

Monitoring and Re-evaluation

The future is uncertain and the project may not deliver as envisaged. Or the environment may turn out to be different from what had been anticipated. Adjustments may need to be made in the project. There is a need to constantly monitor the project and alter its course, if required.

Managers are paid to take decisions. They cannot invest and then simply sit back and watch events unfold. They must constantly evaluate the environment and internal performance to assess the impact of the earlier decision to invest. Such evaluation may lead them to change or even abandon the project, if warranted.

Net Present Value

A project typically involves an initial capital outflow (investment in the project) and a series of positive cash flows later. The cash flows occur at different periods and cannot be compared across time. All cash flows must be converted to their PVs so that a meaningful comparison can be made. The NPV method calculates the PV of future cash flows and subtracts the initial investment from it. The resultant figure is the net PV, it represents the value addition of the project, and the amount by which the value of the company will change if the investment in the project is undertaken. The cash flows must, of course, be discounted at the risk-adjusted cost of capital (COC).

If the net PV is positive, the project is accepted. If the net PV is negative, the project is rejected.

$$NPV = \{C_1/(1 + r)^1 + C_2/(1 + r)^2 + \ldots + C_n/(1 + r)^n\} - C_0.$$

Where C_1, C_2 … C_n are the cash flows in the respective years, C_0 is the cash outflow now (the investment required for the project) and r is the applicable interest rate.

Sometimes, the cash flows generated each year by a project are equal which means that C_1, C_2 … C_n are all equal. Cash flows can then be valued as an annuity, making calculations simpler. Let us understand the calculation of NPV in Illustrations 4.1 and 4.2.

Illustration 4.1

Q. A project's initial cash outlay is ₹100,000. It is expected to generate cash inflows of

₹20,000 in year 1
₹30,000 in year 2
₹40,000 in year 3
₹50,000 in year 4

The interest rate is 10 per cent. Find the NPV of the project. Should the project be accepted?

A. The NPV of the project can be calculated as in Table 4.1.

TABLE 4.1   Project NPV I (in ₹)

Years	C_0	C_1	C_2	C_3	C_4
Initial cost	−100,000				
Cash inflows		20,000	30,000	40,000	50,000
Net cash flows	−100,000	20,000	30,000	40,000	50,000
Present value of cash flow (@ 10%)	−100,000	18,182	24,793	30,053	34,151
NPV = −100,000 + 18,182 + 24,793 + 30,053 + 34,151 = 7,179.					

Source: Author.

The NPV is positive since the PV of the cash inflows is higher than the initial investment outflow. The project is likely to add value and must be accepted. In fact, it will add exactly ₹7,179 value which is its NPV. The market capitalization and shareholders' wealth are expected to increase by a similar amount.

The decision changes if the COC of the company is 15 per cent.

Net annual cash flows	*Year$_1$*	*Year$_2$*	*Year$_3$*	*Year$_4$*
	20,000	30,000	40,000	50,000
Present value (15%)	17,391	22,684	26,301	28,588

The sum of the PVs of the future cash flows is ₹94,964. Since this is less than the initial investment, the project has a negative NPV and is likely to reduce the value of the company. The project should be rejected. Project investments are highly sensitive to changes in COC, which can significantly impact the viability of projects.

Illustration 4.2

Q. AB Power Limited is planning to invest in a power project that it believes will take 2 years to establish and will last for 10 years thereafter. The relevant cash flows are as follows.

The project requires an investment of ₹200 billion in the first year and ₹160 billion in the second year. The cash flows in the subsequent 10 years are

−3,000 2,000 8,000 8,000 10,000 12,000 12,000 16,000 16,000 6,000.

Given a discount rate of 10 per cent, should it go ahead with the project? What should be its decision if the interest rate is 14 per cent?

A. Cash flows on the project can be represented as follows:

	C_0	C_1	C_2	C_3	C_4	C_5	C_6	C_7	C_8	C_9	C_{10}	C_{11}
CF (in ₹)	(20,000)	(16,000)	(3,000)	2,000	8,000	8,000	10,000	12,000	12,000	16,000	16,000	6,000

The NPV of the cash flows have been calculated in Table 4.2.

TABLE 4.2   Project NPV II

Year	DF (10%)	Cash flows (₹)	PV (₹)	DF (14%)	PV (₹)
0	1	(20,000)	(20,000)	1	(20,000)
1	0.9091	(16,000)	(14,545)	0.8772	(14,035)
2	0.8264	(3,000)	(2,479)	0.7695	(2,308)
3	0.7513	2,000	1,503	0.6750	1,350
4	0.6830	8,000	5,464	0.5921	4,737
5	0.6209	8,000	4,967	0.5194	4,155
6	0.5645	10,000	5,645	0.4556	4,556
7	0.5132	12,000	6,158	0.3996	4,795

Contd

Contd

contd

Table 4.2 contd

Year	DF (10%)	Cash flows (₹)	PV (₹)	DF (14%)	PV (₹)
8	0.4665	12,000	5,598	0.3506	4,207
9	0.4241	16,000	6,786	0.3075	4,920
10	0.3855	16,000	6,168	0.2697	4,315
11	0.3505	6,000	2,103	0.2366	1,420
NPV			7,368		(1,882)

Source: Author.

Note: DF = discount factor.

At 10 per cent COC, the NPV is positive and equals ₹7,368. We are aware that COC has a significant impact on PVs. A higher discount rate of 14 per cent yields a negative NPV of ₹1,882, making the project unviable.

Internal Rate of Return

Internal rate of return is the rate that makes the NPV of project cash flows equal to zero. It is the rate which equates the PV of future cash inflows to the investment made in the project now.

The rate is internal to the cash flows of the project. It depends only on the project cash flows and none outside it. It is a single rate that sort of summarizes a project.

Let us assume a project involves investment of ₹100 today and provides ₹108 after a year. What is the NPV of the project?

$$NPV = -100 + 108/(1 + r).$$

Where r is the discount rate based on the COC. Currently, we do not know what the COC is. What we do know is that at NPV of zero, we are indifferent to the project and taking up the project neither adds value nor reduces it. Is it possible to calculate the rate at which NPV becomes zero?

$$0 = -100 + 108/(1 + r)$$

$$r = 8\%.$$

Eight per cent can be defined as the IRR of the project.

Most projects have a life of more than one year, with several cash flows. Calculation of IRR, thus becomes a little more tedious and is possible through trial and error—an iterative process. Different rates must be tried until we find one that makes the NPV of project cash flows equal to zero as shown in Illustration 4.3.

$$NPV = \{C_1/(1 + r)^1 + C_2/(1 + r)^2 + \ldots + C_n/(1 + r)^n\} - C_0 = 0.$$

The manual process of calculating IRR is relevant for learning purposes. In practice, calculations are undertaken on an Excel spreadsheet wherein Excel will itself take care of the iterations.

Once the IRR has been calculated, it is compared with the company's COC. An IRR greater than the COC adds value and the company undertakes an investment in the project. An IRR lower than the COC reduces value and the company should decline the investment.

Illustration 4.3

Q. Consider a project with an initial cash outflow C_0 equal to ₹100,000 and cash inflows in year 1 of ₹60,000 and year 2 of ₹58,241. Find the IRR of the project.

A. The findings are as in Table 4.3.

TABLE 4.3 Project IRR (in ₹)

Year	Cash flow	10%	12%	14%
0	–100,000	–100,000	–100,000	–100,000
1	60,000	54,545	53,571	52,632
2	58,241	48,133	46,429	44,815
NPV		2,678	0	–2,553

Source: Author.

The IRR of the Illustration 4.3 project being 12 per cent, the investment will be undertaken if the COC of the company is less than 12 per cent. On the other hand, if the COC is more than 12 per cent, the project would be ignored.

In this respect, the COC can be considered as a hurdle rate for a project. The IRR must be higher than the COC for a project to become viable. If the IRR is lower than the COC, the project generates negative NPV and is unviable.

If the COC is less than the IRR, the NPV is positive. As the COC goes up, the NPV reduces and becomes zero when the COC equals IRR. As the COC increases even more, NPV becomes negative and the project is no longer viable. The NPV and the project viability are highly sensitive to the COC (Figure 4.1).

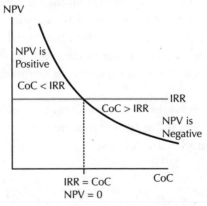

FIGURE 4.1 Relationship between COC and IRR

Source: Author.

Net present value and IRR methods usually lead to the same outcome, and the two methods can be said to be complementary.

If IRR > COC, NPV is positive.
If IRR < COC, NPV is negative.

Both NPV and IRR methods of project evaluation are widely used by companies. In the 1998 annual report of Coca-Cola Inc., the company had clearly stated,

> our criterion of acceptance is simple. New investments are expected to provide cash returns that exceed our long term, after tax, weighted average COC, currently estimated at approximately 11 percent.

NPV versus IRR

Both NPV and IRR are used extensively in capital-budgeting decisions. Given the cash flows, both methods provide the same evaluation of a project. However, that need not always hold. An understanding of the differences between the two methods is instructive and clarifies certain concepts that are useful.

Interim Cash Flow Investment Assumption

There is a difference in the assumption made by the two methods regarding reinvestment of interim cash flows. While NPV assumes reinvestment at the COC, the IRR method assumes reinvestment of the interim cash flows at the IRR of the specific project. Let us spend some time to understand the statement which lies at the heart of appreciating capital-budgeting decisions.

A typical project has a life of a specific number of years. As a manager, we are interested in the returns or value creation over a period that covers the entire life of the project. It would be simple if the project generates a single cash flow at the end of its life (akin to a zero-coupon bond) and the initial and the ending cash flows are the only ones we need to deal with.

Projects, however, generate cash flows throughout their lifespan. The cash flows generated during the interim period need to be reinvested for the remaining period of the project. The rates of return on the reinvested cash flows determine the overall cash flow available at the end of the period. These rates will be known only in the future at the time of the reinvestment. Uncertainty about the rates leads to uncertainty about the returns that will be eventually realized on the project.

To take an illustration, let us assume that a project requires an investment of ₹1,000 and has a life of five years. From the first to the fifth year, it yields a constant cash flow of ₹300 every year. The cash flows can be depicted as follows:

C_0	C_1	C_2	C_3	C_4	C_5
(1000)	300	300	300	300	300

Assuming the COC is 10 per cent, the NPV can be calculated as follows:

$$PVIFA_{10\%,5} = 3.791.$$

Value of 5 years cash flow = 3.791 * 300 = 1,137.30.

NPV = 1,137.30 – 1,000 = 137.30.

The IRR of the project can be calculated as 15.24 per cent, implying that the invested amount should yield a return of 15.24 per cent over the period of five years. Thus, ₹1,000 invested at the commencement of the project should be equal to

$$1,000 * (1 + 15.24\%)^5 = ₹2,032.$$

The problem arises since the project generates cash flows from the first to the fourth year as well. Interim cash flows are reinvested for the balance period of time and the amount available at the end of the five years will be determined by the return at which the interim cash flows can be reinvested. The rate of return is uncertain and unknown at the present juncture, leading to uncertainty in the IRR. For example, in our illustration, the IRR has been calculated at 15.24 per cent. Therefore, the reinvestment rate is also taken as 15.24 per cent, assume that the interest rate declines and is lower at 12 per cent. The invested interim cash flows would, therefore, earn 12 per cent annually.

- The cash flow of ₹300 received in the 1st year is invested for a balance period of four years to yield ₹472.06. $(300 * (1 + 12\%)^4)) = 472.06.$
- The cash flows of ₹300 similarly received in the 2nd, 3rd and 4th periods are invested for three, two and one years at 12 per cent to yield

$$300 * (1 + 12\%)^3 = 421.48,$$
$$300 * (1 + 12\%)^2 = 376.32 \text{ and}$$
$$300 * (1 + 12\%)^1 = 336.00.$$

Cash flow at the end of 5 years = 1905.86 (inclusive of ₹300 at the end of the 5th year).

$$(FV/PV)^{1/n} - 1 = (1,905.86/1,000)^{1/5} - 1$$
$$1.906^{1/5} - 1 = 13.77\%.$$

Thus, the actual or what is technically termed the realized return is substantially lower than the IRR calculated. Longer the life of the project, higher is the impact of changes in the interest rate on the actual return from the project.

It is only when the interest on reinvestment of interim cash flows is 15.24 per cent, the project yields ₹2,032 at the end of the project, providing an IRR of 15.24 per cent. It is unrealistic to expect the company to obtain a return of 15.24 per cent when its COC is only 10 per cent. A lower return on the interim cash flows reduces the return on the project.

The return on the project depends on the rate at which we assume the interim cash flows will be invested. This is where there is a substantive difference between the NPV and the IRR methods of project evaluation.

The NPV method to evaluate projects implicitly assumes that opportunity exists to reinvest the interim cash flows generated at the COC of the company, while the IRR method assumes that interim cash flows can be reinvested at a rate equivalent to the IRR of the project under consideration.

The COC is derived on the basis of the risk profile of the company, and it would be reasonable to assume that the company has opportunities to invest at its COC. On the other hand, the IRR is specific to the given project. There is an underlying assumption that the company will be able to come up with projects in future whose returns are equal to the IRR of the specific project under consideration, an assumption which is hard to justify.

Each project has its own distinct rate of return. Hence, the IRR of each of these projects is calculated on assumptions of different reinvestment rates. Assume that a company is considering three projects with IRRs of 10 per cent, 15 per cent and 20 per cent. The company will have to make different reinvestment rate assumptions for each of these projects, namely 10 per cent, 15 per cent and 20 per cent, which makes no sense.

The NPV method has only one reinvestment rate assumption for all projects. This rate, being the COC, is based on the risk profile of the company. It would be logical to assume that the company would have opportunities to invest its cash flows at its COC.

Hence, in general, NPV is a superior method since it is based on conceptually sound assumption with respect to reinvestment of interim cash flows.

Modified IRR

The problem pertaining to the reinvestment of interim cash flows can be overcome by assuming reinvestment rate equalling the COC and then calculating what is termed as the modified internal rate of return (MIRR). Let us calculate the MIRR for the following project:

C_0	C_1	C_2	C_3	C_4	C_5	IRR	NPV
(100,000)	50,000	40,000	30,000	20,000	10,000	20%	20,921

50,000 at C_1 compounded at 10 per cent will yield ₹73,205.
40,000 at C_2 compounded at 10 per cent will yield ₹53,240.
30,000 at C_3 compounded at 10 per cent will yield ₹36,300.
20,000 at C_4 compounded at 10 per cent will yield ₹22,000.

Together with the cash flow of ₹10,000 at C_5, we will have ₹194,745 which provides a yield or MIRR of 14.26 per cent.

Project Value Addition

The NPV method yields a specific value which the project adds to the company. A company's value comprises the sum of the value of its existing business plus the NPV of all the projects it plans to invest in as shown in Illustration 4.4.

Illustration 4.4

Assume that a company is valued today at ₹10,000. It has the following project options:

Projects	NPV
A	2,000
B	4,000
C	(1,000)

If the company takes up all these projects, its value becomes 10,000 + 2,000 + 4,000 – 1,000 = 15,000. The company would, of course, reject project C which has a negative NPV. If the company invests only in projects A and B, its value will increase to ₹16,000.

The IRR method does not yield a specific value. It only tells us whether investment in a project will add value or not.

Margin of Safety

The evaluation of the viability of projects is based on the cash flows that a project is expected to generate. These cash flows are estimates and may in future turn out to be very different.

It would be useful to know the margin of safety in a project. How much can the cash flows decline without making the project unviable or without generating negative NPV? This information can only be provided by the IRR method as shown in Illustration 4.5.

Illustration 4.5

Let us consider the following two projects:

	C_0	C_1	NPV (10%)	IRR
Project S	10,000	16,500	5,000	65%
Project L	100,000	115,500	5,000	15.5%

For Project L, a drop of a little over 5 per cent in the final cash flows can make the project unviable. On the other hand, Project S will remain viable even with a 33 per cent drop in cash flows. The margin of safety is much higher in Project S which carries less risk.

Managers are likely to have much greater conviction in projects that have a high margin of safety. Knowledge of the margin of safety is extremely useful in analysing the risk embedded in projects. The NPV, which is equal for the two projects, fails to provide the estimate of risk.

Ease of Comprehension

IRR is easier to understand and visualize as compared to NPV. In a sense, IRR is the return on a project which people find easy to comprehend. This return, when compared to the cost (of capital), provides a good decision criterion. The concept of NPV is a little nebulous and difficult to comprehend.

A word of caution is warranted. Capital-budgeting decisions are large-value decisions and have a significant impact on the company over long periods. It would be tragic if such decisions are taken in ways that are easy rather than sound. Decisions involving tens of thousands of billions must be based on clarity of concepts and logical arguments and not on what may be easy to comprehend.

Reduction in Overall Return

Life is never simple. Even successful companies with viable projects face situations that may be difficult to resolve. A company experiencing high returns on investment may, at times, face a peculiar problem. It has an opportunity to invest in a project with a positive NPV, but the return is lower than the company's current return on invested capital. Should the company accept such projects, especially considering the fact that this will reduce the company's overall return?

A retail chain has two outlets, each of which has ₹2,000 invested. The return on investment from each of these stores is 20 per cent. The COC being 12 per cent, the company and its stores are performing exceedingly well.

There is a proposal before the company for a new outlet with the same investment of ₹2,000, but the return is only 14 per cent. If the company takes up investment in this store, the overall return will decline from 20 per cent to 18 per cent (weighted average return of the three stores).

Decision-making in this regard is clear. The objective of the company is the maximization of value. Value will be maximized only if the company takes up all projects with positive NPV. We can compare the values with and without the third store.

Without the third outlet,

$$\text{investment} = 4{,}000 \text{ and}$$

$$\text{value added} = 4{,}000 * (20\% - 12\%) = 320.$$

With the third outlet,

$$\text{investment} = 6{,}000 \text{ and}$$

$$\text{value added} = 6{,}000 * (18\% - 12\%) = 360.$$

The value added with the third outlet is higher because the third outlet will add value equal to 2,000 * (14% – 12%) = 40.

The company must look at value creation. All other objectives are subsumed in this overall objective. It is a fundamental principle of value creation that the more a company invests at returns higher than the COC, the more value it creates.

The differences between the two methods are instructive and critical for a management student to understand. The most critical difference lies in what is called the reinvestment assumption. The NPV method is conceptually superior to the IRR method in this respect.

To recap, we have compared NPV and IRR for mutually exclusive projects on the following aspects:

1. Assumption regarding reinvestment of interim cash flows
2. Value added by the project
3. Margin of safety in future cash flows
4. Easier to understand and apply; widely used and practiced
5. Investment in a project with lower IRR compared to the current return on investment but a positive NPV

Profitability Index (PI)

Profitability index is the ratio of the PV of the expected cash flows after the initial investment, divided by the initial investment. In a sense, PI yields NPV, generated per unit of investment by a project. If this ratio is greater than one, the NPV is positive. If the ratio is less than one, the NPV is negative.

The index is useful when the budget for capital investment is limited and needs to be allocated amongst competing positive NPV projects. A company may have identified various projects for investment, all of which are value accretive. With a limited budget, the funds must be allocated to those projects that will generate maximum value.

What is important in such situations is to find out which projects generate the maximum NPV per unit of investment in the project—in a sense, the highest bang for the buck. The company must select projects with the highest PI.

TABLE 4.4   Project PI

Project	Investment (₹)	NPV (₹)	PI
A	10,000	2,000	1.20
B	10,000	4,000	1.40
C	20,000	12,000	1.60
D	8,000	6,000	1.75
E	2,000	2,000	2.00

Source: Author.

Since the PI for all projects (in Table 4.4) is greater than one, the NPV is positive and all of them must be taken up to maximize the value of the company. In order to take up all five projects, the company requires an investment of ₹50,000 which will add ₹26,000 to the value of the company.

If there is a limitation on the amount the company can invest, the PI can prove to be a useful guide. Project E has the highest PI, thus yielding the highest NPV per unit of investment (Table 4.4). It must rank highest in the selection of the projects. The PI of the other projects will guide the selection, depending on the capital budget available.

Different Techniques of Capital Budgeting

We have discussed NPV and IRR as the two methods of project evaluation and concluded that NPV is superior to IRR. In case of a conflict, NPV should be preferred. Later in Appendix to this chapter, we will discuss two other methods, namely the payback period and the accounting rate of return. Both these methods are conceptually flawed, since they only consider the absolute amount of the cash flows without taking into account the timing of the cash flows. Despite this, we spend considerable time in discussing these methods and even compare them with the NPV method.

The reason is quite simple. It is important to understand a theory in its entirety, its implications and pitfalls and the manner of its application in real life. Blindly taking numbers and filling up an Excel spreadsheet does not help the management take the best possible decisions. Project evaluation is based on projected cash flows—that are mere estimates. While the management is expected to take utmost care to ensure the projections are as credible as possible, it is aware of the fact that the estimates can go wrong and, at times, by a significant margin. Novelis Inc. was acquired by Hindalco Ltd at the height of the boom years in 2007. The financial crisis and the subsequent recession hit the company hard, and it took almost a decade to recover and add value. Similarly, TML started the Nano car project with unprecedented fanfare. The company received global accolades for what was called 'the people's car'. A few years later, the project has been completely shelved and the company no longer manufactures the Nano car.

An assessment of risks inherent in a project can, therefore, be extremely useful. Internal rate of return provides an idea of the margin of safety and, therefore, of the risk inherent in the project which the NPV methodology cannot do. Similarly, PI reveals the value addition per unit of investment which is not only a useful parameter to know but also indicates the level of risk.

Let us assume that an evaluation of a project yields an NPV of ₹0.50 billion. How risky is the project? It is difficult to figure out with only the NPV figure. However, an IRR of 20 per cent and the COC equalling 12 per cent tell us there is sufficient leeway for cash flows to decline without making the project unviable. Similar will be the case with a PI of 1.8. Project evaluation with more varied criteria is likely to give the management a better grip on risk assessment and hopefully improve decision-making in an area that is fraught with significant level of risk.

Advances in Computational Capabilities

Many aspects which we have discussed, including the comparisons made amongst the different methods of capital budgeting, have over the years become redundant due to the development of computing techniques and capabilities. In the pre-computer days, calculating IRR and NPV used to be a tedious task. Estimation of IRR was in fact particularly tough, being an iterative process. Sitting down with long-term cash flows, a calculator in hand, punching figures therein, may present a rather romantic picture now but was not a very pretty sight in those times. Besides the time and effort involved, there were significantly high possibilities of committing an error. Imagine taking up a project only due to a calculation error and later discovering that the project actually destroys value. Simplicity in figures and calculation commanded a premium.

Of course, with Excel spreadsheet and other advanced software becoming ubiquitous, figure work no longer seems daunting. We can easily manage calculations of both the NPV and the IRR for each and every project and need not choose between one or the other. Nor do we need to calculate PI of different projects to budget for limited capital. We can easily look at different combinations of projects to see which of those are within the budget and which amongst those feasible combinations contributes the highest value.

Habits die hard and while logic and intuition tell me to exclude such aspects from discussions in the book in line with changing requirements, I have refrained from leaving them out for the sake of completeness and followed the practice of other comparative books in this regard. Hopefully, future editions of the book will not burden the students unnecessarily and provide more meat per unit of reading. Risk management extends quite obviously to book writing, being for me a long-term project (though, as yet, without positive cash flows).

Project Cash Flow

Accounting and finance are two distinct disciplines. Accounting focuses on earnings and accounting numbers, whereas finance deals mainly with cash flows and valuation. There are primarily three factors which account for the difference between accounting figures and cash flows:

1. Revenue is recognized at the time sale is made while cash comes in later, in accordance with the terms of payment.
2. A profit and loss (P&L) statement records revenues and matching expenses during the year. Actual payment for those expenses need not take place during that period, leading to cash flows being different.

3. A P&L statement does not consider capital expenditure, it only takes into account the depreciation on capital goods for the operating period.

The difference between cash flow and accounting figures has been explained later in Chapter 6, 'Valuation'. Let us illustrate now with an example.

ABC Ltd buys machinery for ₹100,000 to improve the productivity of its workforce. Being a capital expenditure, the cash outflow on account of the purchase of the machine is not reflected in the P&L statement. The expenditure is included in the balance sheet as a capital asset and allocated over its economic life as an expense in the form of annual depreciation.

The machinery is expected to last for 10 years. On a straight-line basis, the depreciation is ₹10,000. The accounting profit and corporate tax will be calculated on the basis of a depreciation expense of ₹10,000 for each of the 10 operating years.

The relevant cash flows relating to the machinery are very different. We have a cash outflow of ₹100,000 in the current period and nothing thereafter. Finance will recognize the cash outflow of ₹100,000 in the initial year (at C_0) while there will be no cash flow thereafter. Capital budgeting is undertaken based on cash flows specific to a project.

Of course, the impact of depreciation on taxes and, therefore, on post-tax operating cash flows in the coming years will be taken into consideration. To the extent that there is a saving on tax liability, cash flows will be positive over the next 10 years. Thus, with a corporate tax rate of 30 per cent, ABC Ltd will save ₹3,000 (10,000 * 30%) in taxes which is an additional cash inflow for the project in each of the next 10 operating years.

A similar treatment is provided for other non-cash expenses such as preliminary expenses and amortization.

The P&L statement does not consider capital expenditure; it only takes into account the depreciation on capital goods for the period. Depreciation is a non-cash expense, cash having already been paid and accounted for when the capital goods were purchased.

Estimation of Project Cash Flows

Capital budgeting is primarily concerned with evaluating project cash flows to decide which projects to invest in and which ones to forego. Once the project cash flows have been estimated, it is not difficult to evaluate them. Various methods, with their relative merits and demerits, have been discussed previously. This is the easy part and today can be done on MS Excel and many other software easily available.

What is more challenging and critical is the estimation of the project cash flows which requires conceptual clarity as well as experience. Management students would be well advised to spend a substantial time learning how to map the cash flows that are generated by the project.

There are three ways in which project cash flows can be estimated. First, past experience of similar projects helps navigate the nuances involved. A cement manufacturer planning to increase his capacity from 10 million to 15 million tons would have precise estimates of the cost of production, sales price and revenue, and the investment required. The estimated project cash flows are likely to be highly credible.

An investment in a new product or customer segment introduces uncertainty. Test marketing may be undertaken to resolve the uncertainty regarding various parameters pertaining to the project, acceptability of the product and the business potential. Test marketing may give us a fair idea of the expected cash flows.

Test marketing is not always feasible, and the third option, scenario analysis, may have to be employed. Scenario analysis refers to the analysis of various scenarios that could unfold in the future and are likely to impact the market for the product and thus the project. Given different scenarios, there will be changes in outcomes of various parameters. Scenario analysis works out the cash flows for the possible outcomes.

For instance, if we assume a booming global economy, the Indian growth rate is likely to be high but the higher global demand will push up the price of oil. On the other hand, the recessionary global environment will lead to reduced growth rates but also keep oil prices at low levels. Instead of altering each parameter and considering the outcome, scenario analysis builds up different scenarios and then looks at how the scenario changes all the parameters that impact the cash flows for a certain project.

A company may plan to invest in a project to manufacture 100,000 litres of paint. It must take into account how various parameters impacting the paint market are likely to pan out. Two of the most critical factors are the growth rate of national income and oil price (oil constitutes a significant component of the paint manufacturing cost). The analysis commences with building scenarios around these parameters.

Principles of Cash Flow Determination

The key question that arises is which cash flows are relevant and must be estimated and included in projects. The answer is quite simply the 'post tax incremental cash flows'. Let us understand this by discussing principles that govern the estimation of project cash flows.

The Cash Flow Principle

While every company prepares accounting statements, what is ultimately relevant is the inflow and outflow of cash. Earnings do not represent real money. A company cannot use accounting earnings to pay the suppliers, employees' salaries or meet other expenses. For that it needs cash. As they say, earnings are an opinion; cash is a fact.

Shareholders pay for their share of ownership by way of cash when they invest in the company. Returns to shareholders are determined on the basis of cash flow generation. Always discount cash flows and not earnings while undertaking a capital-budgeting exercise or corporate valuation.

The cash flows that need to be taken into account for a capital-budgeting exercise are the free cash flows.

Free cash flows are cash flows that remain after the company has used up all the funds required for its business—both for current business operations and for implementing its future plans. Typically, the operations of the company during the year generate profits (or losses). Besides, there are non-cash expenses such as depreciation and amortization. The sum of these two is the cash flow from operations.

In addition, there are investment flows, specifically, capital investments and changes in working capital. These are usually negative, implying that a company would normally invest in projects and that higher working capital is required as sales increase; both lead to cash outflows. Broadly speaking, with minor adjustments, the sum total of the operating cash flows and investment cash flows are termed free cash flows. We will explain free cash flows in more detail later in Chapter 6. It would suffice to point out here that projects comprise free cash flows and not accounting figures.

Capital-budgeting projects are long-term in nature and cash flows occur throughout the life of the project. The value of the project is determined by cash flows over its entire lifespan. Usually, there is a large investment (cash outflow) at the commencement of the project, followed by inflows over the long term. Value creation depends on the company's ability to identify projects with superior long-term cash flows.

Cash flows for a project over its lifespan can be divided into the following:

1. Initial cash flows
2. Operating cash flows
3. Terminal cash flows

Initial cash flows are incurred at the commencement of the project. Typically, this includes investment in buildings, plant and machinery, acquisition of technology and preoperative expenses. Initial cash outflows comprise the total cost of the project.

Operating cash flows consist of profits and non-cash expenses such as depreciation and amortization. Profits accrue from sales revenue after netting of expenses. Initially, operating cash flows may be low or even negative. Slowly, the operating cash flows build up to a high level after the project stabilizes.

Terminal cash flows accrue/are incurred towards the end of the project. Inflows could accrue by way of disposal of assets or through recovery of some of the working capital invested in the project. Alternatively, the company may incur expenditure to wind down a project.

Most of the work relating to capital budgeting involves taking available accounting figures and converting them into cash inflows and outflows, on the basis of the principles enunciated ahead.

Depreciation

An understanding of depreciation, both conceptual as well as its practical implications, is a must for generating appropriate cash flows.

We will revisit the example discussed earlier of the purchase of a machine for ₹100,000 with a life of 10 years. The machine will be in use for 10 years; hence, the entire purchase price of the machine cannot be considered as an expense now. In accordance with the principle of the allocation of cost, the cost of the machine, worth ₹100,000, must be expensed over the 10 operating years. To keep it simple, we can allocate it equally over the 10 years based on what is technically termed straight-line depreciation to arrive at taxable profits.

From a cash flow point of view, the payment for the machinery has been made at the time of the purchase and must be shown as cash outflow of ₹100,000 at C_0. Nothing more will be paid in the subsequent 10 years. In this sense, depreciation is a non-cash expense, meaning, thereby, it is an expense to recognized in the books of accounts and for the purpose of calculating taxable profits. But for the company, there is no cash flow on this account. Thereafter, the depreciation amount must be added back to derive the cash flow from operations.

Thus, the depreciation amount is deducted from sales revenue to calculate taxable profits and then added back to net profit. The deduction of depreciation from sales revenue helps to reduce the tax liability. Showing depreciation as an expense and then adding it back helps calculate real cash flows.

Let us understand this with Table 4.5. The following is a hypothetical P&L statement.

TABLE 4.5 Impact of depreciation on cash flows (in ₹)

	With depreciation	*Without depreciation*
Sales revenues	100,000	100,000
Expenses	75,000	75,000
Profit before depreciation	25,000	25,000
Depreciation	10,000	0
Profit before taxes	15,000	25,000
Taxes (@40%)	6000	10,000
Net profit (PAT)	9,000	15,000

Source: Author.

Notes: Cash flows = profit after taxes + depreciation.
= 9,000 + 10,000 = 19,000.
Without depreciation = 15,000.

Thus, taxes have reduced by ₹4,000 which equals the tax savings due to depreciation (depreciation * tax rate).

Amount of tax reduction = 10,000 * 40% = 4,000.

Depreciation thus increases operating cash flow every year. It must however be remembered that the original cost of the machinery has already been taken into account at the time of the purchase, by showing negative cash flow of ₹100,000.

Incremental Principle

1. Incremental cash flows:

   Cash flows for the project must be calculated on an incremental basis. We should take into consideration the cash flows that can be attributed only to the specific project being considered, and not total cash flows. Calculate the cash flows with and without the project; incremental cash flows will be the difference between the two.

   To take an example, if an old machine is replaced with a new advanced one, only the difference between the new and the previous sales revenue must be taken into account, and not the total revenue. Even without the installation of the new machine, the previous sales revenue was accruing to the company. Also, the cost of purchasing the new machine must be adjusted by the sale proceeds of the old machine.

   Similarly, if a 10-million-ton cement company is adding a 5-million-ton capacity, only the incremental cash flows attributable to the additional 5-million-ton capacity should be taken into account. For instance, the salary of the managing director (MD) should not form a part of the project cash flows.

2. Sunk costs:

   Sunk costs are costs which have already been incurred and cannot be recovered whether the project is undertaken or not. If a student applies to a college for admission, the initial application fee is generally not refundable and is a sunk cost.

   If a company undertakes market research, the cost of the market research is subsequently not recoverable whether the company invests in the project or not. Hence, this is not an incremental but a sunk cost and should be excluded from project cash flows.

   An interesting point is that, prior to the decision to conduct the survey, the survey cost was incremental and needed to be taken into account for estimating cash flows. Having spent the money, the survey cost is not recoverable and, therefore, is not material for the project now. Therefore, whether a cost is a sunk cost or incremental depends on the stage of the project formulation and cash flow estimation.

3. Opportunity cost:

   Opportunity cost is a measure of cost expressed in terms of the alternative given up. As far as capital budgeting is concerned, an opportunity cost refers to the cost of an asset for which the company does not have to bear an expense. Usually, this is because the company already owns the asset. The asset could have been used for an alternative purpose or sold for a consideration if it was not used for the specific project.

   If a company owns a piece of land where a warehouse will be constructed, the opportunity cost for the land must be taken into consideration. The opportunity cost may be the value in the alternative deployment for which the land can be used or the price at which the land can be sold.

4. Side effects:

   Side effect refers to the impact of the project on cash flows of the company outside the project. The impact may be positive or negative.

If a fast-moving consumer goods (FMCG) company introduces a new variant of cream, the entire sales of the new variant may not be incremental. It is quite likely that some of the customers move from using an existing cream to the newly introduced one. This aspect where an existing product loses some business due to a new project is termed cannibalization. Opening a new bank branch may cannibalize customers from an already existing nearby branch. Similarly, online revenues could cannibalize brick and mortar sales. The impact of cannibalization can be considerable and needs to be taken into consideration.

A tire-manufacturing company is planning to form a racing team. The project is expected to lose money. However, the racing team will be an excellent public relations exercise for the company and its brands with positive spin-offs for the sale of its tires. The business plan for the racing-team project must incorporate the incremental cash flows on account of the additional tire sales.

5. Allocated costs:

An expenditure undertaken by a company may benefit more than one project. In accounting terms, such expenses are allocated amongst all the projects it benefits. For the purpose of capital budgeting, however, such costs should be allocated to a project only if it is incremental to the project. If the cost would have been incurred irrespective of the specific project being undertaken or not, then the cost is not incremental for that project.

A company engaged in retail sales currently has 10 outlets. If another outlet is added, normal advertising costs for brand building for the company or the legal and accounting expenses are not incremental for the new outlet.

Interest Exclusion Principle

There are two facets to a project—the investment and the financing side. The cash flows associated with the two should be kept separate. Investment cash flows are a part of the project, financing cash flows are not. The latter represent the way a project is financed and the payments made to the fund providers.

Interest is a financing element which is paid to the debt providers for the borrowing. It should not be included in the project cash flows. Financing cash flows form a part of the COC which is used to discount the cash flows of the project. Thus, interest payment is accounted for in the relevant COC.

Similarly, saving in tax may accrue on account of coupon interest being an expense that reduces taxable profits. Such savings are again not taken cognizance of in the cash flow estimation but are instead captured in the COC. As we will study later, when we estimate a company's COC, the cost of debt is reduced due to the tax deductibility of interest expenses, in what is called the post-tax cost of debt.

A company is considering a project that lasts for one year. The project requires an investment of ₹100 and at the end of the year the project will generate ₹115 (Table 4.6). No other cash flows are involved.

The project will be financed by a loan of one year with a 12 per cent interest rate. Assuming taxes away, the project can be represented as in Table 4.6.

TABLE 4.6 Financing cash flows

Financing		Investment	
Year	Cash flow (₹)	Year	Cash flow (₹)
0	+100	0	−100
1	−112	1	+115
Cost of capital 12%		Rate of return 15%	

Source: Author.

Cash flows on the investment side are not impacted by interest payment which is a financing cost and forms part of the COC.

Post-Tax Principle

Cash flows should be calculated on a post-tax basis. Taxes do not belong to the company, neither do they accrue to the debt providers or equity shareholders; they are paid to the government. Cash flows accruing from the project need to be calculated after deducting the taxes payable.

This principle can be illustrated while calculating cash flows on the disposal of an asset. The asset has a written down value as per the books of account. The difference between the price at which the asset is disposed of and its book value is the capital gain (loss). The price received from the sale of the asset must be reduced by the tax payable on capital gains to obtain the post-tax incremental cash flow.

A machinery had been purchased three years back at ₹100,000. The machine was expected to have an economic life of 10 years. Depreciation is calculated on a straight-line basis. The asset is no longer required and is now sold for ₹82,000. The corporate tax rate is 30 per cent.

Purchase cost of the machinery = 100,000.
Accumulated depreciation = 30,000 (10,000 * 3 years).
Written down value (WDV) = 70,000.
Capital gains = 82,000 − 70,000 = 12,000.
Tax payable on the capital gains = 12,000 * 30% = 3,600.

Hence, the post-tax incremental cash flow on sale of the machine is

$$82,000 - 3,600 = 78,400.$$

There must be consistency in the cash flows and the discount rate. Since cash flows are calculated on post-tax basis, the COC must also be calculated on post-tax basis.

In a nutshell, the rules to remember are

1. ignore sunk costs,
2. take into consideration opportunity costs,

3. recognize the impact of cannibalism,
4. calculate only incremental cash flows,
5. calculate cash flows after taxes,
6. take into account the impact of non-cash expenses.

The objective is to calculate 'post-tax incremental cash flows' as shown in Illustration 4.6.

Illustration 4.6

Q. A company is considering the introduction of a facial cream in the market. The relevant details are as follows.

New machinery required for producing the cream costs ₹1,000,000 and has a life of five years. The company plans to spend ₹100,000 on advertising before the launch of the cream, and this expenditure is amortizable over five years. Each bottle of the cream is expected to sell for ₹15 and has a variable cost of ₹10. Expected sales are 200,000 units per year for the next five years. Working capital is expected to increase by ₹500,000 in the first year, which will be received back at the end of five years. Assume a tax rate of 30 per cent and straight-line depreciation.

Determine the relevant incremental after-tax cash flows accruing on the project.

A. Cash flows can be calculated as in Table 4.7.

TABLE 4.7   Post-tax project cash flows (in ₹)

	C_0	C_1	C_2	C_3	C_4	C_5
Machinery	(1,000,000)					
Advertising	(100,000)					
Revenues		3,000,000	3,000,000	3,000,000	3,000,000	3,000,000
Variable costs		(2,000,000)	(2,000,000)	(2,000,000)	(2,000,000)	(2,000,000)
Depreciation		(200,000)	(200,000)	(200,000)	(200,000)	(200,000)
Amortization		(20,000)	(20,000)	(20,000)	(20,000)	(20,000)
Profit before tax (PBT)		780,000	780,000	780,000	780,000	780,000
Tax (30%)		234,000	234,000	234,000	234,000	234,000
PAT		546,000	546,000	546,000	546,000	546,000
Depreciation added back		200,000	200,000	200,000	200,000	200,000
Amortisation added back		20,000	20,000	20,000	20,000	20,000
Changes in working capital		(500,000)	—	—	—	500,000
Cash flows	(110,000)	266,000	766,000	766,000	766,000	1,266,000

Source: Author.

Inflation

Inflation is another aspect that impacts project cash flows and its valuation. The project cash flows calculated are usually actual cash flows without adjusting for change in prices. In this sense, these are what we call nominal cash flows and not real cash flows.

The impact of inflation is accounted for in the COC which is also nominal, that is, it includes the inflationary element. There must be consistency in the treatment of the cash flows and the COC. If the cash flows are nominal, as they usually are, we must discount these by nominal COC. However, if we adjust the cash flows for changes in prices and therefore the cash flows are real, they must be discounted by the real COC.

A two-bedroom house costs ₹10 million and a three-bedroom house costs ₹12.10 million. You currently have only ₹10 million, with which you can afford to buy a two-bedroom house.

Keen to own a three-bedroom house, you invest ₹10 million at 10 per cent for two years, expecting to get the required ₹12.10 million enabling your purchase of the three-bedroom house.

Prices, however, do not stay constant. Over the two years, property prices may increase by 4 per cent annually, which raises the price of the three-bedroom house to ₹13.10 million, more than ₹12.1 million you will have after two years.

It is important to understand and calculate the real rate of return, adjusted for inflation, and not the nominal return. While the nominal return earned on investment was 10 per cent per annum, the real return was only

$$R = [(1 + 10\%)/(1 + 4\%)] - 1$$
$$= 5.77\%.$$

In order to get a real return of 10 per cent annually, the nominal return must be

$$[(1 + 10\%) * (1 + 4\%)] - 1 = 14.40\%.$$

A return of 14.40 per cent over two years will yield the required ₹13.10 million, which is sufficient to purchase the three-bedroom house.

To calculate the real return, the following relationship can be applied:

$$1 + \text{Nominal return} = (1 + \text{Real return})(1 + \text{Inflation}).$$

Rearranging the preceding equation,

$$\text{Real return} = [(1 + \text{Nominal return})/(1 + \text{Inflation})] - 1.$$

Risk Analysis in Capital Budgeting

> If anything can go wrong, it will.
>
> —Murphy's law

> At the worst possible time.
>
> —O'Reilly

Cash flow projections for any project are just estimates. Rarely do the estimates turn out to be completely accurate. There may be an error in our estimation or the environment may turn out to be different from what had been anticipated.

Managing a project involves more than a one-time estimation of cash flows and calculation of NPV. It is a dynamic process wherein the management keeps revisiting the assumptions, the environment and the decisions taken to see if anything can now be done differently. Maybe there is a sudden increase in oil prices, as had happened globally for the first time in the 1970s. The increase in costs rendered many projects unviable, leading to their abandonment. At the same time, many projects to produce oil which were earlier unviable became value-enhancing. A sudden decrease in the price of rubber, a significant raw material in tires, implies that the project for manufacturing a million tires can now be upgraded to two million tires.

Managers are paid to take decisions. They cannot sit back and relax or spend time playing golf in the afternoon after having once decided to invest in a project. A constantly changing environment leads to the re-evaluation of earlier decisions, as and when warranted.

Changes in cash flows and the consequent risk of the project implies that managers need to estimate and manage such risks. There are various methods to do so. A discussion of these methods is beyond the scope of this book.

KEY CONCEPTS

1. Capital-budgeting decisions have a significant impact on a company's fortunes over long term.
2. A project's worth is based on the cash-flow generation and not accounting figures.
3. A company must select projects that have the potential to generate positive NPV. Net Present Value is superior to alternative capital-budgeting methods.
4. If two projects are mutually exclusive, the one with the higher NPV is selected.
5. The increase in the value of the firm from its capital budget for the year is the sum of the NPVs of all accepted projects.
6. Internal rate of retrun, payback period and ARR are the other methods employed to evaluate projects.
7. Cash flows for a project are incremental in nature, include opportunity costs, exclude sunk costs, recognize cannibalization and take into account taxes and inflation. What needs to be estimated are 'post-tax incremental cash flows'.
8. Cash flows must include depreciation and other non-cash expenses.

9. Cash flows for a project comprise initial, operating and terminal cash flows.
10. The impact of inflation must be taken into account in determining future cash flows.
11. Future cash flows are mere estimates and could turn out to be very different. The risk embedded in cash flow estimation must be taken into consideration.

CHAPTER QUESTIONS

1. Capital budgeting is not a daily activity. Why is it still so critical to a company's long-term future?
2. What are the different categories of projects a company may take up? Give examples of each of the categories.
3. Calculate the NPV and the IRR in the two projects as shown in the following table. The company's COC is 10 per cent. Which of the two projects will you opt for if they are mutually exclusive? Why? Also, why do the two projects give different outcomes?

					(in ₹)
	Year 0	*Year 1*	*Year 2*	*Year 3*	*Year 4*
A	–5,000	1,500	2,000	1,000	1,965
B	–5,000	—	—	—	7,500

4. A company has opportunities to invest in the four projects as in the following table:

Project	A	B	C	D
Investment (₹)	100	80	60	40
NPV (10%)	80	60	40	20
IRR	12%	14%	16%	18%

Which projects should the company invest in if
   a. the four projects are independent of each other,
   b. the projects are mutually exclusive,
   c. the total amount available for investment is (i) 100 and (ii) 140.
5. Let us consider another set of mutually exclusive projects as shown in the following table:

	C_0 (₹)	C_1 (₹)	*NPV (10%)* (₹)	*IRR*
Project P	50,000	60,000	4,545	20%
Project Q	10,000	16,000	4,545	60%

Which project has higher margin of safety?
6. One year ago, ABC Ltd purchased a machine for ₹600,000. The machine was expected to produce a gross margin of ₹120,000 per year and was assumed to have an economic life of six years.

The company now finds that a new machine is available that may offer significant advantages. The new machine can be purchased for ₹800,000, has an economic life of five years, and has no salvage value. It is expected that the new machine will produce a gross margin of ₹220,000 per year. The old machine can be sold now for ₹400,000.

ABC Ltd's tax rate is 30 per cent. At 10 per cent COC, should ABC Ltd replace the old machine?

CASE FOR DISCUSSION

ITS Ltd is an electronics company which commenced business two decades earlier. It has an established product base and a set of loyal customers. The company is planning to introduce a new product that apparently has a tremendous scope in the long run. The capital costs of development would be huge, but if the product succeeds, the demand will be large and stable. The company is considering whether to take up the new product development which will entail substantial outgo initially, followed of course by long-term cash inflows.

The relevant figures are as follows:

- The initial investment will be ₹1 billion in the first year and ₹ 0.50 billion in the second.
- Sales in the year after the project commences are likely to be 1,000 units, with an increase of 200 units per annum in subsequent years.
- The price per unit is ₹600,000. The company is confident of increasing the price by ₹100,000 from the third year onwards every year without impacting the projected sales.
- The variable costs per unit are extremely low at ₹50,000, comprising mainly of marketing expenses.
- The depreciation is calculated at 20 per cent of the gross capital. Investment of ₹1 billion is depreciated from the first to the fifth year, and investment of ₹0.5 billion is depreciated from the second to the sixth year.
- The marginal corporate tax rate is 30 per cent.
- The company must hire 100 software engineers, each earning a salary of ₹2 million in the first year, increasing by 15 per cent annually.
- The working capital requirements are small, amounting to roughly 10 per cent of annual sales by way of credit given to customers. The company gets back the credit given at the end of the project.
- The product is expected to have a life of six years.

1. Find the operating profit and free cash flows of the company.
2. Given the project's rather high COC of 15 per cent, should it invest in the development of the new product?

Appendix

Earlier in the chapter, we have discussed the two most conceptually sound methods of project evaluation, namely the NPV and the IRR methods. In this chapter-end appendix, we discuss more methods of project evaluation. While these methods are not conceptually sound, they are widely used and merit discussion. We also extend our discussion on NPV vis-à-vis IRR.

Payback Period

The payback period refers to the number of years in which the original investment is recovered. A cut-off period is decided. A project with a payback period longer than the cut-off is rejected, whereas a project with a payback period of cash flows shorter than the cut-off is accepted.

Illustration 4A.1

A project needs an initial investment of ₹1,000. It is a seven-year project, with each of the subsequent seven years yielding ₹250 cash inflows.

$$\text{Payback period} = 1,000/250 = 4 \text{ years.}$$

If the company has a cut-off acceptance period of three years, the project will be rejected. A cut-off period of five years will result in the acceptance of the project.

TABLE 4A.1   Expected cash flows for projects (in ₹)

Year	A	B	C
0	–100	–100	–100
1	20	50	50
2	30	30	30
3	50	20	20
4	60	60	60,000
Payback period (yrs)	3	3	3

Source: Author.

From Illustration 4A.1, we can draw the following conclusions about the payback period method.

1. Payback period ignores the time value of money. It takes into account the absolute levels of the cash flows without considering the time of their receipt.

   Both Projects A and B in Table 4A.1 have the same payback period and will be evaluated on par despite the different pattern of cash flows over time. Project B is preferable, since larger cash flows are received earlier rather than later.
2. Cash flows after the payback period are ignored. Project B and C have the same payback period, but Project C gets a large inflow after the payback period.
3. The cut-off period is decided arbitrarily, based in general on the comfort factor of the owner. It usually has no logical basis.

4. However, the payback period method of evaluation of projects is an extremely simple method and is intuitively appealing. It is easy to calculate and is understood by all.

Discounted Payback

A significant weakness of the payback period is that it does not take into account the time value of money and treats all cash flows equally without considering when the cash flows occur. The discounted payback period overcomes this weakness by taking into account the discounted value of cash flows for calculating the payback period of the project.

While the discounted payback method removes a major limitation, it also dilutes the most appealing feature, that of simplicity. Since the discounted payback period no longer remains simple, managers prefer to use what may be a little more complex but conceptually sound methods of evaluation such as the NPV and the IRR methods. Not too many companies use the discounted payback period method in real life.

Accounting Rate of Return (ARR)

Accounting rate of return is the average post-tax earnings as a percentage of average investment (book value).

Earnings after tax are forecast for each year of the project and averaged. The book value of investments in each of those years are calculated, being careful to reduce the accumulated depreciation from the original value of investments. Average profits are divided by the average investments to get the ARR. Let us understand with a hypothetical example.

A project, with a life of five years, needs an investment of ₹1,000. Its profits in the five years are (100), 100, 200, 300 and 400. What is the ARR of the project?

The average profit for the five years is

$$(100) + 100 + 200 + 300 + 400 = 900/5 = 180.$$

The book value of investment in each year, assuming straight-line depreciation is

$$1000, 800, 600, 400, 200$$

and the average investment is ₹600.

Hence, the ARR is 180/600 = 30%.

Accounting rate of return is the only method of capital budgeting which relies on accounting figures. Other methods base the decision on cash flows. Moreover, the ARR method is based on book value and ignores the time value of money.

However, accounting figures are readily available and thus ARR calculation becomes simple and straightforward. There is no need to convert accounting figures to cash flows.

More on NPV versus IRR

Earlier in the chapter we have discussed the relative merits and demerits of the two methods. Here are a few more comments.

1. Multiple rates of return:

    Although not very common, there may be projects which have more than one IRR. As a simple illustration, let us take a project with the following cash flows.

C_0	C_1	C_2
–100	230	–132

    A return of 10 per cent as well as 20 per cent will make the NPV of the aforementioned cash flows equal to zero. The project can be said to have IRR of 10 per cent as well as 20 per cent. If the COC of the company is 14 per cent, we do not know whether to accept the project or reject it.

    Multiple IRRs can arise if there is more than one change in the cash flow signs during the life of the project, that is, negative cash flows changing to positive and vice versa. In the previous equation, we had an initial negative cash flow becoming a positive cash flow in the first year and changing a second time to negative cash flows in the second year.

2. Infeasible IRR:

    Sometimes the cash flows generated may not yield a feasible IRR. It is impossible to find a rate that will make the NPV of the cash flows equal to zero. The NPV of course can be easily determined.

C_0	C_1	C
1,000	–3,000	2,500

    These cash flows have no feasible IRR. However, at 10 per cent COC, the NPV can be quite easily determined to be 339.

Mutually Exclusive Projects

Until now, we have focused on a single project to decide whether the company should invest or not. We have relied on two methods, namely the NPV and the IRR for our decision. The outcome of this evaluation process is quite straight forward—a decision either to invest in or reject the project.

Both the methods, as we have seen, give similar results and there is no conflict in the two methods. A positive NPV is possible only if the IRR is greater than the COC in which case an investment in the project is recommended. If, on the other hand, NPV is negative, IRR is less than the COC. Both methods, therefore, suggest a rejection of the project.

Life is never so simple and usually presents more complicated challenges.

1. We may have projects with more complicated cash flows, and as we discussed earlier, there could be more than one change in the cash flow sign—from negative to positive or vice versa.

2. Though theory assumes that funds in a free financial market would be available for all positive NPV projects, budgetary constraints are a harsh reality·for many companies.

   Budgetary limitations often compel a choice amongst various projects, all of which may be value accretive. How to choose among these projects, to add maximum value to the company, becomes another challenging facet for management practitioners. We have discussed PI as a tool to resolve budgetary constraints earlier in the chapter.

3. At times, two or more projects may be mutually exclusive. The choice of one project implies the exclusion of the other. Thus, only one of the projects can be taken up for investment, but not both. A piece of land that the company owns can be used to either construct a retail mall or a housing complex. When mobile telephony was introduced in India, telecom companies had to choose between global system for mobiles (GSM) and code division multiple access (CDMA) technology. They could not be certain which technology would prevail in long term.

   The Tatas chose the CDMA and failed. They have now practically sold the company for free to Bharati Airtel after incurring huge losses. Capital-budgeting decisions have a long-term impact with significant value implication.

   Mutually exclusive projects often present situations where NPV and IRR provide conflicting choices. A project with a lower IRR may have a higher NPV and vice versa. Such conflicts can arise due to differences in

   a. size of the projects,
   b. life of the projects and
   c. timing of cash flows.

Difference in Size of the Projects

XYZ Limited has acquired a company that has a widespread customer base. The company has not been performing well and needs to be revived by introducing changes in technology. There are two ways to do so.

There is a proven technology that will cost less in terms of investment but the eventual cash flows are likely to be low. On the other hand, the company can be more adventurous and make a larger investment in a recently introduced innovative technology that will generate much higher cash flows. Obviously, a choice between the two must be made and the company cannot undertake both investments.

Given the difference in size of the two investments, there may be a difference in the conclusion reached through the NPV and the IRR method shown in Illustration 4A.2.

Illustration 4A.2

Purchase price = ₹100 million.
Investment in Project X = ₹100 million.
Cash flow after one year= ₹250 million.
Investment in Project Y = ₹500 million.
Cash flow after one year = ₹700 million.

Contd

contd

As always, the COC is 10 per cent.

Total investment in project X = ₹200 million.
IRR: 200 = 250/(1+r) ... r = 25%.
NPV: 250/(1+10%) – 200 = 27.30.

Total investment in project Y = ₹600 million.
IRR: 600 = 700/(1+r) ... r = 17%.
NPV: 700/(1+10%) – 600 = 36.40.

Comparing the two projects as follows:

	NPV	IRR
Project X	27.30	25%
Project Y	36.40	17%

The two methods provide conflicting evaluation; while Project X has a higher IRR, its NPV is lower compared to Project Y. The reason for the discrepancy in outcomes is the size of the projects. Project X requires an investment of ₹200 million, and the additional return over and above the COC (25% – 10% = 15%) generates value for only ₹200 million. On the other hand, Project Y requires an investment of ₹600 million, and the additional return over and above the COC (17% – 10% = 7%) generates value for ₹600 million. Due to higher investments, Project Y generates higher NPV despite having a lower IRR compared to Project X.

Different Project Lives

Two mutually exclusive projects with different lifespans may also provide conflicting evaluation. Let us consider two projects with cash flows as shown in Illustration 4A.3.

Illustration 4A.3

Year	Project X	Project Y
0	–5,000	–5,000
1	6,000	0
2		0
3		0
4		8,745

With a COC of 10 per cent, these two projects have the following NPV and IRR:

	NPV	IRR
Project X	455	20%
Project Y	973	15%

Project X has a much higher IRR, but this generates value only for one year. In comparison, Project Y has a lower IRR but since this IRR is able to generate value for three years, the NPV of Project Y is much higher than that of Project X.

Timing of Cash Flows

Apart from the magnitude and the duration of the projects, the timing of the cash flows is also significant in determining the NPV and IRR of the projects. Let us see how with Table 4A.2.

The COC as always is 10 per cent.

Project X has a higher IRR compared to Project Y but a large proportion of cash flows accrue prior to the ending period of the project, thereby limiting NPV generation. The second project may have a lower IRR but continues to generate NPV throughout the project life for the entire investment.

The NPV of a project is generated from the excess of IRR over COC, over the entire life of the project. Longer this period and higher the investment, higher is the NPV. In all the three discussed cases, for Project X, the difference between the IRR and the COC is higher. Potentially, it can generate a higher NPV. However, compared to Project Y,

1. its net investment is lower,
2. the project life is shorter,
3. a significant proportion of the cash flows are generated before the termination of the project and NPV generation takes place for a lesser period.

Hence, despite the higher IRR, the NPV of Project X is lower than that of Y.

TABLE 4A.2   Impact of timing of cash flows on project NPV and IRR (in ₹)

	C_0	C_1	C_2	C_3	*NPV*	*IRR*
Project X	(10,000)	7,000	6,000	5,000	5,079	39%
Project Y	(10,000)	—	—	25,000	8,783	36%

Source: Author.

CHAPTER 5

Risk and Return

Risk is like pornography. I can't define it but I know it when I see it.

—Potter Stewart, the US Supreme Court Judge

Figure 5.1 shows annualized returns on investment in the US equities over a period of 92 years from 1926 to 2017. The return in any given year varied significantly from the average (10.20 per cent), varying from more than 50 per cent to being significantly in the red. The variability in returns can test the patience of even the most experienced investors. In 1930, the return was –44 per cent. This was on top of a negative return of over 27 per cent in the previous year. An investor who had invested US$100 in the US stocks at the end of 1928 would have been left with only US$41 after two years. Not many investors can bear such significant dilution of their investments. It is the prospect of such losses that keeps stock investors awake at night. It is significant and noteworthy that more than one in four years have experienced negative returns on equity investments.

From 1926 to 2017, the annualized average return on the US large stocks at 10.2 per cent per annum was of course much higher than returns on most other financial instruments (Figure 5.2). Investment in government securities over the same period yielded 5.5 per cent. The gap in returns leads to disproportionate impact in the amount of wealth, especially over a long period. An investment of US$1 in government securities amounts to US$131 (at 5.5 per cent per annum) after 92 years. A similar investment in equity is worth US$7,353 (at 10.2 per cent per annum).

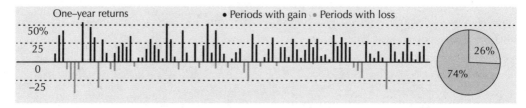

FIGURE 5.1   Annual returns on US stocks from 1926 to 2017

Source: Morningstar Investment Service (2018).

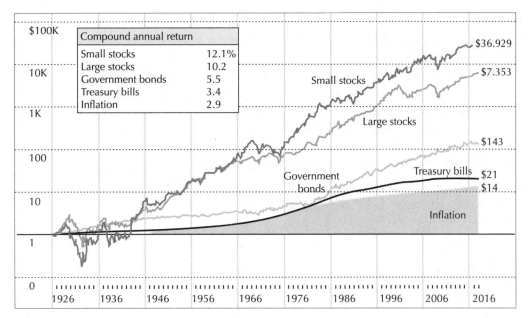

FIGURE 5.2   Annualized returns on different instruments in the US from 1926 to 2017

Source: Morningstar Investment Service (2018).

Inflation (2.90 per cent) adjusted, the difference in wealth in real terms is even greater. Of course, riskier avenues of investment do exist if one has the heart to withstand even greater vicissitudes in return. Return on small stocks are more volatile than that of overall equity, but the return is also higher at 12.1 per cent and the wealth, at the end of a period of 92 years is far greater, at US$36,929.

These two figures aptly describe the risk that investors are exposed to. At the same time, they illustrate the benefits, in terms of additional returns possible, from assuming higher risk. The figures confirm the fact that a higher risk usually provides the investors with a higher return, especially over a long period of time.

Greed and Fear

Stock markets, it is said, are guided by two human emotions, namely greed and fear. That even the most intelligent human beings are not immune from such affliction is clear from Sir Isaac Newton's experience of investing in the South Sea Company.

The South Sea Company, established in early eighteenth century, was granted a monopoly on trade in the South Seas in exchange for assuming England's war debt. This was music to the investors' ears who lapped up the company's shares, taking its price into what can only be described as stratospheric zone. Newton's own investment in the South Sea Company doubled in value in a matter of months. He cashed out with GB£7,000, a

Contd

contd

substantial sum in those times. His logic for selling was simply that the stock had become 'irrationally inflated'.

However, neither his cashing out nor his views about the stock could stop the appreciation of the South Sea Company's share price which carried on its relentless northward journey. All his friends were making huge amounts of money. His greed was satisfied but Newton could not control the fear of being left out.

He jumped into the fray again, investing practically his entire savings, amounting to GB£20,000, incidentally at more than three times his own original price. Not surprisingly, this was almost at the peak price and he promptly lost the entire amount, ruining him financially. He wrote, 'I can calculate the motions of heavenly bodies, but not the madness of men' (*Wall Street Journal*, 2017).

We will try to have a better appreciation of returns before coming back to risk.

Return

The basic concepts of return have already been discussed in Chapter 3, 'Time Value of Money'. It would be useful to elaborate further on the concept and discuss some more ideas here.

Recall the four key parameters pertaining to the time value of money, namely PV, FV, time period and return. If we know the PV, the FV and the time period of the investment, it is easy to estimate the return. Returns are usually calculated in annual terms to make them comparative.

Let us understand with an example.

To make calculations easier, here is the formula for the calculation of annual return if we know the value at the beginning and the end of the period.

$$\text{Return} = (FV/PV)^{1/n} - 1.$$

Q1. Investor A purchases 100 shares of PQR Ltd at ₹40 each. After five years, the shares are sold for ₹100. What is the annual rate of return?

A. Investment in shares is 40 * 100 = ₹4,000.
   Value after 5 years is 100 * 100 = ₹10,000.
   Let us depict the cash flows year wise.

C_0	C_1	C_2	C_3	C_4	C_5
(4,000)					10,000

The PV is ₹4,000, the future value is ₹10,000 and the period is five years. We need to determine the interest rate.

$$\text{Interest rate} = (FV/PV)^{1/n} - 1$$
$$= (10,000/4,000)^{1/5} - 1$$

$$= 2.5^{1/5} - 1$$
$$= 20.11\%.$$

Q2. Another investor has invested in shares of XYZ Ltd. He purchases 100 shares at ₹60 and after holding it for eight years disposes off at ₹200. What is his annual rate of return?

A.

$$\text{Investment in year } 0 = 100 * 60 = 6{,}000.$$
$$\text{Value in year } 10 = 100 * 200 = 20{,}000.$$
$$\text{Return} = (20{,}000/6{,}000)^{1/8} - 1$$
$$= 3.33^{1/8} - 1$$
$$= 16.24\%.$$

While the first investor increased his wealth by 2.5 times over a period of five years, the second increased it by 3.3 times over eight years. It is difficult to evaluate the two investments unless a comparison is made over the same time period. The usual practice is to estimate returns on an annual basis. We have calculated the returns to the first investor at 20.11 per cent per annum, whereas the returns to the second investor are 16.24 per cent per annum. A comparison now becomes meaningful.

Return Calculations

Q3. An investor invests for a period of 10 years, expecting a return of 10 per cent per annum over the entire period. In the first four years, the actual return was only 3 per cent per annum. What should the return be over the remaining six years for him to achieve his original targeted return?

A. Let us assume the original investment is ₹100.

The expected value at the end of 10 years is as follows.

$$FV = PV \, (1 + r)^n$$
$$= 100 \, (1 + 10\%)^{10}$$
$$= 259.37.$$

Actual value after four years is

$$100 \, (1 + 3\%)^4 = 112.55.$$

Return required in the remaining six years is as follows.

$$\text{Return} = (FV/PV)^{1/n} - 1$$
$$= (259.37/112.55)^{1/6} - 1$$
$$= 14.93\%.$$

Dividend Yield and Capital Gains

An investor purchases 100 shares of a company XYZ Ltd at ₹50 per share. The return to the investor accrues in two forms—the dividend and the change in prices. Assume that XYZ Ltd pays a dividend of ₹2 and at the end of the year, the share price is ₹55.

The investment in the beginning of the year will be

$$100 * 50 = 5,000.$$

At the end of the year, the investor has

$$(55 + 2) * 100 = 5,700.$$

The return is

$$= (5,700 - 5,000)/5,000 = 700/5,000 = 14\%.$$

This can be divided into two parts, namely

$$2/50 + (55 - 50)/50 = 4\% + 10\% = 14\%.$$

The first part is the dividend yield which can be stated as the amount of dividend divided by the share price at the beginning of the period. The second part is the capital gain which equals the gain in share price divided by the share price at the beginning of the period. Of course, if the price goes down, the investor incurs a capital loss (technically termed negative capital gain). Whether the investor makes a positive gain or not depends on whether the capital loss is less than the dividend or more.

In our example, if the share price of XYZ Ltd had gone down to ₹45, the investor's return would have been

$$2/50 + (45 - 50)/50 = 4\% + (-10\%) = -6\%.$$

Return Averages

Let us try a simple question. An investor gets a return of negative 11 per cent, 15 per cent and 20 per cent in three years of investment. What is his return per annum over this period?

Taking an arithmetic average, we obtain a return of $(-11 + 15 + 20)/3$ or 8 per cent. An investment of ₹100 at 8 per cent per annum for three years yields

$$100 * (1 + 8\%)^3 = 125.97.$$

However, the amount that the investor will actually have at the end of three years is as follows.

At the end of the first year an investment of ₹100 invested at negative 11 per cent will yield ₹89. An amount of ₹89 invested at 15 per cent will yield ₹102.35 at the end of two years. An amount of ₹102.35 invested at 20 per cent will become ₹122.82 at the end of three years.

This figure is lower than the amount calculated previously through arithmetic average. The reason is very simple. To find out the exact amount of money at the end of a certain period of varying returns, we need to calculate the geometric mean and not the arithmetic mean.

In our example, the geometric mean is

$$[(1 - 11\%) * (1 + 15\%) * (1 + 20\%)]^{1/3} - 1 = 7.09\%.$$

And an investment of ₹100 yielding 7.09 per cent for three years yields

$$100 * (1 + 7.09\%)^3 = ₹122.82.$$

Arithmetic mean provides an unbiased estimate of the expected return next year (or any other period). However, it invariably overestimates the total amount that an initial investment will grow into. Geometric mean provides the correct value.

The return between the two periods is also popularly termed compounded annual growth rate (CAGR). As long as the returns in different years are not equal, the geometric mean will always be lower than the arithmetic mean. Greater the variation in returns over the years, greater will be the difference between the arithmetic mean and the geometric mean. Let us further understand the concept with Illustration 5.1.

Illustration 5.1

Your investment of ₹100 yields 50 per cent in the first year and goes down by 50 per cent in the second year. What is the return per annum?

At the end of first year, ₹100 becomes ₹150, and it becomes ₹75 at the end of the second year.

Average arithmetic rate of return is zero which should yield ₹100 at the end of two years. Correct return can be computed by geometric mean as

$$(1 + 50\%) * [1 + (-50\%)]^{1/2} - 1 = -13.40\%$$

and
$$100 * [1 + (-13.40\%)]^2 = 75.$$

Risk

The quip on risk by the US Judge Potter Stewart, given at the beginning of the chapter, aptly describes how people in general view risk. In our daily life, we face circumstances that have the potential to cause harm. We learn to deal with such situations without even realizing it. While crossing the road, it is instinctive for us to assess the risk of an approaching vehicle and avoid a crash. We do not need to measure the speed at which the vehicle is being driven, its distance from us, the speed with which we will cross the road, the width of the road and other such statistics and enter them on a complicated software on our laptop to find out whether we should cross the road or wait for the vehicle to pass by before making our move. We do this almost instinctively, as a matter of habit.

Life is about risk management; we are faced with risk at every step. There is a risk of falling sick or meeting with an accident, for which we can take health or accident insurance. There is a risk of losing our possessions—the house, consumer durables or jewelry, for which we may take household insurance. A farmer is faced with the risk of crop failure, which he can manage by taking crop insurance. The farmer also faces the prospect of a decline in the price of his product on harvesting, which can be hedged by selling in the forward/future market. We may face impairment in the value of our financial holdings, which we can hedge with options.

There are no guarantees in life and the future is uncertain. Elroy Dimson, Emeritus Professor of finance at London Business School, once described risk as a situation wherein more things can happen than will happen (cited in Bernstein, 2008), meaning that while there will be a single outcome that will accrue, possibly known only after the event, more than one outcome is possible. When you cross the road, chances are that you will safely do so, but there is a slim possibility of accident. When a bank provides a loan to a telecom company, it is expected that the loan would be paid back in accordance with the terms of the agreement, but it is possible that the loan may become a non-performing asset, probably due to a new player entering and introducing predatory pricing. When a company invests in a new cement project, the project is expected to have a positive net present value (NPV). However, the project may become a failure due to slackening demand or an increase in the price of limestone, leading to a reduction in the value of the company.

The different situations we have discussed are uncertain in terms of the outcomes that may be possible. Our actions are premised on the expectations of the future. Reality may, however, turn out to be quite different, jeopardizing our objectives. The future cannot be predicted with certainty; we make forecasts all the time, but the outcome may not match our predictions. Risk refers to the possibility of more than one outcome for any action we take. The more varied the possible outcomes, higher is the risk.

Assume there are two games on offer. The first game offers ₹110 or ₹90 on the toss of a coin. The second, similarly, offers ₹150 or ₹50. Both have an expected value of ₹100, but the second game is considered to be riskier, since the possible outcomes are more varied.

It would be useful here to distinguish between uncertainty and risk. There is a subtle difference between the two. First, an uncertain situation is one where we may not be able to assign probabilities to the occurrence of the possible outcomes. In ancient times, if you asked someone whether it will rain tomorrow, the most likely answer would have been 'only god knows'. The situation was uncertain since no one knew the chances of it raining the next day. In the modern world, while the actual outcome continues to be unknown, the probability of the occurrence of rainfall can be estimated on the basis of historical data and the various meteorological parameters that determine the occurrence of rainfall. In some sense, assigning probabilities to an uncertain situation converts it into a risk. In a risky situation, we know the odds of different outcomes while in an uncertain situation such odds are unknown.

Second, if an uncertain situation has no impact, favourable or adverse, it is not considered to be risky. You are organizing a large party at your house and are wondering how much food to prepare. Invitations have been sent out, but as usual confirmations are slow to come in. The number of persons attending the party is certainly a matter of risk. However, if the party is converted to a potluck one, you are no longer impacted by the number of people attending since each person is expected to bring food sufficient for one person. Thus, while there is no clarity on the number of people attending, the situation can either be uncertain or risky, depending on whether it is a regular party or a potluck one.

Kinds of Risk

Broadly speaking, there are three kinds of risk faced by investors.

Price/Market Risk

Price risk, also termed market risk, is the risk of a change in the price of a security. An investor invests in a security hoping that the price of the security will go up, providing him handsome capital gains. At times, however, the price may go down and the investor suffers a capital loss.

Price risk is an integral part of investment and is usually measured by the volatility in prices. Higher the dispersion of returns around the average, higher is the risk. As we know, there is a direct correlation between risk and return. Riskier securities usually offer higher returns, while safer securities provide lower return.

Acquisition Risk

Tata Steel Ltd acquired Corus, a United Kingdom (UK)-based steel company, in 2006 for US$12.9 billion to gain a foothold in international markets. The markets collapsed soon after, and the company had to write off US$2.9 billion value until 2016. The impairment in its value is likely to continue and further write-offs are expected.

Credit Risk

Credit risk refers to a borrower's failure to meet his obligations in accordance with the terms of the borrowing. It refers to the possibility that the loan given may not return the interest or the principal on the agreed terms or on the due date. A loan that is not paying interest or maturity value on time is termed a non-performing asset (NPA). A high proportion of NPAs weakens a bank's profitability and cash flows and impairs its ability to conduct business. At its extreme, NPAs may even lead to a bank going out of business. Many public sector banks in India have huge NPAs. Some of these banks have had to be bailed out by the government through capitalization, by providing a large amount as capital. Otherwise, these banks may not have survived.

Additionally, credit risk also refers to the violation of the terms of the loan by the borrower. The lender usually imposes certain conditions on the borrower, termed covenants, to ensure the safety of his loan. These conditions may include maximum debt equity ratio, current ratio, prohibition on investment in risky assets and on large payment of dividends and so forth. Any violation of these conditions is also a credit risk, since it compromises the safety of the loan.

Credit risk is an integral part of the business of banks and financial institutions, their main function being lending. Banks take credit risk into account in pricing their lending. Higher the credit risk, higher is the interest that the banks charge on the loan.

Risk in Bank Intermediation

Banks are financial institutions that intermediate funds between savers (mainly the household sector) and borrowers (corporate and retail). Banks take deposits in the form of current and savings accounts, popularly termed CASA deposits, and relatively short-term fixed deposits. Their lending is usually long-term, extending over many years, creating a mismatch in the funds profile, due to which banks are exposed to liquidity risk as well as interest rate risk.

The principal business of banks is borrowing (liability) and lending (asset). Both the borrowing and lending can be at a fixed rate or at a floating one. Usually, there is little change in the price of floating-rate securities, interest rate payable being adjusted to reflect the change in the market interest rate. Fixed-rate securities, however, change in value, consequent to change in market interest rates, exposing the banks to substantial risk.

Banks can hedge interest rate risk through the purchase/sale of interest rate futures and swaps. Exchange rate futures and swaps can also be used by banks to manage exchange rate risks on their balance sheets. The current lack of a vibrant and efficient market in these instruments hampers the ability of Indian banks to manage risk efficiently.

Operating Risk

Operating risk refers to the possibility that a transaction undertaken for investment is not completed in accordance with the terms of the trade.

There are two stages to an investment. The first is the transaction stage, when the purchase and sale of a security takes place. Thus, an investor may purchase 100 shares of Infosys at ₹1,100 per share.

The second pertains to the settlement of the particular transaction. During the settlement, the security is delivered by the seller and the payment made by the buyer. In our example, the buyer will make a payment of 1100 * 100 = ₹110,000 and receives 100 shares from the seller, thus settling or completing the transaction.

There is a time lag between the transaction and the settlement date which may give rise to the possibility that the buyer or the seller either refuses to or is unable to fulfil his part of the transaction. Long gaps between transaction and settlement increases the possibility of default, leading to higher operating risk.

Bond Risks

'Gentlemen prefer bonds' is a statement originally attributed to Andrew Mellon who was the Treasury Secretary to three US Presidents in the early years of the twentieth century. The statement is indicative of the apparently safe characteristics of bonds as an instrument of investment. Cash flows of a typical bond comprise coupons and maturity proceeds. These are fixed, certain and known in advance. Bonds are therefore considered to be safe instruments (and hence, preferred by gentlemen).

We however know better. Bonds carry risks of various kinds. These include

1. price risk,
2. credit risk,
3. foreign exchange risk,
4. reinvestment risk,
5. inflation risk.

These risks have been described in detail in this and other chapters. Investors must take them into account while investing in bonds.

Indian stock markets were in the past characterized by a very high level of operating risk. There was a long gap between transaction and settlement dates, amounting to more than a fortnight. The trading was physical as was the exchange of shares, due to which an effective settlement was always in doubt. Since the mid-1990s, operating issues have more or less been sorted out with the introduction of better processes and surveillance, effective oversight and regulation by the Securities and Exchange Board of India (SEBI) and the exchanges, a T+2 system with settlement taking place two working days after the transaction date, electronic trading and dematerialization of shares. It would be safe to say that since the mid-1990s, the settlement of transactions on Indian exchanges has proceeded smoothly and any transaction undertaken has been duly settled on time. Operating risk has reduced considerably.

Price risk and credit risk are business risks which are an integral part of any investment. Operating risks, however, increase the cost of doing business without adding any value. The virtual elimination of operating risks has significantly reduced transaction costs and turned the Indian stock market into a globally competitive market in terms of operating risks.

Investment Risk

We have defined risk as the possibility of more than one outcome for any action we take. More varied the outcomes, greater is the risk.

Similarly, investment risk refers to more than one possible return on an investment. Greater the spread of returns, higher is the risk. On the other hand, if the possible returns are more closely bunched around the average, the risk is low.

Let us look at the impact of risk on investment decisions. You have a few rupees saved and your thoughts obviously turn to government bonds since they are considered to be a safe security. With its ability to raise taxes and print currency, the government is not expected to default on its obligations. (It is another matter that despite being free of any possibility of default, even government bonds carry risk—price risk and the risk of reinvestment). Currently, government bonds yield 7 per cent. Adjusted for an expected inflation of 5 per cent, this does not leave much in terms of real return for the investors.

You learn that corporate bonds provide a return which is higher than the return on government bonds. You look up the credit rating of different companies and decide to play it safe by investing in bonds issued by Rural Electrification Ltd with an AAA rating, implying the highest possible safety. Instead of the 7 per cent returns provided by the government bonds, you are now able to obtain 200 basis points higher at 9 per cent.

This whets your appetite for more and you do not mind taking a little higher risk by investing in bonds of Rama Shyam Papers Ltd, with a BB rating. The return available now is 13 per cent. As you take a greater risk, the returns are usually higher.

Finally, you decide to test the stock markets, exposing your investment to even higher risk. Stocks in India have yielded a little over 15 per cent per annum between 30 March 2002 and 31 March 2017. At the same time, they also carry a higher risk. Given at the beginning of this chapter is an estimate of the returns on the US stocks over an 92-year period. The Indian stocks data over such long periods is neither available nor reliable, but if we look at the data since the time the Sensex figures are available from 1979 onwards, it shows considerably higher return than other financial instruments, along with a significantly higher risk.

Investment in government securities carries no default risk. Any other investment avenue has an element of risk attached and must provide returns higher than the risk-free rate given by the government securities. The difference between the return on the risk-free security and the return on a risky investment is the risk premium (or the higher return over and above the risk-free rate). The premium is solely due to the risk of the investment.

Attitude to Risk

We have mentioned earlier that investors look for high returns but want a low risk; they are what is technically termed risk averse. They prefer lower risk to higher risk, everything else remaining the same. Technically, this is represented by the following situation.

An investor is offered a choice of playing a game for which he pays ₹100. He tosses a coin. A head entitles him to receive ₹110, whereas a tail gets him ₹90. The expected return of the game is ₹100, the same amount that he pays to play the game. The payment of ₹100 is certain, whereas the outcome of the game is uncertain. He is exchanging a certain ₹100 for a risky, expected ₹100. A risk-averse investor is one who rejects such a game. In order to persuade the investor to play the game, he must be offered an expected value which is higher than the initial payment he makes.

A risk-averse investor expects a higher return for taking on the risk and will not accept an investment that provides the same return but exposes him to a greater risk. Looked at differently, risk aversion refers to the willingness to pay to reduce one's exposure to risk. Purchase of insurance is a prime example of paying to reduce one's exposure to risk. An investor willing to accept a lower return for a security, with a more predictable return, is a risk-averse investor. Investment theory is predicated on the assumption that investors in general are risk-averse.

It is due to the attitude of risk aversion that risky assets require a higher return. To induce investors to take an exposure to risky assets, risky securities need to provide returns that are higher than those of less risky securities. Otherwise, investors will put their money only in safe instruments.

Risk aversion provides us a framework for pricing securities. The return on any security should equal the return on the risk-free security plus a spread for the risk of the security, termed the risk premium. The spread over and above the risk-free rate is a function of the risk embedded in the security. Higher the risk of the security, higher is the spread and therefore, the required rate of return.

The spread depends on the risk-aversive nature of investors. If the investors are highly risk-averse, as happens in uncertain times, the spread over the risk-free rate will be higher and so will the required return on the security. Under normal circumstances, investors are likely to accept risk more easily and the risk premium need not be high. The risk-free return, of course, comprises return for time and inflation.

Grant Thorton (2015), one of the largest global accounting services and consulting firms, has estimated the equity risk premium in India to be approximately 7.4 per cent. Thus, while investments in stocks are fraught with risk, the high-risk premium compensates handsomely for the risk of the investments.

Risk aversion is not constant and keeps changing. In times of crisis, investors become more risk-averse and demand a higher risk premium on investment. After the attack on the New York twin towers in the United States of America (USA) on 11 September 2001, there was a general move towards safety and no one cared to invest in risky assets. Consequently, the risk premium soared to unprecedented levels. Investors demanded a much higher return for investing in risky assets. Given that expected cash flows from businesses did not increase (in fact, many businesses such as hotels and travel experienced a large dip in cash flows!), a higher return was possible only with a large reduction in the price of risky assets. Consequently, prices fell sharply the world over. The extent of risk aversion can have a significant impact on stock prices.

For a long time until the financial crisis in 2008, stocks had been on an upswing. It was widely believed that the ability of investors and financial markets to understand, distribute and manage risk in the economy had improved considerably. Consequently, the risk premium came down substantially, leading to what was believed to be a permanently higher level of stock prices. After the crash in markets and the prolonged recession in the global economy, such ideas have been discarded, hopefully forever.

Inflation Risk or Purchasing Power Risk

One of the greatest sources of risk throughout history has been the risk of inflation or the sustained increase in prices of goods and services. During periods of high inflation, workers demand a large increase in wages to compensate them for the rising prices. Anyone with a fixed income loses out during inflation.

Similarly, investors in bonds will experience a lower real return, that is, return adjusted for inflation. Investment in a 10 per cent bond yields a real return of 6 per cent when the inflation is 4 per cent. However, if the rate of inflation goes up to 7 per cent, the real return falls to 3 per cent.

Governments have at times issued bonds that guarantee a real rate of return. Usually called treasury inflation-protected securities, or TIPS, these bonds pay a nominal return which equals an assured real return plus the prevailing rate of inflation. The nominal return keeps changing in line with the changing rate of inflation.

Risk Calculation

The substantial risk in equity investment arises due to the inability to accurately predict cash flows. Cash flows depend on various parameters that determine the performance of the company and how the economy shapes up, especially in the context of the earlier discussed parameters. For example, for Maruti Udyog Limited, a manufacturer of passenger cars, three key parameters that determine its performance are the price of oil, economic growth and interest rates. The price of oil determines the post-purchase cost of operating the car, economic growth determines the discretionary spending ability of the consumers and interest rates largely determine the monthly EMI payments that need to be made for financing the purchase of the car. Since most vehicles are financed through consumer finance companies, the rate of interest becomes a key determinant of affordability. For Apollo Tires Ltd, two of the most critical factors are the rate of economic growth and the price of rubber. Economic growth determines the demand for tires by influencing the sales of automobiles. Rubber is a major raw material constituent of tires and its price impacts the cost and profits of Apollo Tires Ltd. For an IT company such as Infosys Ltd and Tata Consultancy Services (TCS) Ltd, the rupee–dollar rate and the economic growth in the USA would determine their performance and hence the share price. A large part of the sales of an Indian IT company is in the USA. The rupees available on conversion of dollar receipts on projects depend on the USD/INR rate, a weaker Indian rupee being beneficial to the company.

The standard procedure to estimate the risk is to draw up various scenarios that are possible along with the probability of the occurrence of each scenario. Each of the scenarios yields a specific return on investment. A probability weighted mean provides the expected average return on the stock. A probability weighted standard deviation yields the risk of investment in the stock. The total probability of occurrence should be 100 per cent, covering all possible scenarios.

The standard deviation thus calculated determines the risk of the investment. Standard deviation is indicative of the dispersion of returns around the mean; it shows how closely or how widely the expected returns are bunched around the mean. Standard deviation is a measure of volatility: the more the return varies around the average, the higher is the volatility and the risk inherent in a specific investment.

Let us understand with an illustration by taking the example of TCS. As discussed previously, the rate of return in the shares of TCS is influenced by two factors, namely the growth rate of the US economy and the rupee–dollar rate. There are four possible situations combining the two factors. We need to estimate the returns that would accrue given each of these situations. An estimate of the probability of occurrence of each of these scenarios will enable us to calculate the expected return and the risk associated with an investment in TCS.

Scenario	Probability of occurrence	Expected returns
High growth and weak rupee	25%	40%
High growth and strong rupee	30%	25%
Low growth and weak rupee	10%	10%
Low growth and strong rupee	35%	–10%

Expected return = (25% * 40%) + (30% * 25%) + (10% * 10%) + (35% * –10%),
$$= 10\% + 7.5\% + 1\% - 3.5\% = 15\%.$$

Standard deviation (risk) is

$$(40\% - 15\%)^2 * 25\% = 0.015625$$
$$+ (25\% - 15\%)^2 * 30\% = 0.003$$
$$+ (10\% - 15\%)^2 * 10\% = 0.000025$$
$$+ (-10\% - 15\%)^2 * 35\% = 0.021875$$
$$= 0.04075^{0.5} = 0.2019.$$

Hence, the expected return is 15 per cent with a risk of 20.19 per cent. Let us calculate risk once again in Illustration 5.2.

Illustration 5.2

ABC Ltd is a market leader in real estate. The performance of the company is predicated on two broad factors, namely the growth rate of the economy and the monetary situation which can be tight or benign. The future thus can be portrayed in four distinct situations while combining the growth rate and the monetary environment.

Projected returns in different scenarios	Return	Probability
Low growth/tight monetary environment	–10%	20%
Low growth/benign monetary environment	5%	15%
High growth/tight monetary environment	5%	25%
High growth/benign monetary environment	25%	40%

$$\text{Expected Return} = (-10\% * 20\%) + (5\% * 15\%) + (5\% * 25\%) + (25\% * 40\%)$$
$$= 10\%.$$

Standard deviation is

$$(-10\% - 10\%)^2 * 20\% = 0.008$$
$$(5\% - 10\%)^2 * 15\% = 0.000375$$
$$(5\% - 10\%)^2 * 25\% = 0.000625$$
$$(25\% - 10\%)^2 * 40\% = 0.009$$
$$= 13.42\%.$$

Hence, the expected return is 10 per cent with a risk (standard deviation) of 13.42 per cent.

Stock investment is not the only risky option; investment in other asset classes are also prone to a fair bit of risk. The days of safe, risk-free investments are over, assuming that they ever existed. As investors, we want a higher return but dislike being exposed to risk. Real life is not so benevolent and there is a direct, positive correlation between risk and return. A higher return is accompanied by a higher risk, while if an investor seeks a lower risk, he must accept lower returns.

Financial markets offer a wide spectrum of choices for the investor in terms of risk and return. These choices ensure that the investor takes the minimum possible risk for the return he is getting or that he gets the maximum return for the specific level of risk he is exposed to. Based on his attitude to risk, each investor can opt for the choice that is appropriate for him. It is crucial for the investors to understand the concept of risk and return, the relationship between the two and the method of risk calculation. (And discard the perception of risk being akin to pornography despite the fact that risk is a four-letter word!)

Capital Asset Pricing Model (CAPM)

'Don't put all your eggs in one basket' is a familiar adage. According to the principle of diversification, investments should be split into multiple risky assets rather than in a single asset. Each investment should ideally comprise a small proportion of the total portfolio. If the return on a specific asset is poor or negative, its impact on the overall portfolio is likely to be insignificant.

In fact, undertaken properly, diversification has the potential to reduce the overall risk of the portfolio without reducing the expected return. A popular saying in finance is that there is no free lunch in financial markets, meaning thereby that if you are aiming for a lower risk, you need to accept a lower return. Diversification is one of the rare tools that reduces the risk of investment without lowering returns.

Let us understand how this happens. Finance theory distinguishes between two kinds of risks, namely unsystematic and systematic risks. The risk that a company is exposed to may be

1. unique and specific to the company (unsystematic) or
2. market-wide, impacting all companies (systematic).

Unique and unsystematic factors primarily impact the company under consideration but not others. For instance, the resignation of its managing director has a significant impact on a company as does a labour strike in its manufacturing plant. When the deputy managing director of HDFC Bank resigned in 2018, its share price went down by 3 per cent. The auditor of Manpasand Beverages Ltd, Deloitte Haskins & Sells resigned just before the finalization of its accounts in May 2018. The stock price dropped by 42 per cent over the next five days. These were unsystematic events that reduced the price of HDFC Bank or Manapasand Beverages Ltd shares respectively, but no other company was impacted. The Food and Drug Administration (FDA) Ltd approval of a drug that a pharmaceutical company has been working on will have substantial benefits for it. Other companies are likely to experience only a muted impact.

Systematic parameters are those that have an impact on all companies. These are market-wide factors whose impact is not limited to one company. Different companies are, however, impacted differently. Thus, the extent of the impact on each company may vary depending on the relationship of the different companies to the parameter. The lower growth of the Indian economy over the last few years has had an adverse influence on the performance of all companies. While infrastructure, fast-moving consumer goods (FMCG) and automobile companies have suffered a significant drop, pharmaceutical and IT companies have been affected to a lesser extent. Similarly, high interest rates have adversely impacted infrastructure and automobile companies; at the same time, FMCG companies are much less affected. All companies would be impacted by a lower oil price. The extent of the impact would however vary. A two-wheeler or a paint company is likely to benefit significantly from a fall in oil price, whereas a pharmaceutical company may show a muted impact.

The critical aspect is the relationship between diversification and unsystematic risk in a portfolio. Diversification removes unsystematic risk from a portfolio and an investor does not need to bear it. Unsystematic risk is important to an investor only if the bulk of his investments are in one company. For instance, most of the wealth of Azim Premji is invested in Wipro Limited. If Wipro Limited were to lose value, Azim Premji would experience a substantial erosion in his net worth. He can overcome the impact of unsystematic risks through diversification by spreading his investment in many companies. A diversified investor has limited exposure to unsystematic risks; he only bears systematic risk. All he has to ensure is that he diversifies in a reasonably large number of companies and that such investments are in companies from diverse industries. For example, an investment only in cement stocks is not diversification in the real sense, since all cement companies are impacted by a similar set of parameters. The investor needs to ensure that his investments are in a wide range of industries and in companies that have an exposure to different sets of parameters. Technically, the correlation between stocks in a portfolio must be low.

Correlation between returns on two stocks is the most important determinant of the risk of the portfolio. Correlation refers to the degree to which the rate of return of two stocks vary together. The lower the correlation between return on two stocks, the better is the outcome in terms of the return and risk characteristics of the portfolio.

The correlation between the returns on a security and the returns on the market as a whole is termed beta (β). Beta measures the sensitivity of the returns of a security to the market returns. A high beta, signifying a high correlation with changes in market returns, is indicative of higher risk. On the other hand, a low beta, implying a low correlation with changes in market returns, shows a lower risk of investment.

While detailed mathematical exposition is beyond the scope of the book, it would be useful to describe how beta is calculated.

$$\beta = \frac{\sigma_{im}}{\sigma^2_m}.$$

Where σ_{im} is the covariance of the stock returns with the returns on the market and σ^2_m is the variance of the returns of the market.

Both the covariance and the variance are calculated on the basis of historical returns of the stock and the overall market over a period of time. Brokerages and research firms routinely publish the beta of various stocks and are easily available.

Beta is important since it determines the contribution of a security's risk to a portfolio. The risk that a security adds to a portfolio is not its total risk but only the systematic risk given by beta. The balance unsystematic risk is diversified away as part of the portfolio.

According to the CAPM, diversification removes unsystematic risks from an investors' portfolio. Since a well-diversified portfolio does not bear unsystematic risk, the market does not pay for the exposure to unsystematic risk. It provides returns to the investor for bearing only systematic risk which, by definition, cannot be diversified away.

Required Rate of Return on Equity

Systematic risk is linked to the market risk and can be greater or less than the market risk, depending on the variation in the returns of a stock consequent to the change in returns on the market. As we mentioned earlier, this linkage is measured by beta.

Thus, the required rate of return on a security is determined by three factors. These factors are

1. the risk-free rate (typically the return on government securities, since they carry no risk),
2. the risk premium on the market: the return over and above the risk-free rate that the investor requires to compensate him for the risk of investment in the overall stock market and
3. the beta of the stock or the relationship of the stock's returns with the returns on the market as a whole.

According to the CAPM, the required rate of return is determined in accordance with the following equation:

$$r = R_f + \beta\,(R_m - R_f)$$

where

r is the required rate of return on the security,

R_f is the return on the risk-free security,

beta (β) is the correlation between the security's return and market returns and

R_m is the return on the market. Hence ($R_m - R_f$) is the risk premium on the market.

The CAPM has wide applicability in finance.

1. The CAPM is used to determine the expected return on a stock, or any other security, given its risk. We have seen earlier how the required rate of return can be calculated using the CAPM equation. Illustration 5.3 demonstrates the relationship between expected return and risk through CAPM.

2. The CAPM can be used to price securities. The future cash flows are discounted by the CAPM-determined required rate of return to estimate the present value.

3. The CAPM can be used to evaluate as well as compare performance. Given the risk of the portfolio, the model can be used to estimate its required return. Actual return higher than the required rate shows outperformance. The excess of actual return over the required return given by it is termed alpha. Portfolio managers place a lot of emphasis on a positive alpha to demonstrate their superior investment performance.

4. Project betas and the required return based on the CAPM help in capital-budgeting decisions. While discussing capital-budgeting investment projects, we had evaluated projects on the basis of the cost of capital of the company. This holds only if the risk of the new projects is similar to the overall risk of the company. In case, as often happens, the project risk is different, we need to calculate beta for each of the project, termed *project beta*. Based on the CAPM, project beta can be used to find the required rate of return for each project to calculate their NPVs. The CAPM provides the link between risk and required rate of return of projects.

5. The CAPM also has wide applicability in portfolio formation. According to the model, the contribution of a security to the overall risk of a portfolio is given by its systematic risk. Therefore, unsystematic risk is irrelevant in a diversified portfolio. Thus, it is essential that the constructed portfolio is well-diversified to optimize the risk–return framework.

Illustration 5.3

The risk-free rate in India is currently 6.5 per cent. According to Grant Thornton, the risk premium on Indian stocks as a whole has been 7.4 per cent. Investment in Indian stock market should, therefore, provide a return of 13.9 per cent per annum.

An investor invests in a stock with a beta of 0.7. What return should he expect?

$$r = R_f + \beta (R_m - R_f).$$

$$r = 6.5 + 7.4 * 0.7$$

$$= 11.68\%.$$

An investor who invests in a stock with a beta of 0.7 is investing in a stock which is less risky than the market as a whole. His return will also be less than the market return.

An investor wants a return of 15.38 per cent on his investment. What kind of stock should he invest in?

$$r = R_f + \beta (R_m - R_f).$$
$$15.38 = 6.5 + 7.4 * \beta$$
$$\beta = 1.2.$$

The investor must look for a riskier stock to invest, that is, a stock riskier than the market as a whole. If the stock has a beta of 1.2, he can expect to obtain a return of 15.38 per cent.

Risk Management

Once risk has been identified, it must be managed. Risk cannot be eliminated from the society as a whole. What financial markets do is to offer ways to transfer and trade risks. Risk can be transferred from those who have no appetite for it or can least afford it to those who have the capability to bear and accept risk. Of course, such a transfer takes place at a price and pricing of risk is one of the most critical functions of financial markets. There are three broad methods of risk transfer as follows.

Insurance

Most of us have had some experience of insurance, whether it is our vehicle which we insure or life and medical insurances that we purchase. We pay an annual premium for the right to claim damages to the car or for a large payment to our surviving family in case of death. In a way, we exchange a large uncertain loss for a series of certain but small losses (the annual premiums).

A proper analysis is essential before deciding whether an individual requires insurance, the type of insurance needed and the quantum of such insurance. A married person with young children and a non-working spouse needs a large insurance, since the requirements of the children's education and other costs of raising them need to be protected. The individual's death can have a significant bearing on the family's funds inflow and, therefore, a large insurance is a must.

However, a single person with no dependents needs no insurance but must take a disability coverage. Similarly, if a family constitutes a couple with no kids, the working spouse must take out insurance but the non-working spouse need not.

Insurance can be taken for a variety of unusual risks. Sportsmen and actors insure physical parts of their bodies, their biggest asset and source of their earnings and wealth. Insurance can be taken against the cancellation of an event or a sports competition. Mortgage EMIs can be insured as can the loss of future income.

Like individuals, companies also need to insure against risk. They have valuable assets which are usually insured against disasters such as floods, fire and so forth. Companies must formulate a well-designed insurance policy to clearly specify which assets will be insured by outside insurance companies and which ones will be self-insured.

Self-Insurance

It has been the usual practice for the corporate sector to take insurance for possible loss of their assets. In the early 1990s, British Petroleum, a large oil-refining company, stunned the corporate world by declaring that it will self-insure many assets (bear the risk of those assets on its own), which it used to routinely insure in the past from insurance companies. What was also significant about this move was the fact that most of these assets were large ones.

The move towards self-insurance has received a boost in recent times. The car industry, for instance, is witnessing momentous changes. Manufacturing defects and consequent risks have routinely been covered by product liability insurance. Increasingly confident of their product, some car companies are choosing not to insure product defects and liability. Such trends portend significant changes, especially with the imminent onset of self-driven cars which the insurance industry needs to come to terms with. It is interesting that an industry that insures others against risk is itself now up against it!

Hedging

Hedging is an action that creates a position which offsets the existing position that exposes an investor/a company to risk. The outcome of the underlying position remains the same. A countervailing position is taken whereby, in case of a loss in the underlying position, there is a profit in the hedging position. Alternatively, a profit in the underlying position matches with a loss in the hedging position. Therefore, whatever changes take place in the underlying parameter, the net combined outcome is certain and known.

Let us take an example of the export of auto components by Motherson Sumi Limited. Assume that the company has sold auto components worth US$100 million for which the payment is due in five months' time. The risk for the company is that when it sells the US$100 million after five months, the INR/USD exchange rate may have changed. Hedging typically involves taking a position exactly the opposite of the original position. In this case, the company can hedge the same by selling US$100 million in the forward market for delivery five months hence. With this hedge, irrespective of the INR/USD rate after five months, the company will always be able to realize the amount yielded by the forward rate. Hedging will be explained in greater detail later in chapter 10 on derivatives.

Diversification

Diversification as a concept has already been explained earlier. Suffice it to say that investment in stocks which are uncorrelated with one another or have a low correlation, as means of diversification, can reduce risk substantially without reducing returns. It is amongst the oldest and the most effective tools of risk management known to us.

Strategic Corporate Risk

Apart from financial investors, the corporate sector is also confronted with risk in its business operations. With the liberalization of the Indian economy post 1991, all significant financial variables are market-determined, instead of being fixed by the government or the RBI, as in the past. Consequently, interest rates, foreign exchange rates and commodity prices vary on a constant basis, impacting profitability, cash flows and the value of companies. Many companies that were unable to manage the consequent risk have ceased to exist and have gone out of business. Strategic risk management has become a key aspect of corporate performance. Many companies now have chief risk officers charged with the prime responsibility of understanding, measuring and managing the risk of the company.

Strategic risks based on exchange rate can be classified into three categories as follows.

Transaction Risk

Transaction risk arises out of receivables and payables denominated in foreign currency. The illustration given before the discussion of Motherson Sumi's exposure to the dollar is an example of transaction risk. The risk arises due to a specific transaction, that of the export of auto components that Motherson Sumi has undertaken, and hence is termed transaction risk.

Similarly, a copper wire producer may need to import copper which he uses as raw material. Assume that he purchases copper worth GB£1 million payable in one month's time. Currently, the pound–rupee rate is 90, which means the purchase of copper costs him ₹90 million. However, that would change if the pound–rupee rate were to vary over the next one month. If the pound strengthens to ₹95, the company will have to pay ₹95 million. Alternatively, if pound were to weaken to ₹85, the cost to the company will decline to ₹85 million.

Risk of Education Abroad

Your son is planning to go to the USA for his undergraduate studies. He is currently in the 9th standard and you will need to fund him to the extent of US$100,000 after four years. As per the current exchange rate of ₹70 to US$1, the cost in terms of rupees is ₹7 million. However, a change in either the cost of education or the exchange rate would change the cost in rupees.

Exporters benefit if the domestic currency weakens, since the value of the foreign currency received by them is worth more in the domestic currency. Exporters want a weaker domestic currency. Importers gain when the domestic currency strengthens, since they need less in domestic currency to buy the foreign currency required for imports. Importers benefit from a stronger domestic currency.

Besides exports and imports, borrowing and lending in foreign exchange can also have a significant impact on companies. A company borrows US$100 million at a time when the USD/INR rate is 70. The borrowing is worth ₹7 billion and the annual interest at 5 per cent is 5,000,000 * 70 = ₹350,000,00. However, if the USD/INR rate changes to ₹80, the interest liability will rise to ₹400 million and the repayment of the loan will amount to ₹8 billion. Lending in foreign currency will be similarly impacted by changes in foreign exchange rates, except that lenders will gain when the domestic currency depreciates and lose when the domestic currency appreciates.

Standard derivative instruments exist, which companies can use to hedge transaction risks. A company's overall risk management strategy will decide whether to hedge such risk, how much to hedge and how to hedge.

Translation Risk

Translation risk arises from translating foreign currency denominated assets, liabilities, revenues and profits into a home currency. A company that has invested in a subsidiary abroad needs to convert the profits, assets and liabilities of the subsidiary into domestic currency when it transfers them on its own books.

Assume that the subsidiary has made a profit of US$10 million. At INR/USD rate of 70, the profits amount to ₹700 million. However, if the INR/USD rate is 60, the company makes a profit of only ₹600 million.

Translation risk has no impact either on the strategic business or on the cash flows of the company; it only affects the accounting books.

Economic or Strategic Risk

Economic or strategic risk is a result of the relative movement of exchange rates which may impact competitiveness. A variation in exchange rate alters the final price to the customer, thereby impacts the company's competitiveness, at times forcing the company out of business.

The Indian corporate sector had its first brush with foreign exchange risk when there was a significant rise in the value of the yen in the second-half of the 1980s. The first hesitant steps towards liberalization in the 1980s saw the automobile sector being opened up to foreign companies which were permitted to enter the Indian market through a joint venture with an Indian partner. Consequently, many companies were established including Hero Honda Limited, DCM Toyota Limited, TVS Suzuki Ltd and Swaraj Mazda Ltd, all of which were joint ventures between Indian and Japanese companies. These companies imported engines and kits from the foreign collaborator, payable in yen. They created a further exposure to yen by borrowing from the collaborating companies. When the yen appreciated in the latter-half of the 1980s, businesses floundered and the companies suffered heavy losses. DCM Toyota Limited, in fact, went out of business and others were virtually in a state of sickness until the 1990s brought them relief with the unexpected decline in the value of yen.

The variation in foreign currency rates can have a significant impact on the profitability of a company. Companies devote considerable time, effort and resources to manage the impact of changes in foreign currency rates, commodity prices and interest rates, depending on the extent of the exposure.

KEY CONCEPTS

1. The return on investment between two periods is compounded and annualized.
2. Annualized returns over a time period are estimated based on the geometric mean and not the arithmetic mean.
3. Risk refers to the possibility of more than one outcome of any action we take. The more varied the possible outcomes, the higher is the risk.
4. Investment theory is based on the assumption that investors are risk-averse.
5. There are primarily three ways to manage risk, namely insurance, hedging and diversification.
6. Corporate sector has a significant exposure to risk and must have a well-defined risk management policy to avoid dilution in value and even bankruptcy.
7. Transaction, translation and economic risks are the three strategic risks a company is exposed to.
8. Risk and return are directly related. To earn higher return, we must be prepared to bear higher risk.

CHAPTER QUESTIONS

1. Expecting high returns, you decide to invest in the stock market. The returns will depend on various scenarios that may play out, and the two most important parameters are the growth rate of the economy and the interest rates. The following possibilities exist.

Scenario	Expected return	Probability
High growth/high interest	15%	20%
High growth/low interest	30%	25%
Low growth/high interest	−10%	30%
Low growth/low interest	10%	25%

What is the expected return and risk of your investment?
2. Your investments can either double or become half over the next one year with equal probabilities. What is the expected return and risk?

3. You have invested in the stock markets four years back and realized the following returns.

Year 1	10%
Year 2	–10%
Year 3	20%
Year 4	5%

    What are your annualized returns?
4. Outline the nature of risks a company is exposed to these days. How do these risks impact the company?
5. Explain hedging as a technique of risk management.
6. Grant Thornton has estimated the equity risk premium in India to be approximately 7.4 per cent. How does this impact the valuation of companies in India?
7. Explain the difference between price risk, credit risk and operating risk.
8. An investor invests in the market expecting to obtain a return of 12 per cent annualized over a period of 15 years. His returns in the first four years are 10 per cent, –15 per cent, 5 per cent and 20 per cent. What are the returns over the first four years?
9. Continuing with question no. 8, the next four years' returns are –25 per cent, –8 per cent, 30 per cent and 40 per cent. What returns has the investor obtained over these four years? What returns has he obtained in the first eight years?
10. Continuing with the same question, what should be the annualized returns over the next seven years for him to obtain his targeted return of 12 per cent per annum?

CHAPTER 6

Valuation

What is a cynic? A man who knows the price of everything and the value of nothing.

—Oscar Wilde

The objective of a company is value maximization. Valuation is the theme that runs through the entire gamut of corporate finance; understanding valuation is critical in order to understand corporate finance.

1. Fund managers and equity analysts determine the value of companies in order to take decisions on buying and selling equity shares. Valuation is the basis of equity research and portfolio management.
2. Valuation guides M&A transactions. Acquisitions are undertaken at a certain price; without knowledge of the company's value, it becomes difficult to price mergers.
3. Investment bankers value companies to arrive at the right price for an initial public offering (IPO).
4. Venture capitalists need to value business proposals for them to undertake an investment.
5. The management needs to know the right value of their own company to decide on stock repurchases (shares buyback).
6. And, of course, managers must understand valuation and its principles to be able to maximize value for their ultimate owners, namely the shareholders.

Valuation is an elusive concept which no one has been able to master. It is not a precise science. The speed of travel can be measured to a precise number. Genetic characteristics remain the same irrespective of the scientist studying them. If one valence of magnesium is combined with two valences of chloride, the outcome will always be magnesium chloride. Value is, however, different for different people and even to the same person at different points in time. Vincent van Gogh produced over 800 paintings. In his entire lifetime, he was able to sell only one of them—for US$25. Some years back, one of those unsold paintings was auctioned for US$66 million! Absolute value is a myth.

Beauty lies in the eye of the beholder. Similarly, value depends on how much the buyer is willing and able to pay. The proof of value is when the investors loosen their purse to spend cash and buy the security. Investors need to back up with money what they say with their mouth.

Valuation is a science as well as an art. While it is based on well-defined scientific principles, the application of those principles is a skill that can be honed only through diligent experience.

Value versus Price

Value and price have a very interesting relationship. They also cause much confusion in the minds of people who, in general, fail to distinguish between the two. These are two very different concepts even if they should be equal in an efficient market. If the two are not equal, it is an indication to invest in, or to dispose of, the security.

Price is the amount of money at which a security is traded—bought and sold. If Infosys Ltd is priced at ₹1,100, an investor can pay ₹1,100 to buy one share of the company. Alternatively, the investor can sell one share of Infosys Ltd and realize ₹1,100 from the sale proceeds. Similarly, a Government of India bond maturing in 2022 and paying a coupon interest of 8 per cent per annum may be priced at ₹108.75. An investor can, if he so desires, either buy or sell the bond at the market price.

How does this price of ₹1,100 or ₹108.75 get determined? Investors place a value on the share of a company or the bonds issued by the Government of India. How the value is determined will be explained later in the chapter. If the value they arrive at is lower than the prevailing price, they will sell the share/bond. If on the other hand, the value they estimate is more than the price, they will invest in the share/bond, hoping that the price will come up to the level they have valued it at. Each investor arrives at a different value, based on his own estimate of various parameters and the relationship amongst those parameters. And each investor acts upon his own estimate of value to buy or sell the security.

If a trade takes place of the share of Infosys Ltd at ₹1,100, one investor purchases and another sells the Infosys share. The buyer has estimated a higher value, say ₹1,300, whereas the seller has estimated a lower value, say ₹1,000. Both are faced with the same price, but their respective estimate of value is different, which provides a basis for trading. This difference in valuation may have an impact on the price of Infosys shares which changes depending on the volume of purchases and sales. Eventually, the traded price will converge to the value that the entire market in its wisdom places on the share.

A large volume of trading takes places on the stock exchanges and other trading platforms. Currently, the daily equity trading volume in the Indian stock exchanges ranges between ₹3,000 billion and ₹7,000 billion! The average daily trading volume for a period of 12 months from April 2016 to March 2017 was over ₹4,000 billion, including equity derivatives. This is an ample demonstration of an active and vibrant market wherein investors seek to make profits by trading in those shares whose value and price do not match. Effectively, investors put their money where their mouth is. They do not just estimate value but spend cash to buy shares, or sell, in case the price is different from the value estimated by them.

It would be useful to take cognizance of the following relationship between value and price.

1. Value is not the same as price, although the two should be equal in an efficient market.

2. Price is observable, usually quoted on the exchanges; value must be estimated by each investor on his own.
3. Usually, price is the same for everyone, whereas value differs, based as it is on the investors' own estimation.
4. The difference in valuation of the same security by various investors is the basis for the large volumes of trading that takes place in financial markets.

Different Facets of Value

There are four broad facets of corporate value.

1. Book value: This refers to the value as per the books of accounts. In accounting terms, it equals the net worth, or assets minus liabilities. It represents the company's residual value assuming that assets can be sold for the value on the books and used to pay off the liabilities at the stated value. Whatever remains after the liabilities have been paid off is the net worth.

   Net worth of a company may change due to the following reasons:
   a. Retained profits (losses)
   b. Sale of new shares at a price higher/lower than the book value
   c. Sale of assets at a price different from its book value
2. Liquidation value: This refers to the value that can be realized if the company were to be liquidated and the assets sold.
3. Intrinsic value: This is the value of a company as a going concern. The company is a permanent entity and any cash flows that the company earns in the future is valuable. In this chapter, we will mainly discuss the intrinsic value of companies.
4. Market value: This is the value that the market places on the company, determined through the purchase and sale of equity by investors. Also termed market capitalization, it equals the market price multiplied by the number of shares.

   The market capitalization should, in an efficient market, be equal to the intrinsic value.

Valuation Methods

Various methods of valuation are practised depending on the type of the company and its environment, data availability and the analyst's preferences. These methods can be classified into two broad categories, namely the direct and the indirect or relative methods of valuation.

Direct methods calculate the fundamental value of the company directly from the company's cash flows, whereas indirect methods provide a relative value, benchmarked either to some parameter or compared to another similar company, usually in the same industry. The discounted cash flow (DCF) model is a direct method of valuation which is conceptually the soundest and the most widely used. We will spend considerable time understanding the DCF model now.

Discounted Cash Flow Valuation

The value of an asset is the PV of its expected cash flows, discounted at a risk-adjusted required rate of return.

Termed the discounted cash flow (DCF) analysis, the model is integral to the learning of a student pursuing an MBA, without which his/her knowledge of, and expertise in, the subject would be incomplete. The statement elucidates various concepts, each of which is critical.

1. Value is time-specific and will be different at different points in time. Usually when we calculate value, it is the PV or the value today. The value in the past was different and the value in the future too will vary. It is important to know at what point in time the value of the company is being estimated.
2. Value is calculated on the basis of the cash flows of the company and not accounting earnings.
3. Cash flows, being received in the future, are expected cash flows. Cash flows are estimated based on our understanding of the company's business, an assessment of the environment and various parameters influencing the business.
4. The cash flows are not known with certainty, and there is an element of risk involved. The risk of the cash flows receive due consideration.
5. Cash flows accrue in the future and must be discounted to obtain their PV.
6. The discounting must be done at an appropriate required rate of return. The required rate of return takes into account the risk of the investment in terms of the uncertainty of cash flows.

As indicated in the previous list, valuation is based on cash flows and not on accounting earnings. Invariably, there is a divergence between operating cash flows and profits. Three factors account for the difference.

1. Revenue is recognized at the time the sale takes place while cash comes in later in accordance with the terms of payment. Usually, money is receivable on sales after a period of time. If Apollo Tires Ltd sells tires to Maruti Suzuki Ltd, the sales consideration may be payable after two months. Sale is recorded and revenue is recognized at the time the tires are delivered. Cash may be received after two months as per the terms of the agreement.
2. Expenses are matched with revenues. The profit and loss (P&L) statement records revenues and expenses during the year. The actual payment for those expenses need not take place during that period. Some expenses may be paid in advance while others will be paid later. Cash flow records expenses at the time cash is paid, irrespective of the time the sale pertaining to those expenses occurred.

   Considering this example , Maruti incurs expenses in its books the moment the tires are purchased and delivered. The cash outflow will occur only after two months when the actual payment is made.
3. The P&L statement does not consider capital expenditure; it only takes into account the depreciation on capital goods for the period. Depreciation is a non-cash expense, cash having already been paid and accounted for when the capital goods were purchased.

Corporate Valuation

While undertaking valuation, we must not lose sight of what is being valued. Besides the company in its entirety, we can value debt, equity, a division, an asset or even a brand. The principles of valuation remain the same. Care needs to be taken that cash flows and the time period must correspond to the asset being valued and the required rate of return should be adjusted for the risk applicable to the asset.

When an investor buys an asset, he should be prepared to pay an amount equivalent to the PV of the expected cash flows from that asset. In the context of a company, the appropriate cash flows that need to be valued are 'the free cash flows'.

What Is Cash Flow?

Cash flow has multiple, at times, conflicting meanings. Let us discuss its meaning in its various contexts.

1. Net cash flow = Net profit + Non-cash items

    This has already been explained earlier. Non-cash items include depreciation, deferred taxes, amortization and so forth. Non-cash items are recognized as expenses and deducted from sales to arrive at net profits, but no cash is actually paid out against them in the current year. The actual cash outflow has already taken place earlier when the item, which is being amortized, or the asset being depreciated, was purchased. In some instances, the cash will need to be paid later, as it happens with deferred taxes.

2. While it is useful to calculate and understand the amount of cash being generated from business operations, net cash flow does not account for changes in the current assets and current liabilities. In order to understand whether the company is able to sustain the planned growth, the requirements of current assets and current liabilities must also be taken into consideration. Many companies, over the years, have been undone due to the huge investments the business has required in inventory and accounts receivables, which constrained their cash flows. Therefore, a more comprehensive definition would be

    Cash flow from operating activities = Net cash flow + Changes in current assets and liabilities.

3. Free cash flow refers to the total cash available for distribution to all owners and creditors/lenders after funding all activities worth pursuing. The principal means by which a company creates value for its owners is by increasing free cash flow.

    Free cash flows take into account the capital investments made by the company.

4. The final concept of cash flow is the DCF which refers to a sum of money today having the same value as a future stream of cash receipts and payments. Discounted cash flow techniques estimate the value of an asset that generates a future stream of cash flows.

Free Cash Flows

Free cash flows are cash flows generated by a company which it does not require. The company can carry on its normal business operations and invest in future projects without any need to access these funds. Free cash flows can be taken out of the business without impacting either its current operations, business plans or future investments.

Cash generated by a company from its operations is deployed to support its growth plans and is ploughed back into the business for capital expenditures. Free cash flow is cash flow from operating activities less capital expenditure after taking care of a few technicalities (explained later). These free cash flows are technically what is available to the investors and, therefore, the value of the company is determined by the value of free cash flows.

The business plans of the company usually envisage expansion in capacity, sales and revenues. The expansion in size needs continuous investments in long-term assets and working capital. Consider a cement company with a capacity of 10 million tons which is planning to substantially increase its revenues. It would possibly have to set up greenfield capacity or acquire another cement company. It may also have to extend its markets and customer base, necessitating further investments in marketing and distribution capabilities. Higher sales will need greater level of financing for debtors and inventory. Long-term capital investment and higher working capital need to be taken into consideration and accounted for.

Free cash flows can be positive or negative. In the initial stages, a company invests large amounts in building up capacities and in establishing its brand. The sales and profitability at this stage are low, leading at times, to negative cash flows. Despite the negative cash flows initially, such investments are critical to the organization's future growth and profitability.

Bharti Airtel invested a huge amount in establishing its telecom network and acquiring customers in the initial years of commencing business. Consequently, at the time of its IPO in 2003, the company had large negative free cash flows. Nonetheless, the company was highly valued by the investing community as the telecom license, operating infrastructure and a large customer base ensured consistent and assured cash flows in the coming years. Similarly, direct-to-home (DTH) companies such as DishTV currently have a negative cash flow since they are investing in establishing their operations and acquiring customers. The wide customer base assures them regular cash flows in the years to come. The critical issue is to determine whether the negative cash flows are due to investments in business, marketing, distribution, technology and customer acquisition or these have arisen due to a poor business environment.

Free cash flows reflect the cash flows generated by a company's operations that is available to both debt providers and equity shareholders. Therefore, it must include all cash flows that debt providers as well as equity shareholders are entitled to get.

Alternatively, we can consider the company as entirely equity-financed and then calculate the free cash flows. Any adjustment thereafter is only an allocation between equity holders and debt providers.

Following are the components of free cash flows:

1. Net operating profits after tax (NOPAT)
2. Depreciation and other non-cash expenses
3. Investments in long-term assets
4. Change in working capital

While NOPAT and depreciation are added, investments and change in working capital must be subtracted to arrive at free cash flows (FCF).

Let us understand each of these.

1. The first component of free cash flow is net operating profit after tax or NOPAT which equals

$$EBIT * (1 - \text{tax rate}).$$

Where EBIT is earnings before interest and taxes.

Profits refer to the excess of revenues over expenses. However, it is not the net profits but operating profits that form a part of the free cash flows. While net profit belongs to the equity shareholders, lenders are entitled to interest payment. Therefore, the critical figure is the net operating profit (inclusive of both the net profit and interest payments).

Net operating profit comprises the following:

a. Net profit
b. Corporate tax paid to the government
c. Interest expense
d. Tax saving on account of interest payment, interest being a tax-deductible expense

Net profit belongs to the shareholders while interest accrues to the debt providers. Clearly, both form a part of the free cash flows. Tax paid does not accrue to either the equity shareholders or the lenders. It is paid to the government and must, therefore, be excluded from the calculations of free cash flows.

The final component of operating profits, namely the tax benefit of interest expense presents an interesting conundrum. The payment of interest reduces tax liability and is beneficial to capital providers. This benefit must be recognized. The conundrum is where and how to recognize the benefit of the reduced tax liability. It can be incorporated in the free cash flows (and free cash flows would increase by the amount of tax savings due to the interest expense) or it can be a part of the cost of capital (cost of capital would reduce due to a lower post-tax cost of debt).

The usual practice is to account for it in estimating the cost of capital wherein the cost of debt is taken on a post-tax basis. Incorporating the tax benefit of interest in the cost of capital rather than in free cash flows is conceptually superior. Operating cash flows and financing cash flows are kept separate. (Interest expense is a financing cash flow. Interest is the cost of borrowing that finances an investment. If a company does not borrow, there will be no interest expense.)

Hence, the tax benefits of interest should not be taken into account and NOPAT should be calculated assuming the tax liability that would have accrued from earnings without deducting interest expense.

In a nutshell, the first item in free cash flows comprises operating profits before deducting interest expenses, and of course after reducing them by the taxes payable on operating profits, or the NOPAT. Technically, this would be

$$EBIT * (1 - \text{tax rate}).$$

Assume the following figures for a company, ABC Ltd.

Operating profits = 10,000.

Debt = 30,000 at 10%.

Interest = 3,000.

Profit before tax = 7,000.

Tax (40%) = 2,800.

Profit after tax = 4,200.

Tax saving on interest = 3,000 * 40% = 1,200.

Without the expense of ₹3,000 as interest, the tax would have been higher by ₹1,200 at ₹4,000 (instead of ₹2,800).

$$NOPAT = 10,000 * (1 - 40\%) = 6,000.$$

The balance comprises tax actually paid (₹2,800) plus the savings on tax (₹1,200) due to the interest paid being an expense.

The benefit of tax savings would be accounted for in the calculation of the cost of capital. The post-tax debt cost would be 10% * (1 – 40%) = 6%, compared to the pre-tax debt cost of 10 per cent.

2. Depreciation is a non-cash expense. While it is deducted from sales revenue in order to arrive at NOPAT, there is no actual cash outflow on account of depreciation. It must be added back to the NOPAT to derive free cash flow.

   Depreciation is not the only non-cash expense for a company, although it is the most common, being a part of practically every P&L account. Other non-cash expenses include preliminary expenses and amortization expenses. All non-cash expenses should be added back to NOPAT to derive free cash flows.

3. Enhanced sales and subsequent cash flows are possible only with higher capacities. The future profits and cash flow from operations are based on continuous investments in tangible and intangible assets to generate capacity for the higher level of sales. Without investments in assets, sales revenue and the resultant profits cannot increase and the company will stop growing. Capital investment is a cash outflow and appears as a negative figure. The cash flow generated from operations needs to be reduced by the requirement of capital investment to derive free cash flow.

   At times, a company may decide to dispose of some of its capital assets. This may be due to a change in strategy that requires exiting from a product line, poor returns on investment prompting disposal, cash flow problems leading to forced asset sale or an acquirer offering a very attractive price. Whatever be the reason, sale of assets or divestment generate positive cash flow and can become a source of significant value addition.

   In 2004, L&T Ltd exited the cement business and generated substantial cash flows by selling its cement division to the Kumar Mangalam Birla Group. Many Indian companies which are in financial trouble, having invested in huge capacities mainly through borrowings, have been selling off large chunks of asset to generate cash (negative capital investment).

4. Besides capital investments, increased sales must be supported by higher working capital. For instance, the increased sales of motorcycles by Bajaj Auto Ltd will require higher credit to dealers, higher stocking of components and maintenance of larger inventory of

motorcycles. An increase in working capital results in cash outflow, and the cash flows from operations must be reduced to that extent.

On the other hand, a reduction in working capital generates positive cash flow. A reduction in working capital may be a result of lower sales; new sources of raw material with favourable terms; different operating processes such as enterprise resource planning (ERP) implementation, lower credit period or simply due to greater efficiency. All these factors have the potential, by reducing working capital requirements, to release tied up capital and augment cash flows.

Working Capital Generating Cash Flows

The global aluminum company Alcoa made working capital a priority in 2009 in response to the financial crisis and the global economic downturn, and it recently celebrated its 17th straight quarter of year-on-year reduction in net working capital. Over that time, the company has reduced its net working capital cycle—the amount of time it takes to turn assets and liabilities into cash—by 23 days and unlocked $1.4 billion in cash (Davies and Merin, 2014).

Companies with established brands and sustained demand can reduce the period of credit to their dealers and squeeze better terms from their suppliers to optimize working capital funding. When operating cash flows are at a premium, working capital management offers an attractive way to boost cash flows.

It is not the level of working capital but the change in working capital that forms a part of cash flows. The firm needs to calculate annual free cash flows and, therefore, must consider changes in working capital requirements from one year to the next.

Free cash flow therefore equals

$$\text{NOPAT} + \text{Depreciation and other non-cash expenses} - \text{Capital investment} - \text{Increase in working capital.}$$

Typically, we consider the income statement to assess the performance of the company and determine the cash flow generation. However, without taking into account changes in the balance sheet, the picture would be incomplete. If higher profitability and operating cash flows are a result of unduly high levels of capital investment and working capital, it may not be in the interest of the company and may, in fact, deplete its value. Subhiksha Ltd, was a highly profitable retail chain growing at a rapid pace in the mid-2000s. Buoyed by substantial profitability, it drew up plans to grow at what turned out to be an unsustainable pace. Sales and profits increased but had to be supported by huge investments in stores and inventory. Eventually, the company ran out of cash and became bankrupt. Accounting profits are fine but companies need cash to pay their vendors and meet expenses. As they say, profits are an opinion, cash is a fact. Cash is the lifeblood of an organization, and the value of a company is derived from the cash flows it is able to generate. We need to look at overall cash flows generation by the company and the changes in the balance sheet are as critical as the P&L statement.

Competitive Advantage Period and Residual Period

As is evident, estimating the values of the four components of free cash flow presents quite a challenge. The investor is trying to forecast values that are uncertain and require detailed knowledge of the company's business, its future plans, the environment in which it operates and its competitive position, amongst other things. And to estimate free cash flows far into the future is virtually impossible.

It is a common practice to divide the future into the forecast (or the horizon) period and the residual period. The horizon period is the period for which each component of the free cash flows is derived in detail. After the horizon period, it is assumed that the free cash flow remains constant or grows at a constant annual rate forever. Adding the PV of cash flows in the horizon period to that of the PV of the cash flows in the residual period yields the value of the company.

In order to create value, a company must have some competitive advantage that helps generate the value. The competitive advantage may be due to its brands, patents, superior technology, branch network, marketing strengths or lower costs. A competitive advantage helps the company generate a return which is higher than its cost of capital. The period over which the company has a competitive advantage and is able to generate a return on investment greater than the cost of capital is termed the competitive advantage period (CAP). This is the period over which the DCF model forecasts cash flows and, therefore, becomes the horizon period.

The competitive advantage is never permanent. In a free market, with free entry and exit, competitive forces tend to undo such an advantage. To ensure that the competitive advantage remains with the company, constant investment in resources is required. One of the most important ways to create value is to lengthen the CAP. Usually, the longer the CAP, the higher the valuation. However, at any given point in time, the CAP is fixed and for our valuation purpose becomes the horizon period for estimation of free cash flows. For instance, pharmaceutical companies such as Novartis and Sanofi invest considerable amount in research and development (R&D) in order to discover new drugs and obtain patents for those drugs to establish a competitive advantage in the market. These companies enjoy a long CAP.

The market recognizes the longevity of a company's CAP by giving its equity a higher price earnings (P/E) ratio and, therefore, a higher price. Companies such as Google and Hindustan Unilever Ltd (HUL) have a high value because the market recognizes their extended CAP. Google has a dominant market share in the web search business and it would be difficult for anyone to break its dominance. Hindustan Unilever Limited's dominant brands and a widespread distribution network provide it a distinct advantage over its competitors, and its superior cash flow generation is assured for a long period.

The period after the CAP is the residual period. Since the company does not have a competitive advantage during the residual period, the return on investment is equal to the cost of capital. The residual period cash flows can be valued as a perpetuity—the same cash flow every period continuing forever.

However, this does not mean that the company does not undertake any further investments and will not grow. It assumes that any further investment undertaken will return only the cost of capital, and hence there will be no change in value from such investments. If the company undertakes any investment, the growth rate will be positive and the denominator will reduce, but so will the numerator since a part of the operating cash flows will be invested back and not distributed to the shareholders. The net impact is that the value of the company remains unchanged over this period.

Free cash flows for the horizon period as well as the residual period are discounted at the required rate of return, comprising returns for time, inflation and risk, to obtain the PV of the company. Let us understand DCF valuation with Illustration 6.1.

Illustration 6.1

Current date is 1 January 2017.

1. Revenues in 2016 (calendar year) = ₹10,000.
2. Costs in 2016 = 75% of revenues.
3. Depreciation in 2016 = 5% of revenues.
4. Capital expenditure in 2016 = ₹500.

During the horizon period,

1. revenues increase at 7 per cent per annum,
2. costs increase at 5 per cent per annum,
3. depreciation increases at 5 per cent per annum,
4. corporation tax is 30 per cent,
5. change in working capital is 50 per cent of the change in sales
6. cost of capital or risk-adjusted required rate of return is 10 per cent,
7. forecast period is five years,
8. free cash flows are constant during the residual period.

Find FCF of the company and the value per share are as in Table 6.1.

TABLE 6.1 Free cash flow calculation (in ₹)

	2016	2017	2018	2019	2020	2021	2022
Revenues	10,000	10,700	11,449	12,250	13,108	14,026	
Costs	7,500	7,875	8,269	8,682	9,116	9,572	
EBIDT	2,500	2,825	3,180	3,568	3,992	4,453	
Depn	500	525	551	579	608	638	
EBIT	2,000	2,300	2,629	2,989	3,384	3,815	
EBIT (1 – t)	1,400	1,610	1,840	2,093	2,369	2,671	
Capex	500	525	551	579	608	638	
Change in NWC		350	375	401	429	459	
FCF to firm		1,260	1,466	1,692	1,940	2,212	2,212
PV horizon	6,326						
PV terminal	13,734					22,120	
Total value	20,061						
No. of shares	100						
Value per share	200.61						

Source: Author.

Table 6.2 Change in value due to change in assumptions

Parameters	New assumption	Changed value (₹)	Percentage change
Cost of capital	12%	16,445	(18%)
Increase in revenues	8%	23,084	15%
Initial costs	80%	15,762	(21.50%)
Corporate tax	40%	16,573	(17.39%)

Sensitivity Analysis

The value of the company has been derived on the basis of assumptions about various parameters that impact the company's business and its value. Any departure from the assumptions leads to a change in value. The impact of some of these parameters may be trivial while others have a more significant bearing on the value of a company. The estimated value of a company is not cast in stone but is sensitive to how the assumptions turn out. Any valuation exercise must be accompanied by the resultant impact of the variation in the parameters on valuation. This will reveal the sensitivity of the value to changes in different parameters.

Let us see how the value of the company shifts with changes in the various assumptions in Illustration 6.1 (Table 6.2). We change one assumption only, keeping all others constant.

In order to gain an understanding of the risks embedded in valuation, it is important to look at the values obtained on account of variations in different parameters. Given the probability of changes in these parameters, we can assess the risks in valuation. Sensitivity analysis is an integral part of the valuation process without which risks embedded in the valuation process will not be known and the value derived will seem to have a finality that does not exist in reality. Sensitivity analysis reveals the extent of change in value that is likely and the probability of such a change taking place. Managers can then decide whether possible changes in values, with the given probabilities, are acceptable or not and they are able to improve their decision-making.

Sensitivity in Valuation

The value of a company with an FCF of ₹5,000 next year which grow indefinitely at 7 per cent per annum and an applicable discount rate of 15 per cent can be calculated as follows.

$$5,000/(15\% - 7\%) = 62,500.$$

If the assumption of discount rate and the growth rate were wrong and each could vary by even 1 per cent, the range of possible values would be significantly large.

The value at 14 per cent cost of capital and 8 per cent growth rate is

$$5,000/(14\% - 8\%) = 83,333.$$

Contd

contd

On the other hand, at a discount rate of 16 per cent and a growth rate of 6 per cent, the value is

$$5,000/(16\% - 6\%) = 50,000.$$

If any student has dreams of becoming a fund manager or an investment banker, an estimated value with a range as wide as ₹50,000 to ₹83,333 is unlikely to lead to a lucrative career!

Risk of Abuse

Conceptually sound and extensively used, the DCF model is also widely misused and abused. The results obtained by using the DCF model are very sensitive to the assumptions upon which the model is based. In fact, the user can obtain any value he desires by simply altering a few of those assumptions. Anyone who has worked on Excel and undertaken a what-if analysis knows how this can be done. Assumptions have to be, therefore, carefully thought through, based not on the desired values but on the competitive position of the company, the market structure, the environment and the future that is likely to unfold. For instance, increase in revenues at 7 per cent must be justified on the basis of the key business drivers. What are the likely future growth scenario and the disposable income, where the interest rates are headed as well as oil prices, the future exchange rates, the corporate tax rates and a host of other factors that drive the business and its valuation?

As we have discussed in the previous paragraph, the analyst can derive completely different values with only minor changes in assumptions. A slight tweaking of growth rates or margins and the resultant value could see significant variation. It is possible to obtain virtually any resultant value by changing appropriate assumptions. In practice, many analysts and experts actually plug in the desired number and then make assumptions which will generate that value. For example, in Illustration 6.1, the analyst can easily reduce value by 21 per cent by simply increasing the cost to 80 per cent. This is often done to please the client and bag an assignment. Such instances of abuse are very common in the corporate world and need to be guarded against.

It must be ensured that the assumptions are realistic and based on a genuine understanding of the business, industry, environment and future prospects. Any randomness or arbitrariness will result in a misleading outcome.

The integrity of the analyst is critical. What is required is a thorough knowledge of the business of the company and the market and considerable experience in DCF analysis. As I have mentioned in the beginning of the chapter, valuation is an art which is based on scientific principles. While scientific principles can be easily learned, the application of those principles is an art that can only be honed through practice over a long period of time. The sooner the students start, the better it is.

Another fact that must be borne in mind is that a significant proportion of the total value is contributed by the residual period for which detailed calculations are not undertaken. For

Impact of Long-Term Cash Flows

Some analysts believe, erroneously, as I will show presently, that longer term cash flows should be ignored since these do not contribute significantly to the ultimate value. Assume a company with a cash flow of ₹5,000 growing perpetually at 7 per cent and discounted at 15 per cent.

Value of the cash flows = 5,000/(15% – 7%) = ₹62,500.

Let us consider cash flows only for the first 20 years and ignore subsequent cash flows. These cash flows are like a growing annuity and can be valued as a growing annuity.

The formula for PV of growing annuity is

$$\text{Present value} = \frac{P}{1-g}\left[1-\left(\frac{1+g}{1+r}\right)^n\right].$$

$$\text{Present value} = 5,000/(15\% - 7\%) * \{1 - [(1 + 7\%)/(1 + 15\%)]^{20}\}$$

$$= ₹47,723.$$

Which is a fairly significant 24 per cent reduction in value.

Let us now repeat the exercise for 10 years and ignore all cash flows after 10 years: Value = ₹32,109.

There is an even more drastic 49 per cent drop in value.

It is quite evident that substantial value is created by cash flows deep into the future.

instance, the value of the terminal cash flows is more than twice that of the value of cash flows during the horizon period. This is typical of valuations as per the DCF model. The valuation exercise can only be as good as the validity of its assumptions.

Relative Measures of Valuation

Indirect or relative valuation methods provide a value benchmarked either to some parameter or compared to another similar company, usually in the same industry.

Relative methods of valuation do not derive value directly from a company's cash flows. Instead, they consider a specific parameter and multiply it by an appropriate factor to obtain the value of the share. A higher multiple is based on the assumption of a higher growth in the future, whereas a lower multiple indicates that the future prospects are not considered to be rosy.

The most commonly used relative measure of valuation is the price earnings multiple, popularly called the P/E ratio. To obtain the price of the share, earnings per share (EPS) is multiplied by the P/E ratio. The net profit of the company divided by the number of shares equals EPS.

Assume that a company, HSPE Ltd, has a net profit of ₹100 million with an equity base of 50 million shares. Hence, its EPS is 100/50 = ₹2. If the P/E ratio applicable to HSPE Ltd is 15, the share will be priced at ₹30.

If there is another company, LSPE Ltd, which has the same EPS but poorer growth prospects, it may receive a multiple of only 10 and hence be priced at only ₹20.

There are many other relative measures that investors use such as those based on earnings before interest, tax, depreciation and amortization (EBITDA), cash flow, book value and sales.

Valuation for Acquisition

In 2015, Emami Ltd acquired the Kesh King brand for ₹16.51 billion. The brand's turnover at the time of the sale was only ₹3 billion. The brand was thus valued at 5.5 times its actual turnover. The Kesh King portfolio consists of hair oil, shampoo and an Ayurvedic capsule. The hair oil category contributed 80 per cent to its total sales.

Many acquisition transactions are analysed and undertaken in terms of multiples of EBITDA. Cement companies are valued and acquired as a multiple of capacity to produce. A telecom company's valuation may be based on the number of subscribers. It will receive a value which will be a multiple of the number of subscribers. Companies in the fast-moving consumer goods (FMCG) industry are often valued as a multiple of sales. In 'Valuation for Acquisition', the Kesh King brand is valued at a sales multiple of 5.5. With sales of ₹3 billion, the brand was purchased at ₹16.51 billion. Flipkart was recently acquired by Walmart at 4.5 times its sales.

These are all shortcuts, in a sense rough and ready measures, which save analysts from undertaking the arduous task of valuation through the DCF method. The conceptual basis for relative measures remains the DCF method from which these are derived.

Flow to Equity Method

We have calculated the value of equity by deducting the value of debt from the overall value of the company. Alternatively, we can compute the equity value directly by what is termed the flow to equity method.

The flow to equity method requires estimating cash flows accruing only to equity shareholders. This is equal to the cash flows accruing to the company, less interest and taxes, which are then discounted by the required rate of return on equity to directly obtain the value of equity.

The required return on equity depends on business risk as well as financial risk. Financial risk, of course, is determined by the extent of the borrowings or the debt–equity ratio. Hence, the correct value of equity can be determined by this method only if the debt–equity ratio remains constant; if a significant change in the ratio is expected in the future, the flow to equity method becomes unsuitable.

Practice

The most commonly used methods in practice are the DCF and the P/E ratio. Most analysts use cash flows to value companies, supplemented often by relative valuation analysis. Some methods are sector specific. For instance, price to book value is commonly used to value financial institutions.

As emphasized earlier, valuation is both a science and an art. As students gain experience, they will learn how to apply principles of valuation in practice and be able to decide on the method to be used, given the circumstances and the purpose of valuation.

Firm's Balance Sheet

The balance sheet of a firm, broadly defined, should satisfy the following equation in value terms.

Debt + Equity = Assets (Long-term assets + Working capital).

Thus, if we are able to estimate the enterprise value and subtract from it the value of debt, we will arrive at the value of equity. While it is the assets that provide value to the firm, it is critical to understand how debt and equity on the liability side are valued. Let us start with the valuation of debt and the principles underlying it.

Valuation of Debt

When governments/companies want to raise funds through debt, they issue bonds to the investors. A typical bond pays a periodic coupon interest and has a predetermined maturity period and maturity value. In the past, bonds came attached with a coupon for each period, which the investor had to detach and return to the company in order to get the annual interest. The annual interest payment continues to be termed the coupon interest.

Bonds can be defined completely by their face value/maturity value, coupon rate of interest and the period of maturity. These three parameters determine the cash flows payable by the company to the investor. The investor can then value the bond by finding the PV of the cash flows:

$$V = C_1/(1 + r) + C_2/(1 + r)^2 + C_3/(1 + r)^3 + \ldots + (C_n + M)/(1 + r)^n$$

Where $C_1 \ldots C_n$ are the coupon payments, M is the maturity value, r is the discount rate and V is the value of the bond.

The Government of India issues a nine-year bond with a coupon rate of 10 per cent. If the bond has a face value and a maturity value of ₹100, the cash flows of the bond are as follows:

C_0	C_1	C_2	C_3	...	C_9
	10	10	10		10
					100

The cash flows can be divided into two parts. First are the level coupons of ₹10, providing an annuity of ₹10 for nine years. Second is a single cash flow of ₹100 at C_9 (the maturity proceeds). Adding the value of both the cash flows provides the value of the bond.

It is important to remember that once the bonds have been issued, the coupons, the maturity period and the maturity value remain constant irrespective of the changes in market conditions. Hence, the cash flows available on the bond do not change. Consequently, a change in the required rate of return is possible only by a change in the market price at which the bonds are traded.

Assume that immediately after the bond was issued, there is a general rise in interest rates in the Indian economy. The required rate of return rises and investors now need 12 per cent as the return on their investment. Hence, the cash flows on the bond need to be discounted at 12 per cent. PVIF stands for present value interest factor.

At 12% discount rate, the value of the bond = $10 * \text{PVIFA}_{12\%,9} + 100 * \text{PVIF}_{12\%,9}$
$$= 10 * 5.328 + 100 * 0.361$$
$$= 89.38.$$

Thus, the price of the bond will go down to ₹89.38, and it will be traded at that price in the secondary market. At ₹89.38, the bond now provides a return of 12 per cent to the investors as required by them. The bond is priced at a discount to its face value.

If, on the other hand, the interest rates in the Indian economy drop significantly so that investors now require a return of only 8 per cent, the cash flows on the bond will be discounted at 8 per cent.

At 8% discount rate, the value of the bond can be determined as
$$= 10 * \text{PVIFA}_{8\%,9} + 100 * \text{PVIF}_{8\%,9}$$
$$= 10 * 6.247 + 100 * 0.5$$
$$= 112.47.$$

The price of the bond will rise to ₹112.47, and it will be traded in the secondary market at that price, providing the investors a return of 8 per cent as required by them. The bond is priced at a premium to its face value.

The return on the calculated bond is technically termed the yield to maturity (YTM). It is the rate that equates the PV of the cash flows available on a bond to its current market price. This is the basis of pricing bonds in the debt markets.

You may have observed that when the interest rates increased, the price of the bond came down. On the other hand, when the interest rate dropped, the price of the bond went up. The inverse relationship between interest rates and bond prices is one of the most fundamental theorems of finance.

This theorem is the basis for the interest rate risk underlying debt securities. A mutual fund has a portfolio of bonds valued at ₹1 billion, currently yielding 8 per cent. If the interest rates in the economy go up for any reason, the value of the securities held by the mutual fund will go down. Debt fund managers spend sleepless nights worrying about the impact of interest rate risk on their portfolio.

The large one-time change in interest rate has been assumed mainly to illustrate the impact on bond prices. In reality, the interest rate does not vary by such a sizable percentage. The changes are minor, almost on a continuous basis, and only when something significant takes place such as sudden and unexpected tightening by the central bank, the collapse of a large financial institution or an event such as the 9/11 attack on the World Trade Centre at New York that interest rate changes by more than a few basis points.

Bond Pricing in Practice

Assume that IN0020170026 is a 10-year bond expiring on 15 May 2027. It pays an annual coupon of 6.79 per cent, the coupon being payable twice a year. On 1 August 2017, the bond was priced at a yield of 6.45 per cent. At that yield, the price is ₹102.45. As per the market lingo, the bond is priced at 6.45 per cent.

As can be observed, the fall in the required rate of return raised the price of the bond in accordance with the fundamental theorem of inverse relationship between interest rate and price.

We discovered the new price of a bond consequent to a change in the required rate of return. We can invert the process by finding out the YTM if we know the price of the bond. Thus, if the price of the bond is ₹89.34, based on the cash flows of the bond, we can work out the return at 12 per cent. Thus, just as we can work out the bond price, given the YTM; we can estimate the YTM if we know the price at which a bond is trading.

To recap, once a bond has been issued, the cash flows are known and fixed. The only two variables that can vary are the price and the yield. If the price is known, the yield can be estimated. Conversely, if the yield is known, the price can be worked out. Market participants often do not quote a price but the YTM on a bond. Bond dealers are often heard saying that a specific bond is priced at, say, 7.57 per cent. The yield automatically provides the price of the bond.

Figure 6.1 is a record of the yields on Government of India bonds over the last 20 years. The yield has varied from a high of 14.76 per cent in April 1996 to a low of 4.96 per cent in October 2003. During this period of seven and a half years, the banks enjoyed large profits from their holdings of government securities as a consequence of reduction in interest rates, enabling them to present a rosy picture of the banks' performance. Subsequently, with the increase in interest rates, the banks made a loss on securities, which of course they attributed to market inefficiency and poor luck!

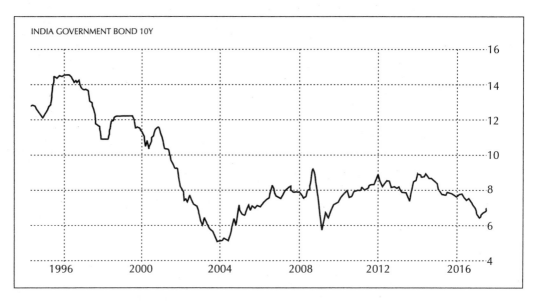

INDIA GOVERNMENT BOND 10Y

FIGURE 6.1   Government of India historical bond yields

Source: https://tradingeconomics.com/india/government-bond-yield. Accessed 28 January 2020.

Debt Holdings and Bank Profitability

Banks in India invest a substantial proportion of their funds in government securities. They are required by regulation to park a certain proportion of their deposits, called statutory liquidity ratio (SLR), in what are termed 'approved securities'. The requirement of SLR in March 2017 was 19.5 per cent of net demand and term liabilities (NDTL). Deposits taken by banks, primarily current and savings account and fixed deposits, comprise NDTL. With NDTL at approximately ₹120 trillion at the end of financial year 2017, the SLR requirement was ₹24 trillion. In reality, the banks held even more than the amount required under SLR, amounting approximately to ₹28.63 trillion.

The huge holdings of government debt in their portfolio is subject to significant change in valuation due to change in the market interest rate. The extent of variation in the value of a debt instrument consequent to a change in interest rate depends on the 'Duration' of the bonds. Bonds held by banks, usually being long-term, show significant variation in values which has a bearing on the profitability of the banking system. However, the RBI has permitted banks to carry their SLR portfolio at book value without subjecting them to market prices.

Zero-Coupon Bonds

The kind of bond discussed in the previous paragraph is termed a level-coupon bond, since it provides a constant coupon interest till its maturity. Issuers sometimes resort to what is termed a zero-coupon bond, which, as the name suggests, does not pay any interest. It only makes a bullet redemption payment on maturity which is usually equal to the face value of the bond. Thus, the cash flow on the bond can be represented as follows:

$$C_0 \qquad\qquad C_1 \qquad\qquad C_2 \qquad\qquad C_n$$
$$M$$

The question one may legitimately ask is why would anyone invest in a bond that does not offer any coupon interest? In financial markets, every security has a value, depending on the cash flows generated. Whether there is a single cash flow or more than one cash flow is immaterial. What needs to be done is to estimate the value of the cash flows. The zero-coupon bond will not be sold at its face value but at a price which discounts the redemption cash flow to the present. The bond will be sold at the present value of the single cash flow.

The Government of India issues a zero-coupon bond maturing in 10 years at ₹100. The cash flows of this bond are as follows:

$$C_0 \qquad\qquad C_1 \qquad\qquad C_2 \quad \dots \quad C_{10}$$
$$100$$

If the required rate of return on this bond is 12 per cent, the bond will be valued at

$$100/(1 + 12\%)^{10} = 100/3.1058 = 32.1973.$$

The issuer receives ₹32.1973 per bond on its issuance and will redeem the same at ₹100 after 10 years. In the interim period, there will be no cash flows.

As in the case of the level-coupon bond, the zero-coupon bond will be traded at its value. If after the issuance of the bond the interest rate goes up to 14 per cent, the bond's price in the secondary market will drop to

$$100/(1 + 14\%)^{10} = 3.7072$$
$$100/3.7072 = 26.9743.$$

If on the other hand, the required rate of return drops to 10 per cent, the price of the zero-coupon bond will rise to

$$100/(1 + 10\%)^{10} = 2.5937$$
$$100/2.5937 = 38.5543.$$

As we had observed earlier, interest rates and bond prices are inversely related. Zero-coupon bonds are also called pure-discount bonds since they will always be priced at a discount to their face value or the maturity value.

Interest Rate and Valuation of Bonds

Let us assume that an investor purchases a zero-coupon bond, as given in the earlier example, for ₹32.1973 at a YTM of 12 per cent. After one year, the bond will be priced at

$$100/(1 + 12\%)^9 = 36.0610.$$

The value of the bond over the one year has gone up by 12 per cent which was the investor's original YTM. The price will keep rising every year by 12 per cent to reach ₹100 at the end of the 10th year.

Interest rates do not stay constant and change almost on a continuous basis. If the interest rate falls to 11 per cent, the price changes to

$$100/(1 + 11\%)^9 = 39.0925.$$

The investor earns a return of 21.42 per cent, partly due to his holding the security for one year and partly due to the reduced interest rate leading to a higher price.

In case the interest rate increases to 13 per cent, the price drops to

$$100/(1 + 13\%)^9 = 33.2885,$$

and the return over one year is a mere 3.38 per cent. Changes in interest rates have a significant impact on the return realized by investors.

Perpetual Bond

A perpetual bond, as the name suggests, is a bond that never matures. The initial face value of the bond is never returned, and the bond is alive forever. It gives an annual coupon interest that is constant and will be paid forever. In Chapter 3, we learnt how to value perpetuities. The cash flow of the perpetual bond is like a perpetuity and can be depicted as follows:

$$C_0 \qquad C_1 \qquad C_2 \qquad C_3 \ldots$$
$$c \qquad\quad c \qquad\quad c \ldots$$

And the value of these cash flows is c/r.

Valuation of Equity

Equity shares can be valued using either the DCF model or the dividend discount model (DDM). While the DCF model takes into account the free cash flows, the DDM considers the dividends that are paid to equity shareholders. A company, as a going concern, is a perpetual entity and unless the company buys its shares back, equity is a permanent security. All that the shareholders get from the company are dividends.

Let us explore this further. When a company makes a profit, it has two options—pay out a part or all of it to the shareholders or retain and invest in projects. A higher dividend payout increases the current income of the shareholders, while retention increases the future profitability of the company, leading to higher dividends in the future. As long as the company is careful to invest in positive net present value (NPV) projects, the PV of the future dividends would be higher than the current dividends foregone. If the entire profit is not paid out as dividends, and a part of it is retained by the company for investment in projects, the company experiences growth and future dividends increase. The fact, however, remains that the shareholders will continue to get their returns by way of dividends, either current or future.

Thus, as per the DDM, the value of the dividends receivable by shareholders will provide the value of equity. A generic method to compute the value of equity with the DDM states that

$$V = \sum_{t=1}^{\infty} \frac{D_t}{(1+r)^t}.$$

We estimate the dividend each year, calculate their PVs and add them to get the value of equity shares. The question that arises is why would anyone be concerned with dividends that accrue in some distant time period.

Let us assume that an investor invests in the equity of a company for one year. The cash flows available to him are the dividends in the first year and the price at the end of the first year when he plans to dispose of his shares.

$$P_0 = (D_1 + P_1)/(1+r).$$

Similar to the current pricing of the share, the price at the end of the first year would be the discounted value of the second-year dividend plus the second-year price.

Therefore,

$$P_1 = (D_2 + P_2)/(1+r)^2.$$

And

$$P_0 = D_1/(1+r) + (D_2 + P_2)/(1+r)^2.$$

A repeat of this chain of substitutions would yield the generic DDM wherein

$$P_0 = D_1/(1+r) + D_2/(1+r)^2 + D_3/(1+r)^3 + \ldots$$

$$= \sum_{t=1}^{\infty} \frac{D_t}{(1+r)^t}.$$

Thus, we derive the DDM wherein the value of a share is the PV of expected future dividends discounted at the required rate of return. The model has two implications for valuation.

1. The value of a share takes into account not just the current or near-term dividends but also dividends in the future.

2. The model incorporates the idea that current pricing depends on not just the future dividends but also on the future prices.

While what we have described is the generic version of the model, it is obvious that dividends cannot be predicted for an infinitely long period. We need to make simplifying assumptions to make it more practical.

No-Growth Company

Let us take a company which is engaged in a mature sector, growth having plateaued. The entire net profits are paid out as dividends and nothing is retained for investment. All that the company does is to maintain its capital, sales revenue and profits. The company will continue in the same state forever. The dividends from such a company will be constant each year. The company can be valued as a perpetuity with D as the cash flow.

$$\text{Value} = D/r.$$

Constant Growth Company

A more common kind of a company is one which experiences a constant rate of growth. The company retains a part of the net profit and pays the balance as dividends to shareholders. The retained profits are reinvested in business to generate growth. The company's cash flows are a growing perpetuity whose value can be calculated as follows:

$$\text{Value} = CF_1/(r - g),$$

where g is strictly less than r (g < r).

CF_1 is the dividend expected next year and can be estimated by multiplying this year's dividend by the rate of growth.

The rate of growth is a function of

1. the retention ratio: the proportion of profits that are retained by the company for investment,
2. return on equity: the return that the company expects to get on invested projects.

The rate of growth can be estimated by multiplying the retention ratio by the return on the invested capital. As we will see, if the rate of return is higher than the cost of capital, the value of the equity will go up. If, on the other hand, our investments return is less than the cost of capital, there will be a fall in the value of the equity.

Let us assume that a company has a net profit of ₹100 million and an equity base of 10 million shares. The EPS is ₹10. The company has no opportunities for growth and will continue as is and generate constant profits for all time to come. Given its business profile, the required rate of return is 12 per cent.

$$\text{Value of equity} = c/r = 10/12\% = 83.33.$$

Let us assume that the company gets an opportunity to extend its business to other parts of the country. This requires an investment equivalent to 60 per cent of its profits. Let us assume, for the sake of simplicity, that these opportunities are permanent and will require continuous investment.

$$\text{Value of equity} = 4/(12\% - g).$$

Since 60 per cent of the profits are reinvested in the business, only ₹4 is paid out as dividends. The growth rate depends on the return on investments. Growth can be derived by applying the return on capital invested to the proportion of earnings ploughed back into operations. Assuming that the return is 15 per cent (a positive NPV investment), the growth rate of dividends would be 60% * 15% = 9%.

Hence,   value = 4/(12% – 9%) = 133.

This is a substantial increase over the earlier value of 83.

On the other hand, if the return on investment is only 10 per cent (a negative NPV investment), the growth rate is

$$60\% * 10\% = 6\%,$$

and

$$\text{Value} = 4/(12\% - 6\%) = 66.66.$$

This is a substantial reduction over the earlier value of 83.

This clearly demonstrates why companies should take up only those projects where the return on investment is higher than the cost of capital. A return higher than the cost of capital increases the value of the company, whereas projects with a return lower than the cost of capital reduce the value of the company.

While it is clear that the value of equity increases if the company takes up projects that yield a return higher than the cost of capital, it would be useful to know what determines the extent of the increase in value. Two factors determine the extent of the increase in value:

1. By how much the rate of return is higher than the cost of capital.
2. What proportion of the net profit is retained and reinvested in business to obtain the rate of return.

If we assume that the rate of return for the company is 18 per cent (instead of 15 per cent), growth increases to

$$60\% * 18\% = 10.80$$

and value increases to

$$4/(12\% - 10.8\%) = 333.$$

If the return were to remain 15 per cent, but the same return can be achieved over a higher investment of 70 per cent of the profits (instead of 60 per cent), the growth increases to

$$70\% * 15\% = 10.5\%$$

and the value increases to

$$3/(12\% - 10.5\%) = 200.$$

Managers have a twofold guideline for maximizing value. First, maximize the difference between the rate of return on investment and the cost of capital.

Second, invest as much as possible at returns higher than the cost of capital. The more the company invests at the higher rate, the higher will be the value added to the company.

The proportion of net profits which is paid out as dividends is termed the payout ratio. In our example, ₹4 was paid from an EPS of ₹10 (dividend of ₹40 million from a net profit of ₹100 million). Hence, the payout ratio is 40 per cent.

The proportion of net profits that are retained for investment is termed the plough back ratio. It must equal (1 – payout ratio). In our example, this ratio is 60 per cent.

What is critical for valuation is not how much dividend is paid out, but what are the returns on investment from the profits retained and invested back into the business. Shareholder value is created through investments that yield returns in excess of the cost of capital.

A growth company is not one whose investments and sales keep growing but one whose value incorporates substantial valuation from fresh investments. In our example, the company's value on a stagnant basis was 83. With opportunity available for further investment, the value increased to 133. Thus, a substantial proportion was contributed by what is technically termed the present value of growth opportunities.

Public Sector Undertakings (PSU) versus Private Sector Companies: Difference in Valuation

It is usually observed that private sector enterprises are valued much higher than comparable public sector companies. The reason is simple. Their value comprises a much larger present value of growth opportunities. Decision-making in PSUs is bureaucratic and much slower, approvals being required from political masters. These undertakings are highly risk-averse and, consequently, investments are much lower than private enterprises, potentially reducing their growth potential. A substantial proportion of the PSU's value comprises only assets in place. Comparatively speaking, private sector companies have a much faster decision-making framework and have a culture that promotes risk-taking. Hence, they grow at a faster rate, yielding higher valuation.

KEY CONCEPTS

1. The difference between price and value is the basis of trading in the financial markets.
2. Value is based on cash flows and not accounting earnings. Cash flows that are taken into consideration are the free cash flows. Free cash flows take into account both operating and investment cash flows.
3. The future is divided into the horizon period and the residual period. The horizon period is the period for which the company has a competitive advantage and the return on investment is greater than the cost of capital.
4. Since cash flows occur in the future, they must be discounted to the PV.
5. The discounting rate must incorporate the risk of investment, in addition to time and inflation.
6. Discounted cash flow is the most common and conceptually sound method of valuation.
7. Future cash flows are uncertain; sensitivity analysis helps resolve the uncertainty.
8. Bonds are valued on the basis of their YTM.
9. The inverse relationship between bond prices and interest rates is one of the most fundamental theorems of finance.
10. Equity can be valued using either the DCF model or the DDM.
11. Value is created by investing in projects with returns higher than the cost of capital. Value is maximized by investing as much as possible at a return higher than the cost of capital.
12. A growth company is one whose value comprises substantially of the PV of growth opportunities.

CHAPTER QUESTIONS

1. ABC Ltd has just paid a dividend of ₹10. The dividend is expected to increase by 4 per cent annually. If the appropriate discount rate is 14 per cent, what is the value of its shares?
   If the price of the share is ₹93.64, what is the market assuming about its growth rate?
   What rate is it discounting the company's shares if the price is ₹86.67 and the growth rate remains at 4 per cent?
2. A zero-coupon bond matures in seven years. The face value of the bond is ₹200. The required return on the bond is 10 per cent. What price should it sell at?
3. Respond to the following statement:
   You say stock price equals the PV of future dividends? That is crazy! All the investors I know are looking for capital gains.
4. Why are cash flows different from accounting figures? Why is this significant?
5. What are the different concepts of cash flow? Discuss them.

6. ABC Ltd has a net profit of ₹400 million. The number of shares is 50 million. Given the nature of its business, the discount rate is 10 per cent. The company invests 30 per cent of its net profit on projects and pays the balance as dividends to shareholders. What is the value of the company if the projects invested by the company yield (a) 15 per cent and (b) 8 per cent?

What is the value of assets in place and the present value of growth opportunities? At what rate is the company expected to grow?

CASE FOR DISCUSSION

Having been established a decade back, ABC Ltd has overcome its initial, teething problems and is now well on course to a period of fast-paced growth. The year gone by saw revenues of ₹10 billion, which establishes a firm basis for the future of the company. The company has, over the last few years, made the required investments and the time has come to reap the rewards of those investments. The cash flow from operations are likely to be strong, without any concomitant need for further funding of long-term assets. In other words, huge free cash flows are expected.

You are running a large fund, planning to invest in ABC Ltd. What, according to you, is the value of ABC Ltd? Assume the following:

Today is the 1 January 2019. The calendar year 2018 had the following figures:

1. Sales value is of ₹10 billion. Number of units sold is 1,000,000, each priced at ₹10,000.
2. Raw material costs ₹5,500 per unit.
3. Operating expenses are ₹1.70 billion.
4. Depreciation is ₹0.7 billion.
5. Tax rate is 30 per cent

There are two phases of high growth for the company. The initial phase of explosive growth lasts for four years, and during this period the sales grow at 30 per cent per annum. Raw material costs grow at 20 per cent per annum, operating expenses at 15 per cent annually and depreciation remains constant. There are no fresh investments required except of replacing the equipment depreciation.

After the initial phase of explosive growth, the next phase lasts for five years during which the growth continues to be high but does not match that in the previous phase.

Sales grow at 18 per cent annually, raw material costs by 12 per cent per annum and operating expenses by 10 per cent. To support sales at high levels, fresh investment is required at ₹10 billion before the second phase of growth. This investment will be depreciated over the next five years.

The working capital requirement is 25 per cent of the current year's sales.

After the second phase of growth is over, the company settles down to normalcy to a new phase of maturity and the free cash flow generation increases constantly at 3 per cent per annum forever.

The company has issued 100 million shares at different prices to finance the investment at various times. The company's operating leverage is quite high, leading to a high risk. The required rate of return (cost of capital) is, therefore, high at 18 per cent.

Find the value of the company.

CHAPTER 7

Capital Structure and Financing

To guess is cheap. To guess wrong is expensive.

—Anonymous

To stay where you are, as the adage goes, you need to keep running. Sustained growth is the mantra of companies. Long-term growth is possible only with continuous investment in projects. Companies can finance investment in projects either through equity or by way of debt. Being a cheaper source of funds, there is a strong temptation to rely on debt rather than on equity. But higher debt makes equity riskier and its returns more volatile. Does the mix of debt and equity have an impact on the value of a company?

Capital structure (debt–equity mix) and its impact on a company's value has, over the years, been one of the most debated and hotly contested issues in corporate finance. Work on capital structure has elevated the theory (and practice) of corporate finance to great heights and earned it the respect it never enjoyed earlier. Corporate finance, in its modern avatar, took root with the Modigliani–Miller (MM) theorem on the capital structure of companies. Capital structure theory is rich in terms of learning and debate and is the kind of stuff that makes its study worthwhile. Not only has it revolutionized the subject but also enabled the corporate sector to formulate its capital structure policy by relying on the work carried out by such luminaries as Merton Miller, Franco Modigliani, Eugene Fama, Stuart Myers, Paul Samuelson, Harry Markowitz, James Tobin, William Sharpe, Fisher Black and Myron Scholes to add value. It is only appropriate that most of these contributors were recipients of the Nobel Prize in economics for their original and outstanding work on the subject. The few who failed to get it died young; Nobel Prizes are not awarded posthumously. The option pricing model was discovered by Fisher Black and Myron Scholes in 1972. Scholes received recognition by the Nobel Committee in 1997. Unfortunately, Black had passed away a few years back and could not be awarded the prize. No one has ever believed Black's contribution to be any less than that of Scholes!

Let us begin by placing the capital structure issue in the right context. Innumerable securities are available to a company for raising funds. Even as we write, new securities are being conceptualized and created in the financial markets, each with its unique return and risk characteristics. Investors are constantly in search of securities with diverse return–risk features.

The corporate sector fulfils this need by creating such securities, in the process satisfying its own requirement of funds in a manner best suited to it. Financial markets are the interface where the two meet and create the ideal conditions for innovation.

Financial securities are distinguished by three features.

1. Investors' claims on future cash flows
2. Their claims on company's assets in case of liquidation
3. Their right to participate in decision-making

Debt securities have fixed returns and a superior claim to the operating cash flows and the assets of a company under liquidation. The return to the equity shareholders is residual in nature and is variable, depending on the performance of the company. Its claim to cash flows and assets of the company, under liquidation, is inferior to the claims of the debt providers.

Equity shareholders are the owners of the company, govern the company on their own and are entitled to take all the decisions for the company. Debt providers have no say as long as they are receiving the interest and the maturity proceeds on time, and the other terms of the agreement are being adhered to.

A company generates revenues by selling its products and services. Various stakeholders of the company have claims to these cash flows. The cash flows are used to pay salaries to its employees, cost of raw material to suppliers, and for general administrative and establishment expenses.

After all the discussed expenses have been paid for, the operating profits (earnings before interest and taxes—EBIT) belong to the debt providers (coupon interest payment), the government (corporate tax) and the equity shareholders (net profit—dividends and retained earnings). The debt providers have the first claim, followed by the government, and the balance cash flows belong to the equity shareholders. The returns to the debt providers are predetermined and defined at the time of the issuance of the bonds. Since the returns to debt holders are (a) known (b) fixed and (c) their claims have priority over the cash flows, debt instruments are a relatively low-risk and safe investment.

On the other hand, the returns to equity shareholders are uncertain. Their claims to the company's cash flows are residual in nature, and they get whatever remains after every other stakeholder has been given his/her due. If the company does not earn sufficient profits, shareholders may not get any return, making equity a very risky form of investment with volatile returns. The required rate of return to equity shareholders is, therefore, much higher than the return to the debt providers.

Since debt provides fixed returns and is safer, the required rate of return on debt is lower than that of equity. Consequently, the reliance on debt presumably increases the return to shareholders. To take an example, assume ABC Ltd has total capital of ₹10,000 with return on assets of 15 per cent per annum. If the company is entirely equity-financed, the overall cost to the company is 15 per cent as is the return to shareholders (₹1,500 in absolute terms). Assume, however, that the company is 50 per cent financed through equity and the balance ₹5,000 by debt, costing 10 per cent.

Return on overall assets = 10,000 * 15% = 1,500.
Return to debt providers = 5,000 * 10% = 500.

Return to shareholders = (1,500 – 500)/5,000 = 1,000/5,000 = 20%.

The return on assets (15 per cent) over and above the cost of debt (10 per cent) provides additional return to shareholders.

Should a company, therefore, take recourse to debt financing to the extent feasible to maximize the return to equity shareholders?

We need to fall back on the objectives that a company seeks to achieve. The objective of value maximization provides the framework for policy action. While debt financing increases the return to the equity shareholders, it is not evident that the company's value also increases. The increase in debt increases risk and, thereby, the required rate of return on equity. The change in value will depend on the impact of change in risk vis-à-vis change in return.

Risk of Debt

We have been referring to debt as a relatively safe instrument whereas equity is considered to be riskier. This fact holds true from the perspective of the investor. From the viewpoint of the company, however, just the reverse holds true, wherein the issue of debt makes equity riskier. Equity in a sense is the company's own capital which is permanent in nature and which the company is under no obligation to return to shareholders. Equity provides a cushion against volatile cash flows and helps absorb any losses the company may make. Unlike the obligatory nature of interest payment on debt, dividend to equity shareholders is paid at the discretion of the company, depending on its profitability and cash flow requirements. Companies are under no obligation to pay dividends.

Debt imposes obligation on the company to pay coupon interest as well as the maturity amount in accordance with the terms of the borrowing. The fixed payment of coupon interest makes the return on equity more variable and hence riskier. In an extreme situation, the company may find itself unable to make the mandated payment to debt providers and becomes a defaulter, inviting severe penalties, including bankruptcy proceedings.

A company resorts to debt because the cost of debt is lower than the return on overall assets of the company. After the debt providers have been paid their dues, the balance that remains adds to the return of the equity shareholders. At times, the return on assets may drop below the cost of debt, leading to lower returns to the equity shareholders. In this sense, borrowing is a double-edged sword.

In the previous example, ABC Ltd borrowed at 10 per cent, which is lower than the return on the company's overall assets (15 per cent), to amplify return to the equity shareholders. The future is however uncertain, and the return may drop, even going below the cost of debt. If the returns drop below 5 per cent, the return to equity shareholders would, in fact, be negative.

Let us understand, with an example, how borrowing makes a company's returns more variable and hence riskier.

Table 7.1 describes two companies with a similar profile. They differ only in terms of their leverage. Under normal expected costs of ₹8,000, the unlevered firm has an earnings per share (EPS) of 1, whereas the levered firm earns an EPS of ₹1.20.

TABLE 7.1 Risk of debt (in ₹)

	Unlevered	Levered	Unlevered low cost	Levered low cost	Unlevered high costs	Levered high costs
Sales	10,000	10,000	10,000	10,000	10,000	10,000
Costs	8,000	8,000	7,000	7,000	9,000	9,000
Operating profit	2,000	2,000	3,000	3,000	1,000	1,000
Interest	0	800	0	800	0	800
Net profit	2,000	1,200	3,000	2,200	1,000	200
No. of shares	2,000	1,000	2,000	1,000	2,000	1,000
EPS	1.0	1.2	1.5	2.2	0.5	0.2
Capital	20,000	20,000	20,000	20,000	20,000	20,000
Equity	20,000	10,000	20,000	10,000	20,000	10,000
Debt	0	10,000	0	10,000	0	10,000
Interest rate	8%					

Source: Author.

There is no free lunch in financial markets. Due to its substantial borrowings, the earnings of the levered firm show far greater variability than that of an unlevered firm. With the change in costs (costs falling to ₹7,000 or increasing to ₹9,000), the EPS of the unlevered company varies from 0.5 to 1.5, whereas the EPS of a levered firm is more volatile, varying from 0.2 to 2.2. In fact, if the margins reduce below 8 per cent, the levered company will be incurring a loss.

We have deliberately taken a very simple example to explain the volatility induced by debt. In real life, the variation in operating parameters such as sales, operating costs and even the cost of debt is much more than assumed here. And the risk is likely to be even higher.

However, since the apparent cost of debt is lower than that of equity, and at times substantially so, there is a great temptation to borrow funds rather than raise equity. How much should a company borrow and the consequent impact of such borrowing on its value is a matter of great debate amongst finance experts.

Maximization of Equity Value

Managers try to maximize corporate value by optimizing the debt equity ratio. There is an underlying assumption that the maximization of the company's value also maximizes value to the equity shareholders. Let us explore this idea.

ABC Ltd has a value of ₹1,500,000, with debt being ₹500,000 and equity equalling ₹1,000,000. It has 10,000 shares, each priced at ₹100.

Let us see what happens when the company borrows an additional ₹250,000, and uses it to pay a one-time dividend of ₹25 per share (250,000/10,000 = 25).

The debt is now ₹750,000 (₹500,000 of the old debt and ₹250,000 of the new). We are aware of the basic relationship wherein the value of the company, V, equals the value of equity, E, plus the value of its debt, D. Hence, the value of equity is V – 750,000. If the value of the company V remains constant at ₹1,500,000, the equity value will reduce to ₹750,000. Along with the dividend of ₹250,000, the total value to equity shareholders remains unchanged at ₹1,000,000.

If, however, the value of the company increases to 1,600,000, the shareholders' value increases to ₹1,100,000 ((1,600,000 – 750,000) + 250,000).

And, if the value of the company decreases to 1,400,000, the shareholders' value also decreases to ₹900,000 ((1,400,000 – 750,000) + 250,000).

Thus, any change in the value of the company accrues to its shareholders, and it would be safe to aver that the maximization of the company's value also maximizes the shareholders' value.

The proposition rests on two assumptions:

1. The change in dividend payout has no impact on the value of the company. This aspect will be discussed in Chapter 8 on dividends.
2. The value of the old debt remains unchanged. Given that a higher debt increases the risk to all debt holders, the old debt may reduce in value, since the interest paid to them remains constant. Any reduction in value of the old debt benefits the equity shareholders.

The debt–equity mix deployed to raise funds for investment by a corporate is termed the capital structure. There are two ways of representing the capital structure. Assume that a company has ₹1 billion equity and ₹0.5 billion debt for a total capital of ₹1.5 billion; the company is thus financed two-third by equity and one-third by debt. In India, we look at the level of debt compared to the level of equity. Thus, debt being ₹0.5 billion and equity being ₹1 billion, the debt–equity ratio is 0.5:1. Both imply the same thing, but look at it from different angles.

Cost of Capital

Cost of capital is one of the most critical parameters for a company. It has three broad applications:

1. The cost of capital is a key determinant of the value of a company. Let us recall the discounted cash flow (DCF) model of valuation. The value of a company is determined by discounting the future free cash flows, the discount rate being the risk-adjusted cost of capital. The cost of capital thus has a significant bearing on the value of the company.

   The higher the cost of capital, the lower is the discounted value of the cash flows and, therefore, the value of a company. On the other hand, the lower the cost of capital, the higher is the discounted value of the free cash flows and that of the company.

   Companies attempt to reduce the cost of capital in order to increase their value. Risk is a key determinant of the cost of capital; therefore, the more a company invests in safer projects, the lower will be the risk and the cost of capital. Whether that maximizes value is not evident, since less risky projects may also generate lower cash flows. The interplay of the cost of capital and the free cash flows must be optimized to maximize value.

Cost of Capital and Valuation

Hindustan Unilever Ltd is a fast-moving consumer goods (FMCG) company. Its revenues, profits and cash flows are largely predictable and stable. The risk is low, resulting in a low cost of capital and a high valuation of the company. Infrastructure projects, on the other hand, have a very volatile business profile with significant variability in revenues and profitability. The cost of capital, being high, has a negative impact on value. A company like IRB Infrastructure Ltd faces a high cost of capital, which depresses its value despite apparently large future cash flows.

The risk that matters is the risk of the cash flows generated by the projects in which the company invests. Technology projects are very risky, with significantly greater volatility in cash flows and returns. Food companies, on the other hand, have relatively stable cash flows.

Companies often attempt to reduce overall risk through diversification. A cement company may decide to invest in the food business, there being a low correlation between the two industries. The financial market does not view such diversification attempts very favourably unless the company can demonstrate a clear business proposition and a competitive advantage in the food business. Desired diversification can be more easily achieved by the investor himself, who can buy shares of a food company, in addition to the shares of the cement company in his portfolio. The market will, in fact, punish the diversifying company by lowering its share price. Each business venture must be looked at and evaluated on its own merits, and not because there is a low correlation between various projects in which the company is contemplating investments.

Unbridled Diversification

L&T Ltd is a technology, engineering and construction company. In the past, it lost focus and invested in many unrelated activities. In fact, at one point in time, L&T owned many such businesses, some of which were insignificant for the company of its size. For example, it had a shoe business amounting to just a few hundred millions. In their desire to do anything and everything, the Indian corporate sector is replete with examples of companies with unrelated businesses in their portfolio.

L&T made large investments in cement, which is typically a commodity business, diluting the image of the engineering division. The markets, of course, did not appreciate L&T's diversified portfolio, which had no synergies with their core business. As a result, the combined valuation of the company was far lower than what the two businesses would have got if they were independent—a clear indication to the management to dispose of the cement business. The company resisted such divestment for a long period, during which its share price and the value remained depressed.

Finally, in 2004, L&T Ltd sold off the cement division to the Kumar Mangalam Birla group. The market gave the transaction its thumbs up by substantially increasing its share price.

2. The cost of capital acts as a hurdle rate for projects that a company may invest in. For a project to add value, the return must exceed the cost of capital. Any project that is not expected to achieve a return at least equalling the cost of capital will be discarded by the company. Cash flows of a project are discounted at the cost of capital to derive the net present value (NPV).

The value addition by a project is a function of the excess of the return on investment over the cost of capital and the amount invested in the project. Lower cost of capital will lead to higher value addition and, therefore, increases the value of the company.

Some of the projects that are not currently viable may turn value-additive if the cost of capital comes down. For instance, if the return on investment of a project is 12 per cent and the cost of capital is 14 per cent, the project reduces value. However, if the cost of capital comes down to 10 per cent, the project becomes value-accretive. Lower cost of capital usually increases the level of investments in an economy and is one of the reasons the corporate sector always wants lower interest rates.

3. Economic value added (EVA) has become an important determinant of corporate performance. The calculation of EVA requires a knowledge of the company's cost of capital. We will discuss EVA later in the book in Appendix I.

Minimization of Cost of Capital

The objectives of value maximization and minimization of the cost of capital are usually thought to be equivalent. It is assumed that a capital structure that minimizes the cost of capital also maximizes the value of the company. While generally true, the basic assumption is that the operating income or the future cash flows remain unchanged, consequent to a change in the capital structure. However, if the future cash flows change as a result of a change in the capital structure, a minimization of the cost of capital may not maximize value.

In general, given the assumptions of the MM Model, future cash flows do remain constant with changing capital structure. Later in the chapter, we will relax the assumptions of the model to see what impact a change in capital structure can have on future cash flows.

Estimation of Cost of Capital

Debt and equity broadly constitute a company's capital. Besides the simple coupon bonds and equity shares, usually termed vanilla instruments, innumerable variations are possible. For example, the government and the corporate sector have at various times issued zero-coupon bonds, floating-rate bonds, commodity-linked bonds, bonds with embedded options, junk bonds, capital-index bonds, convertible bonds, payment-in-kind (PIK) securities and perpetual bonds. Similarly, a company may issue non-voting shares, different class shares and preference shares.

Most securities, in fact, have some features of debt and some of equity. An example would be the issue of bonds attached with warrants that are convertible into equity at predetermined prices.

We could look at each and every security issued by a company and calculate its cost and weightage in the overall capital. Such an exercise is likely to become extremely cumbersome and is futile. In order to understand the calculation of the cost of capital, we classify all securities into either debt or equity, considering those to be the only two categories of instruments that comprise the capital of the company. The cost of capital is the weighted average cost of debt and equity (WACC).

Following elements need to be taken into consideration in calculating WACC:

1. Cost of debt: A typical corporate bond has a defined maturity and pays a fixed coupon rate of interest. The coupons, together with the maturity value, determine the cash flows that accrue on the bond. Given the current price at which the bond trades, the yield to maturity can be easily determined as shown in Illustration 7.1. (This was discussed earlier in Chapter 6 on valuation.). It is the current yield to maturity that represents the cost of the bond and not the coupon interest payable.

   The purpose of estimating the cost of debt, and also the cost of capital, is twofold.
   a. Estimate the current value of the company by discounting the future free cash flows by the cost of capital of the company.
   b. Decide which project proposals on hand add value by comparing the return of the project to the cost of capital.

   For both these purposes, the current cost of debt and capital is applicable. Historical cost has no relevance today.

Illustration 7.1

Assume that Reliance Industries Ltd has a seven-year bond outstanding, with a coupon of ₹12 per year. The bonds were issued two years back and now have five years remaining to maturity. The cash flows on the bond are as follows:

C_0	C_1	C_2	...	C_5
	12	12		12
				100

Assuming the bonds are priced at ₹89.9464 today, the yield to maturity can be calculated as 15 per cent. PVIF stands for present value interest factor.

$$\text{Value of the bond} = 12 * \text{PVIFA}_{15\%,5} + \text{PVIF}_{15\%,5} * 100$$
$$= 12 * 3.3522 + 0.4972 * 100$$
$$= 40.2264 + 49.72$$
$$= 89.9464.$$

Thus, 15 per cent is the current cost of debt of Reliance Industries Ltd (and not the 12 per cent coupon).

It is possible that a bond's yield to maturity is not available if it is not listed or is irregularly traded. The cost of other corporate bonds with a similar risk profile can then be used as a proxy. Risk profile can be compared by looking at the credit ratings of the bonds of the respective companies.

2. The interest paid on debt is an expense recognized by the income tax authorities. The company reduces its taxable profits by the amount of interest paid. The effective post-tax cost of debt is

$$ytm \ (1 - t).$$

For instance, if the applicable corporate tax rate is 30 per cent, the effective post-tax cost of debt for Reliance Industries Ltd is 15% * (1 − 30%) = 10.50%.

(This has been discussed earlier in the Chapter 6. We had discussed why the tax-saving should reduce the cost of debt and not be added to the estimation of net operating profits after tax [NOPAT] and free cash flows.)

The tax rate taken into account is the marginal tax rate applicable to the company and not the average tax rate. Companies are liable to pay corporation tax on their profits at the applicable rate. However, there are various means by which they are able to reduce their tax liability and the actual tax paid by them is much less than the specified corporate tax rate.

The savings on tax payable on account of the interest expense is given by the applicable marginal tax rate. What is critical is the savings in taxes at the margin, that is, the reduction in taxes on account of the interest paid on the debt under consideration. The actual average rate of taxes paid by the company can be different for a variety of reasons and is not appropriate for our purpose.

In order to benefit from the tax deductibility of interest expense, the company must generate sufficiently large profits. If the profits are inadequate and the company is anyway not liable to pay corporation tax, the question of reduction in taxes does not arise. If the company is a loss-making one or if the profits are low, the effective cost of debt would not reduce from its yield to maturity and the pre-tax as well as the post-tax cost of debt will be equal.

3. Cost of equity: The return to the equity shareholders comprises of dividends paid by the company and the capital gains.

Dividends depends on the profits generated and the cash flow position of the company. Dividends are not mandatory, being payable at the discretion of the management. Usually, the dividends constitute a small proportion of the returns. The dividend yield (amount of dividend per share divided by the market price of the share) of NIFTY stocks on 31 March 2017 was 1.25 per cent.

A significant proportion of the return on equity accrues from the capital gains and is determined by the rise in price of the company's equity. Stock price increase is a direct result of the performance of the company, either through higher profitability and free cash flow generation from the existing business or by way of investments in new projects which generate positive NPV.

The capital asset pricing model (CAPM) estimates the required return on equity as a function of three parameters, namely the risk-free return, equity market premium and the risk of the individual stock or its beta. As per the standard CAPM, the required return on equity is

$$Re = R_f + beta * (R_m - R_f).$$

The required return becomes the cost of equity for the company. If the company is unable to provide the required rate of return, the price of the share decreases to the extent that such a return would become available. A fall in the price of the share, of course, reduces the value of the company and is against the objective of value maximization.

Thus, while the return to the debt providers is explicit, accruing mainly from the coupon interest paid, the return to equity shareholders is implicit.

Cost of Equity in India

According to a survey carried out by the consulting firm, Ernst & Young (2014), the average cost of equity in India is upwards of 15 per cent. This rate, however, masks huge variation across different industries. Real estate and telecommunications encounter the highest cost of equity, whereas FMCG companies face the lowest cost.

The cost of equity in India, according to the survey, is higher than international cost. The difference amounts to 3.6 per cent, which is very significant.

4. The last parameter in calculating the cost of capital is the proportion of debt and equity in the total capital, based on their market values.
   a. For equity, the price of the share multiplied by the number of shares provides the value of equity. This value is popularly known as the market capitalization.
   b. For debt too, the price of the bond multiplied by the number of bonds issued yields its total value. If more than one kind of bond has been issued, the value of all bonds should be added together to provide the overall value of debt. The proportion of debt and equity would respectively be

   Value of debt/(value of debt + value of equity),
   Value of equity/(value of debt + value of equity).

   The sum of the proportions of debt and equity, of course, equals 1 (or 100 per cent).

Market Value versus Book Value

The book value of equity reflects historical costs and profits. It has no link to the value that the market currently places on the equity. The market value is forward-looking, based as it is on future cash flows and the current cost of capital.

Investors evaluate the company based on its market values and not on its book value. Moreover, when the investors invest in the company's securities, they do so at market prices of the respective securities and not at their book value. The return required by them is also based on market values.

Summing It Up

We sum up the calculation of the cost of capital as follows:

1. Cost of debt—yield to maturity based on the current market price of the bond.
2. Cost of equity—the risk-adjusted required rate of return.
3. Market values to be taken into consideration for all calculations.
4. Current values to be taken for all parameters; historical values are inappropriate.
5. The costs of debt and equity should be weighted by the proportion of debt and equity in the overall capital respectively, again based on market values.
6. The cost of debt should be adjusted by the marginal corporate tax rate.
7. What needs to be calculated is the investor/market-determined required rate of return for investment in the company.

The equation for the calculation of the cost of capital can be represented as follows:

$$WACC = r_D (1 - t) [D/(D + E)] + r_E [E/(D + E)].$$

Where r_D is the cost of debt (ytm), t is the marginal corporate tax rate, D and E are the market values of debt and equity and r_E is the cost of equity. Calculation of WACC and its application is demonstrated in Illustration 7.2.

Illustration 7.2

Q. DEF Ltd is contemplating a new process of manufacturing which yields annual cost savings of ₹10,000, starting next year. The company has an equity cost of 20 per cent and debt cost of 10 per cent. A portion (25 per cent) of its capital is financed through debt and the balance comprises equity. It is faced with a marginal tax rate of 30 per cent. Should DEF Ltd convert to the new manufacturing process?

A. The cost of capital, WACC, can be calculated as follows:

$$WACC = 10\% * (1 - 30\%) * 25\% + 20\% * 75\%$$
$$= 16.75\%.$$

Value of the cost savings = 10,000 / 16.75% = ₹59,701.

Thus, DEF Ltd should switch to the new manufacturing process if the cost of conversion is less than ₹59,701.

Target Capital Structure

Based on the environment, the operating structure of the company and theoretical considerations, companies usually decide on their optimum or the target capital structure. This is their long-term debt–equity proportion. The actual capital structure at any given time may, however, be different, for various reasons.

1. The operating cash flows and profitability may be volatile, leading to a temporary deviation from the targeted structure.
2. The financing profile of a specific project undertaken by a company may be different from the target structure. The project may be small and only a single-funding source meets the entire requirement. Or market conditions may dictate a different funding pattern. If the equity markets are depressed at the time a project is undertaken, the entire funding could be from debt to be made up later by higher equity in future projects.

If there is a difference between the two, the target capital structure should be used to determine the cost of capital and not the existing debt–equity ratio. Thus, in the formula for WACC, the respective proportions of debt and equity are based on the capital structure targeted by the company.

Use of Funds Determines Cost of Capital

The cost of capital, including the required rate of return on various components of the capital, depends on the use that the funds are being put to. The cost of capital is determined by its risk, and the risk depends on the project in which funds are invested; thus, it is their application and not the source that decides the cost. The cost of capital is the market-determined required rate of return.

We have assumed debt and equity to be the two broad sources of finance and calculated WACC accordingly. In practice, companies resort to various financing options such as hybrid securities, preference shares and different kinds of debt instruments. Ideally, we must calculate the cost and the proportion of each of these instruments and find the cost of capital through what is termed the expanded WACC, which incorporates the cost and proportion of these instruments. Of course, in practice that would become cumbersome and should be used only if it makes a significant difference to the outcome.

While calculation of WACC is a simple process, it is always useful to compare the company's WACC with the industry average. Operating characteristics of different companies in the same industry are usually similar and should lead to a similar WACC. A significant difference could denote an error in estimation or a dissimilar capital structure, both of which need to be further examined.

Industry WACC is especially useful for multi-product companies, where a single company-wide WACC calculation would be meaningless. What needs to be done is to find the WACC of the different industries to which the company's various products/divisions belong and then find the average of these industry WACCs.

There is an intricate relationship between capital structure, the cost of capital and value. Given the future cash flows, the value of a company is determined by its cost of capital. If the capital structure influences the cost of capital, ipso facto, it also impacts the value of the company. If, however, as the MM Model posits, the cost of capital is independent of the capital structure, then it has no influence on the company's value.

Return Variants

We have been using the terms required rate of return and cost of capital interchangeably. The required rate of return on an investment is based on its risk profile. Different investments have different levels of risk and, therefore, their required returns are also different. An efficient market must provide investors the required rate of return.

The return on equity is determined by the cash flows that the company is expected to generate. If the cash flows are expected to be insufficient, the price of the equity drops to ensure that the owners' expectation of the required return is met. The drop in the price of equity, of course, reduces value and is against the objective of value maximization.

As a simple illustration, assume a company, being mature and stable, has earnings of ₹100 million per annum in perpetuity. If the required return is 12 per cent, the company's value would be ₹833.3 million (10/12 per cent). If 10 million shares have been issued, these will be priced at ₹83.33. Assuming a fall in future earnings to ₹80 million per annum, the value of the company drops to (8/12 per cent) = ₹666.6 million and the price of the share to ₹66.66.

For the company to ensure that its value does not decrease, it is imperative that it provides the required rate of return which, therefore, becomes its cost of capital. Thus, in an efficient market, the two terms, the required rate of return and the cost of capital, are one and the same, though looked at from the point of view of the investors and the company respectively.

The interplay of the relationship between these parameters is complex but crucial to the role played by the capital structure in the valuation of a company. Let us start appreciating the relationship by understanding the MM theorem.

Theory of Capital Structure: The Modigliani–Miller (MM) Theorem

Every great theory has two attributes. First, it can be explained in simple terms, even if its implications are wide ranging and transformative. Second, there are always stories—some apocryphal, many imaginary and a few true—pertaining to how these theories were formulated and discovered. The same applies to the MM theory of capital structure.

Franco Modigliani and Merton Miller were both professors at the Carnegie Mellon University when they derived their theorem. They were asked to teach corporate finance despite the fact that they did not have any prior experience of the subject. They started looking for an optimal capital structure which would minimize the cost of capital. What they discovered, to their surprise, was that such an optimal structure did not exist and that there was no relationship between a company's capital structure and its value/cost of capital.

Financial Incentive

Miller taught economic history and public finance at the Carnegie Mellon University (then Carnegie Tech). He was approached by the dean with an offer to teach corporate finance. Economics at that time was a highly snobbish department and Miller refused. The dean then dangled a carrot—business school salaries, at the time, were much higher than salaries at the Department of Economics. Miller's wife had just delivered their second child and the couple was always short of money. He needed no further persuasion. The lure of the lucre can at times lead to noble, path-breaking outcomes!

Interestingly, since Miller was young and relatively inexperienced, Modigliani was asked to keep an avuncular eye on him. The rest, as they say, is history.

Academic literature also could not provide a satisfactory answer to the relationship between capital structure and value. The reading material that existed at the time was inconsistent. Dissatisfaction with the state of the subject led them to undertake their own research. The outcome was the famous MM theorem on capital structure, initially outlined in their paper 'The Cost of Capital, Corporation Finance and the Theory of Investment' in the *American Economic Review* in 1958, later followed by a number of papers delineating their views on various related issues.

Pre-publication Jitters

Their paper caused problems even before it appeared in print. It was one of the first papers to be published under a joint authorship. These days, of course, joint publication of papers is a common practice. The paper was also too long for a journal like the *American Economic Review*, resulting in a part of the appendix, dealing with the macroeconomic implications of the theory, being excluded by the publishers.

It is interesting that the typesetter had no facility to print the statistical symbol for the average, namely x-bar, there being few articles with mathematical orientation. The editor, Bernard Haley, wanted to charge Modigliani and Miller for setting what was then an unusual symbol! The potential impact on the subject is no guarantee for ease of publication.

The MM theory can be simply stated as follows. Assume there are two firms that are identical in terms of operating characteristics, cash flows, investment opportunities and risk profile. One is financed entirely by equity (unlevered firm) and the other is financed partly by equity and partly by debt (levered firm). According to the MM theorem, both the companies will have the same value and their shares will also be equally priced. A difference in capital structure has no impact on the value of the firm or on their share price.

While the statement by itself looks simple and innocuous, its implications for corporate finance have proven to be a game changer. Prior to the MM Model, corporate finance was more a reflection of what happened in the real world, in the corporate sector. Different observations led to different hypotheses, without any underlying theory binding them.

A theory should be based on a proof, premised on assumptions and should provide a framework for analysis and further developments. This is what the MM Model provided and thereby established the foundations of finance as a strong and vibrant subject of study and analysis. For their contributions, both Modigliani and Miller were awarded the Nobel Prize in Economics, though in different years. More than half a century later, the validity of the theory is well-established, given the assumptions of the model. It is the assumptions, as we will study later in the chapter, which provide guidance to finance managers on how to add value to companies. Let us understand the theory and its implications, starting with the assumptions.

Assumptions

Following are the assumptions of the MM Model:

1. There are no income or corporate taxes. This assumption is later discarded.
2. Raising funds through debt and equity is costless, and there are no transaction costs.
3. Investors can borrow on the same terms as companies.
4. Stakeholders are able to resolve any conflict of interest amongst themselves.

The Model

Given these assumptions, according to the MM theorem, capital structure has no impact on the value of the firm. If the company changes the mix of debt and equity in its capital structure, the total value of the company as well as the price of equity remains unaltered. All that happens is that there is a change in the way the value of the company is distributed amongst the debt providers and the equity shareholders.

1. Assume there are two companies, ABC Ltd and XYZ Ltd. Both companies are identical in every respect. They have similar earnings, risk profile and investment opportunities. ABC Ltd has earnings of ₹60 million annually; it has 10 million equity shares and its required rate of return is 12 per cent. There is no debt.

   The value of the company is

   $$60 \text{ million}/12\% = 500 \text{ million}.$$

   And the price per share is ₹50.

2. XYZ Ltd also has earnings of ₹60 million per annum and is similar in risk profile to ABC Ltd. XYZ Ltd is 50 per cent financed through debt (₹250 million) and 50 per cent through equity (₹250 million). The interest rate on debt is 10 per cent.

   The interest cost on debt, at 10 per cent of ₹250 million, equals ₹25 million.

   The balance earnings of 35 million accrue to the equity shareholders whose return increases to 3.5/25 = 14%.

TABLE 7.2   Leverage and risk

	ABC Ltd		XYZ Ltd	
	Total earnings (₹ million)	Rate of return to equity shareholders (%)	Earnings to equity shareholders (₹ million)	Rate of return to equity shareholders (%)
Booming	80	16	55	22
Normal	60	12	35	14
Recession	40	8	15	6
Average	60	12	35	14

Source: Author.

Does the higher return to equity make leveraging a better option? Not really, since the levered equity of XYZ Ltd is riskier and, therefore, the required rate of return is higher than that of the equity of ABC Ltd, an unlevered firm. Higher risk and consequent increase in the required rate of return ensures that neither the value of the company nor its share price changes. The objective of a company is the maximization of its value and not the maximization of the return to equity shareholders. Risk is critical and its impact must be taken into consideration.

Let us understand the risk of debt with the extended version of the example.

The average expected return to equity shareholders for a leveraged company increases but so does the variability in earnings. In Table 7.2, in case of the all equity-financed company ABC Ltd, the rate of return varies from 8 per cent to 16 per cent, while for the levered company XYZ Ltd the rate of return varies from 6 per cent to 22 per cent. In fact, during the period of recession, earnings of equity shareholders of a levered company are lower than that of an unlevered firm. Thus, the risk of equity of a levered company is much greater, compared to that of an unlevered one, and the shareholders need higher compensation for their investment.

Arbitrage

The basic premise of the MM Model is their assertion that capital structure does not impact a company's value. The significance of the model lies in the fact that unlike earlier hypotheses, Modigliani and Miller provided a proof of their model, based on the concept of arbitrage. They showed that a situation in which the value of a company differs, solely on account of the capital structure, is inherently unstable and is subject to arbitrage by investors. (Arbitrage has been explained earlier in Chapter 2 on financial markets.) Arbitrage by investors ensures that the value of two companies, which differ only with respect to their capital structure, will be the same. Let us demonstrate this with the example of ABC Ltd and XYZ Ltd discussed in the previous list.

Assume that the value of the levered company XYZ Ltd is ₹600 million, higher than that of the unlevered company ABC Ltd. Since debt is ₹250 million, the equity is valued at ₹350 million. Given the number of shares at 5,000,000, the price per share is 350 million/5 million = ₹70 which is higher than that of the shares of ABC Ltd.

Such a situation is unlikely to persist for long, and through arbitrage the investors (arbitrageurs) will ensure that the price of the share of XYZ Ltd comes down to ₹50 and the company value is ₹500 million.

For investors to undertake arbitrage, the two assumptions of an active market for short-selling and the ability of investors to borrow at the same rate and on similar terms as corporates are critical. To the extent that personal borrowing is possible on terms different to those of corporate borrowing, arbitrage will not be perfect.

Short-Selling

Short-selling refers to selling an asset without owning it. In the normal course, an investor is unable to take advantage of a possible fall in the price if he does not own the asset. In well-developed markets, there is an active market for borrowing and lending of shares at nominal rates. The short-seller borrows the shares and delivers in the market to conclude the transaction. Later, when he wants to close out his position, he buys the shares back, hopefully at a lower price, and returns the shares he has earlier borrowed. His profits (or losses) depend on the difference in prices at which he has sold initially and purchased later.

What the investor will do is to replicate the debt–equity ratio of XYZ Ltd by

- buying shares of ABC Ltd,
- financing part of it by selling shares of XYZ and
- borrowing the balance amount to offset the impact of corporate borrowing.

In a way, corporate leveraging has been replaced by personal leveraging. By doing so, as Table 7.3 shows, there is an inflow of ₹1 million and no change in the cash flows in the future. As this arbitrage is undertaken in large volumes and by a large number of investors who sell XYZ Ltd and buy ABC Ltd, the prices of the two will converge. The arbitrage opportunity will present itself until there is equality in the value of the two companies and the prices of their shares.

A similar arbitrage can be undertaken if the value of XYZ Ltd is lower than the value of ABC Ltd and the price of a share of XYZ Ltd is less than that of ABC Ltd.

TABLE 7.3   Capital structure: arbitrage I (in ₹)

Action	Cash Flow Now (million)	Cash Flows in Future (annual)
Sell short 1% shares of XYZ Ltd	3.5	– (1% of earnings – 0.25 millions)
Buy 1% shares of ABC Ltd	–5	1% of earnings
Borrow (@10%)	2.5	–0.25 millions
Net Cash flow	1	0

Source: Author.

Table 7.4   Capital structure: arbitrage II (in ₹)

Action	Cash flow now (million)	Cash flow in future (annual)
Buy 1% shares of XYZ	–2	1% of earnings – 0.25 million
Sell short 1% shares of ABC	5	–1% of earnings
Lend 2.5 million @10%	–2.5	0.25 million
Net cash flow	0.5	0

Source: Author.

Assume that the value of XYZ Ltd is ₹450 million, lower than that of ABC Ltd. Since the value of XYZ Ltd's debt is ₹250 million, the value of its equity is 450 – 250 = ₹200 million. Given that the company has 5,000,000 shares, the price per share will be 200 million/5 million = ₹40, which is lower than that of shares of ABC Ltd (Table 7.4).

Again, as in the previous case, what an investor has done is to replicate the debt–equity ratio of XYZ Ltd by

• buying shares of XYZ Ltd,
• financing it by selling shares of ABC Ltd and
• lending the balance amount to offset the impact of corporate borrowing.

As Table 7.4 shows, the investor receives an inflow of ₹0.5 million immediately, and there is no change in the cash flows in the future. As this arbitrage is undertaken in large volumes and by a large number of investors who buy XYZ Ltd and sell ABC Ltd, the prices of the two will converge. The arbitrage opportunity will present itself until there is equality in the value of the two companies and the prices of their shares.

Propositions

Having covered so much ground, let us now discuss the two basic propositions of the MM Model.

Proposition I: The value of a company is independent of its capital structure. If there are two companies that are similar with respect to their business, the growth potential and the risk profile, leverage will have no impact, either on their value or the value of their shares. Leverage increases risk, the impact of which (through a higher required rate of return of equity) exactly offsets the lower cost of debt. The conceptual framework for capital structure agnosticism is provided by arbitrage.

Difference in valuation, solely due to leverage, provides arbitrageurs an opportunity for risk-free returns. All they need to do is to substitute personal leverage for corporate leverage. Any change that managers make in corporate leverage can be undone by arbitrageurs through personal borrowing (or personal investment). The only requirement is that investors should be able to borrow and lend on the same terms as companies.

Proposition II: The expected return on the equity of a leveraged company increases in proportion to the debt–equity ratio. The rate of increase depends on the spread between the company's overall return on assets and the return on debt.

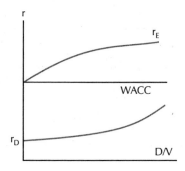

<small>FIGURE 7.1   MM Model</small>

Source: Author.

The proposition implies that the higher the debt component in the capital, the higher is the risk and the required return on equity. Also, larger the difference between the overall required rate of return on assets and the return on debt, higher will be this rate of increase. Thus, the required rate of return on equity is a function of

1. the debt proportion in the funding,
2. the difference between the return on assets and the cost of debt.

   Figure 7.1 can be put down mathematically as follows:

$$r_A = r_D \left[D/(D + E) \right] + r_E \left[E/(D + E) \right].$$

Where r_A is the overall expected return on assets of the company,
r_D is the expected return on debt,
r_E is the expected return on equity and
$D/(D + E)$ and $E/(D + E)$ are the proportions of debt and of equity, respectively, in the capital structure.

By rearranging the equation, we get

$$r_E = r_A + D/E * (r_A - r_D).$$

The equation gives us the framework for calculating the required rate of return on equity of a leveraged company.

To take the previous example of ABC Ltd being an entirely equity-financed company, 12 per cent is the required return for the company overall (r_A) and for its equity (r_E). For XYZ Ltd which is otherwise identical in every respect, the required rate of return on equity can be calculated as follows:

$$r_E = 12\% + 0.5/0.5 \, (12\% - 10\%)$$
$$= 14\%.$$

This is the actual return on equity for XYZ Ltd, ensuring that the value of the company and the share price remains constant.

A change in the capital structure impacts the required return on equity, and possibly, of debt too, given that there is a change in the risk of the two instruments. As we are aware, the risk of a security is given by beta. We can replicate the process of estimating the cost of equity by unlevering and levering beta, instead of the rates of return, as discussed earlier. Asset beta is the weighted average of the beta of debt and equity.

$$\beta_A = \beta_D * [D/(D + V)] + \beta_E * [E/(D + V)].$$

Rearranging it, we get

$$\beta_E = \beta_A + D/E * (\beta_A - \beta_D).$$

A change in the debt–equity ratio changes the risk distribution. The relationship can be used to work out the beta of equity, given a change in the capital structure. Thus, to obtain the required return on equity, we can use either the required return equation or the beta equation.

Thus, according to the MM Model, managers cannot influence the value of a company or its share price by substituting debt for equity. While the cost of debt is lower, less risk gets apportioned to debt, which means that more of the risk of the business is borne by equity. Since the risk to equity shareholders increases, so does the required rate of return as shown in Illustration 7.3. The increase in the cost of the remaining equity is sufficient to offset the benefits of a higher debt–equity ratio. Thus, while the return to equity shareholders increases, the value of equity does not.

Illustration 7.3

Q. ABC Ltd has a return on equity of 16.5 per cent. Its capital structure currently comprises 20 per cent debt and 80 per cent equity. The debt cost is 9 per cent.

The company is planning to change its capital structure to 40 per cent debt and 60 per cent equity by borrowing more and using the proceeds to buy its equity back. What would be the cost of equity with the new capital structure? Assume that the company does not pay any tax.

A. As per Proposition II,

$$R_E = r_A + D/E * (r_A - r_D).$$
$$16.5\% = r_A + 20\%/80\% * (r_A - 9\%)$$
$$r_A = 15\%.$$

Required rate of return on equity with the proposed capital structure would be

$$r_E = 15\% + 40\%/60\% * (15\% - 9\%)$$
$$r_E = 19\%.$$

The overall cost of capital, of course, remains constant at 15 per cent.

Risk is a critical element in understanding the impact of debt financing on valuation. Companies take on debt due to its lower cost. The lower cost is a reflection of the lower risk being absorbed by debt providers. Since the total risk of the company does not change, the remaining equity takes on a higher risk. A higher risk implies that the required rate of return also increases.

The value of a company is determined by the expected cash flows and the risk associated with the cash flows. A change in the capital structure changes neither the cash flows nor the total risk of the company; hence, value remains the same. The only change is in the distribution of the risk between the different components of capital, namely debt and equity?

Creating Value through Assumptions

Given the assumptions of the model, there is a unanimous acceptance of the MM propositions. The question that is often posed is whether the assumptions are unrealistic and whether that makes the model itself unrealistic.

Every theory is based on certain assumptions which enable the model to represent reality in a simplified manner. Without those assumptions, reality proves too complicated for us to arrive at any meaningful conclusions. There is unanimity amongst experts that given the assumptions, the conclusions of the MM Model are valid. It is the assumptions that provide us a framework for action. Let us understand how.

Taxation

Operating profits represent EBIT. There are three sets of claimants to these operating cash flows as shown in Figure 7.2:

1. Debt providers in the form of interest
2. The government by way of taxes
3. Equity shareholders as net profits

Until now, we had assumed away taxes and thus the EBIT was shared between debt providers and equity shareholders. A change in the capital structure of the company did not change the cash flows available to investors; it merely represented a change in the way cash flows were

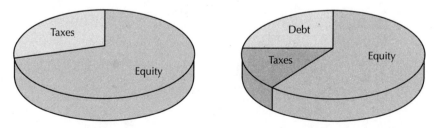

FIGURE 7.2   Change in claims to operating profits as a consequence of borrowing

Source: Author.

distributed amongst the claimants. Taxes are, however, a fact of life and any portion of cash flow that the government takes away means that much less remains for the investors. If the company can reduce the payment of taxes to the government, there will be a corresponding increase in the annual cash flows to investors and thereby the value of the company.

Equity and debt differ in terms of their impact on tax liability. Interest paid on borrowing is recognized as an expense and is deducted from operating profits to calculate profit before tax, leading to a lower tax liability. The return on equity is calculated post-tax. Dividends are a below-the-line item, a part of net profits after the taxes have been paid. The payment of dividends has no impact on corporate taxes. Let us understand with our example of ABC Ltd and XYZ Ltd as in Table 7.5.

When the company (ABC) is entirely equity-financed, its tax liability is ₹18 million and the balance profit after tax of ₹42 million is available to equity shareholders.

When the company (XYZ) is 50 per cent financed by debt, it pays an interest of ₹25 million (10 per cent on borrowing of ₹250 million), leaving ₹35 million as taxable profits. Hence, the tax paid is only ₹10.5 million, resulting in a saving of ₹7.5 million. (₹7.5 million, of course, is equal to 30 per cent of the interest expense of ₹25 million.) The reduction in tax liability because of deductibility of interest on debt as an expense is known as the tax shield.

The earnings of the levered company, amounting to ₹60 million are shared as

- ₹25 million with debt providers as interest,
- ₹10.5 million to the government as taxes and
- the balance ₹24.5 million to equity shareholders as net profits.

The saving in taxes increases the cash flows to investors. A debt-financed company pays less in taxes and, therefore, a higher cash flow from EBIT is claimed by investors. The total cash flow to investors is thus ₹49.5 million, which is ₹7.5 million higher than for ABC Ltd, the pure-equity company.

How does this impact the value of the company? Two assumptions need to be made to value the tax shield.

TABLE 7.5   Tax shield calculation (₹ million)

	Firm ABC	*Firm XYZ*
EBIT	60	60
Interest	0	25
Profit before tax (PBT)	60	35
Tax (30%) on PBT	18	10.5
Profit after tax (PAT)	42	24.5
Income to bondholders and equity shareholders	42	49.5
Tax shield		7.5

Source: Author.

The first assumption is that the current capital structure of the company continues in the future too. Therefore, the available tax shield will continue in the years to follow. If the debt levels and leverage were to change, so will the tax shield and the cash flows.

Second, we assume that the company continues to make sufficient profits in the future. It is self-evident that a loss-making company (or a company with low profits) will be unable to take advantage of the tax deductibility of interest, since it would have anyway not been liable to pay corporate tax.

If these assumptions are valid, the tax shield is available to the company in perpetuity and enhanced cash flow to investors, equivalent to the tax shield, would accrue annually forever. The value of the tax shield can then be estimated as a perpetuity cash flow.

The perpetuity cash flow needs to be discounted, and the appropriate discount rate for the tax shield is equivalent to the cost of debt.

For the previous example, the cost of debt is 10 per cent. Discounting 0.75 by 10 per cent, we get

$$0.75/10\% = ₹75 \text{ million.}$$

Thus, the value of debt-financed company XYZ Ltd will be the value of equity-financed company plus the value of the tax shield.

$$\text{Value of ABC Ltd} = 42/12\% = ₹350 \text{ million.}$$

(The value has reduced from our earlier calculation due to the payment of taxes at 30 per cent. Originally, we had assumed away taxes. Hence, the value of the company has also gone down by (500 − 350)/500 = 30%.)

The value of XYZ Ltd equals 350 + 75 = ₹425 million.

To sum up, a company that takes on debt to partly finance its investment requirements pays coupon interest to the lenders. The interest paid, being an expense, reduces taxable profits and thereby the taxes paid. Assuming that the capital structure remains constant and the company makes sufficient profits to take advantage of the tax deductibility of interest, the tax shield is permanent (perpetuity cash flow) in nature. This leads to an increase in the value of the company, equalling the PV of the perpetuity tax shield.

Tax Shield Value Estimation

Interest paid = debt * interest rate.
Tax saved = (debt * interest rate) * tax rate.

Value of tax shield equals

(debt * interest rate * tax rate)/ interest rate = debt * tax rate.

In our example, the value of tax shield equals

250 million * 30% = ₹75 million.

Given that the payment of interest on debt is a tax-deductible expense, the effective cost of debt becomes much lower. The cost of debt needs to be reduced by the savings on account of the interest expense. The effective post-tax cost of debt is

$$R_D (1 - t).$$

And the weighted average cost of capital can be calculated as follows:

$$\text{WACC} = r_D (1 - t) [D/(D + E)] + r_E [E/(D + E)].$$

The increase in value of the company on account of the tax shield can be substantial. In the previous example, the tax shield amounts to more than 20 per cent, with the value of the company increasing from ₹350 million to ₹425 million. Companies with unused debt capacity must assess the benefit of the tax shield to arrive at an appropriate capital structure.

Personal Taxation

A company is able to increase its returns if it finances part of the capital with debt. It pays less taxes, leaving higher returns for the investors.

What is important to an investor is the return after personal taxes have been paid by him/her, that is, the investor's own post-tax return, and not the company's return. There is a difference in the way debt and equity incomes in the hands of an investor are treated. Based on the income tax rules applicable, the optimum capital structure can be worked out to maximize post-tax returns to investors.

On the whole, the personal tax rules are heavily stacked in favour of the equity investors. While devising its capital structure policy, a company needs to take into account the differential treatment of corporate and personal taxes and accordingly decide on the optimum capital structure from the investors' point of view.

Bankruptcy and Distress

The benefits of the tax shield would appear to suggest the maximization of debt in order to maximize the value of the company. There is, however, a limit to leverage since debt increases risk by making profitability and cash flows more variable. At the extreme, it can lead to cash flow problems or a state of distress. Many companies have gone into bankruptcy due to the excessive use of debt to fund their need for capital. Nortel Networks, the highest-valued company in the Canadian Stock Exchange as recently as the year 2000, filed for bankruptcy in January 2009. Many Indian companies in infrastructure, steel, power and similar areas are in deep trouble, unable to pay their dues to bankers and lenders. The financial crisis of 2008 was rooted in high debt, with some of the financial institutions having a leverage exceeding 30:1! Banks in India, especially public sector banks, are suffering due to the large non-performing assets on their books.

Risk Inherent in Debt Financing

Jaypee Group is a fairly large business house in India, operating primarily in the cement and power industry. During the booming years of the early-twenty-first century, it was optimistic about the future and envisioned great opportunities. It expanded capacities and took on many large projects in its quest for rapid growth.

The proposed investments required large funding. Promoters usually do not like to dilute their equity especially when they are highly optimistic about future prospects. Jaypee Group thus took recourse to massive borrowings, which at one point in time exceeded ₹680 billion.

The power sector business is subject to regulatory and environmental risks, especially hydroelectricity, which comprises a significant part of Jaypee's business portfolio. Delays in project execution and the downturn in the Indian economy have taken a heavy toll on the company. It has defaulted on its borrowing and its market value has been severely impacted. The company is now selling off large parts of its business to meet its commitments and to ensure it does not become bankrupt. The story has been repeated for many industrial groups, including some well-known names. These companies can now be expected to have a better appreciation of the risks inherent in debt and the value of equity funding.

Higher debt leads to greater volatility in cash flows of the company. The impact of volatility on value is a function of the probability of distress and the cost of such distress.

Value of the company = value if entirely equity financed + value of tax shield
– present value of financial distress.

The value of a company will, therefore, be maximized at a level of debt where the marginal benefit of tax reduction equals the marginal cost of distress.

With the introduction of the Insolvency and Bankruptcy Code in India, 2016, bankruptcy resolution is becoming professional and transparent. Companies need to take it into consideration in devising their capital structure.

Financing

The third assumption of the MM Model is that there are no costs incurred while raising funds. It assumes a frictionless world where money flows without any cost. For example, the company may borrow to increase dividend payment to shareholders. It can raise money through equity to pay off existing debt. All these transactions are assumed to be costless, without any impact on decision-making. Reality, as we know, is quite different with significant implications for the company's financing decisions.

There are two kinds of costs in raising funds. First are the transaction costs, inclusive of commissions and promotion expenses. When a company issues shares to the public, transaction costs can be substantial. Depending on the size of the equity issue, transaction costs can range from 5 per cent to 8 per cent of the total amount of the issue. Raising equity directly from large private funds is cheaper and faster, but there are limits to how much can be financed through private funding. Issuing corporate bonds to the public can also be expensive, although it usually costs much less than equity. Other means of raising funds such as term loans, bank borrowing, venture capital and private equity are not as expensive as public issues. All the same, it would be safe to assume that transaction costs of financing are not insignificant as assumed by the MM Model.

More critical are the signalling costs. While it is usually assumed that information about a company is easily and freely available publicly, in practice that may not be true. Insiders, meaning the company's managers, usually have greater access to information than others on the outside. Information asymmetry is a fact of life. Managers of a company know more about its performance, future prospects, technological breakthroughs, customer acquisition, projects in the pipeline and proposed tie-ups or joint ventures with a partner. Such information can have a significant bearing on the value of a company.

Managers often feel the need to convey such information to outside investors, especially if the information is favourable. But, in general, investors and other stakeholders have little faith in what the management says. There is, usually, little credibility in claims made by the company.

Action, as we know, speaks louder than words and can help the management bridge the credibility gap with investors. Investors may not believe what the management says, but they take cues from their actions to infer vital information. For example, managers of most companies believe that their company's shares are underpriced and deserve a higher valuation. Their view, usually, has no conceivable impact on the share price. However, a stock buyback demonstrates to the investors that the company's management is putting its money where its mouth is. No management would buy back equity if it believed that the shares are overpriced. Actions have credibility that words lack, and a stock purchase programme is a credible indication of the management view that shares are underpriced. A change in dividends, as we will discuss in the next chapter, has a similar influence on the investors' perception of the company and the share price.

Conversely, the sale of equity implies that the current value of equity is attractive enough for the company's management to contemplate equity sales. Studies carried out over a long period of time indicate that an imminent prospect of equity sales reduces the price of a share, on an average, by about 3 per cent, which is quite a significant decline. Managers are reluctant to issue equity to fund their investments and may, at times, even forego positive NPV projects if such projects need to be funded by the sale of equity shares.

Given the likely fall in the value of equity, companies prefer to finance their requirements of long-term funding with debt. A reduction in bond price is not significant and the impact on value is only marginal. However, resorting to debt-financing cannot be endless, limited as it is by the current debt–equity ratio in comparison with the targeted debt–equity ratio. If the leverage is already high, further borrowing may not be feasible. Companies like to keep some cushion in their capital structure so that when additional funds are required, they can do so through borrowing and take recourse to equity only under exceptional circumstances. Thus, the capital structure matters and can impact corporate value significantly.

Financing and Strategy

Farm equipment is a highly competitive industry worldwide. During the 1970s, Deere & Company, Massey Fergusson and International Harvester were the three largest companies globally. All of them were adversely impacted by the rising prices of oil and high inflation. The highly leveraged position of Massey Fergusson and International Harvester forced them to curtail their business and extract stiff terms from their dealers. Deere & Company, however, was primarily equity-financed and had substantial capacity to take on debt. It used that capacity to borrow funds for investment in manufacturing and for supporting its dealers, increasing its market share substantially from 38 per cent in 1976 to 49 per cent in 1980. This was a classic case of financial flexibility supporting business strategy with great success.

By 1981, it had exhausted its borrowing capacity but still continued supporting its dealers. The money required was raised through an equity issue of US$172 million. The signalling impact of the equity issue was so strong that the equity value dropped by US$241 million, more than the size of the issue.

The two events, over a period of a decade, provided contrasting learnings to Deere & Company and demonstrated the value of financial flexibility, the use of finance as a competitive tool and the power of market signalling.

Agency Cost of Free Cash Flows

We are by now well aware that debt and equity have different return–risk characteristics. Usually, that does not create a governance problem as management decisions have a similar impact on both debt providers as well as equity shareholders. At low levels of leverage, there is hardly any risk of default and the interests of the shareholders and debt providers are aligned.

However, if the debt component in the capital is high, a conflict of interest becomes a distinct possibility, especially when there is an apprehension of financial distress. Debt holders and equity owners may each prefer the company to follow different, even conflicting policies.

A company is governed by equity shareholders; debt holders have no say in running the organization. If the company is facing troubled times, shareholders are likely to take decisions beneficial to them, often at the expense of the bond holders. For instance, shareholders of a troubled company can pay themselves a hefty dividend, leaving very little remaining for the debt providers. They may borrow significantly large amounts, increasing the risk of the existing bond holders and reducing their value.

Debt providers have claims that are fixed and do not increase if the value of the company goes up. On the other hand, if the company's value deteriorates, they may not get what they have been promised. They have a downside risk to their claims.

The equity shareholders' claims have no upper limit. They get 100 per cent of the gains if the company does well. However, if the company falls into bad times, the risk of the fall in the value will be partly shared with the bond holders. We may often find shareholders of a distressed company undertaking risky projects, since they alone will reap the benefits while sharing with bond holders the risk of failure.

Agency Cost in Practice

The higher management of a ₹10 billion mature company with regular, large cash flows and very little investment opportunities may be staring at a personal future that does not seem very bright. The further growth in the size of the company being limited, the scope for personal advancement is also hampered. A senior manager would be keen to make investments that would take the company towards much higher revenues, reckoning that his chances of promotion would thereby improve significantly. He is personally unaffected by the fact that such investments, returning less than the cost of capital, may reduce the value of the company. His own interests are quite clearly at variance with the interest of the shareholders, and the agency cost may be quite significant.

There is often a tendency on the part of managers to retain free cash flows with the company and not return them to shareholders. They start investing free cash flows in negative NPV projects or undertake diversification through acquisitions in unrelated fields to improve their own personal prospects rather than to maximize the value of the company. Like a rich spoilt kid who wants more and more toys to play with, managers of free cash flow-rich companies want their organizations to keep growing to improve their own future prospects and increase their clout. The interest of the managers may not be aligned with the interest of shareholders, and in fact, the two may be conflicting. Since the companies are doing well and generating large cash flows, equity shareholders are unable to discipline the managers. A failure to pay out excess cash flows negatively impacts value.

What is needed is a disciplining mechanism that reins in the personal interests of the management of mature, large, free cash flow-generating companies. Debt can be handy to tackle the problem.

The ideal solution would be for the company to take recourse to large borrowing and return this amount to shareholders, either through a large one-time dividend, stock buyback or a combination of the two. Given the comfortable cash position of the company, debt would be easily available and is likely to be inexpensive. The resultant obligation to pay interest and maturity value, in place of discretionary dividends, is likely to discipline managers who would hopefully realize the dangers of excessive growth at returns lower than the cost of capital. If subsequent cash flows are impacted and the company faces problems in repayments, creditors are likely to take charge of the company and the current management's control may be seriously jeopardized. Their own personal interest would then ensure that the cash flow of the company is prudently utilized and not wasted in unrelated, negative NPV projects. Borrowing on a large scale, despite there being no requirement for funds, aligns the interest of shareholders and managers and reduces the agency cost significantly.

Agency Cost and Free Cash Flow

For those in the 50-years-plus age bracket, Bajaj Auto Limited was an iconic company that single-handedly catered to the country's demand for two-wheelers, primarily scooters, in the pre-liberalization days. Being a monopoly, there was a waiting period in excess of 10 years for its most popular model, the Chetak. Prices were high, sales volumes were large and assured, and cash flow generation was sustained and enormous. Further boosting the cash flows were the deposits taken from the prospective customers for booking its scooters.

The cash flows were so large that they competed with the core business of two-wheelers in terms of profitability. Financing requirements being non-existent, the company did not need to approach the shareholders or lenders for financing its investments and an attitude developed wherein the interests of the promoters and the management were predominant. The company easily washed off its obligations to the shareholders by giving only a small dividend annually.

There cannot be a starker illustration of the agency cost of free cash flows. If the cash flows with the company were returned to shareholders, the shareholder value would have gone up substantially. Instead, the huge cash flows were invested in various financial instruments that were value-destroying with returns less than the company's cost of capital. Retaining free cash flows (and not returning them to shareholders) can lead to a significant reduction of corporate value.

While the environment, post-liberalization, has become more competitive, the cash flows keep accruing on a regular basis and the problem of agency cost of free cash flows persists, though at a much reduced level. Some of the best companies in the country (and abroad) continue to treat the shareholders merely as an afterthought!

Adjusted Present Value

An alternative method of valuation is the adjusted present value (APV). The APV method first establishes the base value of the company, assuming that the company is entirely equity-financed. Then it finds the impact of various aspects of financing separately such as taxation, distress and government subsidies. The value of each of these is then added or subtracted as the case may be.

$$APV = \text{base case NPV} +/- \text{the value of financing.}$$

The APV method helps to figure out the impact that different financing aspects have on valuation. How much is the cost of securities issue and is it significantly impacting the value of the project? Is the government-subsidized financing option a significant factor? What is the value of the tax shield? Are the liberal financing options provided by the machinery supplier a significant factor in the valuation of the project? The method unbundles the different components of value and analyses each of them separately. It is, therefore, easy to find out the contribution of the different aspects to the project or the corporate value as the case may be. We, therefore, know not only the total value of a company but also where the value has come from.

The APV method is particularly useful in certain specific kinds of transactions, such as the leveraged buyout (LBO). A significant value addition takes place due to the large amount of debt that finances the purchase of the acquired company in an LBO. Similarly, international projects usually come tied up with distinct, specific contracts—financing, suppliers, customers and so forth. There may also be restrictions on repatriation of profits in international projects. The cost of such restrictions should be reduced from the value of the project.

The method is particularly useful when the debt–equity ratio changes significantly in the future, making it difficult to estimate an appropriate WACC for the project. The method does not suffer from such a limitation.

Putting It Together

Following are the four MM assumptions we have discussed earlier:

1. Companies pay corporate tax as per the applicable rates and are able to take advantage of the tax deductibility of interest payments.
2. Debt increases the volatility of cash flows and thereby the risk. At higher levels, this may lead to distress, even bankruptcy.
3. Raising funds is not costless, and financing costs can be significant.
4. Debt and equity providers may have different objectives and payoffs, leading to agency costs. Resolving conflicts between the two is critical but costly.

The capital structure of the company impacts investment and operating decisions, at times significantly; to that extent the capital structure matters. However, to look for value through the capital structure, we need to take into consideration the assumptions underlying the MM Model and not just the propositions of the model.

The assumptions of the MM Model help us understand value creation through capital structure changes. No broad generalization can be made; each company has to be looked at independently to figure out which assumptions are relevant and applicable in adding value to it. A mature company with large regular cash flows is unlikely to reach anywhere near bankruptcy or financial distress but would be in a position to take advantage of the tax deductibility of interest on debt. Such a company adds value by greater borrowing. On the other hand, a company approaching financial distress is likely to gain substantially by infusing equity capital, making the company safer and avoiding a conflict of interest between shareholders and debt providers.

Based on this, two broad theories have emerged on how companies should establish their capital structure. The difference between the two theories lies in the importance given respectively to taxes or bankruptcy costs vis-à-vis signalling and agency problems.

Trade-Off Theory

The trade-off theory, as the name suggests, is a trade-off, or a choice, between the benefits of the tax deductibility of interest expense and the costs of financial distress and bankruptcy as a consequence of high debt. In the initial stages when the level of debt is low, taxation benefits would be predominant. The company is likely to have sufficient profits, and the tax liability can be reduced by borrowing funds. At the same time, low debt levels ensure that the company is safe and far from any semblance of bankruptcy or even distress.

As the level of debt rises, profits may prove to be insufficient. Even if the company is able to avail the tax benefits in the current year, its ability to do so in the coming years may not be assured. Sustained profits at high levels cannot be guaranteed. In addition, at a higher level of debt, there exists a significant probability of financial distress that makes the company risky, negatively impacting its value.

There is a specific level of debt at which the marginal benefit of tax deductibility of interest expense equals the marginal cost of higher financial distress. At that level of debt, the value of the company is maximized, and it is the job of the finance manager to find that level.

The value of the leveraged company equals

the value of the company without leverage (only equity financing) *plus* the present value of the tax shield *less* the cost of financial distress.

While it may be difficult to specify and find out the exact level of debt where the value of the company is maximized, what may be done is to balance the tax benefit and the cost of higher risk to optimize the capital structure.

Financial Distress and Rolling the Dice, Literally

Shortly after launching FedEx, founder Frederick Smith was running out of cash and on the verge of shutting the company's operations. The problem was the massive fixed costs (airplanes, sorting facilities, delivery personnel and so forth) and the low initial volume. 'By 1973, Smith was so desperate for cash that he flew to Las Vegas to play the blackjack tables. He wired the $27,000 he won back to FedEx.'

The company used the winnings to pay its fuel bills, and the rest is history.

Source: Business Week (2004).

The implications are fairly obvious as follows:

1. Companies with safe tangible assets, predictable future and taxable income rely more heavily on debt than on equity. Since the operating risk is low, they can take on a high financial risk.
2. Companies that are risky, whose assets are primarily intangible and which face an uncertain, volatile future rely more on equity than on debt. Already facing a high operating risk, financial risk should be kept to the minimum.

The Pecking Order Theory

The pecking order theory is based on the signalling aspect of raising capital. As already discussed earlier, the sale of securities by a company has significant signalling costs. The investors take the issuance of equity as an indication that the management believes its shares have little scope for further gain. Investors act in accordance with information thus deduced and sell their own holdings, bringing down the price of equity. The fall in price is minimal for debt but significant for equity.

The choice of the issue of security is, therefore, not based on the company's targeted capital structure; rather, there is a hierarchy in terms of accessing funds. Being averse to outside funding, companies rely initially on internally generated funds to finance their requirement for positive NPV projects.

If the internally generated funds are insufficient and outside funding is the only alternative, there is a marked preference for debt rather than equity. Debt has a low signalling cost, which may appeal to many companies. However, the amount of debt a company can raise is limited by its target capital structure. Eventually, external equity may be the only remaining option.

Companies are usually reluctant to issue equity to fund their investments, since equity costs can be substantial. They sell equity only as a last resort and may sometimes even forego value accretive projects if the only way to fund them is external equity.

Thus, there are two sets of choices a company has to make, namely a choice between internal and external funds and a choice between debt and equity, in case external funds are required. There is a hierarchy or a pecking order—internal funds, debt and, only then, equity.

Given this, it is easy to understand, as we will discuss in the next chapter on dividends, why dividend decisions are taken keeping in mind the need for funding investments along with internal generation of funds over a long period. Companies prefer to pay a lower dividend than later being faced with the prospect of accessing equity from outside. The dividend policy is based on the company's expected generation of cash flows from operations along with investment requirements and targeted capital structure over the long term.

Financing Decision and Growth

We have discussed the various ways in which financial choices can impact the value of a company. There is no single, all-purpose strategy that is value-accretive universally. The financial choices a company makes are dictated by the nature of its business and its operations. Financial strategy must support business strategy and structure and never try to be the master. The financial strategy adopted is primarily dependent on the requirements of the business. Different businesses, at different stages, need to be supported by different financial strategies as follows:

1. A high-growth company creates value through new investments, which require capital at frequent intervals. Financing should support such investments by maintaining access to the financial markets. Debt financing should be limited.

   Moreover, high-growth companies generate volatile incomes and cash flows which increases the chances of financial distress. A large proportion of the company's value is represented by intangible growth opportunities. Both these factors rule out high levels of debt.

   What kind of financial policies should high-growth companies adopt?
   a. Leverage should be low and spare borrowing capacity should be available at all times, so that funds can be raised whenever required without constraining and pressurizing equity.
   b. The dividend policy should be conservative, and cash should be retained by the company.
   c. Primary value creation happens through positive NPV investments, which should never be hampered by the non-availability of funding. The company should not hesitate to raise funds externally if required. Any negative impact from signalling will be more than compensated by positive value creation from investments. Investor communication is the key. If the company's story is properly projected and investors can be convinced of the value creation from the investments, they are likely to be supportive of the company's fund-raising exercise and equity prices may not decline.

   In a nutshell, a high-growth company generates value through investments which need to be supported adequately by the financial policy. The role of finance is supportive, and the financial policy should primarily be conservative.

2. For low-growth mature companies, the problem is much easier, since it involves dealing with excessive cash flows. Mature companies do not have to face problems of financial flexibility and market signalling. Such companies no longer have investment opportunities available and must use financial strategy primarily to increase value. Value can be added by borrowing as much as possible and deploying the funds available to buy back stock. Debt financing thus becomes a strategy to improve value.

   Such a strategy adds value in three ways. First, a large debt provides a reduction in tax liability, increasing returns to investors. Second, stock buyback gives a fillip to stock prices. Finally, it aligns management incentives with those of shareholders and reduces the agency cost. The payment of interest and principal imposes discipline on the managers to run the business in a professional manner.

Use of Recapitalization to Increase Value

Colts Industries was a market leader in the aerospace and automotive business. By the mid-1980s, both these businesses had matured with little opportunities available for further investments. At the same time, cash flows were large and regular.

Faced with excessive free cash flows, Colts Industries decided to recapitalize the company and return a large part of the cash flows to its shareholders. It borrowed US$1.4 billion, using the borrowed money to pay each shareholder US$85. Colts Industries also exchanged one share of the old company for one share of the newly recapitalized company. Expecting large cash flows in the future from its operations, it was able to secure financing on competitive terms.

Prior to the recapitalization, Colt's share was trading at US$67. After recapitalization, the share traded at US$10. Along with the received US$85, the value to shareholders increased from US$67 to US$95, a gain of over 40 per cent.

Interestingly, the book value of each share was much less than US$85. Therefore, the payment of US$85 to shareholders reduced the net worth of the company in the balance sheet. The recapitalization was undertaken on such a large scale that net worth actually became negative to the extent of US$157 million, demonstrating dramatically that book value and market value of equity can be at variance with each other.

What Happens in Practice

Research has been carried out to find out how managers determine the capital structure and what are the key practices.

1. Most companies have a low debt in their funding. They seem to give up the benefits of tax saving in order to reduce risk and ensure flexibility for future requirements. This has proven to be a sane practice, given that companies with a high debt are often punished by markets, leading to a reduction in their equity values.
2. Many companies, in fact, have zero debt, validating the pecking order theory, according to which companies with large cash flows fund their needs from internal funds.
3. Most companies have a target debt–equity ratio, and the existing capital structure is a result of a deliberate decision by managers.
4. Companies from the same industry tend to have similar capital structures, whereas there are significant variations across different industries. Thus, operating business characteristics determine the capital structure of companies.
5. General characteristics of an economy are also important determinants of the capital structure. The US economy is a mature one with limited growth opportunities. Despite the prevailing low interest rates and the low cost of capital, the demand for investment is

limited. Need for funds being low, debt can satisfy the entire need for funds. Equity issue by already established companies is a rare occurrence.

India, on the other hand, is still an emerging market with plenty of opportunities for investment. Companies have a significant appetite for growth and raise money through whatever means possible. Any consequent reduction in the value of equity is more than made up by the value addition in invested projects.

At times, the enthusiasm for investment gets the better of the managers who, envisaging promising future prospects, tie up the company in knots, endangering the company's value. The JP Group, Adani, Videocon, Reliance, Essar, GMR and many other well-known companies have found themselves in a debt trap in recent times. These companies would now certainly appreciate the value of financial slack.

Reverse Engineering

Lending is a hopeful act, the hope that the money lent will be returned by the borrower. Corporate debt is risky; the borrowing company's cash flows in the future may be insufficient to pay the coupon interest and maturity value. Some debt is riskier, others less so. Credit rating companies help assess how risky a specific debt is. Typically, the higher the risk, the higher the return required by the investor and hence the higher the cost to the company.

Companies like to maintain a high credit rating in order to reduce their own cost of capital. Higher debt leads to a lower credit rating and vice versa. There is an increasing trend whereby companies are 'reverse engineering' their capital structure. They target a certain credit rating and accordingly work backwards to estimate the maximum amount of debt they can raise, consistent with the desired credit rating.

Let us conclude with some implications based on theory as well as practice.

1. There is no single common target leverage ratio for everyone. It varies depending largely on the nature of the business and operating characteristics.
2. Profitable companies use less debt, since they have cash flow available and do not need to access external funds.
3. Companies prefer financial slack and value the flexibility it gives them. In case of need, they prefer to have choices in terms of raising money. They try and avoid raising funds when market conditions are unfavourable.

KEY CONCEPTS

1. Capital structure refers to the proportion of debt and equity in the total capital of the company. It has the potential to significantly impact the long-term performance of the company and its value.

2. Several luminaries have contributed to the development of capital structure theory, raising the profile of finance and the value it adds to the corporate sector. Most of these luminaries have been recipients of the Nobel Prize for their contribution to the subject.

3. Debt has a lower cost but leads to a higher risk for equity shareholders. The impact on value is debatable.

4. The cost of capital is one of the most critical parameters pertaining to a company. It helps value companies and determines investment in new projects.

5. The cost of capital refers to the investor/market-determined required rate of return for investment in the company. Risk is a critical element of the cost of capital.

6. The MM Model was the most significant advancement in financial theory. The model postulates that the capital structure is irrelevant and the value and share price of a levered and unlevered company, which are otherwise similar, will be the same.

7. Modigliani and Miller proved their theorem on the basis of arbitrage. According to the model, any difference in the price of two securities will be arbitraged away.

8. Assumptions underlying the MM Model provide a guide to valuation. These assumptions include absence of taxes, distress and bankruptcy, insignificant financing cost including the cost of signalling and the resolution of conflicts by stakeholders.

9. Based on these assumptions, trade-off theory and pecking order theory have emerged as popular theories of capital structure.

10. Capital structure should be supportive of the company's business strategy and operations.

CHAPTER QUESTIONS

1. ABC Ltd is an all equity-financed company with a cost of capital of 16 per cent. The current market value of the company is ₹1 billion, and it has 10 million shares outstanding. It has plans to issue ₹200 million debt at 10 per cent interest. The company intends to use the proceeds to repurchase shares of its own stock.
    a. What is likely to happen to the price of ABC Ltd stock?
    b. How many shares will be outstanding after the repurchase plan is completed?
    c. What will be the cost of equity and the cost of capital?

2. Why is debt considered to be risky? Why do companies borrow if debt is so risky?

3. Many hypotheses on capital structure were popular prior to the formulation of the MM theory? What is so special about the MM theory? In what way was the MM Model a game changer in corporate finance?

4. Why is the cost of capital important for a company? What considerations should a company keep in mind while estimating its cost of capital?

5. The cost of capital refers to the investor-/market-determined required rate of return for investment in the company. Elaborate.

6. What are the assumptions on which the MM Model is based? What is the significance of each of these assumptions?

7. What are the two propositions of the MM Model? What is the significance of these propositions?

8. What costs are incurred by a company in raising funds through equity?
9. What do you understand by the agency cost of free cash flow? How can it be overcome?
10. How are the approaches of the trade-off theory and the pecking order theory different? What are the conclusions of the two theories?
11. Three companies have similar business profiles and are identical in every respect, except of their capital structure. Each has an operating income of ₹4,000 and a capital of ₹20,000.

    Company A is entirely financed through equity.

    Company B has ₹5,000 debt, the balance being equity.

    Company C has ₹10,000 debt, and the balance is equity.

    The interest on debt is 12 per cent. There are no taxes.

    What is the return on equity for the three companies in an MM world? What are the share prices of the three companies? Justify your answer. Company A has 500 shares.
12. ABC Ltd has ₹10 billion capital invested. Currently, it has a capital structure whereby 30 per cent is debt and 70 per cent is equity. The return on equity is 16 per cent and on debt is 10 per cent. The company is planning to change the capital structure to 50 per cent debt and 50 per cent equity. What is the likely cost of capital and the required return on equity? Assume no taxes.
13. Infosys Ltd has a market value of ₹3,000 billion. It has a marginal tax rate of 28 per cent. The company decides to change its no borrowing policy to take on a leverage equalling 20 per cent of its current value. What is the value of the tax shield if the new leverage is likely to be permanent?
14. According to the capital structure theory, companies with promising business opportunities should strive to maintain a conservative capital structure. Why?
15. Stockholders can transfer wealth from bondholders through a variety of actions. How would this happen in the following scenarios?
    a. An increase in dividends
    b. A leveraged buyout
    c. Acquiring a risky business

CASE FOR DISCUSSION

A few years back, the Indian economy was facing tough times with surging inflation and high commodity prices adversely impacting operations and profitability of the corporate sector. The RBI had adopted a tight monetary policy in order to curb inflation, leading to an extreme shortage of funds. The situation was so bad that even the Indian government was forced to borrow at an unprecedented rate of 14 per cent per annum. It was precisely at this time that ABC Ltd required a large funding for its expansion in the electronics sector. The funds were required for a long term—the investment in electronics being a long-term project. The company presented a risky opportunity to the lenders who charged a hefty spread of 600 basis points; hence the company's borrowing rate was 20 per cent. Equity issue was not an option, equity markets being depressed, and the large funding would have meant a substantial dilution of equity.

The situation since then has improved considerably with mild inflation and easy availability of funds in the economy. The successful implementation of the capacity expansion has improved cash flows and thereby the credit rating of the company. ABC's stock has performed consistently well, displaying mild volatility, leading to a low beta. The 10-year Government of Indiapaper commands 7 per cent yield to maturity, and the equity risk premium for the market has also reduced to 500 basis points. With a relatively low beta, compared to its levels historically, the cost of equity of the company is 11 per cent.

During a presentation to the board of directors, the CFO of the company patted himself on the back for reducing the cost of equity substantially and in fact claimed that under his charge the company has reached a situation where the cost of equity (11 per cent) is much lower than the cost of debt (20 per cent). He further boasted that the financial reengineering undertaken by the company had enabled him to defy financial theory to take the company's cost of equity below the cost of debt.

Please comment critically on the statement made by the CFO.

What are the different concepts in financial theory that form a part of the events outlined in this section, and which determine the cost of capital of the company and its capital structure?

CHAPTER 8

Dividend Payout

Policy and Practices

Do you know the only thing that gives me pleasure? It's to see my dividends coming in.

—John D. Rockefeller

Microsoft was started, with remarkable success, by Bill Gates and Paul Allen in 1975. Over the next few years, the company established itself as the premier software company in the world. Windows became the standard operating software that everyone installed on their computers. The company earned large profits and accumulated huge cash flows over the years.

However, Microsoft did not pay dividends to its shareholders for the first 28 years of its existence. Then, in 2003, it announced what CFO John Connors (quoted in CBS News, 2003) called 'a starter dividend' of US$0.08 per share. A year later, on 20 July 2004, Microsoft stunned the financial markets by announcing plans to pay the single largest cash dividend in the history of the US corporate sector, a one-time dividend of US$3 per share amounting to US$32 billion. In addition, Microsoft announced plans to repurchase up to US$30 billion of its stock over the next four years and pay regular quarterly dividends at an annual rate of US$0.32 per share.

Over the years, Microsoft has been steadily enhancing its dividend payout. The dividend has increased from US$0.32 to US$1.47 per share which amounts to an annual cash outflow of over US$11 billion. Some analysts have started terming Microsoft as a dividend play; they recommend buying Microsoft for its dividend yield and not for potential capital gains. A software company as a dividend play? That too a market leader!

What is the significance of the company's 'no dividend' policy prior to 2003 and the high dividends now? Is the dividend policy immaterial, as the Modigliani–Miller Model claims, or does it have a significance beyond just the dividend yield a shareholder obtains?

A company can use its earnings in four ways:

1. Retain and invest in long-term projects
2. Pay off liabilities
3. Pay cash dividends to shareholders
4. Repurchase its own equity (stock buyback)

Cash dividends and the repurchase of equity transfer funds from the company to the shareholders and are the primary means by which shareholders earn from their investments in the company.

Earlier in the book, we have discussed the difference between debt and equity. Debt providers are paid an annual coupon rate of interest, usually fixed, which must be paid, irrespective of the profits made or losses incurred by the company. The interest is paid from the operating profits and the coupon interest reduces the taxable profits of the company and thereby the taxes payable. Thus, debt is safer, has fixed returns and the interest paid on debt is tax-deductible.

Equity shareholders receive dividends from the company. Dividends are not assured, depending, as they do, on the profits made and the cash flow requirements of the company. The board of directors decides the dividend payout on a quarterly/annual basis. Dividend payment is uncertain, being paid after the debt providers and the government have got their dues by way of coupon interest and corporate tax. Dividends are paid out of the net profit (or retained earnings) and carry no tax benefits for the company.

Dividends

Dividends may be paid annually, half-yearly or quarterly. Until a few years back, the payment of dividend was a logistical nightmare involving the calculation of dividend amount for each shareholder, the preparation of cheques, putting each in an envelope with an appropriate address, dispatching the same and, finally, the shareholder depositing the cheque in his account at the bank. The subsequent reconciliation was even more onerous. The entire cost was prohibitive, and companies preferred to pay annual rather than quarterly dividends.

In the current technology-enabled environment, the whole process is smooth and fast with automated calculation and electronic credit of dividends into shareholders' designated bank accounts. Most companies now prefer to pay quarterly dividends since shareholders like receiving dividends more frequently, even if the total annual dividend remains the same.

Kinds of Dividends

At times, companies throw in an extra dividend. This may be on account of large cash flows that have accumulated over the years which the company now wants to return to the shareholders (as Microsoft did in 2004). The additional dividend could be on account of the sale of a division, an asset or a brand resulting in the receipt of a substantial one-time cash flow or a special event such as the golden anniversary of the company. Although rare, a company may pay a liquidating dividend when it ceases to exist. After all the liabilities have been paid off, whatever remains is a final payment to the shareholders.

Often, the company pays what is termed a stock dividend. Each shareholder gets additional shares in proportion to the number of shares already owned by him/her. No cash leaves the company or is paid to the shareholders. The number of shares outstanding as well as the number of shares owned by a shareholder increase. The actual increase in the number of shares depends on the ratio of stock dividend announced by the company. Thus, if the company declares a 1:2 stock dividend, each shareholder gets one additional share for every two shares held by him/her or additional shares equal to 50 per cent of his/her current holding. However, this has no impact on the value of his/her shareholding nor does he/she gain anything monetarily. The price of the share adjusts to ensure that the total value remains the same.

Assume a company has 10 million shares priced at ₹300, and the value of the company is ₹3 billion. If the company issues 5 million additional shares (1:2 stock dividend), the price of the share should drop to ₹200 and the total value of the company remains unaltered at ₹3 billion. A shareholder holding 1,000 shares, valued currently at ₹300,000, gets 500 additional shares and now has a total of 1,500 shares. Priced at ₹200 now, the value of his/her holding does not change and remains constant at ₹300,000.

There is no gain or loss to the shareholders or to the company. Stock dividends are similar to exchanging a 100-rupee note for two 50-rupee notes. You may have more notes, but the total value of those notes remains unchanged.

Microsoft raised funds through a public issue in 1986. Since then it has split its stock nine times. A shareholder who owned 1 share in 1986 would by now have multiplied that to 288. Similarly, Walmart has split its stock two-for-one, 11 times since 1970 and one share has now become 2,048.

Companies are also known to provide benefits to shareholders in the form of products or services they produce. Raymond Ltd sends each shareholder discount coupons for its own clothing range. Such gimmicks do not amount to anything substantive but are expected to generate a feel-good factor.

Cash Dividend

The only dividend that has significance in terms of its impact on the shareholders' wealth and is, therefore, relevant for our purpose, is the dividend paid in cash from the net profits of the company. A company can expend its net profits in two ways: it can either retain it for investment in projects for its future growth or pay it to the shareholders as dividends. A dividend payout reduces the cash flow available for investments. It is in this context that dividend is critical to a company. The rest of the chapter discusses cash dividends and its impact.

Theory of Dividend

We visited the Modigliani–Miller theory of capital structure in the previous chapter. Given certain assumptions, Modigliani and Miller have proven that the capital structure does not matter and the value of the company does not change with a change in its capital structure.

Modigliani and Miller have a similar influence on dividend theory. According to them, the impact of a change in dividends can be undone by change in any of the constituents of capital. The company can, for instance, raise dividends, funding it by borrowing which raises the proportion of debt in the capital of the company (or issue equity). Similarly, the company can reduce its dividends and use the extra cash to fund its investments, instead of relying on borrowing. Since the change in debt proportion has no impact on value, it follows that the change in dividends too will have no impact on the value of the company.

Irrelevance of Dividends

The following figures represent the performance of a company, XYZ Ltd.

Net operating profits after tax (NOPAT)	₹10,000
Number of shares	2,000
Cost of capital	12%
Growth rate	7%
Reinvestment needs	₹4,000
Dividends	(10,000 – 4,000) = ₹6,000

Find the value per share.

1. Free cash flows = 10,000 – 4,000 = ₹6,000.
   Value of the company = 6,000 (1 + 7%)/(12% – 7%)
   $$= ₹128,400.$$
   Price per share = 128,400/2,000 = ₹64.20.
   Dividend = 6,000/2,000 = ₹3.
   Value per share = 64.20 + 3 = ₹67.20.

2. Let us say the company decides to double the amount of dividend to ₹12,000. Given its NOPAT of ₹10,000 and ₹4,000 investment plans, the company needs to raise ₹6,000. Let us assume the funds are raised by way of equity.

   The value of the company is ₹128,400 out of which ₹6,000 will be owned by the new shareholders. The value of the company owned by the old shareholders is 128,400 – 6,000 = ₹122,400.

   Therefore, for the old shareholders, the price per share now is 122,400/2,000 = ₹61.20.

   $$\text{Dividend} = 12,000/2,000 = ₹6.$$
   $$\text{Value per share} = 61.20 + 6 = ₹67.20.$$

3. Let us consider the company decides to forego dividends completely. The value of the company is ₹128,400. In addition, the company has ₹6,000 in cash. The total value is, therefore,

   $$128,400 + 6,000 = ₹134,400.$$

   And the value/price per share is 134,400/2,000 = ₹67.20.

   According to the dividend irrelevance theory, a change in the dividends paid by the company does not lead to a change in the value to the shareholders.

Thus, if their proposition of irrelevance of the capital structure holds, it automatically implies the irrelevance of dividends. The value of a company remains immune to changes in dividend payout.

A company generates funds from its operations by way of profits. After paying dividends to the shareholders, the remaining funds are available for investment for future growth. Any shortfall is made up by the company by raising funds through the sale of equity and bonds (debt). As long as the markets are efficient, a positive net present value (NPV) project will not lack funding. Hence, dividend payment is unlikely to reduce funding for lucrative investment opportunities.

Dividend versus Stock Repurchase

There are two ways by which a company can return money to its shareholders. It can pay cash dividends or use the same funds for purchasing some of its stock. Stock repurchase (also called share buyback) reduces the number of outstanding shares. Undertaken at the right price, each share will subsequently be priced higher. In an efficient market, the increase in price due to share buyback will be equal to the dividend forgone. Let us understand with an example.

Assume the following:

Profit after tax (PAT)	₹10,000
Number of shares	1,000
Earnings per share (EPS)	₹10
Price earnings (P/E)	6
Price of share	₹60
Dividend paid	₹4
Total value to shareholders	60 + 4 = ₹64

Assume that instead of paying dividends, the company decides to repurchase shares at ₹64 for a total consideration of 4,000, equalling the total amount of dividends paid earlier.

Number of shares purchased = 4,000/64 = 62.50.
Shares outstanding = 937.50.
EPS = 10,000/937.5 = ₹10.67.
Price of share = 10.67 * 6 = ₹64.

Thus, there is no change in the value of the shareholders' holding. If the company pays dividends of ₹4, the share price is ₹60. Together with the dividend of ₹4, the total value for the shareholders is ₹64. With a stock repurchase, the share is priced at ₹64 but the shareholders do not receive any dividend.

This assumes, of course, that the company does not purchase the shares at a price higher than ₹64. If the shares are purchased at a higher price (> 64), there will be a reduction in value for the remaining shareholders. The post-buyback value of the equity depends on the price at which the buyback is undertaken. The buyback price must be prudently decided to ensure that the company's remaining shareholders do not lose.

Assume for example, the company purchases shares at ₹80. With ₹4,000, it can purchase 4,000/80 = 50 shares and 950 shares will remain outstanding. The new EPS will be 10,000/950 = ₹10.53. Consequently, after the repurchase, the shares will be priced at ₹63.18 (P/E ratio equals 6), reducing the value to the remaining shareholders.

Stock Buyback: Dr Reddy's

On 17 February 2016, Dr Reddy's Laboratory, a leading Indian pharmaceutical company, announced plans for a buyback of its shares as per the following details:

1. Maximum amount ₹15.69 billion
2. At a maximum price of ₹3,500
3. Over a period of six months

This implied repurchase of 4,484,049 shares at the maximum price constituting 2.6 per cent of its equity capital. The promoters' holding would increase partially since they had decided not to participate in the buyback. The share price on 18 February 2016 increased from ₹2,961 to ₹3,094.

Given that the management knows more about a company than outside investors, it is usually assumed that buyback of equity would increase the share price. A company repurchases equity only if the management believes that the intrinsic worth of the equity is not getting reflected in the share price. Contrary to this belief, however, a year and a half after Dr Reddy's undertook equity buyback, the share was ruling at 72 per cent of the pre-buyback price and at 61 per cent of the maximum price at which the buyback was approved by the company. Financial decisions usually have limited, temporary impact and at times, only cosmetic influence on valuation; eventually, the operating and business performance of the company matters. As the MM Model says, the capital structure and dividend decisions have no relevance to the value of a company or of its shares.

Undertaken at the right price, share repurchase and dividend payment provide the same value to the shareholders who should be indifferent between the two.

As is often the case, what happens in practice is different from what theory says. This reminds one of the famous quip by Yogi Berra (a legendary baseball player) that 'in theory, there is no difference between theory and practice; in practice there is'. Usually, the difference is either due to taxation or what the shareholders desire.

Dividend is an income of the person who receives the dividend and is taxable at the rate appliable to his income bracket. An increase in the share price leads to capital gains and is taxable at the rate applicable to capital gains. In most countries, capital gains tax is lower than income tax. Second, capital gains tax is payable only when the shares are sold; a mere increase in value is not taxable. Capital gains tax can thus be postponed to the time when shares are eventually sold. Most investors prefer share buyback which results in an increase in the share price so as to reduce and postpone their tax liability.

The tax on dividend, in fact, amounts to double taxation since the company has already paid corporate tax on its profits earlier. Dividend payments are a mere distribution of what remains with the company after corporate taxes have been paid. Dividend represents the distribution of a portion of the net profits that anyway belong to the shareholders, and taxing distribution after the earnings have already been taxed is unfair in the eyes of many people. Over the years, different countries have resolved the problem in different ways. Currently, in India, the tax provision pertaining to dividends are as follows.

Shareholders are not liable to pay tax on dividends received by them. The company, declaring the dividends, must pay tax on their behalf, termed dividend distribution tax (DDT). This tax rate currently is 15 per cent (gross). Thus, if a company decides to pay dividends amounting to ₹1 billion, it must pay a DDT of ₹150 million to the government and only the balance of ₹850 million will accrue to the shareholders. Assuming that the company has 100 million shares outstanding, each share will be entitled to receive ₹8.5.

The only other relevant provision is that any shareholder who receives a total dividend of more than ₹1 million in a year must pay an additional 10 per cent tax.

Depending on whether the capital gains tax is lower or higher than 15 per cent, the choice of payment in terms of dividends or buyback can be made. In India, any profits made on the sale of shares held for more than a year are treated as long-term capital gains which is taxed at 10 per cent. Profit on shares held for less than a year is termed short-term gain and is taxed at 15 per cent. Capital gains receive a more favourable tax treatment compared to dividends and, therefore, buybacks are preferable.

Since the tax on dividends is paid by the company declaring the dividends, a large number of retail shareholders believe dividends to be tax-free, whereas in fact it is not so.

In the United States of America (USA) and in many other countries, the dividend is treated as an income in the hands of the shareholders and is taxable at the rate applicable to their overall income Capital gains tax is usually lower than income tax, resulting in shareholders preferring share buyback to the payment of dividends.

Share repurchases have assumed critical importance in the USA in recent times with companies purchasing huge volumes of their own shares. The trend has accelerated in the 21st century with companies announcing plans to buyback shares worth over US$1 trillion in the year 2018 alone. This is far greater than the cash dividends paid by the US corporate sector. IBM alone has since 2000 repurchased shares worth US$110 billion. In India, share buybacks have not acquired the prominence that they have in the USA. Share buybacks were allowed in India in 1999, and the Indian corporate sector has not had as much experience with it as the USA corporate sector. Moreover, India is still a growing economy with most companies requiring significant funds for expansion. They would not like to part with large amounts by way of share buyback.

In India, shares that are bought back by companies are extinguished and no longer exist. In the USA, these form a part of the corporate treasury of the company and can be sold again if the company so desires. Different countries have different rules in this regard.

Dividend and Stock Buyback: Shareholder Wealth Agnosticism

Company XYZ Ltd has ₹1 billion in excess cash. The firm expects to generate ₹600 million per year as free cash flows. The cost of capital is 12 per cent. The value of its business is

$$\text{Value} = 60/12\% = ₹5 \text{ billion.}$$

Along with ₹1 billion in cash, the total value of the company is ₹6 billion. The company has 100 million shares. The price per share is ₹60.

The board of directors is considering three options:

1. Use the ₹1 billion excess cash to pay a dividend of ₹10 per share
2. Repurchase shares worth ₹1 billion at ₹60
3. Raise additional cash to pay a larger dividend today and in the future

What would be the impact on share price and on shareholders' wealth for each of the options?

Alternative 1:

Dividend paid = ₹1 billion.
Dividend paid per share = ₹10.
Value of the company post dividend = ₹5 billion.
Price per share = ₹50.
Total value to the shareholders = ₹60.

Alternative 2:

Shares repurchased = 100/60 = 1.67.
Balance shares = ₹83.3 million.
Price per share = 500/8.33 = ₹60.

While the total assets of the company go down from ₹6 billion to ₹ 5 billion, the number of shares also falls, leaving the value of shares unchanged.

Alternative 3: Let us assume that the company wants to pay a higher dividend per share. Since it currently has only ₹1 billion excess cash, it decides to raise ₹500 million by selling equity. Given a price of ₹60, it needs to sell 8,333,333 shares.

After the payment of dividend, the value of the company would be ₹5 billion as calculated on the basis of the future free cash flows of ₹600 million per year. This would now imply a dividend per share of 150/10.83 = ₹13.85 and a price of 500/10.83 = ₹46.15.

Total value to shareholders = 13.85 + 46.15 = ₹60.

The value to the shareholders remains unchanged irrespective of the amount of dividend payout or the shares repurchased. This conclusion, of course, is valid under conditions of perfect capital markets in which transactions are costless and differential taxes are non-existent.

Dividend Decision

Dividend policy requires the company to take two sets of decisions. First, how much of its earnings should be returned to the shareholders. Second, how should the earnings be returned, whether through dividends or by way of share repurchase.

If the company has projects on hand where the return on investment is higher than the cost of capital, it must retain its earnings and invest in those positive NPV projects to maximize the value of the company. Having satisfied its need for investment in value-accretive projects, the remaining earnings must be returned to the shareholders.

While this may be the fundamental theory, there are several other factors that are relevant in determining the dividend policy. For instance, shareholders do not like volatility in dividends. They prefer dividends to be assured and certain. Any variation in the amount of dividends received is not perceived favourably. John Lintner had in 1956 undertaken an extensive survey of the dividend practices of companies. The conclusions he arrived at continue to be valid even after six decades have elapsed!

Lintner Model of Dividend Policy and Practice

One of the most critical findings of the Lintner survey was that shareholders like to receive stable and predictable dividends. They dislike frequent changes. Conforming to the shareholders' preferences, companies establish a stable dividend policy based on long-term trends in profitability, investments and cash flows. They do not change their dividend payout, consequent to a change in performance that may not be permanent and assured. They need to pay stable dividends while facing a rather volatile profitability scenario. Therefore, the dividend policy is a conservative policy that takes into account long-term performance, profitability, investment requirements and cash flow availability. Sudden changes in these variables do not impact dividend payouts; only permanent, sustainable, long-run changes do.

The Lintner survey further documents that shareholders are more concerned about changes in dividend than their absolute levels. Is a ₹10 dividend paid by a company significant? The answer depends on the last year's dividend; it is significant if the last year's dividend was ₹8 and a non-event if it was ₹10. Consequently, managers do not vary dividend payouts that they are unsure of continuing, in particular a dividend increase that may have to be reversed later.

In a nutshell, the dividend policy is devised keeping the long-term in mind. Short-term considerations have little bearing. Over the long period, the earnings, the investment requirements, stability or otherwise of the company's business and its environment decide the dividend policy. It is not a short-term decision amenable to change with every change in profits or cash flows.

Mature companies with stable earnings tend to pay out a high proportion of their profits. They have high earnings that are predictable. Besides, mature companies do not have opportunities for investment in projects. There is a limited need to retain funds, leading to high payouts. A mature company like Hindustan Unilever Ltd (HUL) generates huge cash flows every year. It has limited scope for investments, besides nurturing its various brands. It regularly pays large dividends to shareholders. In fact, its payout ratio has consistently been in excess of 90 per cent of the net profits with dividends in some years even exceeding the net profits.

Growth companies, on the other hand, have low payouts. Such companies, typically in a relatively early stage of growth, generate limited profits which are in any case highly volatile. In addition, they have a ravenous need for funds for investment. Growth companies pay very little dividends, if at all, and retain most of their earnings.

Many companies such as Google and Amazon do not pay dividends, since they are growing companies that need substantial funds for investment. This, of course, is in accordance with what theory says:

- Companies that have a positive NPV projects must retain funds for investment.
- Mature companies that have exhausted investment opportunities, and whose operating cash flow is large and consistent, should pay high dividends.

Signalling

Finance theory is largely based on the assumption that information is freely available to all investors and that no one has private, exclusive information that could be of value in determining the price of securities. In practice, however, managers know more about a company than outside investors. Consequently, investors take an analytical look at decisions taken by the company to infer information that they may otherwise not have. Well-run companies provide a positive spin-on dividend policy and use it as a financial signalling tool. Managers use the dividend policy to often communicate relevant information to investors about the company and its policies.

An increase in dividend payout is usually taken as a positive sign for the future performance and profitability of the company. It is assumed by investors that the company would not increase dividends if it was uncertain of maintaining it. Companies usually increase dividends only when a higher profit is likely to be sustainable.

Conversely, a cutback in dividend conveys tougher times for the company and poor profitability and cash flows. Companies rarely reduce dividends, given the likely repercussion on the stock price. IBM has been paying dividends since 1916 and has paid more than 400 quarterly dividends till date. Any cut in its dividend would have disastrous consequences.

At times, a dividend change may have an entirely different meaning. Dividend payout impacts cash flows, hence dividend decisions are determined by the cash flow requirements of the company. A sudden drying up of investment opportunities reduces the need for funds, inducing the company to increase dividends. On the other hand, fresh projects landing in the company's lap imply a higher requirement of cash flows, necessitating a reduction in dividends.

Communication with investors holds the key. Consequently, the way a dividend decision is projected is critical. A cut in dividend may be a means to conserve cash if the company has come across highly lucrative opportunities for investment. It is imperative that the company keeps the investors suitably informed about the logic for a cut in dividend.

A substantial increase in dividend and a stock repurchase programme may be indicative of a lack of opportunities for investment in projects and a possible slackening of the company's

Royal & Sun Alliance's Dividend Cut

In some quarters, Julian Hance must have seemed like a heretic. On 8 November 2001, the finance director of Royal & Sun Alliance, a United Kingdom (UK)-based insurance group with GB£12.6 billion (US$20.2 billion) in annual revenue, did the unthinkable—he announced that he would cut the firm's dividend. Many observers gasped at the decision. Surely, they argued, cutting the dividend was a sign of weakness. Didn't companies cut their dividend only when profits were falling?

Quite the contrary, countered Hance. With insurance premiums rising around the world, particularly following the World Trade Center tragedy, Royal & Sun Alliance believed that its industry offered excellent growth opportunities. 'The outlook for business in 2002 and beyond makes a compelling case for reinvesting capital in the business rather than returning it to shareholders', explained Hance.

The stock market agreed with him, sending Royal & Sun Alliance's shares up 5 per cent following its dividend news. 'Cutting the dividend is a positive move', observed Matthew Wright, an insurance analyst at Credit Lyonnais.

Source: Berk, DeMarzo and Harford (2011: 520).

growth rate. When Microsoft announced its first-ever dividend, the stock price dropped by 7 per cent. Investors interpreted the dividend as a signal that the technology sector was maturing and that Microsoft had exhausted all opportunities for growth. The importance of investor communication can scarcely be overemphasized in the context of dividend policies and practice.

Factors Impacting Dividends

Theoretical considerations are paramount in determining the dividend policy but ultimately, the company and its management must bow to the wishes of the shareholders. Investors, especially retail investors, have a positive preference for receiving dividends. Having invested their hard-earned money, the shareholders are usually keen to receive regular returns from the company, even if the dividend yield is not very significant. In fact, with the direct electronic deposit of the dividend amount into the shareholders' bank accounts, the charm of physically receiving the dividend cheque has been lost. Nevertheless, most companies pay regular dividends, even if the amounts are small.

Taxability is another factor impinging on how the dividend policy is framed by a company. Before the introduction of the dividend distribution tax in India, most investors did not include dividends in their taxable incomes, choosing not to pay tax on dividend, in violation of the rules of income tax. They, in fact, treated dividends as tax-free. Even now, investors do not realize that dividends are taxable, since the taxes are paid by the company on their behalf and investors themselves have no liability. Given that most investors believe dividends to be a tax-free income, they like a maximum dividend payment.

The assumption of an efficient financial market along with the MM Model makes dividends, borrowing and equity issue fungible, so that each can replace the other without any impact on value. In practice, however, companies do incur transaction and floatation costs in raising funds. Transaction and floatation costs can be substantial, and companies factor these costs in their decision-making. Rarely does a company raise money through an equity issue or even borrow for paying dividends. Companies, in this respect, are conservative in preserving cash, which can be used in tougher times so that they are not forced to raise funds in an unfavourable market environment but instead can do so at a time of their choosing.

The preference of shareholders for receiving regular dividends is a critical factor in determining the dividend policy. The shareholder profile, in fact, becomes a key element in decision-making. For instance, some institutional investors are exempt from tax on the dividends received by them. Other institutions can pay dividends to their own investors only from the current income received by them and not from capital gains. Thus, the sale of shares to pay dividends to their own shareholders is not an option for such institutions who prefer to receive their income from dividends rather than through higher capital gains from share repurchase.

In recent times, companies have started spending considerable time and effort in profiling their shareholding pattern and the preferences of shareholders. They regularly interact with shareholders to fine-tune their dividend policies to match the shareholders' expectations with the business needs of the company. In this manner, the dividend policy is a flexible amalgam of theory, tempered with practical considerations.

Sometimes, a company's management might be of the opinion that its shares are highly underpriced and do not reflect the true value of the company. Buying back shares under such circumstances may increase the price of the share and is beneficial to the shareholders. For example, on 19 October 1987 (Black Monday, as it is commonly referred), share prices in the USA fell by 22.61 per cent and many companies felt that their share prices offered compelling value. Taking advantage, they bought their own shares in large numbers.

Such exuberance must be tempered, and actual buyback should be taken with abundant caution. Managers invariably feel that their shares are underpriced and that markets do not understand the value proposition the company offers. Enthusiasm and optimism on part of the managers is expected but need not necessarily be appropriate.

It is a common practice to reward managers these days with stock options. Stock option gives the holder the right to convert the option into shares by paying a predetermined price (exercise price). The stock-option holders gain when the share price rises and is above the exercise price. The value of stock option falls when the stock price drops. Dividends are cash payments to shareholders which reduce the price of the shares, in accordance with the amount of the dividend payment. Shareholders receive compensation for this fall (the amount of dividend per share) but stock-option holders lose out, given that they do not receive dividends. Hence, if the stock options awarded to managers are significant, they would hesitate to declare large dividends and the return of cash to shareholders is likely to be more through repurchase which boosts share price.

To sum up, the dividend policy in practice depends on the following factors:

1. Desire of shareholders to receive regular dividends
2. Tax provisions relating to dividends and capital gains
3. Transaction and floatation costs and the need to conserve cash
4. Shareholders' profile
5. Managers' assessment of the share value vis-à-vis its price
6. Managers' holding of stock options

Dividend Definitions

There are different conceptual definitions of dividends.

1. Profits made by a company can be used for
   a. reinvestment in business to finance positive NPV projects,
   b. payment of dividends to shareholders.

   The proportion of net profits that is paid as dividends is called the payout ratio. Thus,

   Payout ratio = dividends/net profits

   The proportion of net profits that is retained by the company is termed the retention ratio. Thus,

   Retention ratio = (net profit – dividends)/ net profits

   By definition, the payout ratio plus the retention ratio equals 1.

   Let us assume that PQR Ltd makes a net profit of ₹100 million and pays ₹40 million as dividends. It has 10 million shares outstanding. Assume a face value of ₹1 and market price of ₹200.

   The payout ratio is 40/100 = 40%.

   The retention ratio is (100 – 40)/100 = 60%.

   Thus, the company pays 40 per cent of its profits to shareholders and retains the balance 60 per cent for investment in projects.

2. The total amount of dividends divided by the number of shares is the dividend per share. This is the dividend amount the shareholder gets on each share held by him. The absolute amount received by any shareholder is the dividend per share multiplied by the number of shares held by him.

   For PQR Ltd, the dividend per share = 40 million/10 million = ₹4.

   A shareholder holding 200 shares will get a dividend of ₹800.

3. Next is the concept of the dividend yield which refers to the return based on the market price that a shareholder gets. Thus,

   Dividend yield = absolute dividend per share/ market price.

Dividends in India are declared on the face value which usually ranges from ₹1 to ₹10. The dividend per share divided by the market price provides the dividend yield. The market price may be very different from the face value, so that the dividend percentage (calculated on the face value) may vary significantly from the dividend yield.

For PQR Ltd,

$$\text{Dividend yield} = 4/200 = 2\%.$$

Since the face value of each share is ₹1, the CFO of the company will proudly declare a dividend of 400 per cent. However, if the market price of the share is ₹200, the dividend yield will be only 4/200 or 2 per cent. It is important to comprehend and work out such subtleties about dividends.

In short, the amount of dividend can be expressed as rupees per share (dividend per share), as percentage of EPS (payout ratio) or as percentage of the market price (dividend yield).

High Dividend: Hindustan Unilever Ltd (HUL)

Hindustan Unilever Ltd is a leading player in the fast-moving consumer goods (FMCG) segment. For the year 2017–18, the company declared a dividend of 2,000 per cent on its equity shares. On a face value of ₹1, this was fairly substantial at ₹20 per share. However, given its market price of ₹1,333 at the end of the financial year, the dividend yield amounted to only 1.50 per cent. Incidentally, given the relatively low opportunities for investment, the company paid out almost 90 per cent of its net profit by way of dividends.

Administrative Aspects

The decision regarding dividend payments are taken by the board of directors. After declaring dividends, the board fixes the record date to determine the eligibility for receiving dividends. The investors whose names appear in the company's register as shareholders on the record date are entitled to receive the dividend.

After purchase from the secondary markets, the transfer of shares takes a few days. The stock exchanges fix a date prior to the record date as the ex-dividend date. An investor purchasing shares before the ex-dividend date is entitled to the dividends and the shares are said to be trading cum-dividend (meaning with the dividends). After this date, the purchaser of the shares does not get the dividends (which is received by the seller) and the shares are said to be trading ex-dividend (meaning without the dividends). Usually, the ex-dividend date in India is one business day prior to the record date, since we have a T+2 system of settlement. The actual payment of dividends takes place a few days after the record date and is termed the payment date.

Administrative Aspects of Dividend

Vedanta Ltd declared a dividend of ₹17.70 on 30 March 2017. Its shares had a face value of ₹1. The record date for determining eligibility was 12 April 2017. The stock exchanges declared 11 April 2017 as the ex-dividend date. An investor purchasing Vedanta Ltd shares after 11 April 2017 was not entitled to receive dividends from the company.

The shareholders are entitled to dividend when the shares are trading cum-dividend. They are not entitled to the dividend when it starts trading on an ex-dividend basis. Buyers will, therefore, pay a lower price for shares after the ex-dividend date. Ideally, in an efficient market, the share price should drop by the amount of dividend on the ex-dividend date.

If a share is trading at ₹200 and the company has declared a dividend of ₹8, after the ex-dividend date the share price should fall to ₹192. Reality, as always, is different.

1. Usually the dividend yield is relatively low. The overall dividend yield in the market is between 1 per cent and 2 per cent. Since it is a common practice to pay quarterly dividends, the average dividend paid varies from 0.25 per cent to 0.50per cent. A drop in price by such a small amount is hardly perceptible.
2. If the dividend yield is x per cent and the market on the ex-dividend date rises by y per cent, the share should drop by only x – y%, making the fall even smaller.
3. There are tax implications which reduce the benefit of dividend payment, further impacting the anticipated fall.

Given the listed factors, the drop in the price on the ex-dividend date is hardly noticeable. However, in case of large dividend payouts, the market price does fall significantly on the ex-dividend date. For instance, when Vedanta Ltd paid a large dividend recently, its share price was marked down by more than 6 per cent on the ex-dividend date.

Dividend Reinvestment Plan (DRIP)

In a dividend reinvestment plan, the participating shareholders automatically reinvest any dividend that is receivable to purchase shares from the company. At times, these shares may be sold by the company at a small discount to the market price, benefitting the shareholders who opt for such a plan. The shareholders are able to further invest in the company and increase their shareholding. At the same time, the cash flow of the company is strengthened and the company is able to raise money regularly without incurring the usual transaction cost.

Putting It Together

Dividend policy has stumped many a practicing manager. There are no clear-cut guidelines that can be followed, and confusing signals emerge from what we have learnt. While theory says dividends do not matter, we know that in practice, dividends do have a significance for shareholders and for the market. Even in theory, the dividend policy is irrelevant only when the markets are perfect and the cost of raising funds is ignored. We are well aware that markets are far from perfect and that the cost of raising funds, especially equity, can be substantial. In addition, there are taxation issues to be considered. Complications arise here, since various categories of investors are subject to a differential tax treatment. In the end, the company must make a choice between dividend payouts and stock repurchase as the means of returning cash to shareholders. Quite a complex terrain to traverse for the CFO!

As is usual in such matters, it is useful to follow certain guidelines and start by asking the right questions.

1. Can the company sustain cash dividend over time and, in fact, progressively increase it?
2. Is cash dividend a better return to shareholders than a stock buyback? Such decisions need to be taken with a long-term perspective, keeping in mind the profile of the investors.
3. What is the psychological impact on the investor? We need to take into account the behavioural aspects of the investors. For example, the dividend policy must be aligned to the fact that most investors strongly prefer regular dividends and may not view a cut favourably.
4. Does the dividend policy effectively tell the story of the company and the stock? Is it in line with the strategic and operating characteristics of the company? If compelling growth opportunities beckon, the company cannot be paying large dividends. As in all financial decisions, the dividend policy must be aligned with the fundamentals of the company.
5. What are the relative dividend payouts and the dividend yields of the market and especially of the peers? How does the company compare with them?

In any case, there is no ideal dividend policy. An optimal dividend policy is akin to a moving target which the company is trying to reach but is never able to. The strive towards an ideal framework is nevertheless a continuous one. Even if the company is never able to achieve the ideal policy, the same must be constantly pursued. This holds for most aspects of finance, which is what makes the subject so fascinating.

KEY CONCEPTS

1. According to the MM Model, in a perfect market, the dividend policy has no impact on the value to the shareholders.
2. In real life, however, dividend policy is highly relevant for various reasons. Despite the MM Model, practical considerations have a significant influence on dividend payments.
3. Dividend payment depends on the profitability, cash flows and investment requirements and is a long-term decision for the company.
4. Companies can return money to the shareholders either through cash dividends or stock buyback. Taxes and the shareholders' profile largely determine which of the two the company opts for.

5. Signalling can be a major factor in determining changes in dividends.
6. Dividend policy must be aligned with the business environment facing the company and its requirement of cash flow.

CHAPTER QUESTIONS

1. ABC Ltd has 10 million shares priced at ₹50 each. It plans to purchase 2,000,000 shares at the market price from its existing cash reserves. What will be the market capitalization and share price after the buyback?
2. ABC Ltd has 5 million shares priced at ₹50. It has excess cash of ₹50 million, which it decides to pay out as a one-time cash dividend.
   a. What is the ex-dividend price of a share?
   b. If the board decides to use the excess cash for share buyback instead of paying dividends, what is the price of the share post share repurchase?
   c. As an investor, you prefer to get dividends, but the company is repurchasing shares. How can you leave yourself in the same position as if the company had made a dividend payment?
3. ABC Ltd has a market capitalization of ₹1 billion. It has ₹100 million in cash and the balance ₹900 million in other assets. There are 10 million shares outstanding, each valued at ₹100. What will be the impact on ABC's stock price and the wealth of its shareholders of each of the following decisions? Consider each decision separately.
   a. The company pays a cash dividend of ₹10 per share.
   b. The company repurchases 1 million shares.
   c. The company pays a 10 per cent stock dividend.
   d. The company has a two-for-one stock split.
   e. The company invests ₹100 million in a project whose returns are equal to the firm's cost of capital.
4. What does the Lintner model say about dividend policy? In what way does it differ from the MM theory on dividends? Do companies follow the Lintner model or the MM Model in practice? Explain.
5. Explain the role of signalling in the payment of dividends. Under what circumstances would signalling lead to payment of dividends and under what circumstances would it result in reduction of dividends?
6. What different parameters determine whether a company pays out cash by way of dividends or stock repurchase?

CASE FOR DISCUSSION I

Established two and a half decades back, XYZ Ltd is engaged in Information Technology (IT) for mass consumption. Those were the early days for the IT sector in India, and the company had to battle severe odds in its quest to become a market leader. The presence of some iconic names helped. But the acquisition of technology, product development, establishment of brand and developing a customer base were each a challenge by themselves. Surpassing all these was the challenge posed by financial requirements.

The initial idea for the product was simple but the execution from conceptualization to the final product was quite demanding. From development of the prototype to designing of the product, rolling out its services pan-India, development of the dealer network, and training and development of servicing facilities meant that the initial years were loss-making years and free cash flows were hugely negative.

Obtaining capital when the company was established was an easy task; there was a buzz around it and venture capitalists were only too eager to be a part of what was expected to be an iconic company. The company was, however, conservative in accepting funds, not wanting to dilute equity beyond what was essential. The promoters expected the company to be extremely successful and to generate huge cash flows.

Reality often turns out to be quite different from what we expect. Each of the discussed challenges proved to be stiffer than expected. The result was that while the company was successfully establishing itself during the first few years, profits were long in coming and finances were always strained. Given the uncertainty of operations and cash flows, its funds' management policy was highly conservative.

Huge investment and the consequent negative cash flows in the initial years are absolutely critical to the company's fundamental business and, if successful, leads to a sustained market leadership and a high valuation. While the operating cash flows during this period were positive, the company had immense opportunities for investment in business, building capacities and expanding the scope of their network. This phase lasting for almost a decade, built on the foundation laid in the first phase, made the company one of the best-known names in the country.

The last five years have seen significant changes, with the company's business gaining maturity. It attained a significant size, with cash flow from operations continuing to increase every year. At the same time, new business opportunities have vanished. Fixed costs were high but had already been incurred. The variable cost of each sale was insignificant, with the entire sales consideration contributing to covering the fixed costs and generating profitability. Given the monopolistic nature of its business, there was no need to reduce prices to increase sales, which happened almost on an auto mode. High price of its product, large unit sales and insignificant costs meant a huge free cash flow generation every year. The company has by now accumulated a pile of cash flows for which it has no use. This phase is expected to continue in the foreseeable future.

1. Design an appropriate dividend policy for the company for the three phases of its operations.
2. The dividend policy is largely a financial policy. Does the business environment and strategy have any impact on it? Demonstrate with respect to the dividend policy of XYZ Ltd.

CASE FOR DISCUSSION II

ABC Ltd is a mid-sized company with few investment opportunities. Earnings are stable and there is little excitement around the business of the company. The company is unlevered—it has no debt. The number of shares, issued and paid up, are 100 million, each priced at ₹50.

Some of the more informed shareholders are turning restive and want the company to take a fresh look at its capital structure. They feel the company is not taking advantage of the borrowing potential to enhance its value. There is an increasing clamour to borrow substantial amounts—up to ₹2.50 billion as some shareholders demanded—and return it to the shareholders either as a special dividend or a stock buyback.

The CFO of the company is taking a hard look at the options before him/her. He/she realizes that he/she is paying a tax on profits at 30 per cent, some of which could be saved if the company were to borrow funds. He/she starts asking himself/herself some questions.

1. What are the tax consequences of recapitalization?
2. What is the value of the company today? What is the likely valuation after the recapitalization?
3. How much will be the value of debt and of equity? Who loses out and who gains consequent to the recapitalization?
4. Should the company pay a special dividend or repurchase equity? What considerations weigh in the decision?
5. If the company borrows ₹1.50 billion and uses it to repurchase shares, what are the implications for shareholders? At what price should the company purchase its shares?

CHAPTER 9

Leverage

Give me a lever long enough and a fulcrum on which to place it, and I shall move the earth.

—Archimedes

In physics, leverage is a device to increase force at the cost of greater movement. Companies use leverage to increase profits while being exposed to a higher risk. Leverage uses the concept of fixed and variable costs to understand the impact of a company's cost structure on its return and risk.

Fixed costs do not vary with a change in the volume of production; they stay constant at different levels of production. If the fixed costs at 100 units are X, even at 101 units of production, the fixed costs incurred by the company remain X. Its significance lies in the fact that this leads to a change in the per unit fixed cost. If the production level increases, the same fixed costs are allocated over a larger number of units, leading to a lower cost of production for each unit of output. Managerial remuneration, insurance, interest and depreciation are examples of costs which are fixed. Depending on the nature of a specific industry, some other costs may also be fixed. For example, a flight from Mumbai to Delhi will incur fixed fuel and personnel expenses whether there are 153 or 154 passengers. The additional passenger does not add to the flying cost.

Variable costs vary with the level of output. In general, the per unit cost remains constant irrespective of the level of output. Variable costs include raw material and wages.

Thus, as the level of output increases, while the per unit variable cost remains constant, the per unit fixed cost reduces, leading to a fall in the total cost of each unit of output. This has the potential to increase profits disproportionately at higher level of sales.

In Table 9.1, firm F has low variable costs but high fixed costs. At low level of sales (₹50,000), it incurs operating losses of ₹45,000, being unable to cover the high fixed costs. But when the sales are high (₹200,000), the profits earned are huge at ₹60,000.

In comparison, Firm V has high variable costs and low fixed costs. Even at a low level of sales (₹50,000), the company does not incur a loss. At the same time, when sales shoot up to ₹200,000, it makes a profit of only ₹30,000.

TABLE 9.1 Simplified operating statement of two companies

	Firm F	Firm V
Fixed cost	₹80,000	₹10,000
Variable cost	30% of sales	80% of sales

Sales	Firm F			Firm V		
	VC	*Total cost*	*Profit*	*VC*	*Total cost*	*Profit*
50,000	15,000	95,000	(45,000)	40,000	50,000	0
100,000	30,000	110,000	(10,000)	80,000	90,000	10,000
125,000	37,500	117,500	7,500	100,000	110,000	15,000
150,000	45,000	125,000	25,000	120,000	130,000	20,000
175,000	52,500	132,500	42,500	140,000	150,000	25,000
200,000	60,000	140,000	60,000	160,000	170,000	30,000

Source: Author.

Operating Leverage

Companies face two kinds of leverages, namely operating and financial. The operating leverage arises from the business operations of the company. It involves the substitution of fixed cost methods of production for variable cost methods. It depends on the relative weightage of the fixed cost in the overall cost structure of the company.

Two aspects determine the operating leverage—the industry which the company belongs to and its choice of technology. Hotels and airlines have huge fixed costs, whilst the cost of lodging or of transporting an additional guest/passenger is miniscule. Almost the entire sales realization goes towards contribution and covers the fixed cost. Low capacity utilization leads to large losses, as the high fixed costs cannot be covered. A breakeven occurs at a fairly high level of output. However, once the breakeven is reached, additional sales increase profits disproportionately. Such industries are highly sensitive to capacity utilization.

On the other hand, industries such as textiles have high variable costs and low fixed costs. Each unit sold contributes only a small value to cover the fixed costs. Since the fixed costs are low, the company is able to make profits even at a low level of sales. However, a high output does not lead to excessively large profits.

Leverage in Different Industries

Software products are characterized by high fixed costs, comprising development, technology and marketing. But the marginal cost of providing the service to an additional customer is extremely low. Microsoft spent a huge amount of money in developing and marketing the Windows package, resulting in an extremely high level of fixed costs. The variable cost is low; once the software was developed and launched, the cost of providing Windows to an additional customer is insignificant. A substantial proportion of the revenue from selling every additional package contributes towards covering the fixed costs.

Similarly, mobile telecom companies such as Bharti Airtel had to invest heavily in technology, spectrum purchase, operations and customer acquisition. The cost of providing services to an additional customer is low. Microsoft and Bharti Airtel have a very high operating leverage.

Contrastingly, a retailer such as D-Mart has high variable costs. For every unit sale of a product, it needs to pay the supplier a disproportionately high price. Turnover ratios being high, even a large investment in fixed cost and inventory is not very significant as a proportion of sales revenue.

A company may have a choice of production techniques. A technology may be labour-intensive (high variable cost) and involve less fixed costs. Alternatively, the company may opt for a capital-intensive technology with low variable costs. The choice of technology determines the operating leverage and its risk profile.

Financial Leverage

Financial leverage reflects the extent to which debt is used in funding the capital requirement. In this respect, it is a matter of choice for the management. While every company is subject to some level of operating leverage, depending on the industry it operates in and the technology adopted, the management may choose not to take on any debt and finance itself entirely through equity. A 100 per cent equity-financed company is not financially leveraged. Many companies in India and abroad are almost entirely equity-financed such as Hindustan Unilever Ltd (HUL), Colgate India Ltd and Infosys Ltd.

When companies raise funds through debt, they incur a fixed cost in the form of payable interest. Since interest must be paid irrespective of the level of profits earned by the company, it leads to greater fluctuations in profits. At the same time, the cost of debt is expected to be lower than the return on assets which increases the returns to the equity shareholders. Higher returns combine with higher risk for the company, and, as usual, present a significant decision choice for the CFO.

Leverage and Banks

A bank is a financial institution that intermediates between savers and investors. It leverages on its equity to accept deposits from savers. Deposits are then lent out in the hope that loans taken will be returned by the borrowers as per the terms of the lending. At times, there is a problem in recovering these loans and they become what are technically termed non-performing assets (NPAs).

The bank then has to dip into its equity to stay afloat. Whether the equity is sufficient to take care of the NPAs depends on how much equity the bank has vis-à-vis its lending. This implies that leverage determines the risk of a bank.

Contd

contd

> Assume that a bank has a loan book of ₹10,000, financed ₹2,000 by equity and ₹8,000 by deposits, with the leverage being 4:1. Even in a situation where 25 per cent of the total loans default and are not returned by the borrowers, the bank would be in a position to pay back the depositors, given the large cushion provided by equity. Equity provides a fairly large safety net to the bank's lending.
>
> If the bank wants to enhance its returns significantly, it can increase leverage to, say, 19:1 by contributing only ₹500 equity and funding the balance ₹9,500 through deposits. Now, even a drop of about 5 per cent in the value of its assets will wipe out the entire equity and bankrupt the bank.

Total Leverage

What the company should be concerned with is the overall risk levels which is given by the total leverage. The total leverage is the product of the operating and the financial leverage and shows the impact of the change in sales volume on the earnings per share.

The operating leverage equals the change in operating profits (EBIT) consequent to a change in sales. The financial leverage equals the change in earnings per share consequent to a change in operating profits. The total leverage thus equals the change in the earnings per share (EPS), consequent to a change in sales.

$$\text{Total leverage} = \text{OL} * \text{FL}$$

$$= \text{percentage change in EPS/percentage change in sales.}$$

Companies target a risk level they would not like to exceed. Given the operating leverage which is more permanent than the financial leverage, they can decide on and adjust their borrowings to ensure that the total risk does not exceed the desired level.

The concept of leverage is important for a company. Leverage has the potential to increase returns. There may be a strong temptation to over-leverage to obtain the desired returns. Leverage leads to a fixed obligation of payment which comprises operating as well as financial costs. Companies must take a well-thought-out decision on their ability to meet such payment obligations under adverse recessionary conditions in the market. Financial stress and bankruptcy at higher leverage becomes a distinct possibility which must be avoided.

Leverage makes earnings volatile, thus increasing the risk and the required rate of return on equity. Hence, earnings are discounted at a higher rate. It is important to evaluate whether the increased earnings are sufficient to overcome the impact of the higher discount rate. Certain factors in this context are outside the management's control. Persistent recessionary conditions in the Indian economy have played havoc with the fortunes of many companies which borrowed heavily, anticipating a better environment, higher sales and sufficient cash flows to take care of the debt liabilities. A delay in the revival of the Indian economy has destroyed a large part of the value of such companies. Many companies have had to sell assets and even their entire businesses in order to avoid bankruptcy. Leela Ventures sold four hotels in different cities in India to the Brookefield Group for ₹39500 million in the year 2019 in order to meet its debt obligations. Hotels are a high (operating) leverage business. Large borrowings increased the financial leverage too, leading to an extremely high total leverage.

As always, deciding on the most appropriate level of leverage is not an easy task for any CFO. There is always a temptation to maximize returns by opting for a higher leverage. That may come back to bite the company when the environment turns adverse. Given the industry a company operates in, the CFO may not have enough leeway in deciding the operating leverage. He/she may have greater flexibility in deciding the financial leverage. He/she must ask the right questions before deciding on the appropriate level of leverage.

- How much will a change in volume affect profits and costs?
- At what point does the firm breakeven?
- What is the most efficient level of fixed assets to employ in the company?
- Is the demand for our product highly volatile?
- Are we able to ensure a good credit rating for the company?
- Will the high debt raise risks to unsustainable levels?
- Does the company have access to funds in case of an urgent need?

The nature of the industry and the cost structure influence the CFO's decision. The answers would vary for a low-leveraged industry vis-à-vis one characterized by a high leverage. Knowledge of leverage and cost structure would help the CFO decide on the appropriate level of fixed cost to maintain in the business.

Leverage and the Financial Crisis

According to the legendary investor Warren Buffet, 'When you combine ignorance and leverage, you get some pretty interesting results' (quoted in Nasdaq, 2009). He was, of course, referring to the financial crisis of 2008, which had its genesis in the high leverage of some of the financial institutions.

At the time of the financial crisis in 2007–8, US banks commonly had a leverage greater than 30:1, resulting in an extremely low cushion for their investments. Given the fact that their investments were largely in risky and complex securities, the crisis was an event waiting to happen. The lessons from the crisis are very clear. Notwithstanding the confidence (misplaced?) in their ability to manage any outcome the market may throw, managers would do well to heed the fundamentals of financial theory.

KEY CONCEPTS

1. Leverage represents the use of fixed costs to strengthen the firm's performance.
2. Operating leverage indicates the extent to which fixed assets are utilized in the production by the company.
3. Financial leverage shows how much debt the firm employs in its capital structure.
4. By increasing leverage, the firm increases its profit potential, but also its risk of failure.
5. The combined impact of operating and financial leverage determines the risk of the company.

CASE FOR DISCUSSION

A top-end hotel in a large commercial city has made huge investments in land, building and operations, including salaries and other regular expenses. It is faced with high fixed costs. The variable expenses are not very significant. Any additional room booked by a guest hardly increases the cost to the hotel. How does the hotel price its rooms?

The variable costs are low, and the hotel must aim at maximizing sales, since almost the entire revenue would add to the contribution and thus increase the level of profit. Occupancy rates have a significant impact on the performance. At the same time, there are other issues worth considering, especially in deciding the price for a marginal guest.

- Given that the entire sales price will add to the contribution, how much discount should be offered on the rack rate to improve capacity utilization?
- There are add-on revenues by way of food and other services which need to be taken into consideration.
- Is the industry facing a lean or peak season currently?
- What should be the pricing strategy if a corporate client wants to block 2,500 rooms annually?
- What is the nature of competition faced by the hotel, and what is the cost structure of the competitors?
- Will a lower rate to the marginal customer induce other customers also to demand lower rates?

1. Assume your own figures with respect to the various parameters of a hotel, work out an example and decide your strategy wherein a walk-in customer at 12 pm asks for and tries to negotiate the price of a room for a two-day stay.
2. Similarly, formulate a strategy for a large multinational company (MNC) which wants a corporate deal for 2,500 rooms during the coming financial year.

CHAPTER 10

Financial Derivatives

> Derivatives are financial weapons of mass destruction.
>
> —Warren Buffett

Innovations have been a distinctive feature of global finance over the last half a century. Nothing has, however, been more overwhelming in its scope and breathless advance than financial instruments termed derivatives. Derivatives are not a new concept, having existed in rudimentary forms in the past; nevertheless, in recent times, they have taken the financial world by storm. No company or financial institution can claim to be working in the best interest of its stakeholders without fully taking advantage of derivatives to manage risk and maximize value.

India took its first hesitant step towards offering investors an opportunity to trade in derivatives in the year 2000 when the Securities and Exchange Board of India (SEBI) permitted the trading of equity-based index futures and options on the exchanges. Since then, terms such as index futures, swaptions, programme trading, synthetic cash, equity-indexed bonds, butterfly spreads, inverse floaters and portfolio insurance have become an integral part of the financial market lexicon. We may choose to be overwhelmed by, what to us are, as yet, esoteric terms. Or the excitement generated may lead us to a promising career in a field that has already become an integral part of the corporate life.

The future, of course, holds the greatest promise, and whether it is a career in traditional corporate finance, banking, investments or consultancy, expertise in derivatives would be crucial to success in the corporate sector.

The Concept

A derivative instrument is a financial contract whose pay-off structure is determined by, or derived from, the value of another asset.

A derivative is not an instrument in its own right; it has no direct value of its own but is based on some other instrument called the underlying. The value of the other variable determines the pay-off on the derivative. The pay-off, at any point in time, is a function of

1. the price at which the derivative transaction is undertaken and
2. the price in the cash market of the underlying variable upon which the derivative is based.

The pay-off is, usually, the difference between the two and can be positive as well as negative. As the price of the underlying in the cash market keeps changing, the pay-off also changes. In that sense, it is a derived financial instrument.

If the underlying is the share of TCS, the pay-off and the value of the derivative will be determined by the price of TCS in the spot market. Assume that an investor has purchased TCS futures at ₹2,000. If the cash market price of TCS is ₹1,980, the pay-off on the futures is −₹20. If later, the cash market price of TCS changes to ₹2,070, the pay-off on the TCS futures changes to ₹70.

The underlying can be equity, a debt instrument, commodity, foreign exchange rate, an index or even a derivative itself. Besides, many exotic derivatives are traded and are very active.

Let us understand derivatives with two simple examples.

1. An investor believes that the stock market is currently underpriced and offers a compelling buying opportunity. He/she has no clue about specific companies but is certain of the overall market doing well. How does he/she act on his/her hypothesis?

   In the normal spot market, the investor, taking an index as a proxy for the market, would need to invest in all the shares comprising the index in the proportion the shares constitute it. Constituting a portfolio that mirrors an index is not only tedious but expensive to build and maintain.

   The derivative market enables the investor to profit from his/her hypothesis by simply buying a NIFTY futures contract. The transaction is simple, easy and inexpensive. In fact, the derivative market offers the investor various alternatives including options at different prices. We will explain futures and options later in this chapter.

2. A power utility has a large consumption of oil and is apprehensive of oil prices rising over the next few months, hurting its profitability. In the normal course, the only choice available to the utility is to purchase the required quantity and store it. Not only does it take up unnecessary funding but storing an inventory of oil is costly.

   Derivatives enable the company to hedge its risk of a rise in oil prices by going long in oil futures. Again, the transaction is easy, simple and inexpensive. As in the case of the NIFTY, the market provides alternatives such as options on oil at different prices.

Nature of Derivatives

Corporates and individuals are exposed to risk in their operations or financial transactions. Such risks can be managed by hedging with derivatives. Let us understand the nature of risk with some examples.

1. HCL Ltd bags a project from AIG for US$100 million with the payment to be received one month hence. At ₹70 per US dollar today, the project is worth ₹7 billion. Over the next one month, the value of the US dollar with respect to the Indian rupee may change, altering the Indian rupee value of the US dollars received. If the Indian rupee drops to 80 per US dollar, the project will be worth ₹8 billion. Alternatively, if the Indian rupee appreciates to 60 per US dollar, HCL Ltd will receive only ₹6 billion for the project.

2. Banks borrow money by way of deposits and invest in securities/bonds. They maintain assets and liabilities in both fixed- and floating-rate instruments. The interest payable on the floating-rate instrument is reset in line with the changes in the market interest rate and, consequently, its price does not vary much. However, a change in the interest rate leads to a significant change in the price of the fixed interest rate bonds, thus impacting the value of the bank, depending on the direction of the change in interest rates and the relative values of the bank's assets and liabilities of fixed-rate securities in its portfolio.

3. A copper-wire producer uses copper as its raw material. Its cost of production, sales, profits and cash flows depend considerably on the price of copper.

4. A mutual fund has invested ₹100 billion in the equity markets. If the market falls by 15 per cent, the value of its holding may drop to ₹85 billion.

5. A family is planning a European holiday next summer. At ₹80 to a euro, the cost of the holiday is ₹500,000. If the euro were to appreciate to ₹90, the holiday cost will increase significantly.

6. A farmer producing wheat has a fair idea of the costs. His profit depends on the price at which he is able to sell his produce. The price in the market at the time of the harvest is unknown and leads to variability in the profits the farmer makes.

These cases are illustrative of the risks faced by corporates and individuals when prices of fundamental, underlying variables such as equity, bonds, commodities and foreign exchange change. Such risks need to be managed, otherwise they can create cash flow problems and the value of companies may be adversely impacted. In extreme cases, the company may become bankrupt and go out of business. Derivatives are the tools by which such risks can be effectively managed.

Derivative contracts must be differentiated from a usual cash/spot market transaction wherein the settlement takes place immediately in accordance with the exchange regulations. Indian stock markets currently follow a T+2 delivery system and any transaction undertaken in the spot market must be settled within two working days.

Derivative contracts are undertaken for a time period that is in the future. The time period can be a week, a month, a few months, a year or even longer. The transaction is undertaken now but settled later in accordance with the terms and conditions agreed to. It is a firm legal contract which both the parties—the buyer and the seller, also called counterparties to the transaction—must adhere to. They cannot back out of the contract whether the subsequent market conditions and prices move in their favour or against them. Thus, the settlement must be made as per the terms of the contract.

Since the settlement is undertaken sometime in the future, investors can take a view on the future without having to invest now. Thus, for example, if an investor is of the opinion that a particular security will increase in price, he/she can buy stock futures from the derivatives market without having to pay the full price now. On the other hand, if he/she feels that the stock price will go down over the next few months, he/she can sell the futures now (without possessing the security). Derivatives make it easier for the investor to act on a view he/she has of the market or of a specific financial security or manage the risk the investor may be exposed to over the longer term. (As we will explain later, the investor needs to pay the margin amount which is usually a small proportion of the market price.)

Kinds of Derivatives

There are four broad categories of derivatives. These are

1. forwards,
2. futures,
3. options and
4. swaps.

Let us discuss each of these derivatives.

Forwards

A forward contract is a firm legal contract between a buyer and a seller in which

- the buyer agrees to take the delivery of the underlying at a specified price at the designated time in the future,
- the seller agrees to deliver the underlying at a specified price at the designated time in the future.

Thus, a forward contract has the following features:

1. It is a legal contract that neither the buyer nor the seller can back out of. They must conform to the terms and conditions specified in the contract.
2. The delivery of the underlying must be made as per the terms of the contract. The underlying can be equity, an interest rate instrument, exchange rate, commodity, an index and even a derivative instrument itself. The underlying can also be exotic variables such as temperature, snowfall, volatility and so forth. It can be either standardized, for example, an equity share or needs to be specified in detail such as a commodity or an exotic variable.

Weather Derivatives

Weather derivatives are a very popular category of exotic derivatives. A large part of the economy—agriculture, travel, energy—is impacted by weather conditions, in particular the average temperatures over a period of time. A warm winter reduces the need for heating and adversely impacts the fortunes of utilities and energy companies. An exceptionally cold weather has a negative effect on the business of hotels and travel companies. Weather derivatives quantify and index average temperatures across a wide area and attach dollar values to it.

The first weather derivative was introduced in 1997 as an over the counter (OTC) instrument. From 1999 onwards, Chicago Mercantile Exchange has been trading weather-based futures and options.

3. The date/period of settlement is specified and may be a specific date or a period over which either the buyer or the seller may seek/provide delivery.
4. The price at which the delivery takes place is also mentioned. The price may be either explicitly stated or may need to be calculated. On the settlement date, the seller provides the delivery of the underlying and the buyer makes the payment to conclude the transaction.
5. Forward contracts are direct arrangements negotiated between the two parties who deal with each other without the interface of an exchange. These are technically termed OTC transactions.

OTC trade involves the two parties trading with each other directly and designing the contract as per their requirements. The counterparties take a risk on each other for the fulfilment of the terms of the contract. The contract is negotiated between the two parties and can be customized. The two parties can design a contract with features that they desire. The contract is settled only on delivery since the settlement prior to the delivery date depends on both the parties agreeing to close out the trade which is not very common. Thus, forwards are OTC contracts traded directly between two counterparties. A hypothetical trade demonstrating the use of a forward contract to manage risk is given in Illustration 10.1.

Illustration 10.1

Raymond Ltd has imported raw wool for stitching warm three-piece suits for men. The payment for the wool amounting to GB£10 million is due on 13 September 2019. The company does not wish to be exposed to changes in GB pound/Indian rupee exchange rate which may alter its commitment in Indian rupee terms. It enters into a forward contract with Citibank for the purchase of GB£10 million at ₹90 per GB£1 on 13 September 2019. Irrespective of the prevailing exchange rate in the spot market on 13 September 2019, whether it is lower or higher than ₹90 to GB£1, Citibank will deliver GB£10 million to Raymond Ltd on the payment of ₹900 million. Thus, Raymond Ltd's commitment in terms of the Indian rupee is certain, known and remains fixed irrespective of market fluctuations. The company is no longer subject to risk on account of changes in the foreign exchange rates.

In a forward trade, two parties agree on a contract which will be settled at some later date. All the terms of the contract are agreed on the trade date, but the settlement takes place later. These terms include the specific underlying, the date of settlement, the volume of the underlying and the price at which the trade will go through.

The day a forward contract is entered into is the trade date. The day the delivery is given by the seller and the purchase consideration paid by the buyer is termed the settlement date or the expiry date. The price at which the contract is entered into is the forward price.

Futures

Futures are contracts, similar to forwards but traded on an exchange. This introduces subtle differences. The contract must be standardized to enable large numbers of investors to trade. Thus, the underlying, the settlement date and the number of the underlying in a contract are determined by the exchange. All the features are clearly defined for the contract which is then traded by the investors who, on their own, cannot define or modify the contract.

Futures were created to solve the problem of counterparty risk and the lack of liquidity. In a forward contract, if either of the parties goes bankrupt or is otherwise unable to honour the transaction, the counterparty suffers. Futures solve the problem by making the exchange (rather the clearing corporation) the counterparty for all futures trades. The exchange guarantees the settlement of the transaction, similar to the way it guarantees transactions in the cash market.

Forward contracts cannot be liquidated prior to the settlement date unless both parties agree, which rarely happens. Futures can be liquidated anytime, since these are standard contracts with buying and selling being a continuous process. Thus, the investor need not carry his trade till the settlement date but can liquidate it any time he/she wants.

In India, equity derivatives were introduced in the year 2000 when they began trading on the National Stock Exchange (NSE) and the Bombay Stock Exchange (BSE). Almost from the beginning, the NSE has cornered most of the volume in derivatives trading. Equity derivatives are currently available on 207 companies. Besides, there are index futures contracts wherein investors can trade in futures with various indices as the underlying. For example, on the NSE, futures are available on NIFTY 50, NIFTY IT and NIFTY Bank, amongst other index futures. Futures are also available on international stock market indices such as the Dow Jones, S&P and the FTSE. The equity derivatives follow a three-month trading cycle, and the settlement can be undertaken for the near month (one), the next month (two) and the far month (three). The settlement day is always the last Thursday of the month. On the last Thursday, the near-month contract is settled and a new three-month contract is introduced. In this manner, three contracts are always alive. Most investors trade the near-month derivatives, since these have the maximum liquidity.

As on 25 April 2019, contracts for three settlement dates are available, namely 30 May (near month), 27 June (next month) and 25 July (the far month). An investor can invest in derivatives with a settlement on any of these three dates. On 30 May, all contracts of the near month are settled and a new contract is introduced with 29 August as the expiry day.

The NIFTY Futures

The NIFTY futures on the NSE is a contract with NIFTY 50 Index as the underlying. Each contract is for 75 NIFTY. If the NIFTY 50 has a value of 10,000, the value of one contract is ₹750,000 (75 * 10,000). This is termed as the contract multiple. As per Indian regulations, a contract cannot have a value (the contract multiple) of less than ₹500,000. The contract has a three-month cycle, and there are three contracts, each ending on the last Thursday of the three months respectively.

An investor who feels that the stock market is likely to go down sells NIFTY index futures on the NSE at 10,000 for settlement on the last Thursday of December, which happens to be 29 December. Each contract is for 75 NIFTY. If the NIFTY on 29 December is 9,500, he gains

(10,000 – 9,500) * 75 = ₹37,500. If on the other hand the NIFTY goes up to 10,200, against what the investor believed, he would lose (10,000 – 10,200) * 75 = ₹15,000.

The NIFTY futures is a standardized contract, and its terms cannot be changed to suit the requirements of any investor. If an investor wishes to trade on a contract with different terms, say a different contract multiple or a different expiry date, he must trade outside the exchange which would be then be a forward contract. The terms of a forward contract are flexible, depending on the requirements of the two counterparties. Such flexibility is not available in the exchange-traded futures contract.

Options

Futures and forwards can guarantee the price, cash flow or the value of an asset for an organization which is exposed to risk due to a change in the price of equity, interest rate, exchange rate and commodities. If there is a loss in the cash market position, it is made up by gains in the futures or forward transaction. On the other hand, if there is a gain in the cash market position, the loss in the futures/forwards position neutralizes these gains. Hence, the final price or value is known and fixed. (This is only partially true, since the investor continues to be exposed to basis risk in futures as we will discuss later in the chapter.)

It would be useful for an investor if the losses in the cash market position are made up by the gains in the derivative transaction, but when the derivative position turns unfavourable, the investor can decide not to go ahead with the derivative transaction. He takes advantage of the favourable gains but foregoes the losses. This is exactly what option contracts enable the buyer to do.

An option contract gives the holder the right to buy (sell) an underlying at a specified time in the future at a certain price. However, there is no obligation to do so. Thus, the buyer of the option can decide whether he will exercise the contract which he is holding. He has a right to do so if he so chooses, but he is under no obligation to exercise the contract. If the pay-off from exercising the contract is positive, the buyer will exercise the contract. If the pay-off is negative, the buyer will choose not to exercise the contract and would let it lapse.

The price at which the holder of the option has a right to buy (sell) the underlying is called the strike price or the exercise price. The exchange offers contracts with many strike prices, and the investor can choose to buy/sell an option with any of those strike prices.

The investor is protected from the downside and is able to partake of gains in the stock price. We are aware that there is no free lunch in the financial markets. To obtain such a choice wherein he benefits from a positive pay-off but can walk away from the negative pay-off, the investor needs to pay the option price. The option price, also termed the option premium, is discovered in the market through trading by players. The option price goes to the seller who, in a way, has sold the discussed rights to the buyer and has extracted a price for taking on the obligation. This is similar to an insurance contract wherein the insurer (option seller) charges an insurance premium and indemnifies the insured against any losses he may incur on the insured product. Option contracts at different strike prices are priced differently.

TABLE 10.1 Option price example (in ₹)

Option	Strike price	Option price
Call	1,280	25.90
	1,300	16.75
	1,320	10.70
	1,340	6.80
Put	1,200	4.35
	1,240	10.05
	1,260	15.55
	1,280	23.10

Source: Author.

On 16 August 2019, option prices for Reliance Industries Ltd, with various strike prices, for expiry on 29 August 2019, are given in Table 10.1. Reliance share closed on 16 August 2019 at ₹1,278.50.

As we can see, options at different strike prices are priced differently. The relationship between the strike price and the option price is easy to infer. Lower the strike price, higher is the option price for a call option. On the other hand, lower the strike price, lower is the option price for a put option. This relationship is intuitively easy to understand.

There are two kinds of options, namely call and put options. The call option is the right to buy the underlying at the strike price. The put option is the right to sell the underlying at the strike price. The exchange introduces call and put contracts with several strike prices. Each of those strike prices has one, two and three months to expiry.

Option Outcomes

An investor holding shares of TCS may be apprehensive of the share price going down below ₹2,000 and wishes to protect the value of his holding. At the same time, he does not wish to forego profits in case of a rise in the stock price. The investor can buy a one-month put option on TCS with a strike price of ₹2,000. The put option provides the holder the right to sell TCS shares at ₹2,000. If the price falls below ₹2,000, he can exercise the option by selling his TCS holding at ₹2,000.

If, however, the share price exceeds ₹2,000, he need not exercise the option which lapses. He continues to hold his shares which have gained in value. At the same time, there is no loss from the option position. Options are available to the investor at many strike prices besides ₹2,000.

For buying the put-option contract, he must pay the price of the option also called the option premium. While the options contract is designed by the exchange, the options price is discovered through the trading of the contract by investors on the exchange.

As per the NSE Strike Price policy, the number of call- and put-option strike prices for each scrip would be a minimum of 11 [5 in the money (ITM), 1 at the money and 5 out of the money (OTM) strikes] and a maximum of 21 (10 ITM, 1 at the money and 10 OTM strikes). The NSE may also introduce new strike prices any time it deems fit. The strike prices are based on the volatility of the stock price.

For example, TCS has 10-1-10 option strike prices, with 10 strike prices being less than the current price, 10 being higher than the current stock price and 1 equalling the current stock price of TCS prevailing in the cash market. Both call and put options are offered at each of these strike prices. With expiry in each of the next three months, the total number of option contracts, with TCS as the underlying, is 126 (21 * 2 * 3).

An investor can buy an option contract by paying the option price. The option price is paid to the seller of the contract. The option contract gives the buyer the right to either buy the underlying (for a call option) or to sell the underlying (for a put option) at the strike price specified in the contract. The buyer, however, has no obligation to do so. The choice rests exclusively with him/her whether to exercise his right to go ahead with the purchase/sale of the underlying or let it lapse without exercising.

Alternatively, the investor can opt to sell the option contract and receive the option price. The seller has an obligation to ensure the rights of the buyer. In case of a call option, the seller has an obligation to sell the underlying to the buyer at the strike price whenever the buyer chooses to buy. Alternatively, in case of a put option, the seller has an obligation to buy the underlying from the buyer at the strike price whenever the buyer chooses to sell. The seller has no rights in this respect. He has in fact taken on obligations towards the buyer (explained earlier) by accepting the option premium.

This implies as follows:

1. The buyer's pay-off can never be negative. If the price of the underlying is not in his favour, the buyer will simply choose not to exercise the option and will let it lapse.
2. The buyer can never lose more than the initial premium paid.
3. The seller can never have a positive pay-off. A positive pay-off to the seller implies a negative pay-off to the buyer, which is not possible.
4. The seller can never make more than the initial premium. Having received the premium, his/her pay-off can only be negative.
5. The sum of the total pay-off to the buyer and the seller is zero. The profits to the buyer equal the losses to the seller. It is a zero-sum game.

The exchange defines the various parameters of an options contract. The parameters include the underlying, the strike price, the expiry period and the nature of the option, that is, whether it is a call or a put option. The exchange offers these contracts with the buyers and sellers quoting the option price (the premium) and trading in these option contracts.

There are two categories of options, namely American and European options. European options can be exercised only at the time of the final expiry but not prior to it. American options can be exercised at any time until the settlement day. In India, all options are European options.

Long-Term Equity Anticipation Securities

Long-term equity anticipation securities (LEAPS) are option contracts for a long term, usually over one year. Both call and put option LEAPS are traded. These are offered on individual stocks as well as with the index as the underlying and are available for up to three years. These were first offered for trading at the Chicago Board of Options Exchange in 1990.

An option contract can be defined by the underlying, the settlement period, the strike price and whether it is a call or a put option. Thus, for instance, TCS September 2000 Call

- is a call-option contract
- with TCS as the underlying,
- ₹2,000 as the strike price,
- expiring on the last Thursday of September.

If any of these parameters changes, it becomes a different contract. This is important since an existing position can be squared up by taking an opposite position in the same contract. The gain or loss will be determined by the option price at which the investor is able to square up the contract. The options price is of course determined by the market.

In the Money/Out of the Money

An option is said to be in the money if exercising the option results in a positive cash flow for the buyer. Thus, a call option is in the money if the stock price is higher than the strike price. A put option is in the money if the strike price is higher than the stock price.

An option is said to be out of the money if exercising the option results in a negative cash flow to the buyer. A call option is out of the money if the strike price is higher than the stock price. A put option is out of the money if the stock price is higher than the strike price.

It is easy to surmise that an out-of-the-money option will not be exercised by the buyer who will let it lapse. An option which is in the money can become out of the money, since the stock price can always change adversely. Similarly, an option which is out of the money can become an in-the-money option if the stock price movement is favourable.

At-the-money option is one in which the stock and thestrike prices are equal.

Let us understand this with an example. Please refer to Table 10.2. The following contracts are available on the exchange:

- January Call 100
- February Call 105
- January Put 100
- February Put 105

TABLE 10.2   Derivative positions: ITM, at the money or OTM

Contract	Stock price (₹)	Pay-off (₹)	Position
Jan. Call 100	98	98 – 100 = (2)	Out of the money
Feb. Call 105	98	98 – 105 = (7)	Out of the money
Jan. Put 100	98	100 – 98 = 2	In the money
Feb. Put 105	98	105 – 98 = 7	In the money

Contract	Stock price (₹)	Pay-off (₹)	Position
Jan. Call 100	102	102 – 100 = 2	In the money
Feb. Call 105	102	102 – 105 = (3)	Out of the money
Jan. Put 100	102	100 – 102 = (2)	Out of the money
Feb. Put 105	102	105 – 102 = 3	In the money

Contract	Stock price (₹)	Pay-off (₹)	Position
Jan. Call 100	108	108 – 100 = 8	In the money
Feb. Call 105	108	108 – 105 = 3	In the money
Jan. Put 100	108	100 – 108 = (8)	Out of the money
Feb. Put 105	108	105 – 108 = (3)	Out of the money

Source: Author.

Which contracts are in the money and which contracts are out of the money if the stock price is

1. 98,
2. 102 or
3. 108?

Pay-off for a call is stock price—strike price.
Pay-off for a put is strike price—stock price.

Settlement

A futures transaction gets settled when the seller gives the delivery of the underlying and the buyer pays for it on the settlement day in accordance with the terms of the contract. However, this was a theoretical explanation to elucidate the fundamental concept of a futures instrument. In reality, the delivery is not very common. Recall that the primary purpose of derivatives is risk management. It would become extremely cumbersome and costly if the investor had to receive or provide the delivery for each and every derivative transaction.

Imagine a builder who wants to hedge his large requirement for cement. He gets the delivery from his regular supplier and does not depend on the futures market for his supplies. The futures market is only for the purpose of managing the risk of a change in cement price. The builder buys the futures contract so that he gains in the futures trade when the price goes up, negating the higher cost he has to pay to his actual cement supplier. If on the other hand, the price of cement goes down, he loses in the futures market but that is made up by the lower cost of his supplies in the spot market.

The builder does not intend to take the delivery from the futures market. Taking the delivery in the futures market makes it unmanageable, expensive and exposes the transaction to high volatility that is a characteristic feature of prices close to the settlement period. It is also likely to disrupt his regular supply chain mechanics if derivative purchases were to replace regular supplies.

In fact, in Indian equity derivatives, the delivery is not permitted. What may be done is cash settlement. Under cash settlement, the cash equal to the gains/losses made is exchanged between the buyer and the seller, thus completing the settlement. Assume a transaction in 200 shares of Infosys Ltd futures at ₹1,100. There is no need for the seller to deliver Infosys shares or for the buyer to make a payment for the entire consideration. The transaction will be settled by

- the seller paying ₹80,000 to the buyer if the price of Infosys rises to ₹1,500 ((1500 – 1100) * 200) or
- the buyer paying the seller ₹30,000 ((950 – 1100) * 200) if the price comes down to ₹950.

Cash settlement makes the entire process simple and easy to conclude. There is no need for the clearing corporation to receive the delivery of the underlying asset from the seller and pass it on to the buyer. Cash settlement involves a one-way cash transfer equivalent to the profit/loss through the interface of the clearing corporation.

Futures on Volatility Index

The volatility index (VIX) is a measure of the market's expectation of the volatility in the short run. The NIFTY VIX depicts the expected volatility over the next one month in equity prices. It is an index of volatility of NIFTY options, expressed in annualized standard deviation. Calculated in percentage terms, the values are computed up to four decimal places.

The VIX is sometimes referred to as the fear gauge, with a high index suggesting imminent large changes in equity prices and a low indicating small changes in the coming days.

The Chicago Board of Options Exchange introduced the first VIX in 1993, VIX futures in 2004 and VIX options in 2006.

The VIX derivatives can be used to hedge or diversify the equity portfolio of an investor. Options traders can hedge their volatility risk through VIX. Trading in VIX derivatives has become possible due to cash settlement.

Without cash settlement, contracts with certain underlying instruments could not have been designed and traded, being impossible to deliver. It is virtually impossible to deliver an index.

How does one deliver temperatures, volatility or snowfall? With cash settlement, derivative trading for such underlying has become possible and companies can effectively hedge themselves against various risks they are exposed to.

Many people believe that without the possibility of settlement through delivery, fluctuations in prices are unduly large. High volatility is not considered to be healthy for the market. SEBI is, therefore, in the process of introducing physical deliveries for all equity derivatives. Physical deliveries are likely to be compulsory on the settlement day in all stocks by the end of the year 2019 in a phased manner. Deliveries in commodity derivatives have, of course, always been permitted.

The innovation capability of the financial markets knows no bounds. It is interesting that hardly any transaction is cash-settled. The most common method of concluding a transaction is liquidating or squaring up which involves taking a position that is exactly the opposite of the original position in the same contract. If an investor has bought a one-month futures in Reliance Industries Ltd, he can sell the same contract any time prior to the settlement day, thus squaring his earlier position. A sale position in the three-month NIFTY index can be squared up or liquidated by taking a plus position in the NIFTY index three-monthly contract. The investor must be careful to square up in the same contract which means that the underlying, the settlement date and, in case of options, the strike price and call/put must be the same. If the investor squares up in a different contract, he/she, in fact, adds to his/her position without concluding the earlier position. Most contracts in practice are liquidated and hardly any contract is kept alive by the investors till the settlement day.

Investors and traders prefer to have the flexibility to decide how long they wish to carry a position. Squaring up enables them to dispose of their positions at their will and not having to carry it until expiry. Such flexibility is highly prized by traders and, in general, hardly any position is carried until expiry. They keep trading regularly, altering their positions in the market. Consequently, trading in the market is large and vibrant—either to take fresh positions or to liquidate an already-existing position.

Thus, there are three following possible ways to settle a derivative contract:

1. Physical delivery
2. Cash settlement
3. Squaring up or liquidation

Application

Let us illustrate the applications of derivatives by managing the risk in each of the cases illustrated in section 'Nature of Derivatives'.

1. HCL Ltd hedges the risk of foreign exchange rate fluctuations by selling the US$100 million in the futures market at the exchange or in the forward market outside the exchange by approaching one of the banks or derivative dealers. This will lock in the value of the US$100 million at the current rate available irrespective of changes over the next one

month. HCL Ltd can also use options to hedge the receipt of US$100 million. Forward/futures and options have different risk–return characteristics.

2. A bank which has a different quantum of fixed-rate liabilities and fixed-rate assets can hedge by buying/selling interest rate futures. The change in the value of its bond holdings vis-à-vis its obligations will be neutralized by the gains/losses in the interest rate futures.

3. Instead of buying copper later as per its production schedule, the company can hedge by buying copper futures now. The loss (profits) due to higher (lower) copper prices will be made up by profits (loss) in the futures transaction.

4. The mutual fund can sell index futures to hedge the risk of a falling market. Any losses (gains) in the value of its holdings are likely to be compensated by gains (losses) in the short position in NIFTY futures. It is also possible to hedge by buying put options on the NIFTY.

5. The family can buy the euros now instead of waiting until next summer, but this involves paying and blocking funds. Alternatively, it can take a long position in euro futures and hedge away the risk of appreciation in the euro.

6. The farmer can hedge away the risk of a fall in wheat prices by selling wheat futures in the commodity exchange. He/she will not be impacted by the change in the price of wheat until the harvest time. Any loss due to a fall in spot wheat prices will be made up by the gains in the futures contract and vice versa. Interestingly, organized exchange trading in derivatives commenced in 1848 at the Chicago Board of Trade with wheat futures.

Derivatives are instruments to manage risk. The risk arises from the fundamental operations of a company or investment in financial instruments. Derivatives cannot prevent volatility in the outcome of these operations and investments. What forwards or futures do is to compensate for the losses (profits) by generating equivalent profits (losses) on the derivatives position so that the combined value or cash flows/profits remain constant and known, thus removing the risk from the underlying cash positions. This is termed hedging. A hedge is any action that eliminates/reduces the price risk of an existing or anticipated position in the cash market.

The hedged position in the derivatives is the opposite of the existing spot-market position. A long position in the spot market such as holding a portfolio of securities can be hedged with a short position in the forward/futures market. This position is termed a short hedge. A short futures hedge is appropriate when the investor will sell an asset in the future and wants to lock in a price.

Similarly, a short position in the spot market such as a company requiring the import of capital goods for a forthcoming project investment can be hedged with a long position in dollar futures. This position is termed a long hedge. A long futures hedge is appropriate when the company will purchase an asset in future and wants to lock in a price.

Options, of course, enable the hedging of losses while gaining from the profits in the cash market.

Hedging Mechanics

Derivatives are instruments to hedge risk which implies the following:

1. There must be an underlying risk in the spot market, which creates a need to hedge. The risk arises in the spot market as a part of the fundamental business of a company.
2. Hedging does not change the risk inherent in the spot position which remains unaltered. The basic characteristics of the spot-market position do not change nor do its outcomes.
3. Hedging involves taking a contrary position in the futures/forward contract with the same/similar variable as the underlying. The hedge negates the impact of the change in the price of the variable in the spot market.

There is a need to appreciate the hedging mechanics pertaining to futures. Futures are primarily instruments to hedge risk. Futures can be effectively used by understanding the nature of the risk which an organization or an individual face in the spot market. We must be clear on the following:

1. What variable is the company exposed to? Is it copper, equity markets, wheat or the dollar–rupee rate?
2. What is the nature of the exposure, and how does it impact the organization?
3. Does the company lose when the variable increases in value or vice versa?
4. What is the extent of the loss and over what period?

Once the nature of the risk in the spot market is appreciated, hedging parameters can be decided.

1. Which underlying closely matches the variable that the organization is exposed to in the spot market? Are futures contract available in those underlying, and are they sufficiently liquid?

    For instance, a fund may not find any index that exactly mirrors its own portfolio. Or a copper-wire producer may not find the exact variety of copper it needs for its manufacturing process.
2. Which contract closely mirrors the changes in the risk variable to which the organization is exposed? There are various choices in terms of the index it can hedge with—the NIFTY 50, the BSE 500 and many others. It must make a decision on which of these indices closely tracks the fund's own portfolio.
3. Based on the position in the spot market, the fund must decide whether the futures must be purchased or sold. The position the fund takes must be the opposite of the position in the spot market.
4. What is the number of contracts that need to be traded, given the extent of position in the spot market, the contract multiple and the relationship of the primary spot-market position with the underlying in the futures contract?
5. What should be the period of the contract?

It may not be possible to find a perfect instrument to hedge the risk in the cash market. There may be a difference in the underlying, the quantity or the time period, which introduces

Risk in Hedging

Metallgesellschaft Refining and Marketing (MGRM), as a part of its aggressive marketing strategy, undertook to supply large quantities of refined oil in the US market at fixed rates over a long period. The huge commitments exposed the company to the increase in crude oil prices, which it hedged with oil futures.

The hedge did not work out as anticipated and the company incurred losses exceeding US$1 billion, significantly damaging the fortunes of its own German parent company.

what is technically termed the basis risk. While hedging through futures removes price risk, it exposes the hedger to basis risk.

Basis is the difference between the spot price and the futures price at any given point in time. The difference between the two keeps changing, implying that the basis does not remain constant. On expiration, the two prices are equal; hence the basis is zero and, therefore, known. However, most futures contracts are closed out and liquidated prior to the expiration day when the basis is not known. Since the basis is unknown, the hedger is uncertain of the exact value of his trades. The hedge is thus imperfect and the investor remains exposed to, what is known as, basis risk.

Basis risk is the risk that the spot- and the futures-market positions will not move in the same manner or to the same extent; therefore, hedging is not perfect. Hedging with futures gets rid of the price risk at the cost of assuming the basis risk, which must be clearly understood by the investor.

Let us take a simple example to illustrate the mechanics of a hedging transaction. Assume that today is 3 October 2018. You head a mutual fund which has started a new fund that is currently open for subscription by investors. The fund will remain open for over two months, and you will be able to undertake an investment on 10 December 2018. You expect to collect ₹1 billion for investment.

The risk that the fund is exposed to is the possible rise in the market in the coming two months. The NIFTY is today at 10,000. While it is your view that the markets are attractively priced and you would like to make purchases in the market, you can undertake the actual investment only after the fund has closed for subscription on 10 December 2018. What happens if in the meanwhile the market shoots up 10 per cent to a NIFTY valued at 11,000?

Being a thorough professional, you have already planned your portfolio. The mutual fund has a spot-market position that is exposed to risk—the risk that between 3 October 2018 and 10 December 2018, the market will go up and the investment in the portfolio will need to be made at higher prices.

1. The fund can hedge the aforementioned spot position by taking a futures position on the NSE. The fund manager must understand the characteristics of its spot-market position.

It will be buying securities on 10 December 2018, hence it has a short position in the spot market on 3 October 2018. It must therefore assume a long position in futures to hedge the short spot position.

Another way to understand this is by figuring out whether the fund gains or loses with an increase in the spot market. Clearly, a loss is incurred when the market moves up and vice versa. These are the features of a short position in the spot market. Hence, a buy or long position in the futures is called for.

2. What is the best futures contract that can be used to hedge? Individual stock futures are inappropriate as are sector specific index-based futures. Any one of the general indices may be chosen, depending on the strength of the relationship between the fund's portfolio and the constituents of the index. Assume that the fund selects NIFTY 50 futures, being the most liquid and fairly representative of the overall market.

3. Reflecting the risky profile of the fund, the prospective portfolio which you intend to invest in has a beta of 1.25 with NIFTY 50.

4. The NIFTY 50 futures contract is a standard contract which cannot be modified to suit the requirements of an investor. The fund can either buy the 29 November or the 27 December contract. The usual practice is to buy a contract whose settlement is on a later date. The contract can be squared up on the date the risk of the spot position no longer exists. In our case, that date is 10 December.

5. Assume that on 3 October, when the NIFTY is at 10,000, the NIFTY futures is purchased at 10,050. The number of NIFTY futures contracts to be purchased is

$$1 \text{ billion}/(10{,}050 * 75) * 1.25 = 1{,}658.38.$$

6. On 10 December, ₹1 billion can be invested in the spot-equity market and there is no further need to continue with the hedge. The hedge needs to be lifted by squaring up the futures position. Assume that the NIFTY has gone up by 10 per cent to 11,000 and the NIFTY futures are trading at 11,010. The net position is as follows.

Spot position: the loss in terms of the higher price of purchase is

$$100 \text{ million} * 1.25 = ₹125 \text{ million}.$$

The gains from the futures position equals $(11{,}010 - 10{,}050) * 75 = 72{,}000$ per contract. With 1,658 contracts, the pay-off equals ₹119,376,000.

The hedge has worked fairly well with a little less than ₹120 million of the loss being covered by the hedged futures position.

7. The hedge as pointed out is not perfect.

   a. The contract for the specific date, 10 December 2018, was not available. The fund had to go long in the 27 December contract and square up the position on 10 December.

   b. The price risk was taken care of but the fund is exposed to basis risk. Basis which was –50 (10,000 – 10,050) on 3 October changed to –10 (11,000 – 11,010) on 10 December.

   c. The exact number of contracts that needed to be purchased, being in decimals, could not be traded.

Growth of Derivatives

Over the last few decades, the risk profile of the corporate sector has increased significantly. Their operations have become global instead of being confined within the domestic territory. For many multinational companies, their global operations contribute more to the revenue than the domestic operations. In 2018, more than 60 per cent of Apple Inc.'s sales were outside the United States of America (USA). Even Indian companies have gone global with a vengeance. The Tata Group has more than half its turnover from outside India, having acquired iconic global names such as Corus Steel, Tata Tetley and Jaguar.

For many other companies too exports constitute a significant proportion of their business. Information technology companies, in any case, are predominantly dependent on global revenues as are pharmaceutical, automobiles and many others. With the economy being liberalized, imports have also become increasingly important as are investments abroad and funding in foreign currency.

Corporate Risk Management

An Indian company needs to submit its price quotation for a project in Germany. Assume, the euro–Indian rupee rate is 75 and to recover its Indian rupee cost of 750 million, it can bid €10 million. The German government is likely to take a month to award the project. If in the coming one month, the euro–Indian rupee rate were to change, the cost and the profitability of the project may be impacted, exposing the company to substantial risks. The company can purchase an option on the euro to manage the risk of the change in Indian rupee–euro exchange rate.

Global operations expose companies to significant risks of changes, predominantly in exchange rates, besides interest rates, equity prices and commodity prices. All these parameters significantly impact revenues, profits, cash flows and valuation. Strategic risk management has, therefore, become an integral part of the corporate sector's lexicon.

Derivatives are the main tool that companies rely on to manage their strategic risk. A greater risk exposure means a higher demand for derivatives which has burgeoned to very high levels.

The underlying parameters, including exchange rates, commodities, interest rates and equity prices, have over the years become highly volatile. Until the early 1970s when the Bretton Woods arrangement prevailed globally, exchange rates were fixed by the central banks. Their value seldom changed. Interest rates were also determined by the central banks. Now, of course, all financial parameters are market-determined, fluctuate on a continuous basis and are impacted by global events, making them highly volatile.

Tools available to companies in the form of derivatives have also broadened in scope and become highly sophisticated. The cost of operating in the derivative markets has reduced drastically, trading and liquidity is substantial and contracts can be customized to suit specific organizational requirements. There is widespread expertise available to take advantage of the derivative markets.

Consequently, the market size of derivatives is huge. The market size can be depicted in two ways, namely the notional value of the derivative contracts outstanding or their market value. For instance, a NIFTY 50 futures contract is purchased on 30 June 2018 at 10,800. It will have a market value of ₹15,000 [(11,000 – 10,800) * 75] if the NIFTY value increases to 11,000. The notional value continues to be ₹810,000 (10,800 * 75).

In 2016, the notional value of all derivatives worldwide was US$544 trillion while the market value of the same derivative contracts was approximately US$15 trillion. The huge size reflects the overwhelming need and demand for risk management globally by various entities, the ease of trading and the expertise available. India has been a relatively recent entrant in the derivatives market but the future is highly promising as the regulatory provisions ease and the Indian economy becomes even more integrated with the global markets.

Growth of Equity Derivatives

Equity derivatives in India have grown rapidly and completely dominate trading in the cash market. While in 2004–5, the turnover of equity derivatives was 1.54 times that of the spot market in equities, it has risen to 15.59 times by 2016–17. During this period, while the turnover of the cash equity market rose by 11.39 per cent annually, that of the equity derivatives increased at 35.10 per cent per annum.

Interestingly, during the year 2016–17, over three-fourths of all transactions in derivatives were contributed by index options. The dominance of options in trading becomes risky as the sellers of options have obligations they may find difficult to meet, especially if they are individual players.

Risk Management System by Exchanges

Derivative transactions involve a time lag between the trade date and the expiry date. During the intervening period, the transaction undertaken may move in favour of the investor or the prices may change against him. There is a possibility of the investor not honouring the transaction if he is losing out, technically termed counterparty risk. The whole edifice of the trading structure would break down if investors are able to back out of their commitment. In order to guard against such an eventuality, the exchanges need to have a robust risk management system in place. There is an urgent need to ensure that the long gap between the transaction and the settlement does not lead to defaults and in case an investor does default, it has no impact on the payment mechanism of the exchange and on other investors.

The risk management system that exchanges rely on is primarily based upon the margins that are levied on the transactions undertaken, a kind of a deposit to ensure that the investor does not back out of the transaction. The margin is forfeited if the investor does not fulfil the terms of the contract. The margin is a certain percentage of the value of the transaction and is dependent on the volatility in prices of the underlying. Underlying securities with higher volatility are subject to higher margin and vice versa. In Indian equity derivatives, the margins usually amount to 5 per cent to 10 per cent of the value of the transaction.

Thus, let us assume that an investor buys a contract of NIFTY futures at 10,000. Each contract being for 75 NIFTY, the total value of the transaction is ₹750,000. A margin of 5 per cent implies that the investor must deposit ₹37,500 with the NSE Clearing Corporation Ltd until the transaction is eventually squared up. At the end of the transaction, this amount is returned to the investor.

In addition, the transactions are subject to what is technically termed mark to market. All transactions are equated to the end of the day prices on a daily basis and any difference in price is made up by payment from/to the investors. If the price over the day has moved in favour of the investor, he receives the requisite payment. On the other hand, if the price has moved against the investor, he must make up for the loss. In this manner, the transaction is always in line with the current prices and the chances of default are minimized. The mark-to-market margin is collected from the investors before the commencement of trading the next day.

The exchanges also have limits on the positions that investors and members can take to ensure no investor trades excessively large volumes thereby endangering compliance with the settlement. There are restrictions on volumes for each contract and for the overall position in the market.

Initial margins and mark-to-market margins are the tools that form the basis of minimizing credit/operating risk, and the primary reason exchanges can guarantee transactions. The counterparty risk that is an integral part of OTC transactions is shifted to the exchange and the clearing corporation. The investors take a risk on the exchange and its settlement outfits and not on any trading counterparty. Hopefully, the risk management practices at the exchanges are robust enough for the risk of default to be practically non-existent.

Margins

Assume that an investor buys one contract of NIFTY 50 at 10,000. The contract multiple is 10,000 * 75 = 750,000 (each contract includes 75 NIFTY). The contract is squared up on day 6 at 9,900.

Margin@10% = 75,000.

TABLE 10.3   Daily gains or losses (in ₹)

Trading day	Nifty price	Gain/loss	Gain/loss per contract
Day 1	10,070	70	5,250
Day 2	10,200	130	9,750
Day 3	10,080	(120)	(9,000)
Day 4	9,950	(130)	(9,750)
Day 5	9,975	25	1,875
Day 6	9,900	(75)	(5,625)

Source: Author.

The investor must deposit a margin of ₹75,000 (at 10 per cent of the contract value) which is returned to him/her when the trade is concluded. During each of the six days, he receives credit for the gains and is debited for the losses as calculated in Table 10.3.

Risk in Derivatives

While derivatives are known for their uses, they are also notorious for their abuses. The misuse of derivatives has led to significant disasters which have brought down some well-known companies, besides causing financial loss and damage to the reputation of many organizations. Derivatives share some of the blame for the financial crisis of 2007–8, besides causing substantial financial losses to Metallgesellschaft, Sumitomo Corp., Proctor & Gamble, Gibson Cards and many others, too innumerable to list out. Let us discuss the risk inherent in derivatives operations.

1. Leverage: There is a time lag between the trade date and the settlement date. While the transaction is undertaken on the trade date, the actual payment is made on the settlement date. At the time of the transaction, the investor pays an amount equal to the margin. His investment is limited to the margin amount which is a small proportion of the value of the trade. Consequently, with a given amount of funds, the number of shares the investor can trade in the derivatives market is multiple times the number he/she can trade in the cash market. While this certainly makes derivatives attractive to investors, it also makes trading riskier, since both losses and profits are magnified. Let us see with an example.

   A share is priced at ₹50. With ₹1,000 at his/her disposal, an investor can purchase 20 shares. If the share price moves to 51, he/she makes a profit of ₹20. If the share price drops to ₹49, the investor incurs a loss of ₹20.

   With the same amount of ₹1,000, the investor can invest in 200 futures if we assume a 10 per cent margin (₹5 per share). Consequently, his/her profits and losses get magnified to ₹200, much higher than that in the cash market, making the entire transaction highly risky. Combined with mark-to-market, the cash flows could be very strained.

2. In the rough-and-tough world of derivatives, it is easy for traders to go astray and subject the organization to undue risks. When such risks pay off, the trader becomes a hero. Other stakeholders do not realize or may be apprehensive of pointing out that luck plays a very important part in such profits and that gains made by exposing the company to high risks are not recommended. Such risks eventually come home to roost and many organizations have paid dearly for using derivatives to support their profit targets.

Barings

Established in 1762, Barings was London's oldest merchant bank when it collapsed in 1995. It was a large and a highly respected and revered institution. That amounted to virtually nothing against the unchecked, irresponsible trading of its main trader in Singapore, Nick Leeson.

Contd

contd

Leeson was active on the Japanese market, trading substantially on the Nikkei index. At the time of the crisis, he had built up positions amounting to US$33 billion, which was more than 50 times the total capital of the company. His positions were primarily long forward and short straddle (short put and short call).

Leeson did not expect the Nikkei to fall; hence the discussed positions. Technicalities need not bother us here but when the Nikkei collapsed, consequent to the earthquake in the Japanese city of Kobe, Barings incurred a loss of US$1 billion, wiping out the company instantly.

All the elements of the risks, namely lack of operational control, volatility and leverage contributed to the stated failure outlined. Sitting in Singapore, Leeson single-handedly executed large trades and built up huge positions. He was also in charge of the back office, violating a fundamental tenet of risk management. Leverage enabled him to build up huge positions with little capital. At the same time, high volatility reinforced the losses the company made.

It is interesting that a company headquartered in London was brought down by a single trader located at Singapore who was trading in the Japanese market.

Derivatives are instruments of risk management and should be used by organizations only for managing risk. There is a great temptation to use derivatives for increasing profits. It is important to remember in times of such temptation that speculative derivative trading can also lead to disproportionate losses. The use of derivatives as a profit centre has been the cause of many disasters in the past.

3. Derivatives are easy to trade but difficult to comprehend. Even seasoned players at times do not understand the pay-offs that may be possible from a given derivative position. Organizations must take particular care to establish controls on the derivative traders.
   - What is the total amount they may trade?
   - What is the overall position that can be built up?
   - Will they only hedge an underlying exposure or occasional, independent, profit-seeking trades are permissible?
   - How much exposure should the company take overall?
   - Can the company's cash flow get strained if derivative trades go against the company which then has to pay margins on mark-to-market basis?

   All such aspects must be carefully thought through to devise a policy that is beneficial, given the company's business, without undue levels of risk exposure. Unless a well-thought-out policy is adopted and implemented, companies are likely to meet the fate of Barings, Amarnath Hedge Fund, AIG, Society General, UBS and Lehman Brothers. These are some of the well-known organizations that have suffered due to lack of proper controls and well-defined policy framework while trading in derivatives.

   Companies should ensure that

a. they have an appropriate, logically designed policy to take advantage of derivatives, based on the requirements of the company,

b. they take into account the leverage capability of derivative instruments,

c. they institute proper internal controls, for example, by separating the responsibility of the front and back offices.

Companies need to be very careful in designing their risk management system to decide how much risk they can take. They should be able to draw various scenarios in terms of possible prices of the underlying and consequent pay-offs in order to assess the likely impact on the company and its cash flows.

Given these precautions, there is no reason why derivatives cannot prove effective in managing the risk exposure of a company. Non-existent operational and strategic controls, and a little laxity by the top management, leverage and volatility inherent in derivatives makes them a sure recipe for disaster.

Swaps

An interest rate swap is a contract between two parties for multiple exchange of cash flows based on two streams of interest payments, premised on a common notional principal.

In contrast to a forward contract where only one cash flow is exchanged, a swap contract involves the exchange of multiple cash flows over a period of time. A swap is a long-term contract and is normally used to convert cash flows based on different interest rates—a floating rate of payment for a fixed rate of payment; a fixed-interest receipt for a floating rate receipt. The basis of calculating the interest is decided at the time of the transaction and is applied to a notional principle that is equal and is not exchanged. Only the interest differential is exchanged.

Assume that ABC Ltd has borrowed ₹1 billion at MIBOR (Mumbai inter-bank offered rate) + 200 basis points for five years. Its interest liability is flexible, depending on the prevailing MIBOR rate. The company wants certainty on the interest liability, payable at every six months.

It can enter a swap transaction with a counterparty, swapping its floating-rate liability with a fixed rate of interest, say 7.5 per cent. ABC Ltd takes on a commitment to pay a fixed rate of 7.5 per cent to the counterparty every six months, whereas the counterparty pays ABC Ltd, MIBOR + 200 basis points. ABC Ltd's commitment is ₹37.5 million (100 * 7.5% * 0.5), whereas the counterparty is committed to pay 100 * MIBOR rate * 0.5 by every six months. The two counterparties to the transaction will exchange the difference between their respective commitments every six months and the transaction will be completed.

Neither the actual principal amount of ₹1 billion nor the interest amounts are exchanged; only the difference between the two interest commitments is exchanged. ABC Ltd has thus converted its floating obligation into a fixed and certain one.

Besides interest rate swaps, currency swaps are also common. In currency swaps, both the interest rate and the principal are exchanged. Currency swaps enable the exchange of debt in one currency into debt in another currency. Besides, many other types of swaps exist such as equity swaps and commodity swaps.

KEY CONCEPTS

1. Derivatives are instruments of risk management.
2. Companies are exposed to changes in profits, cash flow and value due to changes in currency rates, interest rates, commodity prices and equity prices. Derivatives help manage such risk.
3. There are four types of derivatives, namely forwards, futures, options and swaps.
4. Futures and options on exchanges have different characteristic features. The structure of trading and the method of settling transactions may also differ amongst exchanges.
5. Companies need to have a well-planned risk management policy to take advantage of derivatives.
6. Derivative trading volumes have shown a significant jump due to a greater exposure to risk, higher volatility of underlying variables, widespread expertise and ease of trading in derivatives.
7. Margins—initial and mark-to-market—are the basis of risk management by exchanges.
8. Leverage, profit-seeking and laxity in controls are the primary causes of disasters in derivatives trading.

CHAPTER QUESTIONS

Are the following statements true or false? Explain logically.

1. Forward contracts and futures contracts are both standardized.
2. All futures contracts are guaranteed for performance.
3. A clearing corporation acts as an intermediary in futures contracts.
4. Futures contracts are usually much more liquid than forward contracts.
5. Collaterals are not required to be kept in futures contracts.
6. In case of forward contracts, profits and losses are booked only on maturity, while for futures contracts they are settled on a daily basis.
7. Both the parties to a futures contract are required to keep margins which are marked to market on a daily basis.
8. If the price of a futures contract increases, the margin account of the holder of the short position is credited for the gain.
9. In case of an option on a stock, the exercise price is decided by the mutual consent of the parties to the contract.
10. It is possible for a futures contract to be the underlying asset for an options contract.
11. The option premium is adjustable against the exercise price for the settlement of the contract if the option is exercised on maturity.
12. If the stock price is less than the exercise price of a call option, it is said to be deep in-the-money.
13. A long position in a call option may be closed out by a short position in a put option with an identical exercise date and exercise price.
14. Other things remaining the same, greater the exercise price of a call option, greater the value it commands.

15. Any call with a greater time to maturity is always valued higher than a call with a shorter time to maturity.
16. At a given point in time, different classes and series of options may be traded.
17. An exchange-traded option contract on stock may involve any number of shares of the stock.

CHAPTER 11

International Finance

> The benefits from a world currency would be enormous.
>
> —Robert Mundell

Laker Airways enjoyed a lucrative business in the 1970s, carrying tourists from the United Kingdom (UK) to the United States of America (USA). The business was highly successful, and the company purchased additional aircraft to cater to the rising demand. It financed the aircrafts by borrowing in US dollars, thus creating a mismatch. While its earnings were primarily in GB pounds, it created liabilities in US dollars. In 1981, the US dollar strengthened and continued to remain strong for a few years. A high dollar (low value of GB pounds) increased the cost for British travellers and reduced the demand, and revenues, for Laker Airways. At the same time, the interest and repayment of loans, being in US dollars, became more burdensome. Eventually, the company became bankrupt.

The foreign exchange market is the market for trading currencies of different countries. Each country has its own currency which can be used to purchase goods and services in that country. Indians earn in Indian rupees and spend in it. The citizens of Thailand earn in Thai baht and spend in the Thai baht. The currency of a country is acceptable within its boundaries but usually not outside it. However, there are currencies such as the US dollar, the GB pound, the euro and the yen, which are widely accepted by traders around the world. All the same, trans-border trade and investment requires converting the currency of one country to that of another.

The Indian rupee is not a widely accepted currency outside India. When we travel abroad, we stock up on US dollars, GB pounds or euros to be able to pay for goods and services we buy locally in the country we visit. Similarly, when corporates make acquisitions abroad, they must pay in the currency of the other country as Tata Sons Ltd did when it paid in GB pound for purchasing the iconic Tetley Group, UK (GB£271 million).

As a simple illustration, when Infosys Ltd undertakes a project for General Electric in the USA, it earns in US dollars for the project. Infosys Ltd needs to convert the dollars into Indian rupees for meeting its expenses in India. MRF Ltd imports rubber from Indonesia for manufacturing tires in its Indian factory. It needs to convert Indian rupees into the Indonesian rupiah to pay for the rubber. Similarly, when Motherson Sumi Systems Ltd acquired two companies of the Reydel Automotive Group, Germany, it had to exchange Indian rupees for euros to pay for the transaction. Thus, exports, imports and investments create the need for the exchange of currencies. Currencies are traded in what we call the foreign exchange markets, which are huge, with more than $4 trillion being traded every day.

The Foreign Exchange Market

The exchange of one currency for another is a foreign exchange (forex) transaction. The foreign exchange market trades various currencies, and the participants can purchase US dollars with GB pounds or sell yen for euros. If the Indian rupee–US dollar rate is 70, it implies that US$1 can be exchanged for ₹70 in the forex market. Conversely, to buy US$1 we need ₹70. A rise (reduction) in the value of a currency is termed appreciation (depreciation). Thus, if the US dollar–Indian rupee rate changes to 80, we can now convert US$1 into ₹80. The US dollar is now worth more in Indian rupees than earlier. Hence, the dollar has appreciated. The exchange rate represents the value of one currency in terms of another. When one currency appreciates, the other currency depreciates or goes down in value. In the example, the rupee has depreciated as ₹80 are now required to buy US$1 instead of ₹70 earlier.

On the other hand, if the exchange rate changes to ₹60, it means that US$1 gets only ₹60. As Figure 11.1 shows, the US dollar has depreciated and the Indian rupee has appreciated; we need only ₹60 to purchase US$1.

It is important to clearly understand the meaning and implications of the changes in the value of a currency, that is, the appreciation and depreciation of a currency. Appreciation refers to the increase in the value of a currency vis-à-vis another, while depreciation refers to the reduction in such a value.

There are two kinds of trade in the forex market. The spot trade is an agreement to exchange currencies on the spot, which implies that the trade will be executed and currencies exchanged in two business days. Alternatively, trading can also be forward (a derivative transaction), which is for a longer period. The forwards trade in forex is similar to a forwards transaction in equity

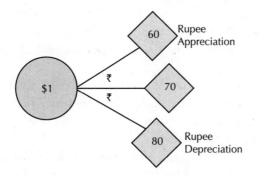

FIGURE 11.1   Appreciation and depreciation of currency

Source: Author.

and other underlying, which has been discussed in the Chapter 10. The trade is undertaken now and the settlement date is sometime in the future.

Besides, foreign currencies can also be traded in the exchange in what is termed the futures market. Options on currencies are also very popular. Derivatives in forex are used by players to hedge underlying exposure to foreign currency.

Currency Derivatives

Currency derivatives in India were launched on 29 August 2008 by the National Stock Exchange (NSE). The underlying in currency derivatives is the exchange rate between two currencies. The first derivative was the US dollar–Indian rupee futures. Futures are now also available for the Indian rupee against the euro, the yen and the GB pound. Options on currency were introduced on 29 October 2010. The contracts follow a 12-month cycle and are cash-settled.

In many countries, currencies can be freely exchanged. We can easily purchase and sell dollars for GB pounds or the euro for the yen. No permission is required for exchanging the currencies, and the price is determined through free trading. Trading is free, simple and large in volume. Other countries impose restrictions and varying degrees of control on the purchase and sale of currencies.

With limited export capability, and the need to import essential items, India had traditionally faced a shortage of foreign currency. Hence, there were severe restrictions on expenditure in foreign currency until 1991. Foreign exchange was released only for transactions deemed essential for the country. Reforms undertaken since then have attracted large inflows, and India currently has comfortable reserves amounting to over US$400 billion, making the RBI's job of managing foreign exchange fairly easy. The RBI has eased restrictions on foreign exchange spending to a large extent, resulting in a relatively free market.

The Indian rupee is fully convertible on the current account, implying that for current consumption and the import of raw materials for manufacturing, foreign currency can be freely purchased. For investments and the purchase of capital goods, the RBI's permission is required. For instance, companies need the RBI's permission before buying foreign currency for acquisitions.

Hindalco Ltd successfully sought permission from the RBI to finance its purchase of Novelis for US $6 billion in 2007. Tata Sons was denied permission by RBI for buying back the stake of NTT Docomo at a guaranteed rate of return. Tata Sons and Docomo successfully approached the courts to overturn the RBI's decision.

In most Western economies, the value of a currency is determined through free trading in the market. Such a system is termed the floating exchange rate. Demand and supply, leading to trading on a continuous basis, determines the price of currencies with respect to one another. The same holds true for India too.

Liberalized Remittance Scheme

Under the Liberalized Remittance Scheme (LRS), individuals are allowed to remit up to US$250,000 during a financial year. Foreign exchange can be remitted only for those activities that are permissible under the Foreign Exchange Management Act (FEMA), 1999. Remittance is permitted for consumption as well as for some capital purposes such as purchase of property, opening an account with a foreign bank or investing in shares of companies abroad and debt instruments.

In other countries, the price is determined by the central bank. Forex trading in these countries can be undertaken only at the rate fixed by their respective central banks. The central bank controls the price of the domestic currency with respect to other currencies, and only occasionally are the rates adjusted, when they get substantially out of sync with the fundamentals of the economy. In India, during the pre-liberalization era prior to 1991, the rate was fixed by the RBI and was seldom changed. At the end of 1990, US$1 fetched ₹17.32!

There are many other variants of the exchange-rate regimes. Some countries, including Hong Kong, have pegged their currency to the US dollar. While their value with respect to the US dollar is fixed, the rate with respect to other currencies fluctuates in accordance with the price of the dollar vis-à-vis those currencies.

Liquidity is another factor that determines the trading of different currencies. For example, the euro can be easily traded with the dollar at the prevailing rate. The market is liquid and significantly large amounts are traded on a regular basis. The market for other currencies may not be so liquid. For the conversion of rupees into the Thai baht, there is little liquidity. Not many people want to exchange Indian rupees for Thai baht or vice versa. There may be no counterparty at the opposite end willing to buy or sell Thai baht for Indian rupees; transactions are limited. In such a situation, what is required is to first convert Indian rupees into US dollars and then further exchange US dollars for Thai bahts. This is termed a cross-currency transaction. Currencies such as the US dollar, the GB pound, the euro and the yen are easy to trade. The market for other currencies may not be so liquid.

The foreign exchange market operates mainly through bank transfers via an electronic transfer system. It is primarily an interbank market with commercial banks, investment banks, corporations, central banks and foreign exchange dealers as the main players. Each forex transaction is fairly large in value, running into millions of dollars.

There also exists a retail market for forex, required for travel abroad, education and other similar expenses. The volumes are too small to hold significance for traders and market participants. Small-value transactions are unlikely to interest bankers or get a competitive quote. Hence, the costs of converting one currency into another, in small denominations, are significantly high.

The dealers and banks provide a two-way quote, that is, they specify prices at which they are willing to buy and sell forex—called bid and ask prices. They act as market makers, willing to buy and sell at the rates quoted. The difference between the bid and ask rates is termed the spread, and it is an indication of the liquidity in the market. Usually, higher the liquidity, lower is the spread and vice versa. Large volumes being the characteristic feature of the foreign exchange market, the liquidity is high and the spread extremely low.

A bank may provide a quote for a US dollar–GB pound trade as

GBP/USD 1.2520/1.2524.

The bank is willing to buy GB£1 for US$1.2520 and sell GB£1 for US$1.2524. A customer who wishes to sell has to strike the purchase quote of the bank, implying that he will get US$1.2520 per GB pound. Similarly, a buyer has to match the sell quote of the bank and must pay US$1.2524 for every GB pound purchased.

The bank makes a spread of US$0.0004 on every transaction which may appear extremely low. However, the large volume, with each deal being worth millions of pounds, rakes in hefty profits for the bank. The huge speculation in forex transactions leads to high liquidity and a low spread with a consequent low cost of trading.

Each currency has been assigned a three-letter code by the International Organization for Standardisation in order to facilitate easier transactions and settlement. The code for the Indian rupee is INR, the US dollar is USD, the British pound is GBP and the Euro is EUR. Currencies are traded in pairs—buying of one currency and selling of another. The first currency is the base currency, and the second is the quoted currency. Thus, GBP/INR is being quoted as the number of Indian rupees per GB pound. Similarly, EUR/YEN refers to the number of yen per euro. The foreign exchange market has its own lingo and jargon, and it is useful to be familiar with the vocabulary even if we are not direct participants.

The forex market is primarily an over the counter (OTC) market. It comprises an electronically linked network of a large number of foreign exchange trading centres. Market participants trade directly with each other. They are connected by the SWIFT (Society for Worldwide Interbank Financial Telecommunication) or some other network to facilitate settlement. In addition, significant business is also conducted on various exchanges. The market works 24/7, spanning all time zones, and it is possible to conduct business at any time of the day or night. London and New York have traditionally been the largest centres for foreign exchange transactions.

Brexit is likely to test the attractiveness of London as a premier centre for foreign-exchange trading. It is possible that some trading moves away to other markets and London loses its prominence.

Impact of Changes in Exchange Rates

We often come across demands from businessmen and economists advocating a lower value of currency in order to improve the competitiveness of the economy. Is a lower value really beneficial? Like everything in economics, the answer simply is 'it depends': depends on who you are—an exporter, an importer, an investor abroad, a borrower or a lender—and on the state of the economy. Let us try and understand the implications of the fluctuation in the value of a currency.

All our examples will assume a base rate of ₹70 to a US dollar, and we will understand the impact of a change in the exchange rate to

- ₹80 per US dollar (depreciation of the Indian rupee) and₹60 per US dollar (appreciation of the Indian rupee).

1. Exporters: Sun Pharma Ltd has significant exports to the USA. Assume that the company receives an order for the supply of drugs worth US$10 million, valued at ₹700 million at the current exchange rate. The export proceeds of US$10 million will be received after a time lag in accordance with the terms of the contract. What is significant is the exchange rate at the time of the receipt of the money. The value of the export proceeds of US$10 million in Indian rupees will depend on the exchange rate prevailing at the time the dollars are actually received. At an exchange rate of ₹80, Sun Pharma will have ₹800 million and will make large profits. However, at US₹60 to a US dollar, the company will be able to convert the US$10 million into ₹600 million only and will end up making a substantial loss. Exporters always clamour for a lower value of the home currency, which increases their cash flows in the home currency.

   The exchange rate has a significant impact on the competitiveness of exporters. An Indian manufacturer exports chocolate to the USA. His/her cost per chocolate is ₹70. At the current exchange rate (US$1 = ₹70), he/she can price it at US$1. Since the domestic producer in the USA prices the same chocolate at US$0.95, the Indian manufacturer is priced out of the US market. If the Indian rupee–US dollar exchange rate changes to ₹80 (depreciation of the rupee), the Indian manufacturer needs to price the chocolate at 70/80 = US$0.875 in order to get ₹70 when he converts his US dollar receipts into Indian rupees. At a price of US$0.875, a large market opens up for the Indian exporter.

   Many companies over time have gained or lost out due to fluctuations in foreign exchange rates despite other fundamentals remaining constant.

   In the year 2011, McDonalds performed well and increased its sales in Europe considerably. However, a strong US dollar meant that profits actually fell. McDonalds generates over three-quarters of its profits from overseas sales, and currency fluctuations have a significant impact on its profitability.

2. Importers: When an Indian company imports from the USA, it has to pay for the imports in US dollars. It must convert Indian rupees into US dollars to finance the imports. The cost in terms of Indian rupees depends on the Indian rupee–US dollar exchange rate.

   Assume imports worth US$1 million. At the current exchange rate of ₹70, it must pay ₹70 million to purchase US$1 million. If the rupee were to depreciate to ₹80, the company will need ₹80 million to import the same quantum of goods valued at US$1 million. An appreciation to ₹60 will, on the other hand, reduce the liability to ₹60 million.

The exchange rate has a significant impact on costs incurred by importers who want a higher value for the home currency. This is in direct contrast to exporters whose interests are better served with a lower value of the home currency.

Impact of Rupee Depreciation

In 2013, the US dollar appreciated by 25 per cent moving from ₹54.73 to a little under ₹68 in a matter of months. Given our annual imports of approximately US$461 billion, largely denominated in US dollars, there was a potential increase in the import burden. In addition, oil prices shot up significantly. The Indian economy had to face highly adverse conditions.

3. Domestic Suppliers: A domestic supplier who does not import any raw material may assume that he/she is not impacted by foreign exchange fluctuations. That would be a mistake, since he competes in the market place with imported products whose domestic price is dependent on the exchange rate. If steel can be imported at US$450 per ton, it will be priced at ₹31,500 at ₹70 to a US dollar. An Indian producer, with a cost of ₹30,000 per ton, is easily able to sell steel manufactured at his domestic factory. However, a change in Indian rupee–US dollar rate to 60 would have an adverse impact, since imported steel becomes cheaper at ₹27,000 per ton. Domestic producers selling in the domestic markets are as much impacted by exchange-rate fluctuations as are exporters and importers.

4. Borrower: The Indian corporate sector is relatively free to borrow overseas in a currency of its choice. A company may choose to borrow in dollars if the interest rate is low and the other terms are attractive. Since the payment of the principal and the interest is denominated in dollars, a significant exposure to the exchange rate is created. Let us see the impact with an example.

ABC Limited borrows US$100 million at an annual interest rate of 5 per cent for 10 years. The repayment will be in 10 equal instalments of US$10 million annually. Converted to Indian rupees, the loan is worth ₹7 billion, the interest of US$5 million equals ₹350 million and the repayment of US$10 million is worth ₹700 million annually.

As expected, the fluctuation in currency rates change the dynamics completely. While the liability in US dollars remains unaltered, the Indian rupee liability changes in line with the changed exchange rate. If the exchange rate becomes ₹80, the interest of US$5 million will amount to ₹400 million and the repayment will need ₹800 million. In fact, even after the first instalment has been repaid, the remaining loan of US$90 million will be worth ₹7.2 billion at the new exchange rate.

Thus, despite having repaid a part of the loan, the liability in Indian rupee terms is higher than when the loan was originally taken. Exchange-rate fluctuations have a significant bearing on the liability and the cash flow of companies. Thus, exchange-rate risks need to be managed carefully.

An interesting option now available to Indian companies are the masala bonds. (Please refer to corporate snippet in Chapter 2, 'Masala Bonds'). Masala bonds are issued by Indian companies in global markets but denominated in the Indian rupee. The payment of interest as well as the maturity amount is in Indian rupees. Hence, the liability of the issuing Indian company raising funds through masala bonds is fixed and does not vary with changes in foreign exchange rates. Masala bonds are relatively recent phenomena but as the Indian economy grows and the Indian rupee gains greater acceptability in global markets, more and more companies are likely to resort to masala bonds to meet their requirement of funds from international financial markets, without exposing them to currency fluctuations.

The Indian corporate sector had its first brush with currency risk when the government permitted joint ventures in the automobile sector, in collaboration with foreign companies, in the 1980s. Many such ventures commenced, especially with Japanese companies as the joint venture (JV) partner. These included Hero Honda Ltd, TVS Suzuki Ltd, Swaraj Mazda Ltd and DCM Toyota Ltd amongst others. In the initial years, completely knocked down (CKD) kits for engines were sourced from the parent companies. The price of the kits was denominated in the Japanese yen. When the yen appreciated, the cost in Indian rupee terms became prohibitive. In addition, most companies borrowed large amounts from their JV partners. The loans being denominated in yen, the liability of interest and the repayment of loans made a huge dent in profitability and cash flows.

DCM Toyota Ltd had to close down while the rest of them flirted with bankruptcy for some time. They were saved eventually by an unexpected decline in the value of the yen towards the end of the 1980s. Their brush with death, in a way, brought home the risk associated with foreign currency borrowing and exchange-rate fluctuations. Risk management tools were not available in those days nor was sufficient knowledge and experience of risk management available. Today, such risk management is a standard practice for any CFO.

5. Lenders: Lenders, of course, have an exposure which is exactly opposite to that of the borrowers. Lenders gain from depreciation in the value of the home currency and lose when the home currency appreciates. Lenders have already given funds in foreign currency to the borrowers and will be receiving these back in the future. Lower the value of the home currency at the time of repayment, the higher will be the amount of repayment in the home currency. We are, of course, assuming that lending is in a currency different from the home currency, for instance, an Indian company lending in Singapore dollars to its Singapore subsidiary.

XYZ Ltd is a mobile-operating company which has set up a subsidiary in Kenya. The Kenyan subsidiary required US$50 million some years back as part of the funding for the project. Being cash-rich, XYZ Ltd funded the requirement entirely through its internal cash flows by converting ₹3.5 billion into US$50 million at ₹70 per US dollar. The interest rate on the loan is 8 per cent, amounting to US$4 million.

At an exchange rate of ₹70, the interest payment of US$4 million is worth ₹280 million. If the exchange rate changes to ₹80 (depreciation of the Indian rupee), the company will get ₹320 million. The appreciation of the Indian rupee to ₹60 will imply an interest of only ₹240 million.

The eventual repayment of the loan is also subject to similar fluctuations. At ₹80, the repayment of US$50 million provides the company ₹4 billion, whereas at ₹60, the company gets only ₹3 billion.

BMW and Exchange Rates

BMW AG is a German automobile multinational company, which is more than 100 years old. Over the years, the company has expanded globally and by 2011, only 17 per cent of its sales originated in Germany. During this period, the USA, China, Russia and India have become critical markets. While rising sales revenues have benefitted the company immensely, its profitability has often taken a knock due to the rising value of the euro. According to the company's own estimates, its exchange rate losses between 2005 and 2009 totalled €2.4 billion.

The company took a two-pronged approach to manage its foreign exchange exposure. First, it built a natural hedge by diversifying its expenses in the same currency as its revenue and set up factories in countries where its sales are significant, including the US, China and India. By 2011, 44 per cent of its production was overseas, up from 20 per cent in 2000. Second, it also increased its purchases in currencies in which its sales were denominated.

Additionally, BMW instructed its regional treasuries to review their exposures on a weekly basis and report it to the group treasurer who recommends necessary action after consolidating the risk globally.

Thus, the impact of exchange-rate fluctuations on a company depends on whether it is an importer, an exporter, a domestic player competing with imported products, a lender or a borrower. Depending on these, the appreciation or depreciation of the home currency may have a positive or a negative impact. What is certain is that exchange-rate fluctuations expose the company to risks—risk of profits, cash flows and value. Every company must establish a well-thought-out risk management policy to manage the strategic risk.

Impact on the Economy

Similar to its effect on the corporate sector, the impact of the variation in the exchange rate on the economy depends on the prevailing conditions. The depreciation of the Indian rupee (the home currency) makes Indian products cheaper in international markets and imported products more expensive in the domestic market. This should boost the volume of exports and reduce the volume of imports. It is not obvious whether the net impact in value terms is positive or negative. Let us discuss this in detail.

Exports

When the rupee (home currency) depreciates in value, Indian exports become cheaper in terms of foreign currency, boosting the volume of exports. Its impact on the value of exports depends on the elasticity of demand for the exported basket of goods. In general, India's exports are highly elastic and react positively to exchange-rate depreciation. Hence, the value of exports usually goes up significantly when the Indian rupee depreciates. Other countries have had similar experiences, including China which ostensibly kept the value of its currency, the yuan, highly depreciated for a long period in order to boost its exports. In times of recession, there is always a clamour for the government to take steps to depreciate the domestic currency in order to encourage exports. Throughout history, exchange-rate management, as a tool of economic policy, has been extensively used by many nations for the benefit of their exporters.

What is important to remember is that the depreciation of one currency automatically implies appreciation of the other currency, which is bound to adversely impact the exports of the other country. The adversely impacted country can be expected to counter-depreciate its own currency, creating a stalemate. A currency war has no winners and eventually leads to a greater demand for protection from all affected parties. The consequent contraction of global trade harms all nations. Currency depreciation is a game which all countries can play. Economists term it 'beggar thy neighbour policy'. It must be initiated with extreme caution, taking into account the possible reaction of other affected economies.

Imports

The flip side to the Indian rupee depreciating is that imports become costlier, reducing the demand. Whether the impact in terms of value is positive or adverse depends on the price elasticity of the basket of imported goods. Unfortunately for India, our import basket largely consists of essential goods which respond poorly to change in prices (inelastic). Being vital to the economy, these goods have to be imported irrespective of their price. Crude oil, capital goods and other products display a low response to price variation, and there is hardly any reduction in the volumes imported. In fact, the import bill in value terms invariably shows a quantum jump consequent to rupee depreciation on account of the inelasticity of the imported basket of goods.

Some years back, the price of oil shot up to US$120 per barrel from US$80 (50 per cent increase). Simultaneously, the exchange rate also changed from ₹55 to ₹68 per US dollar (25 per cent depreciation). Consequently, the effective price of oil increased by over 90 per cent, playing havoc with the Indian economy which is heavily dependent on the imports of oil to meet its needs. The demand of oil is fairly inelastic and did not reduce despite the substantial rise in its price. The country had to spend a significantly larger sum on imports, leading to high external account deficit and problems on the foreign exchange front.

Inflation

An increase in the price of imported goods leads to higher inflation. If the country's imports equal 20 per cent of its national income, a depreciation of 10 per cent in currency value leads to prices going up by 2 per cent (20% * 10%), a substantial rise. An economy already suffering from rising prices may not be able to accept such an inflationary impact of currency depreciation.

Debt

India has large overseas borrowing, amounting to US$529 billion at the end of the financial year 2017–18. The interest and repayment of this borrowing is also subject to the vagaries of the exchange rate. An appreciation in US dollars will increase the liability in Indian rupees while a depreciation in US dollars reduces the liability.

Expectations

A change in the value of a currency induces expectations about its future direction and value. Expectations reinforce the changes that have already taken place, which the policy-makers need to keep in mind. A depreciation of the rupee might generate an expectation of a further drop. Exporters delay bringing their export earnings into the country, whereas importers may hasten payment to their overseas sellers, hoping to escape the adverse impact of a continued depreciation of the Indian rupee. Traders may also speculate by selling Indian rupees against US dollars, worsening the trend.

The previous paragraphs clearly demonstrate two aspects of foreign exchange fluctuations as follows:

1. The impact of foreign exchange rate fluctuations is significant and substantially influences the fortunes of the corporate sector and of other economic entities. Not only does it impact the profits and cash flows, it can also make companies uncompetitive, thereby driving them out of business.
2. Foreign-exchange fluctuations impact economic entities differently, depending on whether they are exporters, importers, lenders or borrowers and what their future plans are. Management practitioners should be able to understand and manage such impacts on their companies.

Toyota's Currency Woes

Subsequent to the financial crisis in 2008, the Japanese yen was considered a relatively safe currency. It experienced significant appreciation and, by September 2010, had reached a 15-year high at ¥84 to the US dollar. Consequently, Toyota found its cars priced out of the global markets, experiencing difficulty in selling against competitors. Companies such as Volkswagen and Hyundai were able to sell easily against the high-priced models of Toyota. Toyota estimated that it lost US$357 million in operating profits for every ¥1 increase in its value. Other Japanese companies such as Honda, Nissan, Sony and Canon also experienced losses, though not to the same extent as Toyota.

The problem was that Toyota manufactured a rather high proportion of its cars in Japan. While the company benefitted when the yen value was low, with the inevitable increase in its value, Toyota's exports were suffering.

Toyota plans to increase its manufacturing outside Japan significantly. As its spokesperson Paul Nalesco mentioned, 'Our goal is to produce cars where they are sold' (quoted in *New York Times*, 2010). But moving production overseas is not an easy decision. It takes time and risks backlash at home where production will need to be cut with a consequent impact on the home economy and implication for jobs.

Determination of Exchange Rates

The exchange rate is the price of one currency with respect to another. As is the case with the price of goods and services, the exchange rate of a currency is determined by its supply and demand. Let us understand this with the example of the Indian rupee vis-à-vis the US dollar.

While exports of goods and services lead to an inflow of US dollars into India, imports lead to an outflow. An excess of exports over imports (current account surplus) results in the country receiving more US dollars than it pays. With the supply of US dollars increasing, its value comes down and that of the Indian rupee goes up.

The appreciation of the Indian rupee reduces the exports of Indian goods and services and increases our imports, thus restoring the balance in the external account.

On the other hand, an excess of imports over exports results in US dollars going out. A reduction in the supply of US dollars increases its value and depreciates the Indian rupee. The depreciation of the Indian rupee should restore the balance in the current account.

Thus, deficit countries will have their currency depreciating and surplus countries will witness their currency appreciating. According to the traditional theory of foreign trade, the adjustment in currency rates will ensure that the economy will move towards a current account that is in balance.

This has been the traditional theory of international trade and foreign exchange, according to which a free market should restore any global disequilibrium. The automatic adjustment of the exchange rate should keep the balance of payments in equilibrium.

The theory, however, ignores movement of funds on the capital account. Capital movement of money can be on account of

1. foreign direct investment (FDI),
2. foreign portfolio investment (FPI),
3. global investment in new issue of equity and debt (global depository receipt (GDR/American depository receipts (ADR) and external commercial borrowing (ECB)),
4. speculation.

These are explained later in the chapter.

Over the years, capital flows across countries have greatly exceeded the flows on the current account and have become far more important in determining exchange rates. Capital flows quickly, in large volumes and has a disproportionate impact on exchange rates. Economies that are promising attract a large amount of capital to take advantage of business opportunities that present themselves. The increasing supply of foreign currency leads to the appreciation of the domestic currency. When conditions turn adverse, the same money exits in large volumes, leading to a sudden and significant fall in the value of the domestic currency. Most economies find it difficult to cope up with such a drastic fall as happened with the South East Asian economies in 1997 and with various other countries at different times.

The Indian rupee is freely convertible on the current account—for consumption and trade. However, India has still not made the Indian rupee convertible on the capital account. This protects the economy from unwanted volatility in capital flows and consequent fluctuations in the exchange rates. However, even the limited capital flows—in the form of portfolio investments and Non-resident Indian (NRI) flows—have often caused a dislocation in the economy and led to a significant fall in the value of the Indian rupee.

There has been an intense debate in the country on the advisability of capital account convertibility of the Indian rupee. A committee was established by the RBI to deliberate and give recommendations on this issue. The committee suggested a framework for and a path towards introducing capital account convertibility. The International Monetary Fund (IMF) has also been exhorting the country to move towards the liberalization of capital account convertibility. However, subsequent to the 1997 South East Asian crisis and more particularly the 2008 financial crisis, the sagacity of having controls on capital movement and the adverse impact of the free movement of money have been acknowledged. Most economists are of the opinion that India is unlikely to be ready for capital account convertibility in the near future.

The theory of exchange-rate determination, being a specialized topic, is beyond the scope of this book. It would, however, be useful to understand the basic postulate.

The change in the exchange rate between two currencies should equal the difference in inflation rates between the two economies, with the currency of the economy with a lower inflation appreciating. Thus, for instance, if the US dollar/Indian rupee rate is ₹70, the inflation rate is 6 per cent in India and 1 per cent in the USA, we should expect the Indian rupee to depreciate by 5 per cent to ₹73.5.

Reality, as we know, is not as simple. Suffice it to say that while the relationship between exchange rate changes and inflation rates may be valid in the long run, in the short run there could be a significant variation. For instance, between 2007 and 2016, a period of one decade, the Indian rupee has depreciated by 53 per cent vis-à-vis the US dollar. However, year-to-year changes in exchange rates have diverged widely from the difference in inflation rates, with the Indian rupee even appreciating in some years, despite a higher inflation in India.

A divergence in practice from what theory says is mainly due to market imperfections and regulatory restrictions. The lack of free capital account convertibility means that capital is not free to move between the two economies. In addition, the market for the Indian rupee–US dollar trade is not as liquid as other markets. Hence, even if the exchange rates are not perfect, arbitrage may be difficult.

International Capital Budgeting

Projects are evaluated on the basis of future cash flows which are discounted by the cost of capital to calculate the net present value (NPV). An investment is undertaken if the project NPV is positive. Does the fact that a project is established in a foreign country, with cash flows in a different currency, change how projects are evaluated?

The answer is both yes and no. Yes, because the cash flows are in a different currency, and that has a significant bearing on the project. No, because the fundamental principles of project evaluation remain the same.

As in the case of a domestic project, the future cash flows from the project must be estimated. These cash flows are denominated in the foreign currency and need to be discounted by the cost of capital in that currency. Thus, an Indian company establishing a project in England must discount the GB pound cash flows by the GBP cost of capital. The NPV that the project yields in GB pound is converted into Indian rupees at the current spot exchange rate to find the NPV in Indian rupees.

It is interesting to observe that there is no need to forecast the change in GB pound/Indian rupee rate. The future receipts in pounds can be hedged forward and, therefore, do not impact the viability of the project. The exchange-rate fluctuation should be kept independent of the assessment of the viability of the international project.

The only remaining piece of the puzzle is the GB pound cost of capital for discounting the cash flows. The critical parameter to estimate is the beta of the UK project. Conceptually, beta measures risk in relation to the investors' existing portfolio. Assuming most of the other investments of the company are in India and denominated in Indian rupees, the risk that the project in England adds to the company depends on the relationship of the UK project with the Indian market. Hence, the beta of the project must be measured with respect to the Indian market.

An alternative is to convert the future cash flows of the project into Indian rupees and then find the NPV. The conversion of the future cash flows requires exchange rates in the future which can be based on the forward exchange rate between the two currencies for the relevant period.

Thus, the NPV of the project can be calculated in two ways.

1. Discount the GB pound cash flows at the GBP cost of capital (based on beta of the project with the Indian market) and convert to the Indian rupee at the GB pound/Indian rupee spot exchange rate.
2. Convert the GB pound cash flows into the Indian rupee based on GB pound/Indian rupee forward exchange rates and discount the Indian rupee cash flows with its cost of capital.

Conceptually, the two are the same and should provide an equal value.

Balance of Payments

The balance of payments is a statement of a country's economic transactions with the rest of the world. It measures the international flow of money and products (goods, services and resources). The balance of payments accounting differentiates between products (goods and services) and financial assets (money). These transactions have an important bearing on the country's economic health.

The balance of payments is broadly divided into the current account and the capital account. The current account refers to trade in physical goods, services, investment income and unilateral transfers. It comprises the following transactions:

1. Trade in goods and services:
   a. The trade in physical goods such as cars, computers, paper, oil and so forth is termed the trade account or the merchandise account.

   The difference between the export and the import of physical goods is termed the balance of trade. India has always had a substantial deficit in its balance of trade. India imports large quantities of oil and capital goods amongst other products, which have always kept the import bill high. The demand for the products that constitute India's imports is highly inelastic and the volume of imports is rather sticky. Imported volumes do not reduce even when prices go up; in fact, the value of imports goes up substantially. Over time, imports have grown significantly, presenting a major problem for the country.

   Many countries with large imports, focus on exports to pay for their imports. India has, however, not exactly been known for its manufacturing capabilities, so the export of goods has always been minimal. The large import of goods cannot be made up by the exports, leading to a high deficit in the balance of trade.

   In recent years, however, there has been a minor shift with automobiles, pharmaceuticals and other products finding some export markets, generating hopes of physical goods exports becoming a significant factor in the economy.

   In 2016–17, which was one of the better years for the Indian economy and its balance of payments, India imported goods worth US$392 billion and exported goods worth US$280 billion. Hence, there was a trade deficit of US$112 billion.
   b. The trade in services includes software, banking, insurance and tourism amongst others. India's services exports are usually higher than its imports of services, helping bridge the deficit in the balance of trade. In 2016–17, India's services exports exceeded imports by US$67 billion.
2. Income accruing to residents from other countries: The second part of the current account is the income account. This includes
   a. net income earned by Indians working for non-Indian organizations,
   b. net income earned on investments abroad such as interest and dividends.
   In 2016–17, the net income on this account was negative to the extent of US$26 billion.
3. Current transfers: The third component of the current account is current transfers, including gifts and grants to foreign individuals, organizations and governments. Foreign aid from international donors and foreign governments used to be significant in the past. Of course, with India becoming self-reliant, that is now a distant memory.

Table 11.1 Current account: inflows and outflows

Year 2016–17 (US$ billion)	Inflows	Outflows	Net
Merchandise	280	392	–112
Invisibles	241	144	97
Services	163	96	67
Transfers	61	5	56
Income	16	42	–26
Total			–15

Source: Adapted from RBI publications, available at https://www.rbi.org.in/Scripts/ PublicationsView.aspx?id=17914. Accessed 28 January 2020.

A significant component of the current transfers are the remittances sent back home by Indians working abroad. The inflow of remittances from NRIs helps to cushion the impact of the deficit in the balance of trade. India is one of the largest recipients of remittances from its citizens living abroad. Without inflows from the NRIs, India's balance of payments and its foreign exchange position would have been extremely disconcerting. In 2016–17, India received US$56 billion as net remittances from its NRIs.

Components of the current account other than the trade in physical goods are often termed invisibles. In recent times, the trade in goods has reduced in importance, whereas invisibles have experienced a significant increase. This is in keeping with the global trend in the composition of national income, in which services are now dominant. The improvement in digital and telecommunication technology has made it easier to trade in services, further enhancing this trend.

Despite the net inflows of invisibles, India's current account has usually experienced a deficit with only stray periods of surplus.

In 2016–17, the imports of invisibles into India were to the tune of US$143 billion, while exports were worth US$240 billion. Hence there was a surplus of US$97 billion in services.

Thus, on the current account, there was a total deficit of US$15 billion as given in Table 11.1.

The Capital Account

The capital account records transactions comprising of the international movement of ownership of assets. It records the financial flows between India and the rest of the world. These include the following:

1. Direct investments comprise greenfield projects and a change in non-resident ownership of companies.

   The investment in a specific project in India by a foreign entity is FDI. For instance, Samsung has invested millions of dollars in India to establish manufacturing facilities and marketing network for its various products. Recently, it increased its mobile manufacturing capacity at its plant in Uttar Pradesh to 120 million units annually at an investment worth US$690 million. Similarly, Hyundai has brought in billions of dollars to invest in its car manufacturing plants in Uttar Pradesh and Rajasthan.

While foreign companies have been making FDI investments in India for a long period, prior to the liberalization in the early 1990s, the amount was quite insignificant. Subsequently, over the years, FDI has increased slowly and steadily. In the year 2016–17, flows on account of FDI were a very healthy US$36 billion.

FDI is beneficial to the country in various ways. First, FDI increases the total quantum of investments in the country. Second, it brings in precious foreign exchange as the companies which set up projects in India, bring in their funds in US dollars and other foreign currencies. Third, the investing companies bring in advanced technologies and modern global ways of doing business, which help in the progress of the Indian corporate sector. Foreign direct investment is a stable investment which is not impacted by the vicissitudes of the financial markets. It is invariably a long-term commitment by the investing company and is not easy to wind up and take back.

2. Portfolio investments refer to the investments in bonds, shares and other financial instruments, purely as a financial investment.

The Indian rupee is not convertible on the capital account. International investors cannot freely take out foreign exchange on the disposal of their investments in India. Converting rupees back to the external currency requires the permission of the RBI. We can safely assume that such investment in foreign currency will not be forthcoming, since repatriation back is not allowed.

Post liberalization in the 1990s, there was a need to attract foreign investors to the Indian financial markets. The government, therefore, introduced the Foreign Portfolio Investment Scheme, under which foreign institutional investors can register themselves with the Securities and Exchange Board of India (SEBI). Once registered, they can bring foreign currency into India to invest in equity and debt, divest any time and convert the sale proceeds back into the foreign currency after paying the applicable taxes. More than 1,000 foreign institutional investors have registered themselves with SEBI under this scheme to invest in the Indian financial markets. Approximately, US$7.5 billion was invested by foreign institutions in the Indian equity and debt market in 2016–17.

3. Issue of equity and bonds in the international markets: Another source of foreign exchange inflow on the capital account is the issue of equity and bonds in the international markets. Equity issuance is undertaken through instruments called the GDRs and the ADRs. Reliance Industries Ltd was the first Indian company to issue GDRs and get itself listed on the London Stock Exchange. Since then, many Indian companies have successfully raised funds from the global stock exchanges, including the US exchanges. Foreign companies have also been permitted to list their shares in India, denominated in the Indian rupee. Standard Chartered Bank was the first company to issue the Indian depository receipt and list on the Indian stock exchange. During the year 2016–17, for the first time, no Indian company raised capital through the issuance of GDR or ADR. They funded their requirements through public issues, private equity and borrowing.

The Indian corporate sector regularly accesses global markets to issue debt denominated in an external currency through ECBs. Various variants of the basic coupon bearing bonds, including foreign currency convertible bonds, have been used to raise money overseas by Indian companies. Usually, the debt of top Indian companies is highly prized in the global financial markets. In 2019, when the SBI wanted to raise US$1.25 billion from global debt markets, it received offers exceeding US$4 billion.

Besides, venture capital and private equity funds have also invested in Indian companies, including various start-ups, leading to a substantial inflow of funds into the country.

Prior to liberalization in the early 1990s, the Indian economy depended on the World Bank and development aid from donor countries to bridge the current account deficit. However, the external scenario was always uncertain.

Liberalization opened up many new avenues for inflow of capital into India, helping the RBI in exchange-rate management. India has built up reserves in excess of US$400 billion and worries about meeting foreign exchange commitments are a thing of the past. Capital inflows into India include FDI, Foreign institutional investment (FII) (portfolio), raising equity overseas through GDRs and ADRs, and ECBs.

The capital inflows have cushioned the impact of the current account deficit since liberalization in 1991 and helped build India's foreign exchange reserves. These reserves are, however, capital investments, which are not only repatriable, but investors also expect high returns. We need to ensure the productive use of such funds to avoid distress in future.

4. Other investments refer mainly to short-term capital flows such as the transfer to overseas banks and the sale/purchase of short-term financial instruments such as treasury bills and commercial bills.

5. Reserve assets reflect changes in the official foreign exchange held by the RBI.

The manner in which the balance of payments are constructed, they must necessarily balance. Surplus (deficit) on the current account, resulting from an excess (deficit) of exports over imports, is balanced by deficit (surplus) on the capital account. The current account surplus must be invested, which leads to the transfer of capital out of the country. Any difference between the current and capital accounts will be reflected in a change in official reserves held by the central bank.

India usually has a current account deficit; it imports more than it exports. It, therefore, needs to attract overseas investment (capital account surplus). Any shortfall leads to a drawdown of official reserves.

In theory, the balance of payments must balance. In practice, that rarely happens, since the accounts are never accurate and there is scope for errors in measurement. Balance of payment (BOP) accounts have a balancing item called 'net errors and omissions'.

Conceptually, exports of one country are imports of another, and, therefore, total global exports must equal the total global imports. It is interesting to note that the two do not match, mainly due to accounting and recognition errors and conceptual differences. Exports by all countries combined are usually higher than imports due to the differences in definition and accounting.

KEY CONCEPTS

1. The foreign exchange market is the market where different currencies are traded. This is a huge market, trading over US$4 trillion daily.
2. The foreign exchange market has its own nuances and distinguishing characteristics, which we must be aware of.
3. Changes in the foreign exchange rates have a significant impact on the corporate sector and the economy.
4. The supply and demand of currencies impacts the exchange rates. This includes both current and capital flows.
5. Balance of payments is a record of the transactions of a country with the rest of the world. Balance of payments is divided into the current and the capital account.
6. India has usually had a deficit in the current account which is made up by inflows on the capital account.
7. Capital account inflows include FDI, FII, ADR/GDR and ECBs.

CHAPTER QUESTIONS

1. The foreign exchange market has its own unique characteristics. Describe some of the features that a manager must be aware of.
2. Why, in your opinion, is the foreign exchange market so large? What attracts participants to the market?
3. What policy measures can the RBI and the government take to encourage greater acceptability of the Indian rupee globally? What hinders the Indian rupee from becoming a globally acceptable currency?
4. HDFC recently issued masala bonds, paying an interest rate of 8.10 per cent, much higher than what it would have paid for a dollar-denominated bond. How did the bank justify the higher interest payment?
5. In 1991, India had foreign exchange reserves totalling US$5.8 billion, sufficient for funding only three weeks' imports. Since then the country has accumulated over US$400 billion despite substantially easing restrictions on spending in foreign exchange and remitting it out for various purposes. How did this happen?
6. What do you understand by current account and capital account convertibility? Would you advise India to move towards capital account convertibility in the near future? What are the likely consequences of such a move?
7. What risks are companies exposed to due to the fluctuations in foreign exchange rates? How can they manage this risk?

CHAPTER 12

Working Capital

> In God we trust. All others must pay cash.
>
> —Anonymous

1. The financial crisis in 2008 caught many companies off guard. They were unprepared for the subsequent recession in the global economy. The large dip in demand severely impacted many companies. Metal manufacturers suffered more than others. Facing a grim future,

the global aluminum company Alcoa made working capital a priority in 2009 in response to the financial crisis and the global economic downturn, and it recently celebrated its 17th straight quarter of year-on-year reduction in net working capital. Over that time, the company has reduced its net working capital cycle—the amount of time it takes to turn assets and liabilities into cash—by 23 days and unlocked $1.4 billion in cash (Davies and Merin, 2014)

2. Fisher-Price Inc.'s *1991 Annual Report* stated, 'The decision to maintain higher inventories was taken to allow Fisher-Price to aggressively support first quarter sales and to further improve our quality of customer service.'

There is a glaring contrast in the working capital policy adopted by the two companies. Alcoa was faced with a tough, recessionary environment where cash was at a premium. Lower demand and a lack of pricing power resulted in poor cash flow from operations and the profit and loss (P&L) account. Alcoa sought to squeeze maximum cash from its balance sheet through the efficient management of the working capital.

Fisher-Price, on the other hand, was operating in a flourishing environment with booming demand and large cash flows from business. The company needed to ensure that its efforts to achieve higher sales were not stymied by inventory constraints and that its working capital was supportive of its aggressive sales strategy. The company had to ensure that there was no let-up in production and that the stocks of the finished products were available to support sales and customer service.

Like other aspects of financial policy, working capital policy must be in consonance with the business strategy of a company. Different business environments and strategies demand different working capital support. It is important to understand the business strategy of the firm and how working capital dovetails in and plays a part in the success of the strategy.

Working capital management is a key determinant of a company's performance. While profit and loss account receives maximum attention in judging how well a company is performing, balance sheet analysis is equally critical. The value of a company is derived from its free cash flows, and changes in the working capital constitute a critical element of the free cash flows. Working capital management is a day-to-day activity, and finance managers spend considerable time and effort in managing it. Companies usually have more control over their working capital than over longer-term aspects.

A company invests in long-term and short-term assets to run its business. Long-term assets include buildings, plant and machinery, technology, patents, brands and other intangibles and involve cash flows that occur over many years.

Short-term assets comprise investments in inventory, debtors (accounts receivables) and creditors (accounts payable). Usually in finance, the distinction between the long-term and the short-term period is taken as one year. Accounts receivables, payables and the inventory cycle generally last for less than one year and are, therefore, considered to be short-term investments.

Concept of Working Capital

Working capital comprises the following:

1. Accounts payable: Corporates are in the business of producing and selling goods and services. The raw material is ordered for production for which suppliers need to be paid. Companies are usually able to get credit on supplies and can defer payments to a later date. The amount of payment, due to the suppliers at any point in time, is termed accounts payable/creditors. The accounts payable reduces the requirement of working capital for the company.

2. Raw material inventory: All raw material purchased may not be consumed immediately; part of it is stocked as inventory to be utilized as and when required. For instance, components required for the production of a laptop are ordered in bulk and then used as per the production schedule. Similarly, Raymond Ltd may order raw wool from Australia in bulk and use it over a period of time for its range of woollen suits. Product and industry characteristics, along with supply chain conditions, determine the inventory level of raw material that needs to be maintained. The raw material may also include spares and replacement parts.

3. Work in process: The raw material becomes work in process once production starts until the final product is ready. During the period of production, the company carries an inventory of work in process. Longer the production cycle, higher is the level of work in process.

4. Finished goods inventory: Even after the final goods have been produced, the sale may not take place immediately. Companies thus carry the inventory of final goods until these are sold. The time taken to conclude the sales determines the inventory of finished goods.

The total inventory of an organization is thus the sum of its raw material, work in process and finished goods.

5. Accounts receivable: Just as it buys raw material on credit, companies offer credit to their own customers. Cash may not be realized immediately after a sale takes place, resulting in accounts receivables/debtors. It is only upon the subsequent payment of the sales proceeds by the customer that cash is realized and the operating cycle is complete.

The entire sequence of raw material supplies, payment to suppliers, production, sale and eventual payment by customers takes place over a period of less than 12 months. In fact, it is common to have many such cycles completed within a period of one year. Working capital refers to the investment required in funding accounts receivable and the stock of the inventory, reduced, of course, by accounts payable.

Inventory—raw material, work in process and finished goods—and accounts receivables (debtors) constitute the current assets, signifying the fact that these are usually converted into cash within a period of 12 months. Companies also need to keep a certain amount of cash and bank deposits, which form a part of the current assets—usually an insignificant proportion of the total.

Components of Current Assets

Following are the components of current assets:

1. Inventory
   a. Raw material
   b. Work in process
   c. Finished goods
2. Accounts receivables
3. Cash and marketable securities/bank deposits

Accounts payable, that is, the amount payable to suppliers for raw materials, constitutes the current liability, again suggesting that the company will have to pay this amount within a 12-month period. There are other expenses such as taxes payable, accrued wages and so forth that also constitute current liabilities.

Components of Current Liabilities

Current liabilities broadly consist the following:

1. Accounts payable
2. Taxes payable
3. Wages and other expenses payable

Current assets (CA) = accounts receivable + inventory (raw material + work in process + finished goods) + cash.

Current liability (CL) = accounts payable + taxes payable + accrued wages.

Working capital = CA – CL.

Operating Cycle

The conversion of the raw material to the work in process, then to finished goods, on to sales and, finally, the realization of cash from accounts receivables is termed the operating cycle. The longer the operating cycle, the higher is the investment required in working capital. Companies go to great lengths to shorten the operating cycle (as we observed with Alcoa) while ensuring that the operations of the company do not get disrupted. The length of the operating cycle is a function of the product line of the company and the industry practices.

- Service companies require less inventory compared to companies producing physical products.
- Products that have seasonal sales require higher inventory.
- A market leader is able to dictate credit terms, and hence needs to extend less credit to its customers.
- Supply chain conditions dictate how much inventory is required to be maintained.
- Imported raw materials require a higher inventory of stock.
- Market conditions—recession or booming economy, structure of the market, competition and customers—determine the level of inventory as well as of accounts receivables.

The operating cycle is the sum of the inventory conversion period and the accounts receivables conversion period.

On the other side, the company also gets credit time to pay the suppliers for its purchase of raw materials, which reduces the investment required in working capital to that extent. The operating cycle minus the payables deferral period is termed the cash cycle. Let us understand this with a hypothetical example. The example is also graphically represented in Figure 12.1.

Assume that on day 0, ABC Ltd places an order for components (raw materials). The components arrive after 30 days, with a credit period of 40 days. The production process starts 15 days after the arrival of the components and goes on for 60 days when the finished product is ready. It takes the company 30 days to sell the finished product and a further 60 days to collect the cash.

The operating cycle commences on day 30 when the components arrive, goes on for another 165 days, which is calculated as follows:

- Raw material inventory of 15 days
- Work in process of 60 days
- Finished goods inventory of 30 days
- Collection period of 60 days, when the cash is actually received from the customers

The cash cycle is 125 days, that is, the operating cycle of 165 days minus the payables deferral period of 40 days.

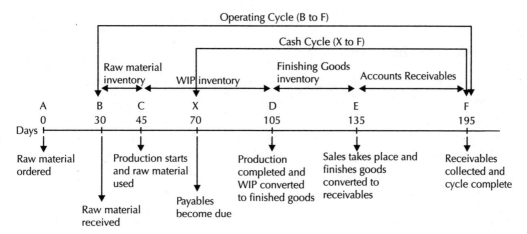

FIGURE 12.1 Working capital cycle

Source: Author.

Industry Characteristics

In 2007, the *CFO* magazine published the results of a survey of working capital in different industries which showed remarkable diversity not only in the level of working capital but also in its constituents.

As can be observed from Table 12.1, different industries have different operating cycles as well as different cash cycles, leading to a significant variation in the level of working capital. In fact, the contrast can be seen in the various components too. The differences are a function of the industry characteristics and the market practices within the industry. Thus, the evaluation of the working capital requirements and its planning must be undertaken in the context of the industry a company operates in. Comparisons across industries may not be very meaningful. If we compare the working capital of Ballarpur Industries Ltd (a paper company) with Speciality Restaurants Ltd, the comparison is likely to produce misleading conclusions.

TABLE 12.1 Survey of working capital in different industries (in days)

	Receivables period	Inventory period	Operating cycle	Payable period	Cash cycle
Electrical utilities	41	18	59	31	28
Healthcare equipment	73	46	119	17	102
Paper products	38	39	77	26	51
Restaurants	10	5	15	14	1

Source: CFO (2007).

Education Industry

Education, as an industry, presents an interesting study with respect to working capital. Let us look specifically at a business school which needs a reasonable capital investment for buildings, IT network, library and so forth. But there is hardly any requirement for stocking inventory. Teaching and academics, including research and training, are intellectual pursuits that do not require physical inventory. Moreover, the students pay their fees in advance, either annually or every semester. In a sense, receivables are negative and are a source of funds. No wonder, there is a big rush to establish and run a business school in India!

Working Capital Planning

There are two competing ideas at work when companies conceptualize and plan their working capital. A higher working capital increases the quantum of funds required for investment in business, resulting in a lower return on assets. Profit has to be apportioned over higher capital employed. Companies are, therefore, quite tight-fisted when it comes to increasing the working capital. Besides resulting in lower returns, the working capital has many ancillary costs that can be very significant. The costs include

1. cost of capital,
2. receivables going bad and being written off,
3. cost of collection,
4. obsolescence of inventory,
5. storage cost,
6. insurance expenses,
7. cost of monitoring.

These costs are termed carrying costs and can be substantial. That is why Alcoa concentrated on reducing the working capital cycle to improve its performance when market conditions turned adverse.

Besides the high cost, an excessive investment in working capital is a prominent reason for the failure of business enterprises. Even if a business idea proves successful and sales are booming, the growth in sales may consume too much cash by way of a huge inventory and debtors, leading to a severe liquidity crunch. Cash gets tied up in production, inventory and credit extended to customers. For every business, there is a sustainable rate of growth, beyond which it may face cash flow problems.

Unsustainable Growth

Subhiksha Ltd was a successful retail chain in the early years of the twenty-first century. It captured the tastes and behaviour pattern of the customers and became a runaway success. While the accomplishments were well-deserved, the inventory and debtors' requirement were largely ignored by the management which focused primarily on sales growth and profitability. While sales grew at a rapid pace, inventories grew even faster. The profit turned out to be largely illusory, showing itself only in accounting books.

The company could not handle the huge volumes, growing beyond what was sustainable, and faced a severe cash crunch. Eventually, unable to pay back its loans and defaulting on payments to its suppliers, it became bankrupt and had to close down. Despite an apparently successful business model, it failed to appreciate the working capital requirements and the consequent cash flow shortages became the cause of its downfall.

Recall the definition of free cash flows. It incorporates the profit and loss statement as well as the balance sheet. It has four components, namely

1. net operating profits after tax (NOPAT),
2. depreciation and non-cash expenses,
3. capital investment and
4. change in working capital.

If the future growth in sales requires an investment in working capital, there are cash flow implications that need to be clearly appreciated.

At the same time, the working capital is an inherent need of the business, without which the entire operations would come to a standstill. A shortage of current assets imposes its own costs on the company, termed shortage or stockout costs.

Stockout costs manifest themselves in many ways. If the company does not give credit to its customers, they may shift their loyalty to competitors and sales would suffer. A lack of adequate raw material may hamper production. A mobile manufacturer must have all the components required for production on hand. The absence of even one of those components may lead to the stoppage of manufacturing. A prospective customer comes to the showroom but the dealer does not have its latest model in stock. The outcome could be a loss of the sale due to a lack of finished goods inventory.

Thus, the shortage of current assets may lead to

1. adverse impact on sales,
2. disruption in the production process.

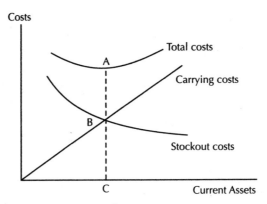

FIGURE 12.2   Cost of current assets

Source: Author.

On the positive side, a higher investment in the working capital can be used as a competitive tool. Fisher-Price used higher levels of inventory to increase sales and profits. We had earlier discussed the use of higher advances to dealers by Deere & Company to gain market share (Chapter 7 on the capital structure and financing).

The CFO must balance the carrying cost and the stockout cost to ensure the maximization of return on investment. As is quite apparent, the size of the inventory and accounts receivable is directly related to the carrying cost and inversely to the shortage cost. The higher the level of current assets, the higher is the carrying cost and the lower the stockout costs and vice versa. At the ideal level of current assets, the marginal carrying costs equals the marginal shortage costs. It should be the continuous endeavour of the CFO to identify and ensure that the company operates at that level.

In Figure 12.2, the shortage/stockout-costs curve cuts the carrying-costs curve at point B, indicating that the marginal carrying cost equals the savings from the stockout cost. At this level of current assets, represented by point C, the total costs are minimized as shown by point A on the total-costs curve.

Dell Computers Ltd

Despite representing the triumph of technology, the computer industry relied on a highly traditional model for the sale of computers in the United States of America (USA) during the 1980s. Computers were assembled and passed on to the dealers who would sell to the end consumers, holding substantial inventory over long periods.

Enter Michael Dell with his direct sales and build-to-order model wherein the customers directly placed orders with the company which then built the specific model as per the requirements of the customer. This had two advantages. First, Dell Computers saved substantially on dealer margins. Second, it did not have to carry large inventories that were a characteristic feature of the industry as the company assembled computers only against orders placed by the customer.

Inventory control is critical for all industries and products. For computer manufacturers in particular, maintaining inventory was expensive. The industry introduced new products and models frequently, rendering older models obsolete at a rate faster than any other industry. Approximately, one-third of the inventory became obsolete annually, extracting a very heavy price in terms of obsolescence in addition to the normal costs of financing, insurance and so forth.

With its build-to-order model, Dell Computers managed to reduce its computer inventory to low levels and became a success overnight, inventory management being a key factor.

Hindustan Unilever Limited

Facing recessionary conditions, the year 1999 proved to be a difficult one for the Indian economy. Company after company declared results that showed the adverse impact of the challenging environment. Hindustan Unilever Ltd (HUL), then known as Hindustan Lever Ltd (HLL), was also expected to show results along similar lines with poor growth in sales and profits.

What actually transpired stunned the market. While the muted sales growth was on expected lines, the company's profits shot up beyond expectations. No one could figure out the reason until the company itself attributed the high profits to the better control and management of its working capital.

Faced with the prospects of low sales and profits, HLL used its monopolistic position and the strength of its brands to reduce the payment period for its dealers. Dealers, in fact, had to pay in advance for the supplies, thus significantly reducing the funding requirements, releasing substantial cash flows and resulting in higher than expected profits.

Credit Management and Policy

There are four elements of a credit policy that a company must establish.

1. Terms of sale: On what terms will the company sell its products? This requires answers to the following questions:
   a. Whether to extend credit at all to its customers or will sales be made only against an immediate payment?
   b. How long would the credit period be?
   c. Will there be any discount on cash payment?

   There are a number of factors that determine the terms of the sale. Every company must have a policy that is in accordance with industry practices. Else, it may find customers moving away if its own terms are more onerous than the competitors. Alternatively, terms that are too generous will impact profitability unnecessarily.

   The following factors need to be taken into consideration in defining the terms of sale:

   a. Life/perishability of the product: The credit period usually does not exceed the life of the product. The shorter the product life, the shorter the credit period.
   b. Consumer demand: established products with rapid turnover have a shorter credit period compared to new ones.

    c. Value of the product: low-value products have a shorter credit period than high-value ones.

    d. Size of the account: Small-size accounts, being of less importance, are given a shorter credit period. The cost of managing small accounts per unit of sales is also higher.

    e. Credit risk: greater the perceived credit risk, shorter will be the credit period and vice versa.

    f. Nature of competition: In a competitive market, a grant of credit is a means to attract customers. A relatively monopolistic position does away with the need to offer credit.

    Companies often offer discount on cash/early payment, which not only reduces the investment in working capital but also cuts down the effort of monitoring the account and the chances of bad debt.

    We often find goods being sold on terms, stated as 2/5, net 50, which means that customers have 50 days to make the payment, but if they pay within 5 days of invoicing, they will receive a discount of 2 per cent on the invoice value. The company is willing to forego 2 per cent of sales value in order to reduce the credit period by 45 days.

2. Credit standards: As a general practice, companies extend credit to their customers. They incur a credit risk in doing so. At times, payments are not made on time by the customers. At other times, the credit may go bad and the payment may not be received at all. Although an integral part of a company's business, the extension of credit is risky.

    Thus, credit given to a customer runs the risk of non-payment or a delay in payment. Risk assessment is a critical element of credit sales. The company must establish standards by which prospective customers would be evaluated for their credit worthiness.

3. Analysis of credit worthiness: Analysing whether a prospective customer merits a grant of credit in accordance with the established credit standards is termed the analysis of credit worthiness. Companies need to evaluate whether a specific customer deserves to be given credit or would it entail too much of a risk. Credit analysis, based on the established credit standards, is a critical element of working-capital management.

    Credit worthiness of a customer is evaluated on the basis of what are called the 5 Cs, referring to

    a. character: willingness and commitment of the borrower towards credit obligations,

    b. capacity to pay: whether the customer has the cash flows to meet his/her obligations,

    c. collateral: asset pledged against credit,

    d. capital: financial reserves as cushion and

    e. conditions: the economic environment prevailing, especially the state of the industry in which the customer operates.

    A detailed analysis based on the 5 Cs determines whether a customer can be given credit and, if yes, on what terms? The terms of credit are based on the risk associated with the grant of credit to him/her.

4. Collection management: Having granted credit to customers, there is a need to ensure that the receivables are eventually collected on time as per the terms of the sale.

    Regular follow-ups and interaction with the customer are critical. Any sign of financial trouble must ring alarm bells and action must be taken before the credit becomes unrecoverable.

Financing of Working Capital

Having decided on the level of working capital and its components, a firm must determine the means of financing. Two decisions need to be taken.

1. What should be the proportion of long-term and short-term funds?
2. What should be the specific instruments by which working capital will be financed?

Working-capital requirements can be highly variable, depending on the inventory levels and receivables at any point in time. This is especially true for industries whose sales are seasonal in nature. However, there is a minimum level that the firm has to maintain at all times. In a sense, this part of the working capital is permanent or long-term in nature. The balance is the fluctuating and variable portion.

Financing working capital is an interesting exercise. While working capital represents short-term investment, a significant proportion is permanent in nature. According to finance theory, a long-term requirement should be met with long-term funding. If short-term funds are used to finance long-term requirements, the company is exposed to a high risk. At the same time, short-term funds are cheaper and cost less.

The CFO must balance these aspects to formulate and implement an optimum financing policy. He/she could adopt a matching strategy which finances long-term working capital requirements with long-term funding and short-term requirements with short-term funding. Or he/she could resort to long-term funding for only a part of the long-term requirements and the balance working capital is funded through short-term means. It is assumed that the short-term instruments can be rolled over and refinancing would be readily available when required. A greater reliance on short-term funding reduces the cost of financing the working capital, while exposing the company to the risk of refinancing.

Working capital can be financed in many ways.

1. Bank finance: bank finance for working capital comes in various forms.
   a. Cash credit: Cash credit is a running account extended for a period of up to 12 months against a collateral of inventory and accounts receivable. Interest is chargeable only on the amount and the period of actual credit utilization.
   b. Overdraft: an access to cash by overdrawing from an existing account.
   c. Export credit: It is credit for export, for both pre-shipment and post-shipment purposes. Pre-shipment credit enables exporters to finance the inventory of goods to be exported. Post-shipment credit enables exporters to finance credit to its buyers. Both these lines of credit are available in Indian rupees as well as in foreign currency as the case may be.
   d. Buyers credit: Importers can avail of a buyers credit to pay for imports in various foreign currencies.
   e. Non-fund-based financing: Firms may also require non-fund-based working capital support. Non-fund-based working capital does not entail actual cash outflow by banks but only involves a commitment to pay. The support may be in terms of guarantees given by the banks on behalf of the company, called fee-based working capital.

i. A letter of credit (LC) is an instrument that enables a manufacturer to sell its products to its customers without assuming a credit risk. There is a time gap between the dispatch/delivery of goods and the receipt of the payment, which exposes the seller to a credit risk. The buyer may later be unwilling to or unable to pay for the goods supplied.

By issuing an LC, the bank certifies the credit credentials of the buyer and guarantees the payment to the seller on behalf of the buyer. The payment is made directly by the buyer's bank to the seller's bank. This is a classic case of the transfer of risk from an unknown customer to a known bank.

An LC is an instrument which is extensively used in international trade. International trade is fraught with risk. A manufacturer selling to a customer in another country may not be comfortable with either the ability or the willingness of the buyer to make the payment as per the terms of the sale. An LC becomes an essential tool to facilitate the sale transaction.

ii. A bank guarantee (BG) is an instrument similar to an LC. It is akin to a guarantee of performance. A BG is often required while bidding for a contract which incorporates penalties for non-performance/non-adherence to the terms of the contract. A failure to perform as per the terms of the contract invokes the BG and the bank pays the company that has awarded the contract an agreed sum. This is an example of the transfer of risk from the bidding company to the bank.

   f. Bank loans: banks also offer companies outright loans for financing their working capital.

2. Commercial paper (CP): It is an instrument for raising short-term funds by the corporate sector from the market. It is an unsecured instrument which is rated by credit-rating agencies. Blue-chip companies are able to raise funds through CP at competitive rates, thereby reducing their funding costs. Some companies have an ongoing CP programme to fund their working capital requirements. Of late, a CP has become a significant avenue of raising funds for blue-chip companies in India.

3. Factoring: Factoring refers to the sale of a company's accounts receivables to a factoring company. A factoring company specializes in collecting and financing outstanding credit. The customers pay their dues directly to the factor. In this manner, the factoring company not only finances the accounts receivables but also takes the onus of collection and the associated risk. Specializing in collections, the factor is able to undertake the job more efficiently. Both the factor and the company gain through the process of the transfer of risk from the seller to the factoring entity. This is termed *factoring without recourse*, implying that the factor has no recourse to the seller in case of a non-payment by a customer. This transfers the risk from the producing and selling companies to the factoring institutions who have much greater expertise and experience in managing debtor accounts.

Often, factoring may be undertaken *with recourse* which means that the risk of non-payment remains with the selling firm and not the factor.

In India, SBI Factors, Canbank Factors and IFCI Factors are a few companies that specialize in factoring. Export Credit Guarantee Corporation (ECGC) Ltd and India Factoring and Finance Solutions Pvt Ltd provide factoring for exports. Few private sector banks such as HSBC and Axis Bank also undertake factoring services.

4. Bills discounting: This is one of the most common methods of working-capital financing. Sales need to be financed until the final payment is made by the buyer. The seller raises an invoice against sales, usually on the delivery of the goods. The bills must be accepted by the buyer as proof of sales having been made and the liability accepted by the buyer.

The accepted bills are presented by the seller to a financial intermediary, usually a bank, which provides finance against these bills. The funding is a discounted value of the total invoice and the discount provides an interest income to the bank. The quantum of the discount depends on the interest rate which the bank wants to charge on the transaction. The buyer, of course, pays the full amount of the invoice on the due date.

Excess Cash

Companies often have excess cash with them. This may be because

1. they have kept aside cash for day-to-day transactions,
2. there is a temporary mismatch between the availability and the requirements of cash,
3. cash may have been accumulated for certain planned expenses in the immediate future.

Cash with the company is not kept idle but is invested in short-term securities to earn a return. While investing, the CFO must judiciously evaluate securities on the basis of certain key parameters.

1. Maturity: Cash is available for a short-term only and hence must be invested in securities with a matching short maturity period. Cash mismatch is temporary; it cannot be invested in long-term securities.
2. Risk: An investment cannot be subject to risk and excess cash must be invested only in risk-free securities. Treasury bills and other money-market instruments are attractive and viable instruments. A short-term maturity of the security, in any case, reduces the interest rate risk.
3. Liquidity: Companies like to have the flexibility of being able to convert their investment back into cash instantaneously, whenever the business requires funds. Liquidity is a critical element of investing cash balances.

The following are the common instruments to park short-term excess cash:

1. Treasury bills
2. CP
3. Certificate of deposits
4. Repurchase agreement (repo) instruments
5. Bank fixed deposits

Strategy

Working-capital management presents a difficult and complex problem for the CFO. There are no straightforward answers. The CFO needs to strike a delicate balance between the apparent costs of higher working capital and the potential disruption due to inadequate working capital.

As always, it is important to remember that financial policy must be supportive of the company's overall strategy in the context of the environment it faces. The financial policy exists to support the strategic plan of the company. As was the case with Alcoa Ltd, if there is an economic downturn, and profitability and cash flows are likely to be strained, the working capital policy must be restrained and conservative. The CFO should try to reduce the working capital cycle and extract as much cash flow from it as possible. On the other hand, if the company is planning to aggressively promote higher sales, as was the case with Fisher Price Ltd, the working capital policy pursued must also be aggressive. It is the CFO's job to ensure that sufficient funds are available for the higher level of working capital required by the company's strategic initiatives.

There are questions the CFO must ask to formulate an appropriate working capital policy. These may include the following:

1. What should be our credit policy? Should dealers be supported with higher credit? Or is there a need to squeeze more cash from them?
2. What is the level of cash the company should maintain for managing smooth operations?
3. What is the appropriate level of the finished goods inventory?
4. Should we seek a longer payment period from suppliers or take advantage of the discounts offered by them for an early payment?
5. How much should we borrow for the short term? What should be the source of such borrowings?
6. Is production likely to be disrupted by a worsening supply-chain environment? Should the company, therefore, stock up on essential raw material? Will the large order size help extract better terms from the suppliers, besides reducing the ordering cost?
7. Should the company explore selling its receivables to a factoring company?

The answers will, of course, depend on the various factors we have discussed in the chapter. Ultimately, these must support the fulfilment of the overall strategic initiative of the company.

KEY CONCEPTS

1. The working-capital cycle refers to the time period starting from the ordering of the raw materials to processing and manufacturing the finished product, on to sales and the final collection of sales proceeds from the customers.
2. An investment in working capital reduces a company's return on investment. It may at times lead to cash flow problems and, in extreme cases, to bankruptcy.
3. At the same time, a low investment may lead to a disruption in operations and lower sales. It is the job of the CFO to find a delicate balance.

4. There is no ideal level of working capital. Working capital must be in consonance with and support the company's strategic initiative.
5. The nature of the industry and the market conditions dictate the requirements of the working capital and its various components.
6. There are various ways to finance working capital—from the traditional bank finance and bills discounting to the more recent factoring services.

CHAPTER QUESTIONS

1. What impact will the following have on the operating cycle? Please explain each separately.
   a. Receivables period goes up
   b. Inventory turnover goes up
   c. Payables turnover goes up
   d. A new manager has been able to reduce the production cycle and manufacture the product faster
2. ABC Ltd has sales of ₹10,000. Its receivables turnover ratio is 5. What is the investment in receivables? Specify the same in terms of the number of days' sales.
3. Name two industries—one which is working-capital intensive and one which has low requirements of working capital. How does this aspect impact decision-making in the industry?
4. XYZ sells its products to customers on credit. The credit terms are 2/10, net 60. Only 80 per cent of the customers avail themselves of the discount and pay 10 days after the billing.
   a. What is the average collection period for XYZ Ltd?
   b. If the annual sales are ₹50,000, how much investment has the company made in receivables?
5. Working-capital policy must dovetail in the overall financial strategy of the company. Discuss.
6. Two companies in the same industry have different current ratios. What could be the reasons?
7. A new player enters the market and provides much more liberal terms to the dealers. What impact can it have on your company and how would you respond?

CASE FOR DISCUSSION

How different were the decades of the 1960s and the 1970s! Those were the days of shortages, waiting, queues, control, licenses and monopoly! Contrastingly, today we are spoilt for choice if we want to purchase any consumer product. Let us take the example of a car. Prior to the 1980s, there were only two brands—the Ambassador and the Fiat. They had limited capacity and were easily able to satisfy the limited market that existed and sell whatever they produced. There was no incentive to reduce costs or improve efficiency, competition being non-existent.

The entry of Maruti in the mid-1980s was a game changer in more ways than one. The way business was carried out became friendly and professional. Dealers as well as suppliers were treated as partners in the business rather than adversaries. The customer became the focus for the industry.

The way a car is manufactured is different from other products. A car has hundreds of components, each of which may be supplied by a different supplier.

Maruti assembles these components to manufacture the car. In addition, Maruti designs the car and the specific features of each component, undertakes quality control, and assumes responsibility for marketing and various other tasks that go along with it.

The role of the component manufacturers is critical. Maruti, therefore, ensures that the component suppliers have an equal stake in the success of the venture. Most of the component manufacturers are located close to its factory in Gurgaon, linked to it through its enterprise resource planning (ERP) network, aware of the production schedule of Maruti on any given day and the number of components it must supply. Maruti, therefore, stocks a limited inventory of components (its raw material) which are supplied daily by the component manufacturers. In addition, no time is lost and no costs are incurred in ordering and transportation, benefitting both Maruti and the component manufacturers.

Currently, Maruti has 246 suppliers, 76 per cent of whom, mainly suppliers of bulky components such as instrumentation panels, fuel tanks, bumpers and seats, are located within 100 kilometres of the Maruti factory. Maruti also has joint a venture with 14 of them.

1. In what way did the entry of Maruti change the way business is conducted in the automotive sector in India?
2. What was the impact of these changes on working-capital management?
3. Is there any other sector that you can think of where similar changes will significantly improve the fortunes of the industry? How?

CHAPTER 13

Ratio Analysis

Financial statements are like a fine perfume, to be sniffed but not swallowed.

—Abraham Brillof

Corporations are complex entities which witness a constant interplay of the policies of the management with the external environment, leading eventually to financial outcomes. At times, the financial outcomes are in accordance with the objectives of the company; at other times, the two may diverge. Whether the desired outcomes are being realized or not, the management needs to continually analyse the performance of the company and consider ways to improve upon it.

Ratio analysis is a tool that is extensively used to scrutinize the performance of a company. Its extensive usage is a reflection of the easy understanding and wide applicability of the concept. A ratio is an arithmetical relationship between two numbers, the numbers being usually picked from the accounting statements. It is important to pick numbers that have a meaningful relationship with each other and whose ratio reveals some key performance parameters of the company. Else, the ratio would be irrelevant, even misleading.

All stakeholders—shareholders, bond holders, bankers, suppliers, employees, customers and, above all, the management—use ratios to monitor various aspects of the performance of the company. Different stakeholders use different ratios, appropriate to their specific requirements. Investors in the stock market are interested in market-based ratios such as the price earnings (P/E) ratio and the market price to book value ratio. Long-term lenders value leverage and debt service coverage ratio. Short-term lenders prefer liquidity and, therefore, are keen to know the current ratio and the quick ratio. No single ratio or set of ratios can be appropriate for all occasions and purposes.

The ratios we calculate and analyse should be appropriate for our objectives, be it performance evaluation, credit analysis or equity investment. Ratios are just numbers that tell us nothing by themselves. The interpretations of these numbers is critical and we must compare ratios across industries and over time in order to draw legitimate conclusions.

Let us try and look at ratios differently, basing our analysis on the return on equity (ROE). It is a key parameter of performance. Given the risk profile of the company, managers try to maximize the return investors get on their equity investments. Let us see how different ratios dovetail into and capture the ROE.

Return on Equity (ROE)

The ROE is defined as the net profit divided by the shareholders' equity.

ROE = net profit/shareholders' equity.

Which can be expanded as follows:

ROE = (net profit/sales) * (sales/assets) * (assets/shareholders' equity).
Profit margin   Asset turnover   Financial Leverage

Return on equity is thus determined by the following three parameters:

1. Profit margin: It is the difference between the sales price and the cost of the products. In a sense, this is the basic reason for the existence of the company; the fact that its products create value and thus are sold at a price that is higher than the cost. Every company tries to increase the margin on sales and, usually, the higher the profit margin, the better the performance.
2. Asset turnover: Investments of the company are in the form of long-term assets and net working capital. These assets are essential for running the business. The sales that can be generated from the invested capital determine the asset turnover. Higher the sales that can be generated with the assets, the better the performance.
3. Financial leverage: A company need not rely only on the funds provided by the shareholders in the form of equity. It can leverage on its equity to raise debt and fund its investments. Higher the total assets (equity + debt) compared to equity, higher will be the ROE. (The fact that higher leverage makes equity riskier and, therefore, increases the required rate of return has already been discussed extensively in Chapter 7, 'Capital Structure and Financing'.)

Any action on the part of the management that impacts these ratios also impacts the ROE. Thus, to improve its ROE, a company can either

1. increase the profit margin,
2. squeeze greater sales from its assets or
3. borrow more to fund the assets.

Given the technology, the industry characteristics, the market structure and the competitive position of the company, there are limitations on each of the three parameters. At the same time, the management does have considerable leeway in influencing them through appropriate policies.

The relationship also reveals the link between performance and financial statements. The profit margin summarizes the company's operating performance by showing profits per Indian rupee of sales. The asset turnover is a reflection of the asset side of the balance sheet, whereas leverage shows the liability side of the balance sheet. Return on equity and its disaggregation into the three parameters, namely profit margin, asset turnover ratio and leverage, thus captures the major elements of the financial statements of the company.

In a competitive economy and market, the ROE of different industries should converge. A high ROE in one industry attracts more players resulting in greater competition and, thereby,

Asset-Light Model

There are two distinct aspects of a hotel—the real estate and the operations and management of its business aspects. Owning a hotel requires huge investments, especially if the property is located in a prime area. The ownership of the real estate adds to the fixed costs which are even otherwise quite heavy. Many hotel chains separate the two, believing that their own competence and value addition lies mainly in the management of the business of the hotel. Thus, they only manage the operations for a handsome fee, leaving property ownership to another party which could be an individual, an investment firm or a PE firm.

Marriot Ltd started selling various hotel properties it owned in the 1970s. As of 2013, it owned only 6 of the 3,400 hotels that bore its name. Similarly, Intercontinental owns only 15 properties, while managing 628 and franchising a further 3,800 with the use of its brands. A substantially lower investment enables the companies to experience high returns on investment.

reduces the ROE. On the other hand, a low ROE discourages investments and encourages current players to leave, with a positive impact on the ROE for the industry. In general, it would be fair to say that overall the ROE in different industries should be similar.

Some industries are asset-light. They require little investments to generate sales. In all likelihood, these industries experience low profit margins. We could include electronics industry in this category. Other industries may require huge investments resulting in low asset–turnover ratios. They make up with high profit margins. Software and jewellery belong to this category.

Let us discuss each of these parameters and the ratios representing them.

Profitability Ratios

Profitability ratios can be estimated with respect to sales (profit margin), assets (return on assets) or equity (ROE). It is important to have conceptual clarity on the profits that we need to consider for different ratios. For instance, assets comprise both equity and debt; profits must include returns to both equity and debt. Hence, EBIT is the appropriate profit figure to take. For the ROE, only the net profits must be taken into account.

Profit Margin

Profit margin reflects the primary reason a company exists, to create value and sell its products at a price higher than the cost. It measures the fraction of each Indian rupee of sales that contributes to profit. Profit margins are a reflection of the company's pricing strategy and its ability to control operating costs.

Gross Margin

Gross margin = gross profit/sales.

The gross margin primarily distinguishes between variable costs and fixed costs. The nature of the two costs is not only very different but is fundamental to the business of any company. The gross margin shows us how much of the sales of a company is taken away by variable costs. The balance is the contribution that covers fixed costs and generates profit.

Higher the gross margin, higher is the contribution per unit of revenue towards fixed costs and profitability. Since the fixed costs are by definition constant, there is a disproportionate rise in profit consequent to higher sales.

The gross margin can be used to work out the breakeven sales level. Each unit of sales contributes an amount equal to the sales price minus variable cost. To get the breakeven sales volume, we need to obtain the number of units that cover the total fixed costs. Hence,

(Price – variable cost) * number of units (N) = fixed costs (FC)

N = FC / (Price per unit – variable cost per unit).

Sales higher than the breakeven volume (N) result in profits for the company.

Net Margin

Net margin = net profit/sales.

The net margin takes out all costs—variable as well as fixed—from the sales revenue, and the balance that remains is the net profit. The net margin shows the net profit made per unit of sales.

Return on Assets

It is a measure of profits per Indian rupee of the assets. The assets comprise of both equity and debt. Hence interest must be added back to the net profit in the numerator, interest being payable on borrowing. Since both debt and equity are included in the denominator, returns to both equity and debt providers must form a part of the numerator.

However, only the interest after the deduction of the tax payable is taken into account. This provides the income that an all-equity-financed company would have earned. It does away with the benefits available from tax deductibility of interest on debt. This also makes it comparable to the weighted average cost of capital which is calculated on a post-tax basis. Additionally, the refinement helps in making comparisons of profitability for companies with varying capital structures. Hence,

return on assets = (net profit + after tax interest)/assets.

Return on Equity

ROE = net profit/equity.

Return on equity is a measure of the profits per Indian rupee of equity. For a leveraged company, usually the ROE is higher than the return on assets. This is based on the assumption that a company would resort to borrowing only if the cost of debt is lower than the return on assets. Borrowing would thereby boost the ROE.

Sometimes, ROE is called return on net worth, since net worth equals the book value of equity.

Return on Capital

The third measure of return is the return on capital. It equals

$$\text{(after tax interest + net profit)/total capital.}$$

You may have observed that the numerator is nothing but net operating profits after tax (NOPAT) for a company.

The return on capital would always be higher than the return on assets, since unlike assets, the total capital does not include current liabilities and will be less than the assets.

Asset Turnover Ratios

Asset turnover is the second parameter that impacts the performance of the company and its ROE. To run their business, companies need to invest in assets. Assets include buildings, plant and machinery, patents and brands as long-term assets, and inventory and accounts receivables (minus payables, of course) as short-term assets. However, it is not the assets per se that provide value to the company but the income and the cash flows those assets can generate. Higher the sales a company can generate with a certain level of assets, higher are the cash flows and thereby the value of the entity. Asset turnover is a critical element of the performance of the company.

The value of a company is determined by the expected future cash flows. Assets are useful to the extent that they produce cash flows. It is a fallacy to believe that higher the level of assets, better it is for the company. The ability of the assets to generate cash flows is far more important than mere ownership of assets.

In fact, a high asset base can be detrimental to the health of the company. Assets need to be financed and if cash flow generation is low or negative, the company can be in financial trouble.

Indian companies traditionally had what can only be termed an acquisition mentality. They kept acquiring large assets, believing their ownership to be valuable. What they overlooked was that without the ability to generate high sales and profits, value will not be created. Without high sales (implying high asset turnover), a large asset base can become a millstone around the company's neck, bringing down the performance and, ultimately, the company itself. Such has been the fate of many companies, especially in the post-liberalization phase in India. Having learnt their lessons, the Indian corporate sector is now, hopefully, more careful in acquiring assets.

Asset Turnover

$$\text{Asset turnover = sales revenue / total assets.}$$

The asset turnover ratio takes into account the entire sales revenue of the company in the numerator and total assets in the denominator.

Higher the sales revenue that can be generated from a certain level of assets, (in other words, lower the assets that are required to support a certain volume of sales), higher is the asset turnover ratio and better is the performance of the company. Asset turnover is an indication of the efficiency with which assets are utilized by a company.

Asset turnover, together with the profit margin, provide the profit per unit of asset. Thus, if a company can generate ₹2 of sales for every ₹1 of asset (asset turnover ratio being 2:1) and the profit margin is 10 per cent, then the return on asset is 20 per cent.

Apart from the total assets, we can also compute and analyse the various components of the assets to determine the performance of each component.

Inventory Turnover

Inventory turnover = cost of goods sold/inventory.

The cost of goods sold is taken in the numerator, since the goods have not been sold as yet and it would be inappropriate to include the profit element. Profits are made only upon actual sales. Alternative definitions of inventory are possible in the denominator such as the average inventory or the ending inventory.

365/inventory turnover = the number of days sales blocked in inventory.

At times, it is useful to look at the number of days' sales blocked in inventory. This facilitates comparisons across companies.

Receivables Turnover

Receivables turnover = credit sales/accounts receivable.

The denominator is the level of accounts receivables in absolute terms while the numerator represents credit sales, since only credit sales lead to accounts receivables. Taking into account the total sales, including sales on a cash basis, would show a misleading picture.

365/receivables turnover = the number of days sales locked up in receivables.

At times, it is useful to look at the number of days' sales locked up in receivables. Again, this eases comparisons across companies.

Payables Turnover

Payables turnover = credit purchases/accounts payable.

Technically, only the credit purchases should be included in the numerator, since only purchases made on credit lead to payables. As in the case of receivables,

365/the payables turnover = the number of days' payables.

Financial Leverage

Financial leverage refers to the use of debt in the capital structure. Given that the cost of debt is lower than that of equity, borrowing increases the ROE and appears to be a very attractive proposition. Its impact on the value of the company and equity is, however, a debatable proposition. This has been extensively discussed in Chapter 7.

Also termed solvency ratios, leverage ratios measure the ability of the company to meet its long-term liabilities. For instance, what is the likelihood of the company being able to pay the borrowing back to the lenders, how likely are cash flow problems in the future or whether the debt level is too high compared to the operating profits of the company? These are some of the questions which solvency ratios can help to answer.

Let us discuss some of the ratios pertaining to financial leverage.

Debt to Assets

Debt to total assets ratio = total debt/total assets.

The debt includes both the short-term as well as the long-term. The ratio gives an indication of the proportion of funds contributed by the lenders. Higher the ratio, higher the ROE is likely to be but with a higher risk.

Debt to Equity

Debt to equity ratio=total debt/shareholders' equity.

This is another way to represent the contribution of debt and shows how much the creditors have provided for every Indian rupee of equity.

Let us assume that a company with an asset base of ₹1 billion is financed ₹750 million by equity and ₹250 million with debt. The debt to asset ratio is 25/100 = 0.25 while the debt to equity ratio is 25/75 = 0.33. What this implies is that 25 per cent of funding comes from debt. In other words, debt equals 33 per cent of equity. Both provide the same information but viewed from different angles.

Equity multiplier ratio equals total assets divided by equity. In the preceding paragraph, assets are ₹1 billion and equity is ₹750 million, yielding an equity multiplier of 100/75 = 1.33. You would have observed that the equity multiplier equals 1 plus the debt–equity ratio.

Coverage Ratios

The financial leverage ratios concentrate on the balance sheet only; debt, equity and asset figures are all a part of the balance sheet. Whether the debt obligations represented earlier are worrisome and risky or not will depend on the ability of the company to meet its obligations from profitability and cash flows. Two companies with similar debt–equity ratios will differ in their ability to service the debt if their profitability from operations is different. Higher profitability will make the balance sheet ratios of debt and equity look safe, whereas low profitability will make the same ratios look extremely risky. We, therefore, need to take into consideration the income statement also, besides the balance sheet.

The income available to service the debt is the operating cash flow represented by the EBIT. The company can use EBIT to meet its obligations of interest and debt repayments.

Interest Coverage

Interest coverage ratio = EBIT/interest expense.

The interest coverage ratio shows the number of times the obligation to pay interest is covered by the income earned. It is obvious that the higher the ratio, the safer is the company.

Having said that, there is no ideal interest coverage ratio. Two factors determine how safe the coverage is. First is the operating business of the company in terms of its volatility. A stable business will be safer even with a low interest coverage as the probability of a significant drop in EBIT is low. A technology company, being inherently volatile and risky, needs to have a higher coverage than say a food processing company. Hence we need to look at the combined impact of the business and operating conditions, on the one hand, and financial leverage, on the other.

Second factor that determines how safe the interest coverage is, is the company's ability to access cash when required.

- Does the company have unused debt limits or investment in liquid securities?
- Does it have assets that can be sold off in case of trouble?
- In general, does the company have the capacity to raise resources when in need?

Times Burden Covered

EBIT/(interest + principal repayment/1 – tax rate).

The interest coverage ratio takes into consideration only the interest liability of the company. In addition, the principal amount also needs to be paid back. What is critical is the number of times the company's overall financial obligations (comprising interest and principal repayment) are covered by the earnings.

There is a subtle distinction between interest and principal repayments as obligations of the company. The interest is an expense and reduces the tax liability of the company. That does not apply to the principal repayment which is a return of the loan amount.

Therefore, earnings required to pay back the principal amount must be calculated on a pre-tax basis. Part of these earnings are utilized to pay taxes and only the balance is available for the principal repayment. What is required is to find out how much earnings are adequate to pay back a certain amount of principal. Let us understand with an example.

If the company has an obligation to pay an interest of ₹100, an EBIT of ₹100 will be adequate to service this interest rate.

EBIT	100
Interest	100
Profit before tax (PBT)	0
Tax (40%)	0
Profit after tax (PAT)	0

However, if the principal repayment is ₹100, an EBIT of ₹100 will not suffice.

EBIT	100
Tax (40%)	40
PAT	60

To have sufficient cash flows to repay the principal, the amount required will be

$$\text{principal repayment}/(1 - \text{tax rate}) = 100/1 - 40\%$$
$$= 166.67.$$

At 40 per cent, the tax on the EBIT of ₹166.67 will be ₹66.67, and ₹100 will remain to repay the principal.

Liquidity Ratios

The ratios discussed until now have mainly been long-term ratios and have included parameters that are long-term in nature. Recall the remarks of John Maynard Keynes that 'in the long run, we are all dead'. A corporate entity is a permanent entity unless it becomes bankrupt and is liquidated or is acquired by another company. To ensure that it does not become sick, the company must be able to meet its obligations in the short run. Long-term sustainability is of no use if short-term cash flow constraints are likely to bankrupt the company.

Liquidity ratios are short-term solvency ratios, useful to assess the ability of the company to pay its dues over the next 12 months. In normal times, the book values and the market values of short-term assets are not very different. However, under conditions of stress, it becomes difficult to dispose of inventories or collect receivables. We must interpret these ratios carefully, going deeper into the composition of the current assets.

Current Ratio

Current ratio = current assets/current liabilities.

Current assets are defined as assets that are likely to be converted into cash within the next 12 months. Current liabilities are defined as liabilities that are due for payment over the next 12 months. Higher the ratio, better is the ability of the company to meet its obligations. However, a high ratio not only involves a higher investment in working capital, it could also be an indicator of inefficiency. As always, industry comparison can nudge us in the right direction.

Business Transactions and Current Ratio

It is interesting to consider the impact on the current ratio of various transactions that may be undertaken by a company. For an example, let us see the impact on the current ratio

Contd

contd

from the following:

1. Purchase of inventory: The stock of inventory, of course, goes up. The inventory can be purchased either with cash or on credit. In the first case, the value of cash comes down and there is no resultant change in current assets or in the current ratio.

    If the inventory is purchased on credit, there is an equivalent increase in accounts payable and current liability. The net impact on the current ratio depends on whether the initial current ratio was less than one or higher.
2. Sale of merchandise: The stock of finished goods goes down, whereas cash or receivables increase. The finished goods inventory is reflected in the books as cost, whereas sales will usually be at a higher price, being inclusive of profits. The net impact is an increase in assets and thereby in the current ratio.

Acid-Test Ratio

Acid-test ratio = (current assets inventory)/current liability.

At times, the inventory with the company may not be as liquid as some of the other current assets. Analysts estimate a more conservative ratio that excludes the value of the inventory from the current assets in the numerator.

There are countless instances of companies that claim to have a robust business model and that are fundamentally sound in the long run, but have collapsed due to a shortage of liquidity and consequent inability to meet their obligations. A company may have a large asset base, which may be much higher than its liabilities, but unless the assets can be converted into cash when the liabilities become due, they are of little use. Usually, lenders and creditors will not accept the inventory of cotton, car radiators or cement in exchange for their dues. They want to be paid in cash. The moot point is how easily can the stock of inventory held by the company be converted into cash when required.

In the course of regular business operations of a company, the inventory held is converted into finished goods, sold subsequently and, finally, money is realized from the sale. In this sense, the inventory is liquid and can be used to pay off dues. However, in times of trouble, when the business cycle gets disrupted, the liquidity of inventory in terms of its conversion to cash is severely tested. Hence, while we may fine tune the calculation of liquidity ratios, the understanding of the company's business is of paramount importance in determining whether the company has sufficient liquidity and is otherwise in sound health.

Market-Price-Based Ratios

Price Earnings Ratio

Equity investors are primarily interested in the valuation of equity. They assign a P/E multiple to companies, popularly called P/E ratio, and multiply it by the earnings per share (EPS) to estimate its value. If the value is less than the stock price in the market, it is time to sell. If the value is greater than the stock price, they go ahead and buy the company's shares.

The critical element in this analysis is the estimation of the P/E ratio. The P/E ratio reflects the expectations of the future performance of the company along with the quality of that performance. Would the sales and profits grow at a fast pace or will the growth rate decline? How confident are we about the estimation or is the performance subject to high volatility? Does the quality of management give us the comfort that earnings growth is likely to be sustained? Does the market structure and the competitive position of the company provide it the latitude to implement its own policies? Or is it likely to follow the market trends? Does the company conform to the highest standards of corporate governance?

Multiplied by the EPS, the P/E ratio determines the price of the company's share. Given the EPS of the company (easily derived from the accounting statements), there is a relationship between the market price and P/E ratio. If we know one, we can easily derive the other. (Refer to Chapter 6 on valuation.)

Market Price to Book Value

The book value is the value of a share as per the accounting books. It equals the net worth of the company divided by the number of shares. The market price, on the other hand, is determined on the basis of the expected future cash flows which are discounted to the present value by the risk-adjusted cost of capital. The market price is forward-looking in nature as compared to the book value which is based on past performance.

Market price to book value ratio is used extensively to analyse banks. Better performing banks have a higher market price to book value ratio compared to poorly performing banks. In India, for example, public sector banks have a much lower market price to book value compared to private sector banks, indicating poor prospects for them. HDFC Bank has always been considered superior to other banks including other private sector banks. As on 3 November 2017, its price to book value was 5.17 compared to 2.29 for Axis Bank and 2.00 for ICICI Bank.

Comparative Analysis

Ratio analysis is a very popular tool of analysis; at the same time, it is also prone to misuse. A better perspective would help in ensuring that we use it for the right purpose and in the right manner.

A ratio is just a mathematical relationship that conveys no information by itself. Any two figures can be taken and their ratio calculated. For instance, one may calculate the ratio of the number of lady employees and the annual export of steel by a company. An extreme example, perhaps, everyone would agree that such a ratio is meaningless. There are other less obvious but equally meaningless ratios that are often employed. The quest to use more ratios rather than meaningful ratios is a tendency that must be resisted. Quality rather than the number of ratios is important.

A ratio by itself conveys no information. It would be meaningful only on a comparative basis. There are three ways to make comparisons and draw meaningful conclusions.

1. External comparison: Companies in the same industry are likely to have similar structures and face a similar environment. They can, therefore, be expected to have ratios that are similar. For example, infrastructure companies usually have very high leverage. Similarly, retail chains have low profit margins but high turnover ratios. A comparison of ratios with its peers can help us draw conclusions about a company's performance.

   Inventory ratios of companies in the car industry can be expected to be comparable. If a company has inventory ratios that are different from its peers, it may be a cause for further investigation. Is it manufacturing too many components in-house; are the suppliers dumping too much inventory instead of supplying as per the planned production schedule; is the production out of sync with expected sales; is the company producing too many models, each with low level of sales, necessitating high inventory levels? A deeper analysis will show why the inventory levels are high compared to the competitors. It is possible that the high level of inventories is a consequence of a different sales strategy adopted by the company in terms of keeping more models and pushing sales. The true picture will emerge with further examination, but it is the ratio calculation and its comparison with competitors that will reveal what aspect of the company's operations needs more detailed analysis.

   We can calculate the level of debtors in terms of the number of days' sales and compare it with competitors in the industry. While a low level may imply a lower investment in debtors, we also need to explore whether the company is offering less credit to dealers, resulting in a reduced interest in our product.

   While easy to understand, in practice such comparisons are not very straightforward. No two companies are alike. While Maruti Udyog Ltd and Honda India are large car manufacturers, they are very different companies in terms of sales volume, technology, targeted customer segment and in many other aspects. A comparison between the two may throw up conclusions that may be misleading. At other times, a company may be diversified and operate in multiple products and industrial segments. Consequently, the comparison of a single product with other companies may not be valid. However, despite these limitations, inter-company comparisons do highlight issues that demand corrective action on the part of the management.

2. Intertemporal comparison is the second way to interpret ratios. Over time, ratios change and the comparison of how these ratios have moved over time provides meaningful conclusions.

   If the gross margins have reduced over the last few years, the management needs to explore why this has happened. Have the raw material prices gone up and the company has been unable to pass on these rising costs to the customers?

   Maybe the accounts receivables turnover ratio has gone up and the company has been carrying a higher number of days' sales in the receivables. Does this mean that the higher revenues that the company has experienced have been a result of pushing sales by giving higher credit to customers? Is this a strategy that is viable in the long run? The company may be in deep trouble due to delayed payments leading to a liquidity crunch. A ratio analysis over time becomes the basis for the evaluation of performance and future health.

3. The third way to compare ratios is by way of what is called common size analysis. Instead of looking at absolute figures, common size analysis standardizes all figures in the profit and loss statement and the balance sheet. The sales figures are taken as 100 and all other figures modified to reflect their value as a percentage of sales. Similarly, the balance sheet figures are changed, with the total liabilities (or total assets, both being equal) taken as 100 and all balance sheet items reflected as a percentage.

Each item, as a percentage of the total sales/assets and changes therein, can reveal meaningful information. Proportionate figures are analytically superior to absolute ones.

Ratio Analysis Application

Ratio analysis has varied applications. Let us look at the most common ones.

1. The most widespread and obvious application is the analysis of corporate performance. Analysis of performance begins with the calculation of appropriate ratios and the implications thereof. The outcome of such an analysis should lead us to
   a. disaggregation of performance into different areas such as margins, liquidity, solvency, risk and so forth;
   b. identifying areas of superior performance and factors that are leading to the improved performance;
   c. identifying areas which are lagging and, therefore, need close attention by the management to figure out what can be done for improvement.

   Ratios, by themselves, do not reveal a complete picture, but they are integral to such an examination. They make the task easier by providing the required intelligence and pointing out the direction that the analysis must proceed. They form the basis of deciding how the company has performed vis-à-vis its objectives, in comparison with the competitors, over time.
2. Creditors are amongst the most extensive users of ratio analysis. A creditor will provide funds to a company only if he believes the company is in sound financial health and will be in a position to return the borrowed funds back, along with the applicable interest. The starting point for judging the financial health of a company is calculating a few basic ratios which will give an overall picture of the viability and solvency of the company. Further analysis will determine the credit worthiness of the company and help judge whether it is advisable to lend funds or not.

   Long-term lenders take into account the long-term viability of the company. Hence they are more concerned with debt–equity ratio and coverage ratios. Short-term lenders, on the other hand, are anxious about the liquidity position in the immediate future. They look at liquidity ratios such as the current ratio and the short-term cash flow position of the company.
3. Ratios are also used to forecast the possibility of corporate bankruptcy. Applying various relevant ratios, analysts forecast how probable it is that the company may become distressed. Edward Altman has devised a bankruptcy model in which he calculates the Z-score of a company, based on specific ratios, which is then used to forecast the probability of a company becoming bankrupt during a specified period.

4. Contrastingly, ratios can also be used to evaluate corporate excellence. Ratios are applied to shortlist companies after which a further analysis determines whether excellence is a trait attributable to the selected companies.
5. Ratios are also used extensively by credit-rating agencies. Credit rating is an assessment of the risks associated with a financial instrument or a financial entity. It assesses the ability of a company to fulfil its commitments towards any borrowing it undertakes. Higher the credit rating, lower is the risk and, therefore, lower is the cost of funding.

In India, CRISIL, IICRA and CARE are the top credit-rating companies while S&P, Moody's and Fitch dominate globally.

While credit rating involves a detailed analysis of the business, its profitability, cash flows, environment and competitive position of the company and an assessment of the management, ratio analysis serves as a starting point. It gives a direction in which the rater should look at while undertaking the rating exercise. It may indicate areas that may be a cause of concern.

Ratio analysis spans a broad canvas; it can be applied for various purposes. An analysis of any nature typically begins with a detailed scrutiny of the ratios of the company's accounting figures. Ratio analysis can thus be employed to answer the following questions:

1. How much has the company borrowed vis-à-vis its equity? Is the borrowing excessive? What is the probability that the excessive borrowing may lead to financial distress?
2. How high is the profitability of the company? Is it mainly due to high margins or low fixed costs?
3. Does the company have sufficient cash to take care of its immediate needs? How likely is the company to experience a liquidity crunch?
4. Is the company using its assets effectively? Can these be employed more productively?
5. Is the company's valuation reasonable? What areas should the company concentrate on to improve valuation?
6. Is the company generating sufficient cash flows to be able to meet its commitments? Does it have a sufficient cushion in case of a downturn in the economy?

Limitations

Ratios must be applied with caution. Being easy to calculate, there is a very high probability of misuse. We have earlier in the chapter pointed out some of the ways in which misuse takes place, knowingly or unknowingly.

1. Ratios, based as they are on accounting statements, suffer from bias and manipulation in the accounting figures. If the figures from which the ratios are derived are doubtful, the use of ratios will also produce doubtful conclusions. Garbage in, garbage out, as the adage goes. Management and accountants have significant discretion in the treatment of intangibles, inventory valuation and depreciation. A considerable variation exists in the accounting rules and practices in different countries.

When Daimler Benz, the manufacturer of Mercedes Benz, decided to raise equity from the New York Stock Exchange in 1993, its modest profits as per the German accounting standards changed to a loss of US$592 million under the US accounting practices. Financial ratios derived from such accounting figures are likely to provide misleading information and may not be suitable for analytical purpose.

2. Lack of underlying theory: In general, there is no coherent theory underpinning ratio analysis which dilutes its usefulness as a tool of analysis. Without an underlying conceptual basis, ratio analysis can degenerate into whims and fancies of the analyst.

   Capital structure, capital budgeting and others are based on a theoretical construct and lend themselves to analysis which is grounded in well-laid-out concepts. Ratio analysis has no such theoretical foundation and is based upon thumb rules and personal biases. Thumb rules and apparent freedom to use any ratio one may wish to, leave significant discretion in the hands of the analyst and make it prone to misuse.

   It is often said that an MBA student who has learnt financial ratio analysis is like a baby with a hammer. To a baby with a hammer, everything looks like a nail, and he keeps hammering at everything he fancies. An MBA will use ratios for any kind of analysis without considering its appropriateness. The greatest danger with financial ratio analysis is the possibility of its overuse and the lack of appreciation of its limitations. While it usually is the starting point for most analysis, ratios can also lead to misleading, and at times false, conclusions. Care needs to be taken before these are applied in practice.

3. As already pointed out, a comparative analysis (comparison with other companies) makes ratio analysis more meaningful. However, no two companies are alike. The differences between two (or more) companies must be recognized and incorporated in our analysis. The problem gets magnified in case of multiproduct and diversified companies where significant data remains hidden and often misrepresented.

   Ratios are like taking a blood pressure reading of a patient which tells us whether something is wrong. However, we need further investigation to find out the cause of the ailment. The blood pressure reading nudges us in the right direction for our diagnosis. Without such a reading, we would not know whether there is something amiss and what our approach towards the diagnosis of the disease should be. Similarly, ratio analysis points out aspects that need further investigation and also areas where there is no cause for concern. Ratios, however, neither tell us what is wrong nor what action may be required by the company's management. That will be known only after further investigation in appropriate areas indicated by ratio analysis. As already pointed out, the greatest danger with ratio analysis remains the possibility of its overuse and the lack of appreciation of its limitations.

KEY CONCEPTS

1. Ratio analysis is a useful tool of analysis for various purposes.
2. It can be used by analysts, long-term and short-term lenders, the management, fund managers, investors and anyone interested in the performance of the company.
3. It can nudge the analyst in the right direction for his analysis. It points out areas which can be a cause for concern and those that are performing well.

4. Since it is easy to use, care must be taken to ensure that it is employed in the right manner.

5. Innumerable ratios can be employed by analysts. Care must be taken to use ratios that are meaningful.

6. Ratio analysis becomes meaningful only on a comparative basis. Comparison can be either across peers or over time.

7. Analysts must be aware of the limitations of ratio analysis and must be cautious in its use.

CHAPTER QUESTIONS

1. Why are ratios so commonly used? What precautions are called for in their use?

2. Provide three ratios that each of the following stakeholders use for their analysis. Justify the use of each of those ratios.
   a. Management
   b. Creditors
   c. Lenders
   d. Equity investors

3. Financial statements are like a fine perfume—to be sniffed but not swallowed.
   Critically evaluate the statement.

4. Given that there are varying characteristics of companies with respect to assets, margins, profitability and so forth, why are returns on investment of different companies expected to converge?

CASE FOR DISCUSSION

Calculate and evaluate the various ratios discussed in the chapter.

Balance sheet as on....

	31 Mar. 2016	31 Mar. 2017
Liabilities		
Paid up equity	300	300
Reserves and surplus	200	265
Net worth	500	565
Debt	200	215
Total liabilities	700	780
Assets		
Gross Plant and Machinery	600	680
Accumulated Depreciation	150	210
Net Plant and Machinery	450	470

Inventory	125	150
Receivables	200	250
Less payables	100	120
Cash	25	30
Current assets	250	310
Total assets	700	780

Source: Author.

Profit and loss statement

	2016–17 (₹)
Sales	1,000
Cost of goods sold	700
Gross margin	300
General expenses	100
Operating margins	200
Interest	50
Profit before tax	150
Tax	45
PAT	105
Dividends	40

Source: Author.

Appendix

Efficient Market Hypothesis

Efficient markets hypothesis (EMH) is the foundation of the entire edifice of corporate finance theory. The conceptual framework of corporate finance is premised on the existence of a vibrant, efficient financial market. EMH has two attributes.

1. Prices fully reflect all available information that is relevant to the valuation of securities.
2. Future price movements are random.

Investors in the financial markets trade securities on the basis of their assessment of the worth of those securities. They continuously evaluate securities and compare their value with the price in the market. Value is estimated on the basis of information about the security with respect to the economy, the industry, the company and various other parameters. An efficient market is one where the price of a security is derived on the basis of all the information that is relevant and publicly available.

Since the current price incorporates all the information that is known and available, a change in price can take place only with new information becoming available. By definition, new information is random in nature. Hence, the future price movement is also random.

The implications of the EMH are fairly simple but significant. Since future prices are random in nature, they cannot be predicted. By definition, securities are efficiently priced and are unlikely to give extra-normal returns. The fierce competition amongst the large number of extremely savvy and knowledgeable investors ensures that it is difficult to beat the market on a consistent basis, especially after risk is accounted for.

The EMH does not imply that the returns from all investments are equal but that the returns are determined by the risk of the security. Higher the risk, higher is the return and vice versa. An investor can get a higher return if he so desires. However, for that he would need to assume a higher risk of investment. Similarly, the investor may have an appetite for safe investments and less risk which in turn would be associated with lower returns.

Thus there is no free lunch in the financial markets. This is aptly illustrated by the apocryphal story of a finance professor and his student walking down the street when they come across a ₹2,000 note lying on the sidewalk. When the student bends down to pick it up, the professor admonishes him saying the note is an illusion and that if it was real someone would have already picked it up!

Indexing

Given efficient pricing and the random nature of stock price movements, the active management of funds to beat the market is likely to be unsuccessful. There is sufficient evidence that most fund managers fail to earn extra-normal returns, especially after accounting for the higher cost of active fund management.

Consequently, investors have wondered at the futility of managing funds on an active basis. They increasingly invest in the market portfolio, in what is termed as the passive style of investing. Since investing in all securities comprising the market is extremely tedious and costly, a suitable index is selected as a proxy for the market. Funds are invested in the securities comprising the index, in the same proportion, as they form a part of the index.

For instance, if ITC Ltd has a weightage of 7.5 per cent on the National Stock Exchange (NSE) NIFTY index, a fund managing ₹10 billion will have invested ₹750 million in ITC Ltd. Investment in other companies will also be similarly determined by their weightage in the index. Constituting the fund is likely to be less costly and the transaction costs are minimal. The returns from passive investing should equal the returns from the market, more specifically the returns on the index that has been selected for investment.

Indexation as a strategy of investment is extremely popular, with substantial funds being invested on a passive basis, both in India and globally. Depending on their objectives, different funds opt for different indices to anchor their portfolio.

The EMH is premised on the assumption of rational behaviour on the part of the investors. It is assumed that investors are able to overcome the 'noise' in the market to optimize decision-making.

Practical experience suggests otherwise. Investors, even professional ones, are known to use shortcuts and rules of thumb in their decision-making. Gathering relevant information and then analysing it in a rational manner is not only tedious and time-consuming but also beyond the capability of all but a handful of investors. The future is uncertain, and the theory of choice under uncertainty is not a precise science. Faced with a complex problem, the investors display a lack of rationality, if not outright irrationality, in making their choices.

The observation of decision-making by people, when faced with choices, has led to the emergence of a field of study widely known as behavioural finance. Behavioural finance is the application of psychology to financial behaviour. Instead of assuming rationality, as the traditional finance theory does, behavioural finance makes systematic efforts towards studying how people take decisions in practice. Human decisions are based on a wide array of errors that stem from perceptual illusions, overconfidence, emotions and rules of thumb. Investors behave in a manner that is different from, even contrary to, the assumptions of the rationality model, often leading to errors creeping in the investors' analysis.

People are usually overconfident of their own ability. For instance, most people believe themselves to be better than average drivers which is statistically not possible. People also have similar faith in their own investment acumen. When such belief is built into their actions, there is room for trouble. Investors are subject to biases which impact their decision-making. Behavioural finance believes that investor psychology has an impact on stock prices which cannot be explained by the pure rationality school of thought.

Given the number of securities and the huge volume of trading, there are frequent deviations from efficient pricing. For example, small firms with low price earnings (P/E) ratio or low price to book values often provide higher return than large firms. There also exists what is termed the calendar effect. Returns in January are found to be higher than in other months (the January effect). Returns on a Monday are usually lower than the previous Friday (the weekend effect).

Some of these anomalies can be explained by the higher risk of investing in firms with the given features. If the higher risk embedded in such firms is taken into account, the extra-normal return disappears or is no longer significant. Calendar effect is also transient and has been found to provide no basis for consistent profits.

The more critical issue is whether behavioural finance and its findings render the rationality-based model of finance invalid. Do theories and concepts that currently form the basis of finance need significant revision?

As they say, it takes a new theory to discard an old one. While behavioural finance does specify lacunae in the rational school and points to the fact that its assumption of rational investor behaviour may not be factually correct, it is unable to provide an alternative theory of the determination of security prices. In defence of the rationality school, it can be pointed out that the EMH does not preclude the existence of anomalies which lead to superior returns. It does not even require all securities to be fairly priced all the time. Securities may be undervalued or overvalued on a random basis and subsequently return over time to an efficient price. As long as the deviations from fair value are random in nature, no strategy based on such anomalies can produce consistently superior returns. Given the number of investors and analysts tracking the market, by normal laws of probability, some of them will beat the market while some will underperform consistently. That, in no way, negates the EMH.

All the same, behavioural finance serves a useful purpose in pointing out the limitations of the EMH and focuses attention on the decision-making process, especially under uncertainty. Behavioural finance has enriched our knowledge of how people in the real world make choices and arrive at decisions. We need not choose between the two models; together they enrich our knowledge about corporate finance and financial decision-making.

Fintech

Fintech (short for financial technology) refers to the use and application of information technology and telecommunication to offer and enable banking and financial services. It describes a business that relies on software and modern technology to provide financial services.

The use of technology has made the delivery of financial services efficient and more inclusive. People at the margins who had no hope of ever being a part of the formal financial services are now integral to the industry and the financial system. While start-ups and technology companies have been pioneers in the development of fintech, even established companies have

SingX

SingX is a Singapore-based fintech company which has launched a funds remittance platform. The high cost of funds remittance for small and medium enterprises (SME) and individuals has provided SingX with an attractive opportunity. It has the potential to disrupt the funds remittance business and reduce the cost of funds transfer between different countries and currencies.

adopted it in a big way. In fact, it is difficult to imagine financial services now without thinking of technology. The lines between the two are getting blurred, and it is difficult to figure out where one ends and the other begins.

Following four sets of players constitute the fintech industry:

1. Large, well-established financial institutions, often called incumbents.
2. High-tech companies which are active in financial services but whose main business lies elsewhere, primarily in technology (Apple, Google and Facebook).
3. Companies which provide infrastructure or technology that facilitate financial services (Master Card, NSE).
4. Fast-moving start-ups, focusing usually on a particular innovative technology or process, such as Paytm (mobile payments), Betterment (automated investing), Prosper (peer-to-peer lending), Moven (retail banking) and Lemonade/Policybazaar (insurance).

The sector is in a state of flux and no one knows what the future may unfold. Established financial institutions are focusing more and more on technology, technology companies are offering financial services and disruptive start-ups are providing services which, until recently, were available only from banks. Money transfer, lending, payments, investment advisory and wealth management are some of the services where fintech now has a significant impact. Thus, fintech fits into all three business verticals, namely lending, wealth and asset management, and payments.

The use of algorithms for trading and investment advice is on the upswing. While in the West, more than 40 per cent of trading is computer-based, without any human intervention; even in India, algorithm-based trading is significant and increasing in importance. Machines are becoming more and more intelligent and artificial intelligence is enabling computers to adapt to changing market situations. As this trend continues and gathers pace, there is hope (and apprehension!) that all investment decisions would eventually be computer-based. The experts with their algorithms would apparently figure out what drives market outcomes and reduce it to a seamless system.

When all investment decisions are taken by intelligent machines, without being prone to human fallibility, markets will become perfect and all securities will be priced efficiently. Efficient markets which have existed only as a theoretical construct will become a reality. Termed financial singularity, this is analogous to technological singularity which refers to

Robo Advisors

One area where fintech is beginning to have a significant impact is automated investment services or robo advisors. Robo advisors offer investment advice online without human intervention; they automate the process of asset allocation and wealth management. Automation is premised on the belief that the functions of a human wealth advisor can be replicated by an advanced intuitive software.

There exists huge potential for automated wealth advisory services for fintech companies to exploit. Millennials in particular are attractive potential customers for robo advisors, being online savvy but not yet possessing the huge wealth to be able to afford the services of a personal wealth advisor.

BlackRock, the largest asset manager in the world, with US$6 trillion assets, has introduced a set of exchange traded funds in which securities will be chosen by a computer rather than by tracking an index.

the creation of super-intelligence wherein computers control human life with humans having virtually no say in it.

Real Options

Real option applies option valuation techniques to capital-budgeting decisions. An option contract gives the holder the right to buy (sell) an underlying at a specified time in the future. However, there is no obligation to do so.

Options thus provide the holder a choice, enabling him to benefit from the uncertainty in the values of an underlying. If the underlying variable moves in favour of the investor, he exercise the options contract and gains a positive pay-off. However, if the pay-off is negative, the investor can choose not to exercise the option and lets it lapse.

There are many financial securities with option features embedded in them. Housing loans usually incorporate the right of prepayment of the loan by the borrower. Similarly, a car lease provides the lessee the right to buy the car at a specified price at the end of the lease. Many bonds have callable features with the company having the right to buy the bonds back prematurely. All these are examples of financial options.

Options that do not involve financial securities but are based on real products are called real options. The most important real options involve capital-budgeting decisions. Investments in projects involve cash flows over a long period of time. The cash flows are not assured but uncertain. In an uncertain environment, the ability to delay a decision until some of that uncertainty has been resolved offers value. Managers take decisions based on information and data available at a given point in time. If new information emerges, they may change their earlier decision. The management needs to be proactive in responding to the changes in the environment.

The net present value (NPV) method assumes decision-making based on the estimated cash flows. It does not take into account any change in data that may occur in the future. We are aware, however, that with time, additional information may emerge about the project. Real option analysis is a way to make use of uncertainty for better decision-making.

Changes in investment include the decision to expand, abandon, defer or reduce the scope of a project. A company may be planning an investment in a cement project, based on the highway construction planned by the government. It could defer its decision until the government decides whether to go ahead with the highway project or not.

Real options, as mentioned earlier, apply option valuation techniques to capital-budgeting decisions. Usually, real options as well as the underlying variable are not traded as a financial security. Since there is no history of trading, past prices are not available and volatility cannot be calculated, as is the case with financial options. Real options are not available from the markets and need to be created or discovered. At times, the holder of the option can influence the value of the underlying.

Performance Metrics

The objectives that a company seeks to achieve must reflect the demands of the changing times. While value maximization continues to be the single most important objective a company seeks to pursue, the changing complexity of the society we live in compels companies to consider alternate metrics of performance too. We will discuss a few of them in short.

Economic Value Added

Economic value added (EVA) has over the years gained considerable popularity, with many organizations extensively using it for evaluating overall performance, as well as the performance of various divisions and employees. In its simplest form, EVA equals the net operating profit after taxes, minus a charge for the capital employed to produce those profits. The capital charge is the required rate of return necessary to compensate all the firm's investors, the debt holders as well as the shareholders for the risk of the investment. A consistently high EVA generation over a period of time is the best indicator of the good health of an organization. A consistently negative EVA, on the other hand, indicates value dilution by the organization and is reflective of its poor health.

The evaluation of the performance of a company is usually based on its profit and loss statement. A positive profit is what people seek, since profits are derived after deducting expenses. However, while all other expenses, including the interest on debt, are deducted from the sales revenues to arrive at a net profit, the cost of equity capital is ignored. Is it advisable to evaluate performance based on a metric that ignores a major component of cost?

The capital of a company comprises both equity and debt. While the return to debt providers is deducted from the earnings before interest and tax (EBIT) by way of coupon interest, to arrive at the net profit, the return to equity shares is implicit and is not accounted for in the profitability statement. The question that needs to be asked is whether net profit is the real return the company has earned if the cost of equity is not taken into account.

TABLE A.1 Understanding EVA (in ₹)

Assets and liabilities		*Profit and loss*	
Assets			
Current assets	450	Sales	1,200
Current liabilities	200	Cost of goods sold	770
– Net working capital	**250**	Expenses	280
Capital investment	500	Net operating profit	150
Total assets	**750**	Interest	30
liabilities		Profit before tax (PBT)	120
Debt (10%)	300	Taxes	36
Equity	450	Net profit	84
		Net operating profits after tax (NOPAT)	**105 (14%)**

Source: Author.

To obtain the real value addition by a company, the cost of equity, based on its risk profile, must be deducted from the profits. Equity has cost, like any other funding mechanism, and that must be taken into consideration. Positive profit is not enough; the company needs to generate a value that is positive after the risk-adjusted cost of equity has been provided for. Only then can it be said that the company has added value through its operations. If we get a negative profit after taking into account the cost of equity, the company has reduced value. Positive profit by itself has no meaning. Let us understand EVA in Table A.1 as an example.

Net return on investment equals

$$105/750 = 14\%.$$

If the cost of capital of the company is 12 per cent, the returns are higher than the cost of capital and the company is adding value. If, on the other hand, the cost of capital is 17 per cent, the returns are less than the cost of capital.

At 12 per cent cost of capital, the company must return

$$750 * 12\% = 90.$$

The excess of the absolute Indian rupee returns over the Indian rupee cost of capital is termed EVA. In the current example, EVA is

$$105 - 90 = ₹15.$$

This is the value that the company has added during the given period.

If, however, the cost of capital is 17 per cent, the EVA is

$$105 - (750 * 17\%) = 105 - 127.50 = ₹-22.50.$$

And there has been a reduction in the value of the company during the year. Thus,

$$EVA = net\ income - (investment * cost\ of\ capital).$$

The term EVA has been popularized by the firm Stern Stewart & Co. Other companies have their own method of calculating the value added. Terming it as economic profit, McKinsey & Company calculates it as follows:

$$EP = (ROI - r) * investment.$$

$$(14\% - 12\%) * 750 = 15,$$

or $$(14\% - 17\%) * 750 = -22.50.$$

The EVA is based not only on the profits made by a company but on the value added after the cost of capital invested is taken into account. Hence, the amount of invested capital is a crucial determinant of performance. Managers, therefore, become stingy in their use of capital. They employ only those assets that return at least the cost of capital. They try and squeeze the most value from the assets that have been employed in the business. The return on assets becomes more critical than the mere acquisition of assets. The benefits of the efficiency of assets eventually accrue to the company.

Total Societal Impact

A company is a vibrant entity whose existence is relevant as a part of the overall society and the environment in which it operates. It cannot be satisfied with achieving a single objective but must pursue multiple aims in accordance with the requirements of the society. Companies must be cognizant of the overall impact they are having on the society, technically termed total societal impact (TSI). It captures the economic, social and environmental impact (both positive and negative) of a company's products, services, operations and core capabilities. A negative TSI is likely to dilute the company's value while a positive TSI can give it a sustainable competitive advantage.

Balanced Scorecard

Another metric that has gained popularity over the years is the balanced scorecard. The balanced scorecard believes that success in the modern competitive business environment is predicated on a combination of parameters that together determine success. Focus on a single financial metric makes the company's performance imbalanced and is likely to lead to failure. While financial returns are undoubtedly important, it is even more critical for companies to invest in long-term value creation, particularly in intangibles and intellectual assets that generate future growth.

To achieve this, the balanced scorecard seeks to evaluate the company along four different objectives and measures. These include financial, customer, internal business processes, and learning and growth. The balanced scorecard is a measure of the different objectives that companies must pursue to guarantee long-term success. The objectives are looked at from the perspective of different stakeholders including shareholders, customers, suppliers and employees.

Bibliography

Acharya, V. V. and M. W. Richardson, eds. *Restoring Financial Stability*. Hoboken, NJ: John Wiley and Sons, 2009.

Allen, F. and R. Michaely. 'Payout Policy'. In *Handbook of the Economics of Finance: Corporate Finance*, edited by G. Constantinides, M. Harris and R. Stulz, 337–429. Amsterdam: North-Holland, 2003.

Altman, E. I. *Corporate Financial Distress and Bankruptcy*, 3rd edn. New York: John Wiley, 2005.

———. 'A Further Empirical Investigation of the Bankruptcy Cost Question'. *Journal of Finance* 39, no. 4 (September 1984): 1067–89.

Altman, Edward. *Corporate Financial Distress: A Complete Guide to Predicting, Avoiding, and Dealing with Bankruptcy*, 2nd edn. New York: John Wiley and Sons, 1993.

Amram, M., F. Li and C. A. Perkins. 'How Kimberly-Clark Uses Real Options'. *Journal of Applied Corporate Finance* 18 (Spring 2006): 40–7.

Apte, Prakash G. *International Finance*, 2nd edn. New Delhi: Tata McGraw Hill, 2008.

Asquith, P. and D. Mullins, Jr. 'The Impact of Initiating Dividend Payments on Shareholder Wealth'. *Journal of Business* 56, no. 1 (January 1983): 77–96.

Becht, M., P. Bolton and A. Röell. 'Corporate Governance and Control'. In *Handbook of the Economics of Finance*, edited by G. Constantinides, M. Harris and R. Stulz, 1–109. Amsterdam: North-Holland, 2003.

Berk, Jonathan, Peter DeMarzo and Jarrad Harford. *Fundamentals of Corporate Finance*, 2nd edn. Prentice Hall, 2011.

———. *Fundamentals of Corporate Finance*, 2nd edn. Boston, MA: Prentice Hall, 2012.

Bernstein, Peter. 'What Happens if We're Wrong?' *New York Times*. 22 June 2008.

Bhattacharya, S. 'Imperfect Information, Dividend Policy, and "the Bird in the Hand" Fallacy'. *Bell Journal of Economics* 10 (1979): 259–70.

Bodie, Zvie and Robert C. Merton. *In Finance*. New Jersey: Prentice Hall, 2000.

Brealey, Richard A., Myers C. Stewart and Allen Franklin. *Principles of Corporate Finance*, 10th edn. New York: McGraw Hill-Irwin, 2011.

Business Week. 'Frederick W. Smith: No Overnight Success'. 20 September 2004.

CBS News. 'Microsoft to Pay Dividends (Finally)'. 17 January 2003. Available at https://www.cbsnews.com/news/microsoft-to-pay-dividends-finally/. Accessed 20 October 2019.

CFO. 'Working Capital Survey'. 2007.

Cornell, B. *The Equity Risk Premium: The Long-Run Future of the Stock Market*. New York: Wiley, 1999.

Davies, Ryan and David Merin. 'Uncovering Cash and Insights from Working Capital'. *CFO*. 24 July 2014. Available at https://www.cfo.com/cash-flow/2014/07/uncovering-cash-insights-working-capital/. Accessed 30 September 2019.

DeAngelo, H., L. DeAngelo and D. Skinner. 'Corporate Payout Policy'. *Foundations and Trends in Finance* 3 (2008): 95–287.

DeAngelo, Harry and Linda DeAngelo. 'Payout Policy Pedagogy: What Matters and Why'. *European Financial Management* 13, no. 1 (January 2007): 11–27.

Dimson, E., P. R. Marsh and M. Staunton. *Triumph of the Optimists: 101 Years of Investment Returns.* Princeton, NJ: Princeton University Press, 2002.

Dixit, A. and R. Pindyck. 'The Options Approach to Capital Investment'. *Harvard Business Review* 73 (May–June 1995): 105–15.

Duffie, D. and K. J. Singleton. *Credit Risk: Pricing, Measurement and Management.* Princeton, NJ: Princeton University Press, 2003.

Earnst & Young. *India's Cost of Capital; A Survey.* January 2014.

Eckbo, B. E., R. W. Masulis and O. Norli. 'Security Offerings: A Survey'. In *Handbook of Corporate Finance: Empirical Corporate Finance*, edited by B. E. Eckbo, 233–371. Amsterdam: Elsevier/North-Holland, 2007.

Ehrbar, A. *EVA: The Real Key to Creating Wealth.* New York: John Wiley and Sons, 1998.

Eiteman, D. K., A. I. Stonehill and M. H. Moffett. *Multinational Business Finance*, 11th edn. Reading, MA: Pearson Addison Wesley, 2007.

Elton, E. J., M. J. Gruber, S. J. Brown and W. N. Goetzmann. *Modern Portfolio Theory and Investment Analysis*, 7th edn. New York: John Wiley and Sons, 2007.

Esty, B. C. *Modern Project Finance: A Casebook.* New York: John Wiley, 2003.

Fabozzi, F. J., ed. *The Handbook of Fixed Income Securities*, 6th edn. New York: McGraw-Hill, 2005.

Fabozzi, F. J., S. V. Mann and M. Choudhry. *The Global Money Markets.* New York: John Wiley, 2002.

Fama, E. F. 'Efficient Capital Markets: A Review of Theory and Empirical Work'. *Journal of Finance* 25 (May 1970): 383–417.

———. 'Efficient Capital Markets: II'. *Journal of Finance* 46 (December 1991): 1575–617.

Fama, E. F. and K. R. French. 'Dissecting Anomalies'. *Journal of Finance* 63 (August 2008): 1653–78.

Froot, K. A, D. Scharfstein, and J. C. Stein. 'A Framework for Risk Management'. *Harvard Business Review* 72 (November–December 1994): 59–71.

Goetzmann, W. and R. Ibbotson. *The Equity Risk Premium: Essays and Explorations.* New York: Oxford University Press, 2006.

Graham, J. and C. Harvey. 'How CFOs Make Capital Budgeting and Capital Structure Decisions'. *Journal of Applied Corporate Finance* 15 (Spring 2002): 8–23.

Graham, John R., and Campbell R. Harvey. 'The Theory and Practice of Corporate Finance: Evidence from the Field'. *Journal of Financial Economics* 60, nos. 2–3 (2001): 187–243.

Graham, John. 'How Big Are the Tax Benefits of Debt?' *Journal of Finance* 14, no. 1 (Spring, 2001): 42–54.

Grant Thorton. 'Valuation Insights on Equity Risk Premium {ERP} for Indian Market'. October 2015.

Harris, M. and A. Raviv. 'The Theory of Capital Structure'. *Journal of Finance* 46 (March 1991): 297–355.

Hill, N. C. and W. L. Sartoris. *Short-Term Financial Management: Text and Cases*, 3rd edn. Englewood Cliffs, NJ: Prentice-Hall, Inc., 1994.

Hull, John C. *Options, Futures and Other Derivatives*, 6th edn. Upper Saddle River, NJ: Prentice Hall, 2005.

Ibbotson, R. G., J. L. Sindelar and J. R. Ritter. 'The Market's Problems with the Pricing of Initial Public Offerings'. *Journal of Applied Corporate Finance* 7 (Spring 1994): 66–74.

Jensen, M. C. and W. Meckling. 'Theory of the Firm: Managerial Behavior, Agency Costs, and Ownership Structure'. *Journal of Financial Economics* 3, no. 4 (1976): 305–60.

Knowledge@Wharton. 'The Cost of Entrenchment: Why CEOs Are Rarely Fired'. Wharton School, University of Pennsylvania, 19 January 2011.

Koller, T., M. Goedhart and D. Wessels. *Valuation: Measuring and Managing the Value of Companies*, 4th edn. New York: Wiley, 2005.

Lintner, J. 'Distribution and Incomes of Corporations among Dividends, Retained Earnings, and Taxes'. *American Economic Review* 2(May 1956): 97–113.

Luehrman, T. A. 'Using APV: A Better Tool for Valuing Operations'. *Harvard Business Review* 75 (May–June 1997): 145–54.

Malkiel, B. G. 'The Efficient Market Hypothesis and Its Critics'. *Journal of Economic Perspectives* 17 (Winter 2003): 59–82.

———. *A Random Walk Down Wall Street*, 8th edn. New York: Norton, 2003.

Malkiel, G. Burton and Charles D. Ellis. *The Elements of Investing: Easy Lessons for Every Investor*. Hoboken, NJ: John Wiley & Sons, 2013.

McDonald, R. L. 'The Role of Real Options in Capital Budgeting: Theory and Practice'. *Journal of Applied Corporate Finance* 18 (March 2006): 28–39.

———. *Derivatives Markets*, 2nd edn. Reading, MA: Pearson Addison Wesley, 2005.

Merton, R. 'A Functional Perspective of Financial Intermediation'. *Financial Management* 24 (Summer 1995): 23–41.

Miller, M. 'Financial Innovation: The Last Twenty Years and the Next'. *Journal of Financial and Quantitative Analysis* 21, no. 4 (December 1986): 459–71.

Miller, M. and K. Rock. 'Dividend Policy under Asymmetric Information'. *Journal of Finance* 40(1985): 1031–51.

Miller, M. H. 'The Modigliani-Miller Propositions after Thirty Years'. *Journal of Applied Corporate Finance* 2 (Spring 1989): 6–18.

Miller, Merton. 'Debt and Taxes'. *Journal of Finance* 32, no. 2 (May 1977): 261–75.

Modigliani, F. and M. Miller. 'The Cost of Capital, Corporation Finance and the Theory of Investment'. *American Economic Review* 48, no. 3 (June 1958): 261–97.

Morningstar Investment Service. 2018. *2018 Fundamentals for Investors*. Ibbotson® SBBI 2018 Morningstar, Inc., 2018. Available at https://advisor.mp.morningstar.com/resourceDownload?type=publicForms&i d=3f9dff3c-f085-47a1-98ba-0bc008df9f25. Accessed 16 September 2019.

Myers, S. C. 'Finance Theory and Financial Strategy'. *Midland Corporate Finance Journal* 5 (Spring 1987): 6–13. Reprint, *Interfaces* (January–February 1984).

———. 'Financing of Corporations'. In *Handbook of the Economics of Finance*, edited by G. M. Constantinides, M. Harris and R. Stulz, 215–53. Amsterdam: Elsevier North-Holland, 2003.

———. 'The Capital Structure Puzzle'. *Journal of Finance* 39, 28–30 December 1983 (July 1984): 575–92.

Nasdaq. 'Should You Use Leverage?' 15 December 2009. Available at https://www.nasdaq.com/articles/ should-you-use-leverage-2009-12-15. Accessed 20 October 2019.

New York Times. 'Toyota Feels Exchange-Rate Pinch as Rivals Gain'. 2 September 2010. Available at https://www.nytimes.com/2010/09/03/business/global/03toyota.html. Accessed 20 September 2019.

Philippon, Thomas. 'Has the U.S. Finance Industry Become Less Efficient? On the Theory and Measurement of Financial Intermediation'. Stern School of Business, New York University; NBER; and CPER, September 2014.

Porter, M. 'What Is Strategy?' *Harvard Business Review* November–December 1996, 61–78.

Rajan, R. G. and L. Zingales. 'What Do We Know about Capital Structure? Some Evidence from International Data'. *Journal of Finance* 50 (December 1995): 1421–60.

Reinhart, C. M., and K. Rogoff. *This Time Is Different: Eight Centuries of Financial Folly*. Princeton: Princeton University Press, 2009.

Ritter, J. R. 'Investment Banking and Securities Issuance'. In *Handbook of the Economics of Finance*, edited by G. M. Constantinides, M. Harris and R. Stulz, 254–89. Amsterdam: Elsevier Science, 2003.

Ritter, Jay and Ivo Welch. 'A Review of IPO Activity, Pricing and Allocation'. *Journal of Finance* 57, no. 4 (August 2002): 1795–828.

Ross, S. 'The Determination of Financial Structure: The Incentive Signaling Approach'. *Bell Journal of Economics* 8, no. 1 (1977): 23–40.

Ross, Stephen A., Westerfield W. Randolph and Jordan D. Bradford. *Corporate Finance*, 9th edn. New York: McGraw Hill-Irwin, 2010.

Saunders, A. and L. Allen. *Credit Risk Measurement*, 2nd edn. New York: John Wiley, 2002.

Scherr, F. C. *Modern Working Capital Management: Text and Cases*. Englewood Cliffs, NJ: Prentice-Hall, Inc., 1989.

Schwert, G. W. 'Anomalies and Market Efficiency'. In *Handbook of the Economics of Finance*, edited by G. M. Constantinides, M. Harris and R. M. Stulz, 939–74. Amsterdam: Elsevier Science, 2003.

Sercu, P. *International Finance: Theory into Practice*. Princeton, NJ: Princeton University Press, 2009.

Shapiro, A. C. *Multinational Financial Management*, 8th edn. New York: John Wiley & Sons, 2006.

Shefrin, Hersh M. and Meir Statman. 'Explaining Investor Preference for Cash Dividends'. *Journal of Financial Economics* 13 (1984): 253–82.

Shiller, R. J. 'From Efficient Markets Theory to Behavioral Finance'. *Journal of Economic Perspectives* 17 (Winter 2003): 83–104.

———. *Irrational Exuberance*, 2nd edn. Princeton, NJ: Princeton University Press, 2005.

Shleifer, A. and R. W. Vishny. 'A Survey of Corporate Governance'. *Journal of Finance* 52 (June 1997): 737–83.

Shleifer, Andrei. *Inefficient Markets: An Introduction to Behavioral Finance*. Oxford: Oxford University Press, 2000.

Smith, C. W. and J. B. Warner. 'On Financial Contracting: An Analysis of Bond Covenants'. *Journal of Financial Economics* 7, no. 2 (1979): 117–61.

Smith, K. V. and G. W. Gallinger. *Readings on Short-Term Financial Management*, 3rd edn. New York: West, 1988.

Smithson, C. H. and B. Simkins. 'Does Risk Management Add Value? A Survey of the Evidence'. *Journal of Applied Corporate Finance* 17 (Summer 2005): 8–17.

Smithson, C. H. *Managing Financial Risk*, 3rd edn. New York: McGraw-Hill, 1998.

Stern, J. M. and J. S. Shiely. *The EVA Challenge—Implementing Value-Added Change in an Organization*. New York: John Wiley and Sons, 2001.

Stern, Joel M. and Donald H. Chew, eds. *The Revolution in Corporate Finance*. New York: Basil Blackwell, 1986.

Stulz, R. M. *Risk Management and Derivatives*. Cincinnati, OH: Thomson-Southwestern Publishing, 2003.

Thaler, R. H., ed. *Advances in Behavioral Finance*. New York: Russell Sage Foundation, 1993.

Triantis, A. and A. Borison. 'Real Options: State of the Practice'. *Journal of Applied Corporate Finance* 14 (Summer 2001): 8–24.

Wall Street Journal. 'Isaac Newton Learnt about Financial Gravity the Hard Way'. MoneyBeat blog, 10 July 2017.

White, M. J. 'Bankruptcy Costs and the New Bankruptcy Code'. *Journal of Finance* 38, no. 2 (May 1983): 477–88.

Index